Feminist Ethics and Social Policy

A Hypatia Book

Feminist Ethics and Social Policy

EDITED BY
Patrice DiQuinzio
AND
Iris Marion Young

Indiana University Press

BLOOMINGTON AND INDIANAPOLIS

The paper used in this publication meets the minimum requirements of American National Standard for Information Sciences—Permanence of Paper for Printed Library Materials, ANSI Z39.48–1984.

MANUFACTURED IN THE UNITED STATES OF AMERICA

Library of Congress Cataloging-in-Publication Data

Feminist ethics and social policy / edited by Patrice DiQuinzio and Iris Marion Young.
p. cm. — (A Hypatia book)
Includes bibliographical references and index.
ISBN 0-253-33296-6 (cloth : alk. paper). —
ISBN 0-253-21125-5 (pbk. : alk. paper)
1. Feminist ethics. 2. United States—Social policy—1993– . I. DiQuinzio, Patrice, date. II. Young, Iris Marion, date. III. Series.
BJ1395.F446 1997
170'.82—dc21 96-53431

1 2 3 4 5 02 01 00 99 98 97

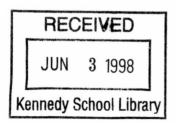

CONTENTS

INTRODUCTION

PATRICE DiQUINZIO AND IRIS MARION YOUNG

For more than twenty years feminist philosophers have been mapping new territory in ethical theory. This theoretical work has had a noticeable influence, moreover, on ethics and political philosophy more generally. Much of this work in feminist ethics has been rather abstract, however, referring little to living contexts of moral action, and that which has referred to contexts of actions has tended to focus on individual action. The essays in this volume bring feminist ethics to interrogate practical contexts of public and collective action. In collecting them, we are motivated by the conviction that the important paradigm shifts in normative analysis produced by feminist ethics can enable creative ways of reflecting on social policy.

Most generally, we mean by ethics the normative analysis of issues and concepts concerning right action, the human and nonhuman good, and social justice. Feminist ethics criticizes the gender blindness and biases in much traditional ethical theory. For example, traditional ethics has tended to assume a public-private dichotomy according to which the primary characteristics considered to be part of the "moral point of view"—universality and impartiality—correspond implicitly to institutions and activities dominated by men: contract making, statecraft, the application of legal principles (Friedman 1989, 1991; Young 1987; Held 1993). Many feminists have questioned the opposition between reason and emotion presumed by much traditional ethical theory, for example, and have offered important accounts of the role of emotions in moral reason (Okin 1990; Jaggar 1989).

Feminist ethics has developed new theories and concepts that are more gender sensitive and has worked to conceptualize issues of right action, social justice, and the human good from out of the specifically gendered experience of diverse groups of women. The most famous of these conceptualizations, perhaps, is the ethic of care first proposed by Carol Gilligan (1982) and pursued and refined by many philosophers (e.g., Noddings 1984). But other concepts that are sensitive to women's experiences and critical of the individualist contract society model of human interaction typically underlying moral theory have also been developed. For example, feminist philosophers have elaborated concepts of trust (Baier 1991) or of lesbian community (Hoagland 1988).

Both in the philosophical literature more broadly and in this collection of essays, feminist ethics has no single set of questions or propositions but includes a variety of approaches. Some of these essays operate within a liberal framework of equality, freedom, justice, and rights, while others are more critical of mainstream liberal versions of these concepts. Some use an experiential approach to moral inquiry, while others speak of principles or practices in more general terms. Three essays use the care ethics that has become influential in feminist ethics, but others criticize it. Two rely on postmodernist approaches to discourse analysis to draw conclusions about the moral context of public discourse. Despite this diversity of approaches and language, the essays share a commitment to the analysis of concepts such as freedom, equality, and justice, and the recognition that most social policy problems have no simple answers.

The referent of social policy is just as diverse in this collection. We conceive social policy most generally as about issues of institutional decision or regulation, particularly but not exclusively public institutions. The essays cover a diverse range of institutional arenas of social policy. Some, such as the ones by Mary L. Shanley on father's rights and Judith Wagner DeCew on women in the military, critically reflect on the content of legal decisions. Sharon E. Hartline interrogates the legal definition of self-defense in the context of battering. Other essays, such as Eva Feder Kittay's on the Family and Medical Leave Act, analyze specific legislative acts. Several reflect on the policies of specific regulatory bodies, including those by Uma Narayan on Immigration and Naturalization Service regulations, Naomi Zack on the race classification policies of the U.S. Census Bureau, Lisa S. Parker on the Food and Drug Administration's regulations on breast implantation, and Anita Silvers on Oregon health care rationing policies.

Several of the essays refer less to specific policies and more to analysis of the general terms of a policy issue. Thus Carolyn H. Magid proposes two conceptualizations for understanding the strategy and policies of comparable worth. Several essays analyze the discursive frameworks of particular contexts of social policy. These include Janet R. Jakobsen on public discourse about sexuality, Alisa L. Carse on pornography debates, Gail Weiss on dilemmas arising from possible practices of sex-selective abortion, and Kate Mehuron on women and AIDS. The policy context for Selma Sevenhuijsen's essay is the Netherlands, and several essays refer to the international implications of policy issues.

We believe that bringing feminist ethical theory to reflect on specific social policies is productive for both theory and practice, raising important questions for each. Do feminist ethical critiques and positive concepts suggest directions for policy other than those that currently predominate? Do the demands of reasoning in specific policy contexts require problematization or refinement of concepts in feminist ethics? We think that the answer to both questions is often affirmative and that this collection of essays shows why.

Many of these essays operate with concepts relevant to modern liberal democratic law and policy at the same time as they interrogate them. Most salient are the discussions about individuality, equality, and freedom.

Several essays question the abstract concept of individuality as an independent and autonomous agency that liberalism presupposes as the ground of equality and freedom. For instance, Kittay argues that John Rawls's account of equality makes this presupposition and thus does not take into account the reality of dependency in social interactions. Sevenhuijsen likewise criticizes the tendency in Western democracies to identify citizenship with independence and self-sufficiency. Shanley locates this concept of individuality in the assertions of rights that dominate discussions of adoption and child custody. Weiss detects this concept at work in certain evaluations of sex-selective abortion. Jakobsen argues that the very possibility of political participation requires that citizens constitute themselves as independent and autonomous agents.

Many of these essays raise questions about the meaning of equality for women and the best ways to promote equality. At least two themes concerning equality emerge. The first asks whether equal treatment is best promoted through rules of formal equality that aim to be gender, race, and ability neutral or whether promoting equality requires the explicit recognition of difference. The second asks about the meaning and limits of equality in the distribution of resources, income, and positions.

Whether equality implies treating women in the same way as men or, on the other hand, noticing gender-specific differences has been a longstanding debate in feminist theory. DeCew's analysis of the U.S. Supreme Court's reasoning in cases challenging the exclusion of military women from combat argues that at least in this case treating women in the same way as men would be an improvement over current policy. On issues of women and combat, policy and the court have never been gender neutral. The court appeals to the intentions of Congress with respect to women in combat to argue that requiring draft registration of men but not women is not unequal treatment. But DeCew shows that the court's deference to congressional intention is problematic because congressional debate on this matter relies heavily on traditional ideas about women's proper roles.

Several other essays, however, challenge the efficacy of gender neutrality in promoting women's interests. Shanley argues that accounts of unwed fathers' rights that appeal to gender neutrality overlook both men's and women's different situations with respect to pregnancy and the inequality characteristic of the social structures of sexuality and reproduction. Narayan shows the implicit gender biases in U.S. immigration regulations. Failing to notice the specific circumstances under which many immigrant women enter and live in the United States, these regulations subject some women to threats of violence and deportation that men do not, as a rule, experience. Hartline argues that traditional legal understandings of self-defense presuppose relations among strangers. Neutral application of traditional meanings of self-defense to women who kill their batterers thus sometimes does injustice. Hartline does not argue for a special definition of self-defense to apply to battered women, however, but for an altered general meaning of self-defense that would be neutrally applied.

Magid raises the question of whether policies and proposals to alter the wage structure of traditionally female jobs should be thought of primarily as an antidiscrimination strategy of compensatory justice or as a distribution according to the intrinsic worth or merit of jobs. She argues against the idea that jobs have any kind of intrinsic worth and suggests that thinking about comparable worth policies in this way perpetuates a hierarchical view of the workplace. Seeing comparable worth as a remedy for discrimination is more egalitarian. Sevenhuijsen criticizes a distributive paradigm of justice in health care policy because it presupposes that health care needs are already defined. She argues for a more participatory approach to health care policy in which citizens would discuss not only the efficient and just meeting of needs but also the meaning of the needs themselves.

Several of these essays take up issues of freedom of speech or choice in a liberal democratic society. They argue that where questions of gender oppression or sexuality are at stake, the simple alternative of either allowing or forbidding speech and/or choice is not adequate to the subtlety of the issues. Thus both Carse and Jakobsen give compelling reasons why those who care about the status of women should roundly condemn much pornography, yet both also offer clear accounts of why legal regulation of pornography is problematic. Weiss wrestles with dilemmas for freedom of choice raised by sex-selective abortion. While she argues against restricting freedom of choice, she also shows how the policy alternatives of allowing or forbidding are not adequate to this issue. In criticizing restrictions on breast implants, Parker reiterates the importance of a woman's right to choose what to do with her body. She works with the concept of informed consent but shows how women's informed consent can be undermined by the effects of patriarchal beauty standards on medical practices of informing and assessing patients. Zack's argument for racial self-identification takes seriously the social construction of racial identities as well as the history of racism in the scientific study of race and in the use of such studies in public racial classifications. She nonetheless concludes that, given the importance of self-determination and freedom of association in U.S. political culture, the opportunity for racial self-definition should be available to persons of mixed race.

Many of these essays presuppose the critique of principle-based moral theories that has emerged in feminist ethics and has some of the same implications as the critique of gender neutrality as a standard for equality. By principle-based moral theories we mean those that propose a basic moral principle to guide and evaluate all action, defend this principle on universal grounds, and argue that considerations not universally true of all contexts of moral choice and action are insufficient for establishing the truth of a moral principle. According to feminist ethics' critique, principle-based moral theories fail to consider morally relevant aspects of the contexts of moral choice and action. Applying this insight to social policy makes even clearer the need for contextualization in ethical theory and social policy. Analyses of the specificity and complexity of the sociocultural contexts in which policy issues arise and must be addressed, as well as analyses of the institutional contexts of policy making and implementation, show that policies must be carefully designed for specific contexts if they are to be successful.

Several of these essays show how a principle-based approach leads to unsatisfactory policies. Narayan argues that failure to consider the specific circumstances of women with dependent immigration status leads to flawed immigration policy. Hartline shows how the criteria for evaluating self-defense that the law insists are universally relevant to all incidents of threatened harm are actually most relevant to those involving strangers and less applicable to threats of harm in domestic contexts or personal relationships which women are more likely to experience. She argues that the legal understanding of self-defense must be expanded to include a concept of intimate danger, specific to threats of harm in domestic or interpersonal contexts. Shanley argues that a policy on custody and adoption disputes between unwed parents that adjudicates the conflict between the mother's right to have her child adopted and the father's right to parent the child overlooks the different and usually unequal situations of men and women with respect to pregnancy and child care. Analyzing the variety of circumstances in which unwed parents may find themselves, she argues that parental claims should be based on a combination of genetic relationship, assumption of responsibility, and provision of care to the child (including gestation) and that these factors should be assessed in terms of the specific situations of the parents.

This emphasis on contextualization also applies to the contexts of policy implementation and policy formation. So, for example, Parker argues that whether consent to breast implantation is truly informed depends on specific aspects of the medical practice of assessing and evaluating candidates. And Jakobsen examines the specific contexts that distinguish different instances of alliance building, such as that of feminist antiviolence advocates, conservative Christians, and the state that resulted in the Meese Commission's report on pornography; the "sex wars" within lesbian and feminist communities in the 1980s; and the attempted alliance between members of the white feminist media and Anita Hill.

Weiss argues that a morally adequate approach to sex-selective abortion must consider the interdependent relationships that connect mother, fetus, father, other children, and other family members. It should also consider the larger sociocultural context which shapes these relationships, influences the values and priorities of these persons, and may determine what options are realistically available to them. Weiss's argument suggests that social policy on sex-selective abortion should not only enable individuals to make the best decision about sex-selective abortion in their circumstances, as opposed to punishing those who choose it, but also change social circumstances so that there is less need to make such a decision. Thus this application of feminist ethics' critique of principle-based moral theories and of its emphasis on contextualization shows that moral evaluation of the contexts for individual decision making created by specific social policies should also be an important element of feminist approaches to social policy.

In addition to working with these critical aspects of feminist ethics, some of these essays use and further refine the positive contributions of feminist ethics, one of which is the ethic of care. Two of the essays work within the framework of care ethics, although each offers a somewhat different interpretation of what this means. As an alternative to principle-based moral theories, Weiss turns to Sara Ruddick's work on maternal thinking, a moral theory associated with an ethic of care. Weiss argues that preserving familial and community relationships of care should be one goal of social policy on sex-selective abortion. Kittay, on the other hand, uses an ethic of care to show that dependency concerns fall within the scope of both the political and justice as fairness. Justice thus requires both a public conception of social cooperation that includes dependency concerns and institutions that provide for and facilitate dependency relationships. On this basis Kittay evaluates the Family and Medical Leave Act of 1993. While this policy recognizes and makes provision for dependency concerns in a way that U.S. social policy has rarely done before, its limited scope and benefits make only a limited contribution to fairness and equality for all.

Sevenhuijsen makes a similar critique of health care policy in the Netherlands. The report of the Dutch Commission on Choices in Health Care does notice the position of women as dependency workers and caregivers, but not in order to give recognition and social support to the work that women do. Instead, the report looks upon women as health care gatekeepers who can regulate the health care consumption of family members and thus reduce the costs of public health care. The Dutch state continues to use a model of citizenship as independence and self-sufficiency, Sevenhuijsen argues, thus devaluing people who need care.

While Weiss, Kittay, and Sevenhuijsen articulate an ethic of care and find it an appropriate basis for policy making and policy evaluation, a number of these essays express reservations about the implications and effects of a care-based approach to moral decisions and policy making. Silvers voices the strongest of such objections, arguing that an ethic of care leads to a theory of justice that grounds just treatment on considerations of difference. Moral theories that advocate caring treatment based on empathetic perception of the feelings and needs of the less advantaged, however, may require their continued submissiveness and compliance. She concludes that social policy should recognize difference but should work at reconciling equality and difference without abandoning equality of treatment as a goal. The Americans with Disabilities Act of 1990, according to Silvers, meets this standard, recognizing the complexities of difference but insisting on an end to practices and institutions that preclude equal treatment of disabled persons.

The concern that policy making should at least preserve if not enhance the autonomy of persons historically disadvantaged is shared by several of the authors. For instance, Parker argues that culturally dominant ideas and values about female beauty and appropriate roles for women do not prevent women from making competent and voluntary decisions about breast implantation. Even given this cultural context, women are, and must be regarded as, autonomous agents, as long as they are adequately informed and appropriately assessed as candidates for breast implantation. While this may regrettably perpetuate these dominant ideas and values, failure to respect women's autonomy is a worse outcome. Carse evaluates the legal regulation of pornography partly in terms of the value of autonomy. She argues that if the legal regulation of pornography would lead to the legal regulation of other expressions of sexuality, this would be harmful, because it would limit sexual exploration and expression, which are important to self-possession and self-mastery. Narayan's assessment of immigration policy also considers the value of autonomy. Current immigration policies in practice may disempower women with dependent status, especially if they have experienced battering. A battered immigrant woman may not be in a position to exercise the autonomy required to secure permanent status without her husband's cooperation. Immigration policies should be changed so as to enhance the autonomy of women immigrants, for instance by enabling women with conditional status to self-petition for change to permanent status. Thus these essays also implicitly question whether social policy making informed by an ethic of care will enhance opportunities for the exercise of autonomy. While the impact of care ethics has been considerable, its interrogation in the context of social policy shows the variety of feminist interpretations and responses to it, and the application of care ethics to social policy brings some of its problems to the surface.

Several of these essays demonstrate how important are the terms and images in which a policy issue is framed. They show that a shift in terms can radically affect understanding of the political issues at stake, often with specific practical consequences. Thus Hartline examines the specific definition of self-defense commonly applied in the United States today, noting that it usually operates to exclude women who kill their batterers. Mehuron thinks about the AIDS epidemic from within the discourse of conspiracy theories that have arisen in African American and urban gay communities, analyzing them as subjugated knowledges which illuminate important aspects of the social phenomenon of AIDS which are otherwise masked by the dominant discourse of medical and public health experts. She shows how AIDS and policy responses to AIDS can fruitfully be conceptualized as a case of genocide and that doing so importantly shifts our understanding of responsibility and victimization in connection with this disease. She argues that such an approach contributes to the feminist genealogical practices needed to surface and address the specific health care needs of women and members of minority communities with respect to AIDS.

In recent years feminists have also been occupied with a discussion of "identity politics," exploring the social construction of female, African American, Chicana, or lesbian identities and asking what differentiates these identities and puts them in solidarities with others of the same identity. A position that identity is socially constructed, however, quickly sees that the very notion of a single identity for a person and one common identity for a group is problematic. Responsible action and policy in a complex social world of plural and shifting identities must negotiate the borders and aim to break down rigid categories of identity. These are themes of Jakobsen's analysis of discourse about sexuality and Zack's critique of race classifications. Jakobsen focuses on the overdetermination of identities by the demands of political participation in liberal societies but shows that this does not preclude alliance building, which recognizes and even makes use of the instability of identities. Zack analyzes the history of racial classification in the United States, showing that racial identities originate not in biology or genetics but in the sociocultural interpretation of physical traits. Because these interpretations have historically been inflected by racism as well as by economic structures such as slavery, social policy on racial classification today should emphasize self-determination based on self-classification by those historically disadvantaged by racial classification.

Bringing feminist ethics to social policy thus has the effect, first, of focusing a gender lens on policy. A feminist approach to policy issues asks about the differences between men and women that neutral policy evaluation has failed to notice. Normative approaches to this gendering of policy often reveal the need for more contextual applications of principles and methods and for understanding the plural identities that claim most people's lives. They also tend to show that simple alternatives between formalized equality and special treatment, or allowing or forbidding actions, often do not adequately address policy issues, especially those involving sexuality and the sexual division of labor.

Feminist ethical analyses of social policy thus call for rethinking such basic concepts as freedom, equality, justice, and rights. We offer these essays as a sampling of the diversity of subjects and approaches possible in doing feminist ethical analysis of social policy. We hope they will inspire others to put their minds to interrogating the actions and policies of institutions which profoundly affect the opportunities of women and men to realize their capacities and execute their decisions.

REFERENCES

Baier, Annette. 1991. *A progress of sentiments: Reflections on Hume's Treatise*. Cambridge: Harvard University Press.

Friedman, Marilyn. 1991. The impracticality of impartiality. *Journal of Philosophy* 86 (November 1989): 645–58.

Friedman, Marilyn. 1989. The social self and the partiality debates. In *Feminist Ethics*, ed. Claudia Card. Lawrence: University of Kansas Press.

Gilligan, Carol. 1982. *In a different voice: Psychological theory and women's development*. Cambridge: Harvard University Press.

Hoagland, Sarah. 1988. *Lesbian ethics: Toward new value*. Palo Alto, CA: Institute of Lesbian Studies.

Held, Virginia. 1993. *Feminist morality: Transforming culture, society, and politics*. Chicago: University of Chicago Press.

Jaggar, Alison M. 1989. Love and knowledge: Emotion in feminist epistemology. In *Women, knowledge, and reality*, ed. Ann Garry and Marilyn Pearsall. Boston: Unwin Hyman.

Noddings, Nel. 1984. *Caring: A feminine approach to ethics and moral education*. Berkeley: University of California Press.

Okin, Susan Moller. 1989. *Justice, gender, and the family*. New York: Basic Books.

Young, Iris Marion. 1987. *Justice and the politics of difference*. Princeton: Princeton University Press.

Feminist Ethics and Social Policy

1

Taking Dependency Seriously

The Family and Medical Leave Act Considered in Light of the Social Organization of Dependency Work and Gender Equality

EVA FEDER KITTAY

Dependents require care. They are unable either to survive or to thrive without attention to basic needs. Dependency needs range from the utter helplessness of a newborn infant to the incapacity of illness or frail old age. Dependency can be protracted (e.g., the extended dependency of early childhood) or brief (e.g., a temporary illness). An individual who is dependent may be able to function otherwise independently if only she is given needed assistance in limited areas, or she may be dependent in every aspect of her being, that is, utterly dependent. At some stage in the lives of each of us we face at least one period of utter dependency; and, with accident and disease forever a danger to the most independent of us, we are all, at least potentially, dependents. In our dependency, we not only require care, but require a sustaining relation with a care-giver who provides this care—for *who* does the caring is often as important as the care itself. These dependencies may be alleviated or aggravated by cultural practices and prejudices, but given the immutable facts of human development, disease, and decline, no culture that endures beyond one generation can secure itself against the claims of human dependency. While we are

Hypatia vol. 10, no. 1 (Winter 1995) © by Eva Feder Kittay all dependent on some form of care or support, at least minimally, and although dependencies vary in degree, those that involve the survival or thriving of a person cut most deeply through the fiction of a social order presumably constituted by independent equal persons.

For the past two decades, feminists have argued that this fiction is parasitic on a tradition in which women attend to those dependencies. The labor has been seen as part of their familial obligations, obligations that trump all other obligations. Women who have been sufficiently wealthy or of sufficiently high status have sometimes had the option to confer the daily labor of dependency care to others—generally other women, mostly poor and ill-situated. Poor women who have had dependency responsibilities along with paid employment have often relied on female familial help. The gendered and privatized nature of dependency work has meant, first, that men have rarely shared these responsibilities—at least with the women of their own class—and, second, that the equitable distribution of dependency work, both among genders and among classes, has rarely been considered in the discussions of political and social justice which take as their starting point the public lives of men.

As women from many different classes increasingly participate in paid employment, adequate provisions for dependency care—child daycare, care for the elderly, time for family members to care for ill children, and so on—have surfaced as a major social concern. One response has been various kinds of social legislation that provide for leaves for parents with newborn children and for workers with family members who are ill or temporarily disabled. It is no secret that among industrialized nations, the United States, in spite of its early history of equal opportunity employment legislation, is especially primitive in its response to the concerns of dependency work. At long last, in 1993, a national piece of legislation, The Family and Medical Leave Act (FMLA) (Public Law 103–3, February 5, 1993, 107 Stat., 6–29) provides for some parental leave and some leave time to take care of ailing family members. The act is a rare piece of social policy insofar as it recognizes a public responsibility for dependency care.

The standard liberal tradition that policymakers appeal to, most especially in the United States, but to varying degrees in other Western democracies as well, does not acknowledge the claims of dependency. The liberal political philosophy that supplies the idealizations and the utopian visions of which contemporary society is an (albeit poor) approximation have as little to say about dependency as do the policymakers. The result is particularly detrimental to women's aspirations to empowerment and equality. And this despite the pretensions to a gender egalitarianism in the rhetoric of Western democracies and in the presumed gender-blindness of liberal political philosophy.

This neglect suggests that the ability to incorporate dependency concerns serves as a criterion of adequacy for any theory of a just social order that purports to advocate gender equality. John Rawls's egalitarianism will serve as the case study for the adequacy of liberal philosophy in recognizing dependency concerns. Elsewhere I discuss the adequacy of Rawlsian contractual liberalism to dependency concerns in detail (Kittay, N.d.). Here I focus on the notion of social cooperation as a keystone of that theory. The egalitarian ideal informing and informed by the idea of social cooperation leaves no space for dependency concerns because it requires the idea of mutual reciprocity by cooperating members. But such reciprocity cannot always pertain to persons in a relation of dependency, that is, between dependent and care-giver. In order to include the fact of dependency and its impact on those who do dependency work, we are compelled to enlarge the concept of social cooperation to consider a form of social interaction that, without being exploitative or neglectful of the concerns of any party, does not presume equality in power and situation of all parties. In the FMLA, we find elements of the expanded notion of social cooperation I advocate. But it falls short of what the crisis requires, and its limitations can be attributed to its fundamental adherence to the liberal model that is being criticized. The inadequacy of the FMLA reveals the failure of liberal theories to conceptualize social cooperation in such a way that provides women with the gender equality they purport to endorse.

THE DEPENDENCY CRITIQUE OF LIBERAL EGALITARIANISM

Contemporary liberal egalitarians tend to regard gender as a morally irrelevant category and endorse the ideal of sexual equality. Feminists, however, have asked not only what it will take for women to achieve equality but have interrogated liberal understandings of the ideal itself. Some feminists have evoked both women's difference from men and women's differences among themselves.[1] Their *difference critiques* of equality have pointed to the implicit use of men—*more specifically white middle-class men*—as *the* standard against which equality is assessed. These feminists have argued that this norm is unfit for incorporating all whose identity is marked by their gender, race, class, and other socially salient difference.[2] Other feminists, elaborating a *dominance critique*, have underscored the power difference between men and women. Men's entrenched dominance over women means that gender-neutral, equality-based policies either fail to address issues that specifically affect women or merely preserve the relations of dominance that are already in effect.[3] The considerations to which I have alluded in the introductory paragraphs of this essay form still another critique of dominant views of equality. This I call the *dependency critique*.[4] The dependency critique maintains that by construing society as an association of equals, conceived as individuals with equal powers, equally situated in the competition for the benefits of social cooperation, one disregards the inevitable dependencies of the human condition, thereby neglecting the condition both of dependents and those who care for dependents (see Kittay, N.d.).

The dependency critique looks beyond women's socially prescribed differences from and subordination to men by considering the difficulties in assimilating women to the liberal ideal of equality. Its focus is on the circumstances under which the ideal was conceived and, more specifically, on the presumption that inevitable human dependencies and the consequences of such dependency for social organization are outside the political sphere for which the ideal of equality was articulated. Traditional formulations of liberal equality which originated as a challenge to feudalism posited an ideal for male heads of household. The feudalistic dependencies inherent in political hierarchy were targets of liberal thinkers such as Locke and Rousseau. Yet by positing equality for the male heads of households the dependencies of human development and frailty can remain unaddressed, at least as long as the household can accommodate these needs—an accommodation made possible by the privatized labor of women. The dependencies that cannot be banished by fiat are sustained by a social organization that creates a secondary dependence in those who care for dependents. They remain outside the society of equals insofar as they cannot function as the independent and autonomous agents of liberal theory who are presumed to be equally empowered and equally situated to engage in a fair competition for the benefits of social cooperation. For the woman who cares for dependents, the *dependency worker*, is not so situated—not as long as her responsibilities lie with another who cannot survive or thrive without her ministrations. Her attention is directed to another's needs; even her understanding of her own needs are enmeshed with the needs of a vulnerable other whose fundamental well-being is entrusted to her. And yet, within a liberal doctrine of society as a contractual agreement between equals, she should be an autonomous and independent individual. Liberalism constructed an equality for heads of households (wherein dependencies exist within the household and are attended to by women), and then counted the head of household as an *individual* who is independent and who can act on his own behalf. The equality for individuals overlays the equality for household heads, creating the illusion that dependencies do not exist and that the extension of equality to all, not only heads of households, is easily accomplished.

The illusion sustains a fiction that society is composed only of independent individuals who come together to form associations of social cooperation[5] and that an egalitarian notion of justice is served by considering those individuals to be free and equal (that is, self-originating sources of claims) who are equally situated and equally empowered. But social cooperation is required not only by autonomous and independently functioning individuals for the purposes of mutually improving life chances, but first and foremost for the purpose of sustaining those who are not independently functioning, those who are not equally situated, and those who are unable to benefit from an equal empowerment. They are persons who are too young, too ill, too disabled, or too enfeebled by old age to care for themselves and to speak for themselves. These persons are our children, our parents, our siblings, our companions, and, at some points in life, ourselves. In states of dependency, we are unable to discharge the responsibilities and carry the burdens of the *equal* citizen; we have to rely on our caretaker to fulfill our basic needs; and we have no public or political voice except the voice of the dependency worker charged with articulating as well as meeting our needs. These dependencies are part of a network of interdependencies that form the central bonds of human social life. The care and attention to the vulnerabilities of dependent persons on the part of the dependency worker and the trust invested by the dependent in the dependency worker are among the most essential of social interactions.

When the fact of dependency and its social dimensions within the political conception of society is omitted, the secondary dependence of the dependency worker and the contribution of even the most dependent to the fabric of human relations is missed. The dependency worker acquires a dependence on others to supply the resources needed to sustain herself and the dependents who are in her charge. The dependency relation is a cooperative arrangement sustained by these resources, the labor of the dependency worker, and the responsiveness to care on the part of the cared-for.[6] The dependency worker may be unpaid, caring for familial dependents, or paid, caring for dependents in an institutional or home setting. Whether her work is done for pay or as a familial obligation,[7] the dependency worker attends to and voices the needs and desires of her charge in addition to, and sometimes at the expense of, her own; she assumes the same responsibilities other citizens have to each other and to themselves and assumes the added responsibility on behalf of one who cannot meet these responsibilities alone. In the distribution of burdens and benefits, most liberal egalitarian theories count each person as one. The incapacity of the dependent—to sustain her share of burdens and claim her share of benefits—and the obligation of the dependency worker—to assume the burdens of more than one and, at times, to put the benefits to her charge ahead of her own—ill-suits an economy of social cooperation presumed for an association of equals: that each will equally assume a share of the burdens and each will claim her own share of benefits. That women historically and customarily assume the role of dependency worker means that such an account of equality leaves out many women who retain their role and status as dependency workers. Because a redistribution of dependency work has too often exploited the situation of poor women, the dependency critique provides a framework for investigating theories and policies of equality across race and class as well as gender, and looks toward a more adequate understanding of gender equality.

PRESUPPOSITIONS OF RAWLSIAN EQUALITY

Rawls identifies society "as a fair system of social cooperation" and looks for "principles specifying the basic rights and liberties and the forms of equality most appropriate to those cooperating, once they are regarded as citizens, as free and equal persons" (Rawls 1993, 27).

Free and equal persons come together in the initial situation to choose principles of justice they can accept when they do not know their own status in life, their own conception of the good, their own particular dispositions and psychological propensities, and to what generation they belong. In *Political Liberalism* Rawls again characterizes the modeling of the equality of citizens: "To model this equality in the original position we say that the parties, as representatives of those who meet the condition, are symmetrically situated. This requirement is fair because in establishing fair terms of social cooperation (in the case of the basic structure) the only relevant feature of persons is their possessing the moral powers . . . and their having the normal capacities to be a cooperating member of society over the course of a lifetime" (Rawls 1993, 79). He speaks of the "representation for equality" as "an easy matter" of situating the parties to the original position symmetrically to one another and describing them identically. And yet in this easy and seemingly transparent move, so much is presumed.

First, *all* citizens are idealized as "fully cooperating members of society *over the course of a complete life*" (Rawls 1980, 546; emphasis mine). Rawls continues, "The idealization means that everyone has sufficient intellectual powers to play a *normal* part in society, and no one suffers from *unusual* needs that are *especially difficult* to fulfill, for example *unusual and costly medical requirements*" (1980, 546; emphasis mine).[8] The theory is constructed for the "normal" situation and only afterwards made to accommodate *unusual* circumstances. But if the normal situation is not that of a fully functioning person who is a cooperating member throughout his or her lifetime, if we are instead all potential dependents and the "unusual" needs are an inevitable feature of any human community, and if these needs demand dependency workers constrained in the degree of their full cooperation as *independent* citizens, then the idealization does not merely grease the wheels of the Rawlsian construction but renders it of questionable value in providing a theory that will deliver justice for dependents and dependency workers.

Second, the symmetry that Rawls posits for the representatives in original position is bound to a notion of persons as *free* and equal. For a person to be free means here, in part, to view oneself as a "self-originating" or "self-authenticating source of valid claims." But can the dependency worker be seen as "a self-originating source of valid claims"? She is as likely to put forward the claims of her charge as she is to put forward her own. Furthermore, there is often no clear separation between claims that she makes on her own behalf and those that originate with the charge—even though the conflict between these sets of claims can sometimes be palpable. If there is an important notion of freedom for the dependency worker, it is often one that recognizes the bond she shares with her dependent, even as it recognizes her own independent personhood.

Third, equality requires a measure. In Rawls's theory the comparative measure of interpersonal well-being is the index of primary goods, a list of goods that all persons require if they are to be able to realize their own conception of the good, given the moral powers that we have as free and equal persons. Rawls's moral powers do not include the responsiveness to vulnerability needed for care; nor do they include the good of being cared for when we become dependent or having the support we require to care for another if another becomes dependent on us. Consequently, the centrality of dependency in human life, and the concomitant value of human relationship and care in a relationship are absent from the list of primary goods.

Fourth, Rawls, building on Hume, identifies the "circumstances of justice." These are the circumstances under which the constitution of a society of free and equal persons who cooperate in the benefit and the burdens of social organization takes place. Missing from these is the circumstance of human development that incurs a period of dependency for each of us, a period during which we are unequally situated relative to those who are independent.[9]

Last, a sense of justice depends on an acceptance of a conception of social cooperation. Rawls writes of "the equally sufficient capacity (which I assume to be realized) to understand and to act from *the public conception of social cooperation*" (Rawls 1980, 546; emphasis mine). It is this notion of social cooperation that I explore here.

THE RAWLSIAN CONCEPTION OF SOCIAL COOPERATION

Social cooperation, writes Rawls, involves "fair terms of cooperation," not "simply . . . coordinated social activity efficiently organized and guided by publicly recognized rules to achieve some overall end" (1993, 300). That is, along with coordinated self-interested activity—what Rawls calls the *rational*—social cooperation demands a sense of what is fair—what Rawls calls the *reasonable*.

If they are both rational and reasonable, dependency concerns ought to be included within the features of a well-ordered society reflected in the public conception of social cooperation. To insist that it is reasonable to expect that the social order consider the care of dependents follows directly from the observation that any society into which we are born and expect to live out our lives contains those who are dependent and thus unable to realize any of their moral capacities—much less survive or thrive—independently. Only if a human society exists under especially hard conditions would we exempt its members from the moral responsibility to care for its dependents. Thus it is reasonable to expect that a well-ordered society is one that attends to the needs of dependents and whatever else that necessitates.

Furthermore, we can argue for the rationality of each individual—acting in their own self-interest—to choose principles that would include such concerns among the terms of social cooperation, for given the developmental nature and the fragility of human life, it is likely that dependency will touch each of our lives in some form. Whether we find ourselves dependent or needing to care for a dependent, it is rational to suppose that we would wish to be cared for or to be provided the resources by which we can provide care.

Although the inclusion of dependency concerns within a conception of social cooperation is both reasonable and rational, the mention of such are not to be found. The acknowledgment of "*normal* health care" (1993, 21; emphasis mine) covers some dependency concerns, but leaves out the daily care of infants and young children—which are not *health* care—and prolonged illness or states of diminished independence (e.g., a handicapping condition), which arguably are not conventionally understood as "normal" health care.

Rawls has many times acknowledged limits to his theory and expressed hopes that the theory could be extended, but the omission of dependency concerns is a result of the characterization of social cooperation—a characterization which it is the goal of this essay to identify and dispute. "Fair terms of cooperation," according to this view, articulates "an idea of reciprocity and mutuality: all who cooperate must benefit, or share in common burdens, in some appropriate fashion judged by a suitable benchmark of comparison" (Rawls 1993, 300). The point is made still sharper when Rawls writes, "Those who can take part in social cooperation over a complete life, and who are willing to honor the appropriate fair terms of agreement are regarded as equal citizens" (1993, 302).

But this understanding of social cooperation leaves out many persons. The second quotation cited in the preceding paragraph even suggests that Rawls does not extend *citizenship* to those who are permanently and so sufficiently incapacitated that they cannot be expected to restrict their freedoms in relevant ways[10] or to participate and so reciprocate in relevant ways. But why should the contingent fact that someone is born, let us say, sufficiently mentally disabled necessitate his or her exclusion from citizenship? There are some political activities the mentally disabled may not be able to engage in—for example, they may be incapable of enough political understanding to vote—but surely they need to receive the protections of political justice all the same.[11] The temporarily dependent can defer reciprocating until the individual regains full capability. But during our period of dependency we cannot reciprocate. Those who restrict their liberty, or use their labor, resources, or energy on our behalf cannot be repaid by us as long as we remain dependent. We may or may not be able to reciprocate at some future time, but the labor expended on our behalf cannot be so expended on the condition that we will reciprocate: a child may not reach maturity; an ill person may die; a now needy and elderly parent may not have been an adequate provider or nurturer. Who then is to reciprocate the efforts of the caretaker?[12] Unless the needs of their caretakers are to be met in some other form of reciprocity, the only available moral characterizations of the caretaker's function is as exploitation or supererogation. When we consider relations of dependency, we see that they are not characterized as social cooperation according to fair terms of cooperation, and those whose social relations are defined by the dependency relation then fall outside the bounds of social cooperation as understood by Rawls's characterization.

Relations of dependency may be excluded from the discussion either because (1) they are not appropriately characterized as pertaining to *political* justice or (2) they pertain to political justice but not to a theory that holds that justice is fairness.[13] Is it then appropriate to exclude the dependent and the dependency worker from a fully adequate conception of social cooperation? First, if political justice is to express the principles of a well-ordered society, then it seems that dependency concerns do fall within the scope of political justice. A society that does not care for its dependents or that cares for them only by unfairly exploiting the labor of some cannot be said to be well-ordered any more than a society that enslaves part of its population. I cannot see how any thoughtful reflection would yield an opposing insight. Second, if the "fair terms of cooperation" are identified as the reasonable and the rational, then I have already shown that it is both reasonable and rational to consider dependency matters in formulating principles of justice for a well-ordered society. Furthermore, if we reorient our political insights so that we see the centrality of human relationship to our happiness and well-being, and we recognize dependency relations as foundational human relations, then it becomes obvious that such concerns are among the basic motivations for creating a social order, and that a just social order must concern itself with what fairness requires for both dependents—who, even in their neediness, contribute to the ongoing nature of human relationships—and the one who cares for dependents—whose social contribution is invisible when dependency is thought to be outside the social order. If our reflective judgments confirm that those who are dependent (whether temporarily or permanently) ought to be appropriately cared for, and if those reflections focus on the importance of the central human bonds that form around dependency needs, then a society is well-ordered only if it offers adequate support to dependents and those who care for them in relations of dependency.[14]

SOCIAL COOPERATION AS *DOULIA*

If fairness obtains only for those who are themselves fully functioning, have normal capacities, and are in social interactions with others who are similarly endowed, then even if we insist that dependency concerns have a political dimension, justice as fairness will not pertain to dependency concerns. This idea of fairness and social cooperation is grounded on a notion of reciprocity alien to those in dependency relations. But if social cooperation can be seen to involve a second sort of interaction (similar to, but distinct from, the reciprocal interaction among those equally situated and equally empowered), then there is a way we can expand the conception of justice as fairness. Cooperation between persons where intergenerational needs are to be met will illustrate the point. When we consider the Family and Medical Leave Act, we see how it incorporates, to a limited degree, an expanded notion of reciprocity and social cooperation.

Families in modern industrial and urbanized societies are often not grounded in a community and often live far from other family members. Periods in which some family members are stressed by special dependency cares are particularly difficult. These are the stressful times that the FMLA is meant to alleviate. The situation of the postpartum mother who is caring for her newborn is especially interesting. Her need is most acute directly after childbirth when her infant is utterly dependent and her own body requires healing and rest—even for the production of her infant's food. Traditional societies sometimes mark this period as a time when the mother is entitled to special privileges and care. Contemporary mothers in the United States have had to make do with very inadequate provisions. At least until the enactment of FMLA (which as we will see only applies to some, not all, workers), the father (if present) has rarely been released from his employment, regardless of employment status; the mother is often pressured to return to paid employment as soon as possible, a situation alleviated but not fully remedied by FMLA; friends and relatives, whose assistance is not an option in FMLA, since it defines family narrowly, are rarely available to help and less so since so many women are now in the paid work force; and paid help, for those who can afford help, is the "baby nurse." Generally, however, it is not the baby who needs a nurse; the recuperating mother is normally capable of caring for the baby only if someone helps her take care of herself and her other duties. Adapting a strategy found in a number of traditional cultures, some have instituted a form of caretaking whereby the postpartum mother is assigned a postpartum care-giver, a *doula*, who assists the mother, and at times relieves her.[15] *Doula* originally meant slave or servant in Greek, but it is appropriated here to mean a person who renders a service to another who renders service to a dependent. A doula is not provided for in the FMLA, nor am I arguing here that it be provided. But I want to reflect on the principle embodied in the person of the doula and in the practice which we will call *doulia*.[16]

Let us extend the idea of a doula beyond one who provides a service to the postpartum mother, so that it describes those who attend to the needs of those who attend to another who is utterly dependent upon them (whether temporarily or permanently). In so doing we displace both the relation of servant and served and the traditional relation of reciprocity among equals as models of cooperative activity and put at the center a relation of *nested dependencies*. These nested dependencies link those who help and those who require help to give aid to ones who cannot help themselves. Extending the notion of the service performed by the doula, let us speak of "doulia" to indicate a concept by which service is rendered to those who become needy by virtue of attending to those in need, so that all can be well cared for.[17] The form of social cooperation that emerges from the relation between the doula, the mother, and the infant is captured by the colloquial phrase "What goes round comes round" when it is used to describe a form of cooperation often engaged in by members of poorer communities:[18] I, as a member of the community, help another who requires my help, with the expectation that someone in the community, not necessarily the individual whom I helped, will come to my aid if and when that is required.

This notion of social cooperation is not as far from the Rawlsian project as it may at first seem. Rawls understands that society is an association that persists through generations and that our efforts to pass the world on to the next generation without depleting its resources—a responsibility entailed by the "just savings principle"—is not reciprocated to us by those we benefit. The "chronological unfairness" to which Rawls refers resembles the cooperative idea embodied in doulia. And indeed, both the savings principle and doulia are consequences of the facts of human development and generation: as the benefit of the previous generation passes through us to the next and so on, the care a mother bestows on her child calls not only for reciprocation from the adult child but also for the grown children to care appropriately for a future generation.[19]

But how, one might ask, does this private interaction of mother, infant, and doula translate into a public conception of social cooperation? For this we need a public conception of doulia. To urge that the well-being of dependents *and* their caretakers *and* the relation itself between caretaker and dependent must be seen as requirements of public understanding of social cooperation, I invoke the fact that dependency is inherent to the human condition, that it often marks our most profound attachments, that care of a dependent morally obliges the dependency worker to give a certain priority to the welfare of her charge, and that the constitution of dependency relations is such that the parties are of necessity unequal. That is, it is the responsibility of the public order to ensure that a dependent has a caretaker, that the dependency relation is respected, and that the caretaker is adequately provided for so that her dependency work does not in turn deplete her. Without a broadened conception of reciprocity and a suitably modified sense of fairness, the dependency worker and dependent cannot be embraced within the bonds of social cooperation and accorded their full moral worth as equals in a well-ordered society.

In the next section, I argue that to the extent that the FMLA recognizes the dependency responsibilities of those engaged in paid employment and accepts a public responsibility to assure that those in a relation of dependency have adequate care and can give adequate care, it identifies social cooperation in the enlarged sense of doulia. Where it restricts leave time and opportunities, and where it limits resources allocated to those in relations of dependency, it reverts to the traditional liberal model.

READING THE FAMILY AND MEDICAL LEAVE ACT OF 1993

The FMLA is, in many ways, emblematic of the sort of legislation and social policy that is required to meet dependency needs of paid workers. It permits up to twelve workweeks of unpaid leave within any twelve-month period for one or more of the following reasons:

> (A) Because of the birth of a son or daughter of the employee and in order to care for such son or daughter.
> (B) Because of the placement of a son or daughter with the employee for adoption or foster care.
> (C) In order to care for the spouse, or son, daughter, or parent of the employee, if such spouse, son, daughter, or parent has a serious health condition.
> (D) Because of a serious health condition that makes the employee unable to perform the functions of the position of such employee. (Public Law 103–3—Feb. 5, 1993, 107 Stat. 9)

This law expressly recognizes the dependency relations that I have argued are so grievously ignored in much political theory. And it recognizes the importance of acknowledging some of the demands of dependency not only of the employee herself, but those of the individuals who depend on her. Given that the United States has had no provisions set by law to address the needs of paid employees with such concerns, the Family and Medical Leave Act is an immensely important piece of legislation.

But the law is relatively limited in its scope and in the real benefits it provides, and so its contribution to fair equality for all is circumscribed. I suggest that the limitations are traceable to an ideology of reciprocity and equality that continues to push dependency concerns back into the domain of the private, that is, to a conception of dependency concerns which still fails to recognize the extent to which addressing these needs is a matter of the social cooperation required for a well-ordered and just society.

Among the limitations of the act are the following: leave is unpaid; employers with less than fifty employees are exempt from the FMLA; and the FMLA construes family in relatively traditional terms. Let us look at the "Findings and Purposes" of the FMLA, and then return to consider if these bear on the limitations of the act.

(a) FINDINGS.—Congress finds that—

> (1) the number of single-parent households and two-parent households in which the single parent or both parents work is increasing significantly;
> (2) it is important for the development of children and the family unit that fathers and mothers be able to participate in early childrearing and the care of family members who have serious health conditions;
> (3) the lack of employment policies to accommodate working parents can force individuals to choose between job security and parenting;
> (4) there is inadequate job security for employees who have serious health conditions that prevent them from working for temporary periods;
> (5) due to the nature of the roles of men and women in our society, the primary responsibility for family caretaking often falls on women, and such responsibility affects the working lives of women more than it affects the working lives of men; and
> (6) employment standards that apply to one gender only have serious potential for encouraging employers to discriminate against employees and applicants for employment who are that gender. (Public Law 103–3, 107 Stat. 6–7)

First among the findings is that the number of single-parent households and two-parent households in which the parent(s) all work has significantly increased. The fact that this counts as a finding for a bill such as the FMLA is indicative of the way in which the breakdown of the sexual division of labor on the male side of the divide—expanding the paid labor force to include more women—is putting pressure on de-genderizing the female side of the divide—the largely private and unpaid care for dependents. This is the first significant step in understanding that dependency concerns need to be a part of the public understanding of social cooperation: that decisions to undertake dependency care cannot remain matters of private decision making with only private consequences, but belong within the public arena.

The second finding serves to recognize the nonfungibility of many dependency relations—e. g., the need of a sick child to have a parent attending her—but also moves retrogressively in the direction of the privatization of dependency care by suggesting that the importance of early child rearing and care of family members who have serious health conditions is for "the development of children and the family unit" rather than for the general welfare of the nation and so a public feature of social cooperation.

The third finding points to the need for policies that avoid pitting job security against parenting demands. Both job security and parenting are regarded as matters that are important for the well-being of individuals. The law recognizes the importance of the state in assuring both goods to those individuals who may be torn between competing concerns, and so it establishes a responsibility of public institutions to assure that individuals can fulfill dependency responsibilities as well as job-related duties, and that the burden of dependency work must sit not solely on the shoulders of those who undertake these obligations.[20] But how far does it go? Not very far. The leave is unpaid and the exemption for employers of fewer than fifty persons is not insignificant. There is no acknowledgment of public responsibility to assure job security, given parental responsibility for children. Why should parenting responsibilities be privileged with respect to job security? The basis for securing such a privileged relation is tenuous indeed, as the law's limited scope indicates.

It is here that a public conception of doulia needs to be brought into play—the reciprocity of doulia. More than "accommodation" is required. Accommodation presumes the situation of employment as it is now; accommodation neither challenges concepts of what counts as part of the economy nor employment conditions that presume privatized dependency arrangements. To acknowledge the contribution of those engaged in dependency work to the larger society—the contribution to the continuity, stability, and resources of society—means that the larger society has an obligation to support dependency work. Supporting dependency work means relieving the dependency worker of some of the costs and burdens of responsibility for the care of dependents. The argument from a public conception of doulia is that *fairness* demands that business or government—whatever public institutions are appropriate—carry some of the costs of dependency work so that dependents within our society can be properly cared for without exploiting dependency workers.

The fourth finding, which addresses the inadequate job security for workers with serious or prolonged health conditions, is an acknowledgment of the vulnerability to dependency that is shared by all employees.

The fifth and sixth findings are of special interest, for they acknowledge the inequity that results from the gender-specific nature of much dependency work. That work has occupied the female side of the sexual division of labor. The fifth and sixth findings call our attention to the failure of efforts to bring about gender equality on the side of the sexual division of labor traditionally occupied by men when the labor on the other side of the divide—the side traditionally occupied by women (see Hadfield 1993) remains the sole, and unsupported, responsibility of women. The justification for the bill that can be garnered from findings five and six is an equality argument, an inference sustained by the fourth and fifth stated purposes of the bill (see below). But until we reconstrue equality and political conceptions such as justice and social cooperation, and until it becomes a public priority to refashion sensibilities accordingly, the FMLA cannot alter the gender-structured nature of dependency concerns nor can it move us sufficiently in the direction of understanding that dependency work cannot be privatized and genderized without violating justice and equality.

Now let us now look at the "Purposes" of the act. I reproduce these in full: (b) PURPOSES.—It is the purpose of this Act—

> (1) to balance the demands of the workplace with the needs of families, to promote the stability and economic security of families, and to promote national interests in preserving family integrity;
> (2) to entitle employees to take reasonable leave for medical reasons, for the birth or adoption of a child, and for the care of a child, spouse, or parent who has a serious health condition;
> (3) to accomplish the purposes described in paragraphs (1) and (2) in a manner that accommodates the legitimate interests of employers;
> (4) to accomplish the purposes described in paragraphs (1) and (2) in a manner that, consistent with the Equal Protection Clause of the Fourteenth Amendment, minimizes the potential for employment discrimination on the basis of sex by ensuring generally that leave is available for eligible medical reasons (including maternity-related disability) and for compelling family reasons, on a gender-neutral basis; and
> (5) to promote the goal of equal employment opportunity for women and men, pursuant to such clause. (Public Law 103–3, 107 Stat. 6–7)

The purposes of this act recognize "national interests in preserving family integrity." But the act does not identify what about family integrity is important for the national interest, and so it cannot count anything but a limited set of traditional structures as family. The purpose stated in (3) is to "accomplish the purposes described in (1) and (2) in a manner that accommodates the legitimate interests of employers." But if there are national interests in preserving family integrity, why should (1) and (2) not trump the interests of employers? And if they don't, what are the consequences?

In the light of the reading of the "Findings and Purposes," let us consider what I have listed as the limitations of the act. First, the leave is unpaid—all twelve weeks of permissible leave time are unpaid. To take off from work to attend a sick child then remains a luxury, or a factor moving one closer to impoverishment. Not only is the United States one of the last industrialized countries to have a family leave policy, it is also the only one in which the leave is entirely unpaid.[21] One of the purported findings to which the act is addressed is the increase in the number of single-parent households. But how many single-parent employees can afford to be without pay for three months of the year? How are they supposed to put food on the table of a sick and needy person? One need not argue that the full twelve weeks ought to be paid, but surely some of that time needs to be paid leave—by law, not merely by the goodwill of some employers who provide paid leave—if it is to have a substantial impact on the practices of single-parent households—which now constitute one-fourth of all households.[22]

Second, employers with fewer than fifty employees are exempt from the family leave policy. But employees in companies with fewer than fifty employees make up a very large portion of the American work force. In fact, they make up the *majority* of the work force.[23] That means that a majority of paid employees in this country are not covered under the FMLA! What is clear, again, is that heeding dependency concerns is not viewed as a general responsibility. These can be trumped by the employers' needs—benefits for whom are not only thought to be personal but also to be part of the economic well-being of the wider public—and nothing is put in place to meet the putatively *personal* demands of the employee, even when family integrity is identified as a "national interest." Dependency care is not counted as part of the economic structure; it does not figure into the Gross National Product.

Third, the FMLA construes family in relatively traditional terms. Although *parent* includes not only biological parents but also any individuals who have stood in *loco parentis*, and the term *son or daughter* is defined as "a biological, adopted, or foster child, a stepchild, a legal ward, or a child of a parent standing in loco parentis," the term "spouse" is restricted to husband or wife, leaving out nonmarried adults who are cohabitating, gay and lesbian families, extended families, and so forth. Contrast this with the "nurturance leave" proposed by feminist legal theorist Nadine Taub (1984, 85), which argues for nurturance leaves for any adult members of a household. If the stress in our policies is to support dependency relations because the fabric of social structure is founded on the maintenance of such relations, then the relations themselves and not the social institutions in which they have traditionally been lodged ought to become the focus of our concern.

The decisions or situations from which these dependency relations result may appear to be private decisions between the parties involved—decisions between parties which do not devolve obligations on third parties. But there are some social institutions which appear to be formed by private decisions between the parties involved and which nonetheless induce obligations in third parties.[24] Marriage is such an institution. The private decision another and I make to be a married couple means that socially and legally certain actions are binding on my employer, my landlord, hospitals, insurance agencies, the IRS, and so on. In an analogous fashion, the private decision to take on the work of dependency and to form a dependency relation with a charge ought to induce third party obligations to support the dependency worker in his or her care for the charge. In the case of marriage, the binding obligations are part of a larger societal interest in maintaining the institution of marriage. Recognition of its legal and social status means that the existence of a connection between two individuals is acknowledged.

A major reason, however, to recognize such institutions is that they are the loci of the care and sustenance of dependents. The relation of dependency is morally and socially still more salient and fundamental than marriage, and so forms the very ground of this feature of the marriage relation. But the social technology of traditional marriage and family makes the dependency worker and charge within the nuclear family vulnerable to the vicissitudes of the marriage arrangement and vulnerable in a relation of (to use Amartya Sen's term) "cooperative conflict."[25] The claim on third parties to support and help sustain the dependency relation, independent of a particular arrangement such as marriage, has morally the stronger claim. This claim is realized in the public obligation of social cooperation I have called *doulia*. The argument for such doulia transcends the institution of marriage as traditionally understood and family arrangements sanctioned by traditional marriage and biological relation. Its basis is the undertaking of care, and responsibility for care, and the dependency to which the caretaker then becomes vulnerable.

The FMLA is an example of the legislative and policy directions in which the dependency critique urges us, but it remains still all too firmly grounded in a conception of society primarily constituted by those who are healthy, autonomous adults, who, as Rawls would have it, are "fully functioning" and for whom justice requires the reciprocity of those equally situated. We need to shift our vision and see society as constituted by the nested dependencies that require a concept of justice between persons who are equal in their connectedness but unequal in their vulnerability and for whom a notion of doulia—of caring for those who care—is central.

The arguments in this essay have been directed at demonstrating that the Rawlsian and the liberal account of social cooperation is at best incomplete and at worst inadequate, and that legislation such as the FMLA falls short of meeting the needs of dependency demands as long as it remains within a framework which is represented in the Rawlsian account. The claim here is that a society cannot be well-ordered, that is, it cannot be one in which all its members are sustained and included within the ideal of equality, if it fails to be a society characterized by care. For a society to be characterized by care, we need something other than the affirmation of the importance of family integrity. We need structures that will assure that dependency work, whether done in families or other social institutions, can be carried out under nonexploitative conditions. What is required is that the public understanding of social cooperation include respect for the importance of caring for one another and the value of receiving care and giving care. It then becomes a matter of political justice for basic institutions to *make provisions for and facilitate satisfactory dependency relations*. The only assurance that both dependents and dependency workers are well cared for and can benefit from an egalitarian ideal is the inclusion of enabling conditions and resources for care through the social institutions that reflect the public understanding of social cooperation. For a well-ordered society, therefore, to instill in its citizens a sense of justice and a sense of what is right, it must also be sensitive to our vulnerability to dependency and to the vulnerability of those who attend to dependents.[26] Rawls speaks of the need to give priority to the basic liberties and points out that even when the political will does not yet exist to do what is required (as it does not in the society in which we live), "part of the political task is to help fashion it" (1993, 297). The possibilities of the FMLA and its shortcomings indicate that it is no less the case that since the political will to imbue citizens with such a sensitivity and sense of priority for care does not yet exist, "part of the political task is to help fashion it."

NOTES

I thank the editors of this special issue and the anonymous reviewers for their suggestions. I also thank Lisa Conradi for her comments at the Conference on Feminism and Social Policy, the audience at the session for their remarks, and members of the New York City Society for Women in Philosophy Research Group in Ethical, Social and Political Philosophy for their helpful discussion of an earlier draft.

1. The literature is extensive. I mention but a few discussions of difference feminists. See Allen (1987); hooks (1987); Kay (1985); Littleton (1987); Minow (1990); Scales-Trent (1989); West (1987); Williams (1982, 1985); Wolgast (1980).

2. bell hooks (1987) asks, "Since men are not equals in white supremacist, capitalist, patriarchical class structure, which men do women want to be equal to?" The point stressed by a number of feminists and captured by hooks is that the striving for equality on the part of the largely white and middle-class women's movement presumes an egalitarianism into which women can integrate themselves. In Kittay (N.d.), I call this the "heterogeneity critique." It speaks to a heterogeneity among women not acknowledged in demands for sexual equality. Because the heterogeneity critique is aimed less at any particular formulation of equality than at a prevailing formulation of sex equality which masks intragender inequalities, inequalities that result from race, class, sexual orientation, age, and disabilities, as well as cross-gender inequalities, it is orthogonal to the other critiques. The force of the heterogeneity critiques emerges with special poignancy

when one looks at the racial complexion of dependency workers in countries blighted by racial inequity.

3. Catharine MacKinnon is the main exponent of this view (1987, 1989).

4. Several feminist theorists have regarded the work of liberal political philosophers with an eye toward issues of dependency without articulating the dependency critique. Those who have done so have spoken of "the need for more than justice," as Baier (1987) entitles one work expounding this theme (see also Baier 1985, 1986). Others, such as Patemen (1988) and Held (1987a, 1987b) have shed light on the unacknowledged gender considerations that undergird a social contract engaged in by men. The work of Okin (1979, 1989a, 1989b) brings the historical and contemporary neglect of women's involvement in dependency to the forefront of her political considerations. Okin has been the most articulate, yet sympathetic critic of the influential political theory of John Rawls on matters that concern familial dependency relations. Tronto's (1993) work bringing the notion of care into the arena of political theory may also be seen to be a contribution to the dependency critique.

5. See Young (N.d.) for an interesting discussion of a false ideal of independence in understanding citizenship.

6. Tronto (1993) points out that caring is an activity that requires several stages for its completion: caring about, caring for, response to care. We may note that the person cared for need be only potentially responsive in order for her to be a part of a dependency relation.

7. I thank John Baker for suggesting that I make explicit my view that the dependency critique is meant to hold for dependency workers whether they voluntarily take on that task or whether they are perforce burdened with it.

8. Rawls repeats a similar statement in *Political Liberalism*: "The normal range is specified as follows: since the fundamental problem of justice concerns the relations among those who are full and active participants in society, and directly or indirectly associated together over the course of a whole life, it is reasonable to *assume that everyone has physical needs and psychological capacities within some normal range. Thus the problem of special health care and how to treat mentally defective are set.* If we can work out a viable theory for the normal range, we can attempt to handle these other cases later" (Rawls 1993, 272 n. 10; emphasis is mine).

9. Each of the above points, as well as a discussion of social cooperation are elaborated in Kittay (unpublished).

10. In *A Theory of Justice*, Rawls writes: "The main idea is that when a number of persons engage in a mutually advantageous cooperative venture according to rules, and thus restrict their liberty in ways necessary to yield advantages for all, those who have submitted to the restrictions have a right to a similar acquiescence on the part of those who have benefitted from their submission" (Rawls 1971, 112).

11. I thank Susan Okin for valuable discussion on this point.

12. It needs to be pointed out that the paid dependency worker is often paid not by the dependent, but by someone who stands in a relation of guardianship or stewardship to the dependent.

13. "How deep a fault this is must wait until the case itself can be examined," says Rawls and reminds us that political justice needs to be complemented by additional virtues (1993, 21).

14. When we look back to *A Theory of Justice*, we see that for Rawls the problem appears to be how to have strangers cooperate. Friends and intimate associates, so the

supposition goes, cooperate because they have ties of sentiment. But consider, when a mother acts toward a child through ties of sentiment, many of her own needs—often including the need to earn an income—go unattended unless she has intimate ties to someone who is willing to cooperate and attend to her needs. That is, her ties of sentiment provide little in the way of societal cooperative efforts that suffice to sustain her and her children. (Furthermore, the assumption that the mother's cooperative behavior toward her children is motivated by parental ties of sentiment makes a puzzle of the apparent frequency with which men so often feel less obligated by ties of sentiment to provide for their children when no longer involved with the mother—U.S. fathers currently owe mothers $24 billion in unpaid child support, according to the *Report of the Federal Office of Child Support Enforcement [1990].*) It is just such a precarious dependence on ties of sentiment on the part of those (women mostly) who do dependency work, especially when it is unpaid—that leave them (again, women for the most part) so vulnerable to exploitation, (male) domination, and poverty. It is such precariousness that makes her inclusion in the political sphere so tentative.

15. See Aronow (1993). One of the doulas "recalls arriving at home late in the morning to find mothers who haven't eaten or dressed. 'They are so concerned that the baby is O.K., they forget to take care of themselves'" (Aronow 1993, 8).

16. I wish to thank Elfie Raymond for helping me search for a term to capture the concept articulated here.

17. See Stacks (1974) for a discussion of this ethic in the African American community. What Stacks describes as "swapping" is more like a one-to-one reciprocal arrangement than what I am trying to characterize by *doulia*. However, it resembles *doulia* insofar as reciprocity is deferred and is geared to the meeting of needs as they arise rather than as payment qua tit-for-tat exchanges.

18. This is a phrase Rawls borrows from Alexander Herzen. See Rawls (1971, 291).

19. I do not mean to suggest that we have a duty to *have* children because we have been cared for, but that we owe to any children we may have a quality of care at least as high as the care we received. And furthermore that the care bestowed on us is, in fact *reciprocated*, through care to the next generation.

20. That burden can be measured, in part, in economic terms. Estimates of the costs to workers of not having a parental leave only are $607 million versus approximately $110 million as based on the more generous leave policies of earlier versions of the act (Spalter-Roth and Hartmann 1990, 42). The cost is greatest to those least able to bear these costs, namely workers with the lowest incomes, with African American men doing worse than white men, white women doing worse than white men, and African American women doing worse than white women (Spalter-Roth and Hartmann 1990, 2833). See Spalter-Roth and Hartmann (1990) for a detailed analysis. It is curious that in speaking of the cost of meeting dependency needs, the cost to businesses is seen as a public concern, while the cost to the workers who bear the major burden is regarded as a private concern.

21. Ellen Gilensky, Families and Work Institute, personal communication with author, New York City, 1 August 1994.

22. On the morning of the day I was to read this paper at the Feminist Ethics and Social Policy Conference held at the University of Pittsburgh, the public radio station announced on its news program that in Pittsburgh the figure was one-third of all households.

23. Only 44 percent of women workers and 52 percent of men workers are covered

by the current act which exempts employers with fewer than fifty employees (see Spalter-Roth and Hartmann 1990, 44).

24. This idea can be found in Kaplan (1993).

25. Sen (1990) has argued this point with respect to certain third world countries. Borrowing from the work of Okin (1989) and others, I extend Sen's argument to apply to traditional marriage within the industrialized world as well (Kittay N.d.).

26. See Goodin (1985) for a very useful discussion of our obligations to protect those who are vulnerable.

REFERENCES

Allen, Anita L. 1987. Taking liberties: Privacy, private choice, and social contract theory. *University of Cincinnati Law Review* 56(1–2).

Aronow, Ina. 1993. Doulas step in when mothers need a hand. *New York Times*, 1 August, 1, 8, Westchester Weekly.

Baier, Annette. 1985. Caring about caring. In *Postures of the mind: Essays on mind and morals*. Minneapolis: University of Minnesota Press.

———. 1986. Trust and antitrust. *Ethics* 96: 231–60.

———. 1987. The need for more than justice. In *Science, morality and feminist theory*, ed. Marsha Hanen and Kai Nielsen. Calgary: University of Calgary Press.

Daniels, Norman. 1990. Equality of what: Welfare, resources, or capabilities? *Philosophy and Phenomenological Research Supplement* 50: 273–96.

Goodin, Robert. 1985. *Protecting the vulnerable*. Chicago: University of Chicago Press.

Hadfield, Gillian K. 1993. Households at work: Beyond labor market policies to remedy the gender gap. *Georgetown Law Journal* 82: 89.

Held, Virginia. 1978. Men, women, and equal liberty. In *Equality and social policy*, ed. Walter Feinberg. Urbana: University of Illinois Press.

———. 1987a. Non-contractual society: A feminist view. *Canadian Journal of Philosophy* 13: 111–37.

———. 1987b. Feminism and moral theory. In *Women and moral theory*. See Kittay and Meyers 1987.

hooks, bell. 1987. Feminism: A movement to end sexist oppression. In *Equality and feminism*, ed. Anne Phillips. New York: New York University Press.

Jaggar, Alison M. 1985. Women: Different but equal? Douglass College, Rutgers University.

Kaplan, Morris. 1993. Intimacy and equality: The question of lesbian and gay marriage. Paper delivered at the Stony Brook Philosophy Colloquium Series, 4 March.

Kay, Herma Hill. 1985. Equality and difference: The case of pregnancy. *Berkeley Women's Law Journal* 1.

Kittay, Eva Feder. N.d. *Equality and the inclusion of women*. New York: Routledge. Forthcoming.

———. Unpublished. Equality, Rawls and the dependency critique.

Kittay, Eva F. and Diana T. Meyers. 1987. *Women and moral theory*. Totowa, NJ: Rowman and Littlefield.

Littleton, Christine A. 1987. Equality across difference: A place for rights discourse? *Wisconsin Women's Law Journal* 3: 189–212.

MacKinnon, Catharine A. 1987. *Feminism unmodified: Discourses on life and law*. Cambridge: Harvard University Press.

———. 1989. *Toward a feminist theory of the state*. Cambridge: Harvard University Press.

Minow, Martha. 1990. *Making all the difference: Inclusion, exclusion and the American law*. Ithaca: Cornell University Press.

Okin, Susan. 1979. *Women in western political thought*. Princeton: Princeton University Press.

———. 1989a. *Justice, gender, and the family*. New York: Basic Books.

———. 1989b. Humanist liberalism. In *Liberalism and the moral life*, ed. Nancy L. Rosenbaum. Cambridge: Harvard University Press.

Pateman, Carol. 1988. *The sexual contract*. Stanford: Stanford University Press.

Public Law 103–3, 5 February 1993, 107 Stat., pp. 6–29.

Rawls, John. 1971. *A theory of justice*. Cambridge: Harvard University Press.

———. 1980. Kantian constructivism in moral theory: The Dewey lectures. *The Journal of Philosophy* 77(9): 515–72.

———. 1993. *Political liberalism*. New York: Columbia University Press.

Scales-Trent, Judy. 1989. Black women and the constitution: finding our place, asserting our rights. *Harvard Civil Rights-Civil Liberties Law Review* 24: 9–44.

Sen, Amartya. 1990. Gender and cooperative conflict. In *Persistent inequalities*, ed. Irene Tinker. Oxford: Oxford University Press.

Spalter-Roth, Roberta M. and Heidi I. Hartmann. 1990. Unnecessary losses: Cost to Americans of the lack of a family and medical leave. Washington, DC: Institute for Women's Policy Research.

Stacks, Carol B. 1974. *All our kin: Strategies for survival in a black community*. New York: Harper and Row.

Taub, Nadine. 1984–85. From parental leaves to nurturing leaves. *Review of Law and Social Change*, 13.

Tronto, Joan C. 1993. *Moral boundaries: A political argument for an ethic of care*. New York: Routledge.

West, Robin L. 1987. The difference in women's hedonic lives: A pheno-meno-logical critique of feminist legal theory. *Wisconsin Women's Law Journal* 3: 81–145.

Williams, Wendy W. 1982. The equality crisis: Some reflections on culture, courts, and feminism. *Women's Rights Law Reporter* 7: 175–200.

———. 1985. Equality's riddle: Pregnancy and the equal treatment/special treatment debate. *New York University Review of Law and Social Change*, 13.

Wolgast, Elizabeth. 1980. *Equality and the rights of women*. Ithaca: Cornell University Press.

Young, Iris Marion. N.d. Mothers, citizenship and independence: A critique of pure family values. *Ethics*. Forthcoming.

2

Reconciling Equality to Difference

Caring (F)or Justice for People with Disabilities

ANITA SILVERS

WOMEN MERELY "EQUAL" TO MEN WOULD BE "LIKE THEM," THEREFORE NOT WOMEN AT ALL.

—LUCE IRIGARAY, *THIS SEX WHICH IS NOT ONE*

WOMEN CANNOT GIVE UP "DIFFERENCE"; IT HAS BEEN OUR MOST CREATIVE ANALYTIC TOOL.

—JOAN SCOTT, "DECONSTRUCTING EQUALITY VERSUS DIFFERENCE"

THE DILEMMA OF DIFFERENCE

Of feminism's many transformations of the social thought we have inherited from the Enlightenment, the advancing of difference as a key to moral value has been most influential in theory yet most problematic in application. The difficulty with difference is that legitimating it, along with the disparate treatment it appears to promote, threatens to attenuate our devotion to equality. Embraced as our paramount American ideal, it is equality that has propelled us toward progressively inclusive social practice. Yet, whether equality's route to social inclusiveness marginalizes whoever cannot or will not be homogenized is the troubling question raised by feminist reappraisals of difference. And this leads to the equally troubling question of whether, so as to give

Hypatia vol. 10, no. 1 (Winter 1995) © by Anita Silvers

differences their due, we are compelled to retreat from the heretofore cherished goal of inclusiveness.

"Dilemmas of difference appear irresolvable," warns Martha Minow in beginning *Making All the Difference: Inclusion, Exclusion and American Law.* "The right to be treated as an individual ignores the burdens of group membership; the right to object to the burdens of group membership reinvokes the trait that carries the negative meanings. . . . Why do we encounter this dilemma about how to redress the negative consequences of difference without reenacting it?" (Minow 1990, 49–48). According to Minow, dilemmas of difference confront those who seek justice for such historically subordinated groups as women, racial and ethnic minorities, children, and people with disabilities. For instance, Minow maintains, we should not deny someone with a serious disability the same medical treatment available to nondisabled people, yet in satisfying a principle of neutrality toward disability we may victimize the disabled person by inappropriately disregarding how her needs, expectations, and outcomes differ on account of her situation.

Unlike the ethics of equality, which explicitly eliminates individuals' special affiliations or stations from the foundational considerations that structure morality, ethics associated with feminism—namely, those which elevate such values as caring or trust over equality as being central or crucial to morality—build recognition of differentiating relational characteristics such as dependence, vulnerability, or special need into morality's base. But by magnifying the importance of positional differences, these ethics seemingly cast equality as illusory or irrelevant, thereby challenging the priority our institutions assign to uniform over disparate treatment.

To be most just to previously marginalized people, is it equality or is it difference which most deserves preeminence?[1] In this essay, I argue that social policy that reconciles equality with difference can advance historically subordinated groups but that displacing equality in favor of positional ethics merely reprises the repression of those already marginalized. In my exploration of how certain negative social consequences of difference may be repaired through equal treatment, I follow Minow's suggestion that persons with serious disabilities are among the most stubbornly limiting cases in respect to the homogenization of moral personhood. I will show that this is so as well as why it is so.

Having established the pervasiveness with which serious physical or mental impairment is viewed as an intractably negative difference, I will consider how individuals with disabilities are treated by the ethics of caring and trust, moral positions that advocate grounding just treatment on difference. Here I will disclose why difference is not an effective foundational notion for remedying the negative consequences attendant on how the disabled are different. Recognizing that my previous discussions follow current feminist practice in assuming difference to be a product of social construction, I will turn next to a view which rejects this assumption; namely, the belief that inequality follows naturally rather than artificially on disability. Having firmly disposed of this suggestion, I will consider the conception of equality embedded in the 1990 Americans with Disabilities Act (the ADA) and argue that it resolves both theoretical and practical aspects of the dilemma of difference.

JUSTICE, EQUALITY, AND DIFFERENCE

First, though, let us recall why (some) feminist theory takes equality to be a repressive rather than a liberating notion. In the service of equalizing, it is charged, our Enlightenment tradition imposes uniformity on the core descriptions of moral agents, stripping them of their differentiating particularities and positions so that what counts toward moral personhood is neither multifarious nor susceptible of much variation. Forms of recognition responsive to race, culture, sex, gender, class, and other features that diversify us thus are dismissed as not vital to moral identity, a repudiation that implicitly confers permission to marginalize individuals for whose personal or social identities these differences are inescapable. Far from liberating members of groups subordinated on account of difference by demonstrating their underlying identity with dominant kinds of persons, the conceptual device of abstracting from difference to uniformity is thought by feminist critics and others to become just another instrument furthering social repression. As Charles Taylor observes in commenting on the new politics of identity: "Not only contemporary feminism but also race relations and discussions of multiculturalism are undergirded by the premise that the withholding of recognition can be a form of oppression" (Taylor et al. 1992, 36).

So is it difference rather than sameness which policy should privilege? With equality dominant, justice prohibits individuals being treated disparately, while, when difference displaces equality, justice encourages diverse treatment for different groups. Roughly, when identified with equality, justice usually is construed as an attribute of those distributive systems that are effectively constrained by the assumption that people are essentially the same, regardless of the individuating accidents of their different personal and social histories and positions. Typical of schemes that comply with this standard are distributive systems that adopt either equality of opportunity or equality of outcomes as necessary to justice.[2]

However, feminist and other critiques challenge the serviceability of a conception of justice that demands construction of an ideally impartial point of view on which all, both the viewer and the viewed, appear to need identical opportunities or outcomes. Among the charges brought against such a standard of impartiality are that it fruitlessly attempts to escape from the particularities of position (e.g., desires, interests, affinities, and impairments) which inescapably influence our actual actions, that it deceptively disguises dominant groups' viewpoints as "everyone's," and that, consequently, differences distinctive of subordinated groups are labeled as inferiorities, liabilities, menaces, or risks. From these objections to conceiving justice as bound to the formal interchangeability of agents emerges an alternative construal of justice as the virtue exhibited by social arrangements that encourage the satisfaction of personal need and desires through inclusive positive interaction of individuals or groups.[3] Rather than abstracting from personal and social positionality, justice as diversity embraces difference, which is seen as energizing rather than impeding progressively inclusive moral and social practice.

These paradigms agree that just policies are neutral to difference just to the point at which difference converts to disadvantage by being viewed as deviation from a standard or norm. At which point, formal justice, which idealizes equality, deals with deviance by discounting it, while interactive justice, which celebrates difference, deals with deviance by revaluing it positively. Whether a dissimilarity is better ignored or better acknowledged is relative to many variables, including the kinds of group identities that figure in social interaction within a society. Thus, for instance, in a persistently racist society where race intractably matters, exalting previously deprecated attributes of a racial group (such as its African heritage) may be more effective in improving the social standing of the group's members than trying to neutralize those attributes (such as requiring Africans to become competent in the European tradition).

On the other hand, it may not. For to characterize the alternatives thus is to discount the dilemma of difference, which as Minow reminds us is precipitated where group membership is a negative and burdensome trait, not a transformable positive one, yet is also unavoidably an element of the groups' members' social identity. Research into the psychology of cognition generally agrees that, in vague or sparse perceptual contexts, differences are cognized as deviant. Where context makes a difference salient, its perceived strangeness amplifies the insecurity we experience when what we encounter is alien. Thus, absent clear and replete contexts that the discordant discomfort the perception of anomaly provokes, a group's salient differences may persist in being cognized negatively as fearfully socially deviant (Wright 1988, 5).

Abundant research has shown that Americans with disabilities are subject to persisting and generalized negative bias in social relations.[4] By the nature of their difference, the presence of individuals with disabilities in social interactions tends to amplify aggravating ambivalence in other people. For a nondisabled person, both a friendly response made towards a disabled person—that is, someone who is regarded as unworthy and burdensome—and a hostile response made against a disabled person —that is, someone who is regarded as unfortunate—casts the "defective" person as an irritant to the nondisabled person's sense of self-esteem (See Katz, Hass, and Bailey 1988, 47–57).

Given its salience, disability thus appears to have a prima facie negative impact on interpersonal relating. Here then is a dilemma triggered by difference. Disability tests to the limit whether the irreducibility of difference is central to morality or whether even for the disabled equality eclipses alterity. Disability tests as well which paradigm of justice best resists marginalization or repression attendant on the negative consequences of difference.

Members of the group differentiated in respect to disability deviate from the norm in virtue of having a physical or mental deficit severe enough to bar their performing one or more major life activities. I adopt this definition of "the disabled" from the legal definition of the class granted equal treatment by the ADA—that is, by the civil rights legislation that specifies the extension of Fourteenth Amendment protections to individuals so defined. As the discussion progresses, I will provide more detail regarding some of the provisions and conceptions found in this law, particularly those which elucidate how being equal can be responsive to being different.[5]

HOW "DEFECTIVE" AGENTS FRUSTRATE EQUALITY

From the thirteenth century, it has been widely held that indulging, exempting, or shielding people with disabilities or placing them in specially protective care is more realistically to their benefit than giving them access to merely equal treatment (Stone 1984, chap. 2). Thus, to clarify why these people need to be protected, and in what their protection effectively may consist, probes the contrast between equal and disparate treatment.[6] Commenting on this contrast, Joan Scott observes: "Equality, in the political theory of rights that lies behind the claims of excluded groups for justice, means the ignoring of differences between individuals. . . . This presumes a social agreement to consider obviously different people as equivalent" (Scott 1990, 142). But serious impairment so resists being thus dismissed through social agreement that individuals with disabilities customarily are conceptualized as irremediably unequal.

To illustrate, a remark offered offhandedly by Charles Taylor in his recent *Multiculturalism and "The Politics of Recognition"* illustrates why the existence of defective agents frustrates the leveling tendencies of progressive social agreements. Commenting on the extent to which egalitarianism characterizes modern moral thought, Taylor identifies "the basis for our intuitions of equal dignity" as "a universal human potential, a capacity that all humans share." But, he continues, "our sense of the importance of potentiality reaches so far that we extend this protection even to people who through some circumstance that has befallen them are incapable of realizing their potential in the normal way—handicapped people . . . for instance" (Taylor 1992, 41–42). By assuming that being handicapped places an individual in global deficit, Taylor suggests that it is only in virtue of an intervening fiction that such "defective" agents have equitable access to the categorical principles on which humans generally are accorded dignity or respect. Far from flattering the egalitarian project, this way of putting things deconstructs it by intimating that "handicapped" people are equal only by extension or derivation or fiction because they really don't possess the essentially humanizing capacity to fulfill their potential 'normally.' (And if so for the handicapped, for whom else is equality thought to be only a fiction?)

But it is delusive to purport to delineate normal, or full, from abnormal, or restricted, realization of potential as Taylor does. For not just the disabled but every human being has potentials which through circumstance remain unrealized, and whether these could have been fulfilled "in the normal way," and whether any loss accrues in not realizing them, is merely speculative. We would not dream of declaring that an athletically gifted person who cannot realize his potential as a professional boxer because he wants to play the concert violin is equal only in some extended sense. So, but for the degree to which disability resists equality, why place an artistically gifted violinist like Itzhak Perlman, who has not actualized whatever potential he has for boxing because he cannot walk unaided, in this inferior category?

As Taylor's comment indicates, moral thought in the Enlightenment tradition has not construed disability as being like other particularities which differentiate moral agents one from another. While most other differences between persons are dismissed as contingent and external, and thus as accidental to a person's moral being (this being the maneuver of which radical feminist theory complains), disability unmistakably has been embraced as a morally essential attribute, one which assigns those who have it to the borderline of moral worth. The moral status of individuals with disabilities thus is impaired because the stereotype of them defeats a condition imposed by most and perhaps all rational moral systems, namely, that reasons for action must not be opaque to normal adults.

Able-bodied persons often say they cannot imagine wanting to live if they became confined to a wheelchair.[7] For instance, despite the preexistence of the ADA and the publicity occasioned by its passage in 1990 and its phased-in implementation beginning in 1991, Oregon's public policy makers did not shrink from dictating that having an irreparable disability should be sufficient ground for being denied health care, and even life itself.[8] As originally proposed, the Oregon Health Plan internalized ancient exclusionary prejudices and stereotypes. Being impaired in *some* way that defies medical restoration automatically reduced one's eligibility for *many kinds* of care because the system's conceptual framework assumed that to be disabled is without question to live an inferior quality life. This ranking was arrived at through a telephone survey of able-bodied individuals who surmised, for example, that they would rather be dead than confined to a wheelchair. (Parenthetically, such morbid counterfactual speculation by the able-bodied often is utilized in public policy contexts to justify exclusion of people with disabilities from many parts of life.)

But that their testimony expressed myths about disability rather than empirically confirmable wants is evidenced by how far from accurate they are in predicting the actual behavior of persons with disabilities.[9] The suicide rate among persons with disabilities would be much greater than it is if the survey had reported actual preferences instead of fearful fantasies. Employed in the original version of the Oregon Health Plan to prioritize treatments, the survey was used to impose somebody else's suicidal fantasies on disabled individuals, thereby diminishing their access to health care and denying them recognition as self-determining moral beings. This basis for rationing health care subsequently was judged by the U.S. Department of Health and Human Services to be in violation of the ADA.

What obstructed ethical thinking here is that reasoning responds to the common, not the deviant, case. In general, the compulsion to dismiss the disabled as abnormal—that is, as being in a state unthinkable for oneself—renders all appeals to such criteria as what one would wish done were one in the other person's place ineffective where persons with disabilities are concerned. For a moral reason to have motivating power, moral agents must understand it or "get it." If this is so, but "normal" individuals cannot accurately estimate what they would be like if in a "damaged" individual's place, then truths about how one would want to be treated if one were disabled are opaque to "normal" individuals and cannot motivate them morally. (A similar point sometimes is made by denying that men can imagine themselves in a pregnant woman's place, but here the argument is somewhat more tenuous because it is unclear whether the denial extends to women who have never been or cannot become pregnant but who do not fear or abhor pregnancy. To be so different as to be unimaginable, an individual's perspective must be thought so unbearable or otherwise appalling as to forestall others from partaking of it even vicariously.)

Thus the requirement of experiential accessibility does not always succeed in furthering equality. Far from extending morality so that it cloaks even individuals with disabilities, this condition seems to magnify the impact of their deficits, so as to exclude these individuals from normal moral recognition. Parenthetically, the opacity of disabled people's experience seems to preclude their being subject to Martha Minow's resolution of the dilemma of difference. For, at the close of her book, Minow avers:

> By taking difference into account, we can overcome our pretended indifference to difference and our tendency to sort the world into "same" and "different," . . . "equal" and "unequal." . . . Admitting the partiality of the perspective that temporarily gains official endorsement may embolden resistance to announced rules. But only by admitting that rules are resistible—and by justifying to the governed their calls for adherence—can justice be done. . . . What we do with difference, and whether we acknowledge our own participation in the meanings of the differences we assign to others, are choices that remain. The experts in nineteenth-century anesthesiology did not stop to ask whether they properly understood the pain of others. We can do better. (Minow 1990, 389–90)

As we have seen, our aversion to the very idea of being disabled forestalls our understanding the disabled from their perspective. But perhaps the standard of understanding from the other's point of view is not germane. For, as explicated earlier by Minow, the risk incurred by the dilemma of difference lies in the probability not of misunderstanding but of mistreating those who are different. So what Minow might mean by "proper" understanding of those who are different might take the form not of imagining oneself in their place but rather of acknowledging their difference with an empathy sufficiently forceful to stand proof against their mistreatment.

EQUALITY OR CARING

To explore this suggestion, I propose to consider the view of Lawrence Blum (1991), who insists that it is not by *reasoning* about whether defective individuals are equal, but rather by *feeling* about their situations as they do themselves, that we can conduct ourselves morally toward them. Blum's diagnosis grows from his conviction that logic driven judgment stumbles where agents must behave ethically to persons less advantaged than themselves. Rather than trying to judge neutrally—that is, by constructing judgments that endeavor to be from no point of view—advantageously positioned agents should respond so sensitively that their perceptions of the particularities of any situation validate the perspective of whoever may be victimized by it.

For Blum, the possibility of interpersonal moral agreement in these cases lies not in abstracting from the experiential multifariousness of each unique perspective on a moral situation, but rather in engaging with uninviting perspectives so as to acknowledge them. Blum thus relaxes the standard for interpersonal moral reasoning by realizing that the perspectives of better- and worse-positioned agents may be so polarized by both concept and affect as to be experientially inaccessible to each other. Nevertheless, Blum advises, it is quite possible to acknowledge someone else's perspective while recognizing the impossibility of imagining one's self as that other person.

Blum explores the case of a disabled worker, debilitated by distress and treated unfeelingly by a supervisor who refuses to adjust her standards to his impaired performance. In Blum's view, it is natural to recognize the reality of others' pains, even if one cannot imagine having them. Other people's pain is invisible only to the morally blinded. Patterning his account on an actual case, Blum describes a supervisor, Theresa, who accepts her company's legal obligation under federal law to accommodate to the disability of an employee, Julio, but "who offers Julio less than he needs and is entitled to. . . . It is not that Theresa fails entirely to see Julio as 'disabled' and as 'in pain,' but she does fail fully to grasp what this means for him and fails fully to take in or acknowledge that pain. . . . Theresa is failing to perceive or acknowledge something morally significant—namely, Julio's physical pain and his distress at the impact of his condition on his work situation" (Blum 1991, 704–5).

Blum attributes Theresa's impaired moral vision to emotional blockage against certain threatening aspects of moral reality. Advantaged persons dread beholding damaged persons out of fear that they in future might themselves become impaired (Blum 1991, 718). Because the worker's debilitating despair is real, Blum addends, it is only the supervisor's impaired perception that blocks her from accepting the pained person's estimation of the incapacitating impact of his pain and his assessment of what she owes him in regard of it. But is this so?

I do not think it can be so, for to condemn the supervisor's moral proficiency in this way has some bizarre implications. First, although Blum condemns Theresa for offering Julio less than he needs and is entitled to, he seems to locate her deficiency on her failure to validate Julio's suffering. For, in respect to what Julio is entitled to, both Title I of the ADA and its predecessor, Section 503 of the 1993 Rehabilitation Act, provide that she need offer *only* what's required for him to do his job, as long as the cost of accommodation is not unreasonable when compared to the employer's entire budget. Legally, Theresa surely does not owe Julio *all* that he needs. Moreover, even on the most indulgent needs-based model of moral and social justice, it is irrational to demand for everyone *everything* they need, since satisfying some needs may prevent satisfying others. This suggests that the needs of whoever is disadvantaged constitute no clearer a standard of just interactions between superiors and their inferiors than the needs of whoever is advantaged do.

Second, however, Blum privileges Julio's judgment over Theresa's on the ground that the former, rather than the latter, has the veridical point of view regarding the reality of the debilitation attendant on his impairment. Blum thus seems to think Theresa *owes* forbearance to Julio to compensate for his position's being opaque to her. But a common experience in learning how to be disabled is to regret, when looking backward, one's initial debilitating panic and abdication. This process is recounted again and again in anecdotal and autobiographical material authored by persons with disabilities.

On Blum's account, which for this reason cannot be right, persons reconciled to their disabilities must be guilty of moral insensitivity to themselves. But it is absurd to think that disabled persons' earlier despairing states always are opaque to their later, more hopeful selves. Nor can it be from the former position only that disabled persons' moral identities can reflect their difference. Nor do disabled persons owe it to their earlier selves to regard self-pity as credible. Concomitantly, there is a logical flaw in thinking that the supervisor owes either the despairing or the sanguine disabled employee acceptance of his own assessment of the quality of his life, nor, more generally, does position, whether of more or of less advantage, establish what precedence should be afforded alternative moral perspectives. No more does any disabled or otherwise marginalized individual owe "normal" persons acceptance of their assessments of the quality of her life.

To summarize: recognizing that (dis)advantage and (mis)fortune are gauged from social points of view, Blum presents the disabled person (the worker) as positionally inferior to someone not impaired (the supervisor).[10] Subsequently he proposes to remediate inequality in the positions of interacting moral agents by assigning moral priority to the way whoever is *disadvantaged* desires to be treated. Thus the inferior positionality stereotypically assigned to individuals with disabilities is equalized by allowing them to designate the conduct advanced toward them as well as their own conduct. But privileging the perspectives of disabled people is no improvement on disregarding them. In short, to indulge the disabled *because* they are disadvantaged entails that, for them, submissiveness remains the price of good treatment. For, if forbearance for subordinates, rather than respect for equals, motivates moral conduct toward the disabled, their abandoning the compliant behavior that marks them as subordinate inevitably will dissolve or at least weaken the moral bonds that link others to them.

To acknowledge this is, however, to challenge stereotypes that are stubbornly embedded in our social perceptions. As Ron Amundson observes, "the 'sick role' . . . relieves a person of normal responsibilities, but carries other obligations with it. The sick person is expected to . . . regard his or her condition as undesirable. These requirements resonate with the attitudes of society towards disabled people. . . . One interesting correlation is that able bodied people are often offended by disabled people who appear satisfied or happy with their condition. A mood of regret and sadness is socially expected" (Amundson 1992, 114, 118).

THE PRACTICE OF CARING

Amundson is accurate in remarking how commonly it is supposed (and frequently resented) that persons with disabilities must be relieved of responsibility—that is, indulged. This is not surprising, for whoever treats the disabled badly is easily seen as deficient in the very dispositions that all of us, in a generalized way, rely on in others whenever we are vulnerable to them. If moral and social operations are thought of as expansions of basic caring, it is no surprise that whether someone treats the disabled caringly becomes a test of that person's trustworthy dispositions. So we can see why adverse treatment of disabled persons, though a natural reaction to perceived deviance, is deprecated on accounts like Blum's, which take another natural response, caring, as the foundation of moral and social value. It is not that the object of the treatment is owed better, but that agents who treat dependents uncaringly appear for that reason disposed against treating almost anyone well, since almost anyone might present as deviant under some circumstances.

Nevertheless, systems focused exclusively on protecting those seen as deficient too readily lend themselves to harming the putatively dependent by requiring them to accept lesser quality care than they could administer to themselves. For a dependent stance is advantageous only if genuine—that is, if the putative dependent is truly incompetent. But in a social system in which caring-for is the primary way able-bodied relate to disabled, it becomes socially incumbent upon the latter to profess incompetence even where they are more competent than the former. It was not too long ago, recall, when women were expected to dissemble this way to men.[11]

Surely, some of us shouldn't be obligated to let ourselves be harmed simply to afford others opportunities to be virtuous. Is it reasonable to insist that some citizens must voluntarily be poor simply so that the rich have the opportunity to act charitably, or that some are obligated to expose themselves to criminals to give the police somebody to rescue? In a framework of moral relations in which some must make themselves vulnerable so that others can be worthy of their trust, the disabled are typecast as subordinate. So modeling morality on being cared-for and caring appears to make such self-sacrificially compliant behavior obligatory for persons with disabilities, and this is morally counterintuitive.

Although an advocate of the ethics of caring, Joan Tronto notes that "in focusing on the preservation of existing relationships, the perspective of care has a conservative quality" (Tronto 1987). If this is so, an ethics of caring may be impeded in empowering corrective justice where existing relationships are themselves a source of repression. However, because I believe that the very structure of helping or caring relationships invites the marginalization of whoever is consigned to the position of dependence, my apprehension is more global than Tronto's caution. For, far from vanquishing patriarchal systems, substituting the ethics of caring for the ethics of equality threatens an even more oppressive paternalism. We can grasp this by noting that helping relationships are voluntary, but asymmetrically so. Help-givers choose how they are willing to help, but help-takers cannot choose how they will be helped, for in choosing to reject proffered help one withdraws oneself from being helped as well as from being in a helping relationship. To relate to others primarily by being helped by them, then, implies subordinating one's choices to one's caretakers, at least insofar as one remains in the state of being helped. Of course, helping need not be repressive, for bonds of affection encourage mutual helping, and bonds of respect support reciprocal helping. This suggests that if being cared for is to advance those previously subservient, helping cannot itself be institutionalized but must instead be permitted to transpire within a frame of sharing or collectivizing or equalizing practice which corrects its fundamental asymmetry. But, as Marilyn Friedman observes, even "in a close relationship among persons of comparable moral personhood, care may degenerate into the injustices of exploitation, or oppression" (Friedman 1987, 96).

DEPENDENCE AND MORALITY

We should recall here that some philosophers, notably Annette Baier and Laurence Thomas, might be less cautious, for they seem to suggest that it is precisely from relations between unequals that morality commonly flows. That is, they propose that the typical moral case involves one person being vulnerable to, and thereby having to rely on, another. They see the contractual relation, so often taken by modern moral thought as basic, as being only a special case of morality wherein otherwise independent individuals enter into a relation of mutual dependence. But these autonomous agents' artificial interchanges by no means should be supposed to contain morality's pivotal plot. In "Trust and Anti-Trust" Baier writes:

> Relations between equals and nonintimates will *be* the moral norm for adult males whose dealings with each other are mainly business or restrained social dealings with similarly placed males. But for lovers, husbands, fathers, the ill, the very young, and the elderly, other relationships with their moral potential and perils will loom larger. For Hume, . . . the rights and duties of equals to equals . . . could only be *part* of the moral story. . . . For those most of whose daily dealings are with the less powerful or the more powerful, a moral code designed for those equal in power will be at best nonfunctional, at worst an offensive pretense of equality as a substitute for its actuality. But equality is not even a desirable ideal in all relationships—children not only are not but should not be equal in power to adults, and we need a morality to guide us in our dealings with those who either cannot or should not achieve equality of power (animals, the ill, the dying, children while still young) with those with whom they have unavoidable and often intimate relationships. (Baier 1986, 248–49)

Baier chides contractarians for focusing on persons bound together by temporary rather than enduring relations, for the commitment forged by a promise appears less persistent than that which fastens children and parents. Here she associates herself with the proponents of the ethics of caring, who distinguish themselves from the adherents of the ethics of obligation in part because they argue that social intimacy or closeness between persons, originating from the natural affection felt by parents for their helpless young, is the foundation of morality.

In favor of casting caring as a moral foundation adequate to the challenge posed by defective agents, it should be remarked that, within a (functional) family, defects in persons cause them to be cared for rather than condemned. Indeed, a main objective of family structure is precisely to provide for this kind of care. With such protective advantages borne in mind, those who would substitute a feminist for a patriarchal point of view often model moral motivation after the affectional engagements of family feeling. Concomitantly, they reject impartial or equalizing criteria for moral judgment as depersonalizing.

On this alternative to the ethics of equality, utility renders protection of the vulnerable not quite an obligation, but certainly a socially salutary disposition. As Baier notes, the eighteenth-century philosopher David Hume depicts these socially extended relationships of trust as an "artificial contrivance for the convenience and advantage of society" and as requiring constant education and effort to maintain (Hume [1739] 1975, 525). Notice, however, that tender feelings for familial dependents are not infinitely extendable to total strangers. Consequently, for the ethics of caring it becomes incumbent on whosoever must rely on nonfamilial protection, as must most of the disabled, to conduct themselves in general so as to stimulate protective behavior in others.

This demand, I believe, violates Baier's condition for the moral decency of a trust relationship. She says:

> I . . . propose a test for the moral decency of a trust relationship, namely, that its continuation need not rely on . . . successful cover-up of breaches of trust. . . . We could . . . generalize this test into a version of an expressibility test, if we note that knowledge of what the other party is relying on for the continuance of the trust relationship would . . . itself destabilize the relationship. More generally, to the extent that what the truster relies on for the continuance of the trust relation is something which . . . is likely to lead to destabilization . . . of that relation, the trust is morally corrupt. . . . A trust relationship is morally bad to the extent that either party relies on qualities in the other which would be weakened by the knowledge that the other relies on them. (Baier 1986, 253–55)

In respect to the disabled, morality would be destabilized were the trusted caregivers to be forced to admit that their moral practice requires the *pretense* of helplessness on the part of the trusting disabled. Moreover, the trust that flourishes even in morally decent dependence relationships may not be much more durable than the (sometimes enormously long-term) contracts Baier derides. It is notable that some kinds of dependent referenced by Baier above—children while young or the dying—retain this status relatively transiently, while a third kind—animals—must be domesticated into dependence. This leaves the ill, who either recover or evolve into individuals with disabilities. And in their case, as we have seen, being compelled to accept care rather than command respect invites their being driven into the kinds of relationships Baier condemns as morally bad. This suggests once again that no acceptable morality, feminist or otherwise, can flourish on dependence.

Let me clearly delimit what I am arguing here: although it is too strong to hold categorically that being cared for abrogates commanding respect, this is the regrettable repercussion when caring becomes conventional. Institutionalizing caring depersonalizes whoever is cared for by shifting the source of the care-giver's motivation from affectional, admirational, or reverential regard for the particular recipient of care to diligent regard for the social role of caregiver. Consequently, institutionalizing caring to achieve the scope required of any foundational mode of moral association deforms caring, converting its other-regarding function into a form of self-regard. Absent the motivation that affection, admiration, or respect afford, those assigned to socialized roles as caregivers require supporting casts of compliant care receivers to stimulate them.

In being subjected to institutionalized caring, those already marginalized, for whom being the object of other people's other-regarding actions might have been supposed to realize advancement, instead are diminished. For in these institutionalized relationships, the devalued find themselves perceived merely as means for furthering other people's self-regard, not as the valued ends of other people's actions. I maintain that socially devalued people—those perceived as defective or deviant—generally cannot help but occupy inferior positioning when drawn into such conventionalized asymmetrical associations, although, of course, so sweeping a view of the matter is not precisely warranted by the arguments I have been able to present here. Nevertheless, the considerations I have raised should cast grave doubt on whether the moral foundation for corrective justice can effectively rest on practices for which such positional difference is crucial.

THE SOCIAL HISTORY OF DEPENDENCE

To consign individuals with disabilities to such subordinating relationships takes a complex social structure which has been fashioned to propel them into dependency. Since the thirteenth century modernizing laws began to group persons with quite different disabilities into a single inferior class, one which the dominant class found to its own advantage to claim to treat exceptionally protectively, and one which consequently excited the envy of other subordinated groups. From this institutionalizing process emerged the concept of "the disabled," individuals who would have worked but for their unfortunate impairments. To be a member of this class was to be distinguished from the undeserving, willfully malfunctioning poor, and was to be in virtue of this status the object of envy by this latter class, as well as the object of pity by the superior class.

By definition, then, the "deserving" poor must be incompetent to be deserving. Their treatment, while technically benevolent, must make their condition seem unattractive to those capable of work. In view of their definitively deficient state, the deserving poor are not conceivably capable themselves of the responsible use of whatever means charity bestowed on them. So another social group emerges: care-givers, persons whose profession it became to channel charity by administering it properly to damaged individuals. Thus, as a social class, the disabled became required by definition to be non-productive. They also became the means of production for members of another group, professional care-givers.

To legitimate such an arrangement, it is advantageous to regard the disabled as *essentially* defective and, as well, to disregard the extent to which the social arrangements that confine them infiltrate what we imagine them to be. In a report commissioned for the Winter/Spring 1993 issue of *Report from the Institute for Philosophy & Public Policy* on the 1990 Americans with Disabilities Act, David Wasserman exemplifies this regard by contending that nature has made persons with disabilities "less equal" than other Americans and so *irremediably* inferior. I have two reasons for examining this view in some detail here. First, identifying the flaws in Wasserman's claims about the inferiority of the disabled will help us clarify the actual source of their inequality. Second, we will be furthered in finding a remedy for their inequality by observing how Wasserman's objections to the ADA also are flawed.

According to Wasserman, the law itself defines the class it protects in terms of "biological" defects that render the class's members irreparably inferior in respect to warranted claims to fair or equitable treatment. (I summarized the definition of disability actually used in the ADA at the end of Section II.) I do not know whether Wasserman would want to be so blunt about the implications of his position, but this conclusion is the unavoidable result of maintaining, as he does, that there are biological differences that constitute the definitive characteristics of the class protected by the ADA. These differences are supposed by Wasserman to be irreparable and, for that reason, are taken by him to naturalize the inferiority of individuals with disabilities in respect to claims of justice, fairness, or equitable treatment. For example, he professes: "The fact of biological impairment, recognized by the ADA in its definition of disability, makes the notion of 'equal opportunity to benefit' problematic. This is a serious defect in a statute that treats the denial of such opportunity as a form of discrimination" (Wasserman 1993, 10).

That this argument is made central to an analytical report on the ADA should not pass without comment. For the strategy of arguing that biological impairments or inferiorities justify the inequitable social arrangements visited on a repressed class is a familiar but discredited one. Egalitarianism has advanced to the point that these claims now would almost automatically be branded as racist or sexist. In view of the philosophical community's overwhelming opposition to defending discriminatory practices in this way, it seems to me that whoever adopts the strategy of invoking biology as a natural cause that justifies prolonging exclusionary social systems must bear a considerable burden of proof.

But Wasserman's report simply takes as self-evident that the "natural" impairments or inferiorities of persons with disabilities confound legislation the stated purpose of which is simply to furnish them equal protection under the law. To foster this assumption, the report systematically misreports the language of the law, for the term "biological" *never* appears in the law's text. (Nor is it factual that the impairments of members of the class it protects are definitively or even preponderantly "biological," adherents of eugenics to the contrary. While some such impairment originates genetically or chemically, much of it results instead from traumatic injury generally understood as a mechanical, not a biological, process.)[12]

In a penetrating essay listed as a reference in Wasserman's report but apparently ignored by him, Ron Amundson explains why no obfuscation of this matter should be tolerated: "If handicaps are natural consequences (rather than social consequences) of disabilities, the victims' loss of opportunity can be thought of as beyond the resources, or at least beyond the responsibility, of society to remedy. Someone whose disadvantage comes from a natural disaster may be an object of pity, and perhaps of charity. Pity itself is a 'devaluing' attitude. Someone whose disadvantage occurs as a result of social decision has a more obvious claim for social remediation" (Amundson 1992, 113).

Nevertheless, those mired in the social arrangements that *define* the disabled as recipients of care simply cannot comprehend that equal opportunity, not exceptional treatment, could be the objective of legislation protecting the disabled. Wasserman, for instance, cannot imagine anything other than a mandate for treating these individuals exceptionally benevolently to be the ultimate objective of the ADA, despite the explicit protestations of the language of the law itself. Yet, as he himself recognizes, such a mandate would be absurd: "More broadly, we cannot reasonably expect to raise all people with disabilities to a level of functioning where they can receive the same benefits from facilities and services as able-bodied people" (Wasserman 1993, 10).

But to argue this way is to interpose a straw man, for neither the ADA nor any disabled advocacy group I know of proposes this kind of goal. Reforming the functioning of disabled people to make them whole does not appear as a standard in the ADA. Nowhere does the ADA propose changing the members of the class it protects to make them more like other, more socially favored people. This is the goal of medicine, not of law. To the contrary, the ADA proposes changing social practice to eliminate its favoring non-disabled persons. That is, the ADA proposes that equality of treatment become equally responsive to those differences that define the disabled as a protected class under this law. (In the next section I examine this proposal more schematically.)

Wasserman's report goes on to criticize the ADA as follows: "However much they [the public transit regulations] required, they would fall short of assuring equal mobility. The fact of . . . impairment . . . makes the notion of 'equal opportunity to benefit' problematic. This is a serious defect in a statute that treats the denial of such opportunity as a form of discrimination" (Wasserman 1993, 10). But within the context of the ADA benefiting equally from public transportation means no more than being able to travel the same public routes with approximately the same expenditure of time and money as other individuals. The ADA does not demand that society render mobility-impaired individuals fully mobile and in so doing extricate them from the class the law protects, for where accessibility regulations have been properly rather than mean-spiritedly implemented, persons in wheelchairs use public transit with as much facility as able-bodied persons do. So Wasserman's criticism that full implementation of the regulations would still "leave most people with disabilities with a far greater burden of mobility than most able-bodied people" is worse than irrelevant (Wasserman 1993, 10).[13]

Does he mean that the ADA is an ineffective law because it cannot make a cripple run, rather than wheel, a winning marathon? Not only is it demeaning to caricature disabled persons by imputing to them fantasies that are Wasserman's own obsessions, but it is inconsistent to criticize the ADA on such a ground unless one also criticizes earlier civil rights legislation for failing to make black people white or to transform women into men. By importing a class structure which isolates a class of "deserving" dependents, confusing this with the class protected by the ADA, and then assuming that elevation from this class is the overriding desideratum, Wasserman condemns the ADA from the point of view of the social arrangements it is designed to dislodge. Moreover, in maintaining that "the ADA itself recognizes that the physical endowment of people with disabilities contributes to their disadvantage," (Wasserman 1993, 8) Wasserman neglects to disclose that the ADA *nowhere* cites a direct causal connection between physical state and disadvantage. On the contrary, the language of the law explicitly conjoins the disadvantaged status of disabled persons not with their inferior "physical endowment" but with the social status to which they are consigned. The term "disadvantage" occurs in its text only in Finding 6, which asserts that empirical research shows people with disabilities to "occupy an inferior status in our society, and (be) severely disadvantaged socially, vocationally, economically, and educationally."

Agreed that having a disability, or equally being believed to have one, is a *necessary* condition for triggering contemptuous interpersonal responses to disability. But acknowledging this only replays the Congress's finding that our culture ranks disabled people as social inferiors. Only in the circumstance of enabling social conditions does having a disability become a *sufficient* condition for being treated shoddily or victimized. Wasserman's report shifts the blame for being victimized to the victims in a way reminiscent of how the myth of biological determinism has fueled eugenically sanctified liquidations of "defective" populations. In contrast, the ADA repudiates this sad history by banishing any legal presumption that "normal" and "disabled" are categories created by natural law.

In sum, the idea diffused throughout the ADA is that only by acknowledging, rather than by ignoring, how a history of inferior social positioning fuels inequality do we effectively guard against imagining the accidents of personal and social history to be essential advantages or defects. In institutionalizing this approach to implementing the Fourteenth Amendment, the ADA constructively reframes the "equality versus difference" controversy in a way that would be tolerable to at least some feminist scholars. For instance, in the essay earlier cited, Joan Scott goes on to argue: "To maintain that femininity predisposes women to certain (nurturing) jobs or (collaborative) styles of work is to naturalize complex economic and social processes and . . . to obscure the differences that have characterized women's occupational histories" (Scott 1990, 145). Scott here embraces what is also a framing notion of the ADA, namely that accounts of social, legal, and moral personhood must concede the relevance of contingencies which differentiate agents in ways relating to the historical record of the domination or subordination of the classes to which they belong.

HISTORICAL (IN)EQUALITY

So inured are our historically conditioned feelings of superiority to individuals with disabilities that it is almost automatic for us to join Wasserman in equating disability with disadvantage. However, even though an impairment is no advantage, it does not follow that to be impaired or disabled is to be disadvantaged per se. For disadvantage is relative to context and end. A specific impairment need have no natural or necessary deleterious impact on a life. Indeed, what counts as an impairment is itself relative to what is imagined to be normal, the last being, of course, a famously procrustean concept.

To illustrate, in an age of corrective lenses and supermarkets, your nearsightedness is not the disadvantage it would be for a Neanderthal hunter. Another illustration: deafness is not a *natural* disadvantage in interpersonal communication. Signing members of the Deaf community communicate with one another as effectively as do hearing persons who speak to each other. That the majority of Americans know speech rather than sign may be thought of as simply another in a long list of practices imposed by the dominant group to suit its members while suppressing a minority whose practices are otherwise. However, history itself might have been otherwise. Were the majority of hearing persons positioned by having had Deaf rather than hearing parents, so that as children they were subject to and dependent on persons who signed rather than spoke, most of us would sign adroitly, a skill typically possessed by hearing as well as Deaf children of Deaf parents.

We should not protract Wasserman's confusion of two very different questions. Whether a departure from "normal" physical or mental states *is* correctable is a medical issue. But whether a deficit *should* be repaired, or adapted to, or exploited by society, is an open social and personal question which Wasserman arbitrarily slams shut. And this last answer will be swayed by yet another consideration: is inequality, cast as an intractable aspect of a person's experience, definitive of individuals with disabilities, as Wasserman has it, or is it merely the unyielding artifact of historically exclusionary social arrangement?

In the everyday life of persons mobilizing in wheelchairs, their inequality, both as experienced by them and in the eyes of others, manifests itself not in the inability to walk but in exclusion from bathrooms, from theaters, from transportation, from places of work, and from life-saving medical treatment. Suppose that most persons used wheelchairs? Would we continue to build staircases rather than ramps? Suppose most were deaf? Closed-captioning would be open-captioning and would have been the standard for television manufacture long before July 1, 1993. By hypothesizing what social arrangements would be in place were persons with disabilities dominant rather than suppressed, it becomes evident that systematic exclusion of the disabled is a consequence not of their natural inferiority but of their minority social status. In keeping with this realization, it is the strategy of the ADA to require that whoever operates a facility or program must reform arrangements that exclude individuals with disabilities unless doing so would constitute an undue hardship, as measured against the overall financial resources of the facility or program. (To provide for fair distribution of the responsibility to alter exclusionary practices and their durable results, the "undue hardship" provision caps the resources which any entity can be required to expend for accessibility in proportion to the entity's total expenditures. But the Congress explicitly rejected an amendment which would have capped expenditure on each disabled employee in proportion to her salary.)

What informs this mandate is recognition that accessibility would now be a commonplace, not a novelty, were the majority, not the minority, of the population disabled. Thus the ADA sets neutralizing historical inequality as the benchmark against which to assess whether current practice is just. Rather than speculating on how the *subjective personal response* of unimpaired agents would be transfigured by the onset of physical or mental impairment, this standard calls for projecting how *objective social practice* would be transformed were unimpaired functioning so *atypical* as to be of merely marginal importance for social policy. Note that this counterfactualizing process reconfigures the operation of moral imagination so as to comprise social rather than psychological extrapolation. The standard introduced by historical counterfactualizing thus is operational, for it realistically accepts that able-bodied persons do better envisioning anyone but themselves as disabled. Instead of the able-bodied being required to imagine themselves as seriously impaired, they need imagine no more than that they are personally unchanged but socially ignored by and isolated from most beneficial institutions and practices in virtue of their being able-bodied.

In examining how the ADA references the conditions under which difference becomes damaging, we are reminded of the dilemma of difference. Will we find that acknowledging the history through which difference becomes deleterious "reinvokes the trait which carries the negative meaning"? Even where referencing difference mainly involves explaining its history, Minow is apprehensive that it does:

> The dilemma for decision-makers—courts, states, employers—is how to help overcome past hostilities and degradation of people on the basis of group differences without employing and, in that sense, legitimating those very differences. Put in these terms, the dilemma of difference appears in debates about affirmative action in employment and educational practices. How can historical discrimination on the basis of race and gender be overcome if the remedies themselves use the forbidden categories of race and gender? Yet without such remedies, how can historical discrimination and its legacies of segregation and exclusion be transcended? Should nonneutral means be risked to achieve the ends of neutrality? A similar conundrum arises over how to acknowledge victimization without repeating the victimization in the process of acknowledging it. . . . Demanding that those who have been injured by others present their injuries in the often brutal process of adversarial litigation may inflict new injuries. Yet new injuries can also be induced if the legal system denies access to this process. (Minow 1990, 47)

Minow accurately observes here that accentuating a dismally different past can prolong rather than redress inequality, for merely excavating past repressions serves neither for reparation nor atonement. As Alexander Crummell writes about African Americans, "dwelling morbidly and absorbingly upon the servile past" threatens to arrest future moral, social, and economic development (Crummell 1969, 13, 14, 18). Moreover, this devastating process leaves those who are vulnerable to it with what W.E.B. Du Bois calls "double consciousness," the debilitating awareness of stifled ambitions which result from "measuring one's soul by the tape of a world that looks on in amused contempt and pity" (Du Bois [1903] 1965, 214–15). But that there are dangers in dwelling on historical exclusion does not settle the question of whether prior repressions may be referenced in a manner that liberates us from, rather than mires us in, reliving the awful past.

What is important to notice in this regard is that historical counterfactualizing as activated in the ADA neutralizes difference without delegitimating it. Acknowledging, rather than ignoring, whether social institutions have historically embraced or excluded certain kinds of selves alerts us to how what we take to be essential conceptions of these excluded persons may in actuality be the product of historical contingency. Historical counterfactualizing then strips differentia of their negative meanings by disclosing that the source of adverse signification lies in the remediable accidents of social arrangement, not in the immutable inferiority of the alienated group. By doing so, historical counterfactualizing deflects the regrettable tendency abstract thought has of equivocating between what has been accidentally true of certain kinds of people and what is inescapable about them. It thus counters one of the criticisms levied by advocates of the ethics of difference against the ethics of equality.

Because it projects how lives would be different had history been otherwise and had different social practices or arrangements obtained, historical counterfactualizing maintains consciousness of crucial difference(s). Thus, in step with many feminist reappraisals of the moral importance of difference, historical counterfactualizing assesses the justice of proposals regarding equality of treatment by taking into account whether an agent is of a group whose domination, or else whose suppression, has historically shaped our moral associations. Historical counterfactualizing thus fosters recognition of how social identities have been formed in the crucible of oppression without miring those same identities in retribution and regret. Noticing this suggests how to transcend the dilemma arising out of the putative impasse between equality and difference, for counterfactual projection realizes difference free of its deleterious meanings.

Here I discount Minow's apprehension in regard to "legitimating those very differences" which have been the basis of "past hostilities and degradation." For to the extent that current social practice is the product of these "past hostilities and degradation," it is already far from neutral. Consequently, the question is not whether to legitimate difference but rather whether to continue to legitimate practices that already prefer some sorts of differences to others. But Minow would be right were her concern about a somewhat different question: whether preferential treatment responsive to difference can ever be equitable.

To respond to this misgiving we need to return to that distinction, lost on Wasserman, to the effect that the ADA seeks equal, not exceptional, treatment to secure protection of its subject class. Comparing two kinds of different treatment, one required by the ADA and one omitted by it, illuminates the contrast. By requiring bus ramps and lifts (devices different from steps) and teletyping phones (devices different from voice phones), the ADA effects equal access to standard public utilities for taxpayers who happen to be disabled. Notice that it is only equal, not advantageous or preferential, access which is afforded; moreover, were a majority rather than a minority of users disabled, the initial designs of public transportation and communication systems would have accommodated them with no differential expenditure needed to include them later on. Thus, the ADA designates failure to provide such accommodation as inequitable treatment in virtue of disability, even though the remedy itself is responsive to disability.

In contrast, despite explicitly recognizing the historical exclusion that bars most individuals with disabilities from employment, the ADA makes no requirement for compensatory income. We can comprehend this aversion by noticing how infeasible such a system would be were most people disabled, for how could a system be long sustained if its dominant majority depends for care on a subservient minority. (Systems of slavery inevitably collapse when slave drivers become too helplessly dependent on their slaves.) Indeed, by affirming that individuals with disabilities can, with or without reasonable accommodation, perform the essential functions of many types of jobs and by declaring that the denial of employment in virtue of disability to otherwise qualified disabled applicants violates their civil rights, the ADA deconstructs that current practice that ratifies the expectation that the disabled do not work.

Bernard Williams writes about slavery in Athens that no Greek but Aristotle seems to have questioned the practice precisely because "considerations of justice and injustice were immobilized by the demands of what was seen as social and economic necessity" (Williams 1993, 125). Williams then declares: "We have social practices in relation to which we are in a situation much like that of the Greeks and slavery. We recognize arbitrary and brutal ways in which people are handled by society, ways that are conditioned, often, by no more than exposure to luck. We have the intellectual resources to regard the situation of these people, and the systems that allow these things, as unjust, but are uncertain *whether* to do so" (Williams 1993, 125; my emphasis). But what could prompt us to regard an arbitrary social system as unjust? In *Human Morality*, Samuel Scheffler proposes that being socially marginalized is an enabling condition for perceiving injustice (Scheffler 1992, 142–43). Here, I add that for those who by good luck do not now occupy an historically inferior social position, the device of historical counterfactualizing creates cognitive contexts in which the (in)justice of current social practice can be perceived. On a practical level, historical counterfactualizing compels us to recognize that the exclusion of those who are different is not natural, which in turn permits us to regard such exclusionary practice as unjust. To accomplish this result, historical counterfactualizing dissipates the dilemma of difference by elaborating and explicating historical contexts so that salient differences recede until they cease to strike us as being deviant. For, in regard to individuals with disabilities, as well as to members of other habitually devalued social groups, historical counterfactualizing transforms the sparse and vague contexts within which they appear so alien by conceptualizing what an environment that welcomes them would be. Historical counterfactualizing thereby equalizes by reducing the distance between those well-intentioned able-bodied individuals who are so well-integrated socially and psychologically that they have internalized prevailing social norms and those others who, like the marginalized disabled, are different in that their vision is not shielded from the perception of injustice.

A decade ago, in arguing against the polarization of social theory into "feminine" and "masculine," Linda Nicholson wisely observed: "There needs to be more stress on the point that gender has been an important factor in influencing moral perspective and moral theory because gender has been an important factor in influencing the concrete circumstances of people's lives. . . . Other factors, such as race, class, and the sheer specificity of historical circumstances also profoundly affect social life and thus a moral perspective" (Nicholson 1983, 516). What I have argued here echoes part of Nicholson's point, in that the dilemma for individuals with disabilities lies not in their personal differences but in how the sheer specificity of historical circumstance marginalizes them socially and, consequently, morally as well. It is from the latter diminution that policy makers routinely have gained permission to debar the disabled from the benefits of public programs, from participation in such public institutions as marriage, and even from presenting themselves to the public's sight.[14]

Forged by disabled persons out of their experiences of such circumstance, the 1990 Americans with Disabilities Act dissolves their dilemma by boldly endeavoring to neutralize exclusionary social practice in a way responsive to the complexities of our lives. Thus this law becomes a paradigm for reconciling equality to difference, for, as conceptualized in the legal and moral framework of the ADA, equality, although complex, is neither conflicted nor (d)elusive. And this is important for progressive social thought, for by ascertaining how even the disabled are equal, we create a framework accessible to all those groups whose historically devalued differences—whether of gender, race, ethnicity, sexuality, age, or other category—still screen them from corrective justice.

NOTES

I am immensely grateful to Susan Wendell, author of the forthcoming *The Rejected Body: Feminist Philosophical Reflections on Disability* (Routledge), for recommending revisions to an earlier draft of this essay; to Ruth Ginzberg and to another, anonymous reviewer for very helpful comments; and to Iris Marion Young and Nancy McDermid for their moral support of this work.

1. Because I take the policy issue inspired by the dilemma of difference to be whether justice is best assessed against a standard of equality (understood as neutrality) or against a standard of difference (understood as corrective partiality), I do not construe it as forcing a choice between caring, which is a type of partiality, and justice itself. In this way of construing the issue I believe myself to be in agreement with Young (1990) and Friedman (1987).

2. See Gutmann (1980, esp. 218–22) for an excellent summary of this conception of justice. Cambridge: Cambridge University Press, 1980.

3. See Young (1990, esp. 121, 173) for a compelling account of this approach to justice.

4. Among the negative attributes this group is assigned are the following: required to grieve permanently for the loss of function, globally incompetent because of a specific deficit, provoking guilt, punished because sinful, punished unjustly and seeking retribution, inherently inferior, ugly, or offensive, a reminder of what could happen to anybody, kindling fear of mutilation or death, threat to body image or physical integrity, burdensome, irritating or awkward in social interactions. For a review of this literature, see Livneh (1988, 35–46).

5. Because my objective here is to disclose, and then analyze and apply, the moral, social and legal foundation on which the 1990 Americans with Disabilities Act rests its instruction that people with disabilities can and must be repositioned so as to secure social equality, I have had to sacrifice presenting a more detailed treatment of and commentary on the ADA's text.

6. I have made some of these points with the same or similar examples in an essay on egalitarianism in health care distribution which is forthcoming in the 25th Anniversary issue of *The Journal of Social Philosophy* (see Silvers 1994a) and in Silvers (1994b). Together with this essay, these are part of a larger project which contrasts the "minority" and the "medical" models of disability as strategies for correcting the repression of individuals with disabilities. I borrow this way of designating the contrasting conceptualizations of disability from my colleague, Professor Paul Longmore.

7. In using the expression "confined to a wheelchair," I am attempting to speak in the voice of someone who cannot imagine wanting to live if she became disabled. This is not an expression most wheelchair users find acceptable.

8. See *New York Times*, 20 March, p. 8, for a synopsis of the Oregon Health Plan.

9. It is a commonplace of social psychology that devalued groups are judged much more unfortunate, or as having much less satisfying lives, than the group's members judge themselves. Physically disabled persons rate themselves as average in fortune, while others see them as below average. See Denbo and Wright ([1956] 1975).

10. In fact, Blum depicts the supervisor as being "morally" impaired. However, in Silvers (1994c) I demonstrate how problematic such a construal is. Because of the close relation the subject of that essay bears to this one, much of the factual material about the history of disability, and some of the conclusions I draw from that history, are repeated there.

11. Cf. Scott (1969). This study shows how agency-dependent blind persons are conditioned to be docile, acquiescent, even ascetic and melancholy, by social acquaintances as well as agency personnel regardless of whether these are advantages survival traits beyond the agency setting.

12. Ron Amundson (1992) makes a similar point by carefully arguing the difference between disability and disease in "Disability, Handicap, and the Environment," which Wasserman cites in his bibliography (1993).

13. As a public policy analysis, Wasserman's argument functions to offer public officials an excuse for not enforcing regulations. In the case of the complaint filed on June 28, 1993, by the California Council of the Blind against the San Francisco Municipal Railroad System, Wasserman's position would excuse the MUNI's systematic, pervasive, and prolonged failure to comply with federal and state regulations requiring that stops be announced for visually impaired passengers. Note that enforcement of the regulation has no fiscal implications for MUNI, but being deposited at unfamiliar locations

beyond their stops creates serious hazards for blind MUNI riders. Wasserman's position permits MUNI officials to excuse their practice of permitting drivers to ignore blind riders' requests to be notified aurally of their stop. It does so by reenforcing the drivers' attitude, once sanctified by exclusionary laws, that presence of persons with disabilities in public is an imposition.

14. United States legal history evidences very many public laws and court decisions that banned individuals with disabilities from such institutions as public schools, marriage, air travel, and even from being seen on the public streets. Lest anyone believe such exclusions to be phenomena of a distant clouded past, it should be understood that, for example, it took the 1988 Air Carrier's Act to secure the right to air transportation for ticketed disabled passengers. Until that legislation was implemented, airlines could and did arbitrarily refuse to carry ticketed disabled passengers, regardless of whether the passenger traveled with no need of assistance and regardless of whether the airline had any factual basis for its fear of the passenger's disability. In this country at this time, relatively few disabled adults have escaped experiencing segregation and exclusion arising out of false beliefs about, or fears of, their disabilities.

REFERENCES

Amundson, Ron. 1992. Disability, handicap, and the environment. *The Journal of Social Philosophy* 23(1): 114, 118.

Baier, Annette. 1986. Trust and antitrust. *Ethics* 96(2): 248–49.

Blum, Lawrence. 1991. Moral perception and particularity. *Ethics* 101(2): 701–25.

Crummell, Alexander. 1969. *Africa and America: Addresses and discourses*. Miami: Mnemosyne Publishing Company.

Denbo, Tamara, Gloria L. Leviton, and Beatrice A. Wright. [1956] 1975. Adjustment to misfortune: A problem in social psychological misfortune. *Rehabilitation Psychology* 2: 1–100.

Du Bois, W. E. B. [1903] 1965. The souls of black folks. In *Three negro classics*. New York: Avon Books.

Friedman, Marilyn. 1987. Beyond caring: The de-moralization of gender. In *Science, morality, and feminist theory*, ed. Marsha Hanen and Kai Nielsen. Calgary: University of Calgary Press.

Gutmann, Amy. 1980. *Liberal equality*. Cambridge: Cambridge University Press.

Hume, David. [1739] 1975. *A treatise of human nature*. Ed. Lewis Amherst Selby-Bigge and Peter H. Nidditch. Oxford: Clarendon Press.

Irigaray, Luce. 1985. *This sex which is not one*. Trans. Catherine Porter with Carolyn Burke. Ithaca: Cornell University Press.

Katz, Irwin R., Glen Hass, and Joan Bailey. 1988. Attitudinal ambivalence and behavior toward people with disabilities. In *Attitudes towards persons with disabilities*. See Yuker 1988.

Livneh, Hanoch. 1988. A dimensional perspective on the origin of negative attitudes toward persons with disabilities. In *Attitudes towards persons with disabilities*. See Yuker 1988.

Minow, Martha. 1990. *Making all the difference: Inclusion, exclusion and American law*. Ithaca: Cornell University Press.

Nicholson, Linda. 1983. Women, morality, and history. *Social Research* 50(3): 514–36.
Scheffler, Samuel. 1992. *Human morality*. Oxford: Oxford University Press.
Scott, Joan W. [1985] 1990. Deconstructing equality-versus-difference. In *Conflicts in feminism*, ed. Marianne Hirsch and Evelyn Fox Keller. New York: Routledge.
Scott, Robert. 1969. *The making of blind men: A study of adult socialization*. New York: The Russell Sage Foundation.
Silvers, Anita. 1994a. Defective agents: (In)equality, (ab)normality and the tyranny of the normal. *The Journal of Social Philosophy*, forthcoming.
Silvers, Anita. 1994b. (In)equality, (ab)normality, and the "Americans with disabilities" act. *Philosophy and Medicine*, forthcoming.
Silvers, Anita. 1994c. Damaged goods: Does disability disqualify persons from just health care? *Mount Sinai Journal of Medicine*, forthcoming.
Stone, Deborah. 1984. *The disabled state*. Philadelphia: Temple University Press.
Taylor, Charles et al. 1992. *Multiculturalism and "The politics of recognition."* Princeton: Princeton University Press.
Tronto, Joan. 1987. Beyond gender difference. *Signs: Journal of Women in Culture and Society* 12(4): 644–63.
Wasserman, David. 1993. Disability, discrimination, and fairness. *Report from the Institute for Philosophy and Public Policy* 13(1/2): 10.
Williams, Bernard. 1993. *Shame and necessity*. Berkeley: University of California Press.
Wright, Beatrice. 1988. Attitudes and the fundamental negative bias. In *Attitudes towards persons with disabilities*. See Yuker 1988.
Young, Iris Marion. 1990. *Justice and the politics of difference*. Princeton: Princeton University Press.
Yuker, Harold, ed. 1988. *Attitudes towards persons with disabilities*. New York: Springer Publishing Co.

3

Feminist Ethics and Public Health Care Policies

A Case Study on the Netherlands

SELMA SEVENHUIJSEN

INTRODUCTION

The reform of public health care policies is high on the political agenda nowadays. Several governments have installed special commissions to produce proposals for new systems of insurance, for norms of admission and application of medical technology, or for the provision of care for the elderly. There is also a search for new institutional settings and decision-making procedures that can change the deeply entrenched power relations in the medical sector. The context of these new policy designs is that of the restructuring of modern welfare states. There are of course many relevant differences between countries in this respect. While in the United States the Clinton administration has tried to introduce a scheme of mandatory health care insurance, several Dutch governments in succession have tried to save public funds by distinguishing a "basic package" of necessary health services from less necessary services to be paid for in the private market. A common denominator in both these policies is, however, that new relations and balances between public and private health care provisions are being discussed. There seems to be a broadly shared awareness that on the one hand national states cannot make available all the health care service technologically possible, but that, on the other hand, market forces can't deliver the goods in accordance with basic principles of social justice and political solidarity.

In 1992 the Dutch government published a remarkable policy document, "Choices in Health Care." This report presents a framework for public decision-making about the availability of and access to health care services as well as a proposal for a public debate on these issues. After its publication a wide variety of organizations in the medical field as well as political and cultural organizations and media were invited to participate in this debate, including women's health organizations and the National Women's Council. Positive as this might be from a feminist perspective, it also confronted the leadership of women's organizations with a complex situation. It was by no means clear with which voice, about which issues, or from which position to speak in the public domain when discussing health care policies. And in spite of the open invitation to participate in the public discussion, it was striking that the main text of the report that was to serve as the basis for the public discussion referred neither to feminist approaches to health care nor to women's complex position in the care system. This pointed, in turn, to the necessity of making a critical analysis of the terms of political discourse when the public discussion was started and reflecting upon the way these terms are channeling political judgment.

In a sense this avenue was suggested by "Choices in Health Care" itself, because a considerable part of the report is devoted to an evaluation of normative frameworks that can guide public decision-making on health care. This facilitated the idea to start the feminist involvement with an analysis of the normative frameworks in the report and to evaluate these from the perspective of feminist ethics and feminist political theory. In this essay I have laid down several of the insights that have grown from these discussions.[1] My approach can be taken as an exercise in a gender reading of a public policy document. Policy documents can be analyzed as vessels of normative paradigms that define a social problem in order to prepare it for regulation. A paradigm can be defined as a configuration of knowledge that brings order into social diagnoses and modes of action and intervention. Here Iris Young's definition of a paradigm is a useful tool of analysis: "a configuration of elements and practices which define an inquiry: metaphysical suppositions, unquestioned terminology, characteristic questions, lines of reasoning, specific theories and their typical scope and mode of application" (Young 1990, 16). Policy texts are sites of power because their modes of speaking structure the way individuals and social groups (in this case women and their political representatives) can profile themselves in the public sphere by constructing legitimate speaking positions and acceptable considerations. By establishing narrative conventions, authoritative repertoires of interpretation, argumentation, and communication, they confer in systematic ways power upon preferred modes of speaking and judging and upon ways of constituting moral and political subjectivity. I use this approach because it can be of help in tracing the open and hidden gender load of the vocabularies of official documents. And it can help us to analyze the inclusionary and exclusionary effects of texts with regard to gender: to see how they can and cannot speak about women and gender issues.

By starting from an analysis of the way in which women, women's issues, and women's speaking positions are conceptualized in the terminology of "Choices in Health Care," I will work my way through its text and analyze the gender load of its leading normative concepts and normative frameworks. By taking its speech patterns about women as a starting point I intend to use gender as an analytic category (Harding 1986; Scott 1986), with the aim of reflecting upon the way sexual difference assigns meaning to seemingly gender-neutral concepts like "necessary care" and "normal social participation," concepts that are proposed as crucial guidelines for political judgments about public health care policies. An analysis of the gender load of these concepts and the surrounding normative frameworks will in the end enable me to make an evaluation of the effects and the value of these frameworks for feminist concerns. I then argue that an ethic of care, conceptualized in a communicative and relational paradigm of politics, has the capacity to reformulate several of the leading normative concepts that are used as guidelines for thinking about health care policies.

In doing so I have two goals. My first interest is in reflecting upon the best possible framework for public policy making when it would have to include feminist concerns about women as receivers and providers of care in its considerations. My second interest is even broader and more ambitious. By reflecting upon the gender dimensions of public speech about health care policies, I hope to contribute to a more general discussion about the policy frameworks concerning health care as a part of the care system of modern societies.[2] Bringing the hidden gender dimensions of "care talk" into the daylight of public speech can, in my view, enrich our normative thinking about the availability and the quality of care in modern societies. I will do so by situating discussions about care in conceptions of citizenship. Public discourse constructs "citizenship positions," images of how a good citizen should think and act, in this case when engaging in political action concerning care or when making use of the health care system. By analyzing the vocabularies of citizenship that have implicitly informed "Choices in Health Care," I try to develop discursive spaces for integrating feminist political theories of care into the public discussion: these theories have in my view the potential of talking about care in a more solid manner than the frameworks proposed in "Choices in Health Care." First I will, however, sketch the outlines of the report.

THE NORMATIVE FRAMEWORK OF "CHOICES IN HEALTH CARE"

In 1990 the Dutch state secretary for welfare, health and cultural affairs, Hans Simons, formulated the leading question for the commission on choices in health care as follows: how to put limits on new medical technologies and how to deal with problems caused by scarcity of care, rationing of care, and the necessity of selection of patients for care. The commission should not only present normative considerations and criteria about these questions but also stimulate a public discussion of the question of whether everything possible should be done.[3]

The report, published at the end of 1991, argues the necessity of choice by referring to the rising part of the national income spent on health care, to waiting lists for operations, and to a growing scarcity in the availability of medical provisions for mentally handicapped, elderly and psychiatric patients.[4] Scarcity is, according to the commission, not just a financial problem but also a moral problem of just distribution. The report operationalizes this issue of distribution in the question of how we can protect the weakest parties (the elderly and the chronically ill) in a situation in which the possibilities of prolonging life are steadily growing. By making the health care system more efficient or by making more money available, the problem of scarcity could not be solved, because, in the words of the report, "we are caught in an upward spiral of expectations. . . . in an understandable desire to banish all illness and defect, we expect often the impossible from our health care system, and certainly so if this system contributes itself to this expectation." To counter this development, political choices should be made about which care is necessary, and which forms of care should be taken as an individual responsibility.

The report goes on to argue about how to find a framework for criteria for decision making about "necessary care." It distinguishes three approaches to questions of health and health care. The first is labeled the *individual approach*. Health would here be linked to self-determination, autonomy, and the fulfillment of individual life plans. It would be dependent upon the goals, needs, and preferences of individuals. The commission condemns this approach because it would deny the possibility of collective choices. The range of individual preferences would be too broad, and it would not be possible to make demarcations between individual health preferences and social problems. Descriptions of basic needs differ from one to the other, and it would thus be impossible to make decisions about necessary care.[5]

The second approach is labeled the *medical-professional approach*. Here health would be defined as normal biological functioning or the absence of illness and defects. Biomedical knowledge about the internal construction and the biological functioning of the body would then lead to statements about what is necessary health care. The commission criticizes this approach with two arguments. First, it would not allow for psychic and social determinants of health and cannot thus argue, for example, the necessity of contraceptives in an overpopulated society. Second, the complaints of patients could only be understood in the languages of medical professionals. Medical and economic norms would then remain dominant in the process of choosing.

The commission sees the solution in a third approach, the so-called *community-oriented approach*. Here health is perceived as a "means for every member of a community to function normally according to the prevailing norms in Dutch society." The commission argues for this approach in the following terms:

> The choices here are made at the level of the society because individual health is seen to be linked to the possibility of participation in social life. According to the community-oriented approach care is necessary when it enables an individual to share, maintain and if possible to improve his/her life together with other members of the community. Individual preferences and needs are not given priority here; the central question is which care is necessary care from the point of view of the community. ("Choices in Health Care" 1992, 54)

The commission acknowledges that there resides a problem in this approach: not every society will give the same answers to this question of "normal social functioning" because there is a great variety in norms and values. This problem is then solved by the statement that in the Dutch democratic social-constitutional state the most important norms and values are laid down in international treaties and the constitution. This would lead to three fundamental norms that should be applied in the processes of choice: the fundamental equivalence of all human beings, as laid down in the constitution; the fundamental need for the protection of human life, as laid down in international conventions; and the principle of solidarity, as laid down in the construction of the public health care system.

The community-oriented approach would allow for a description of necessary care separated from individual needs. It would enable limits to be placed on individual choice and patients' autonomy as well as limiting the professional autonomy of the medical professions.[6] The report argues for a system of distributive justice in which principles of equal access can be combined with just distribution of resources. In this way care could be guaranteed for members of society who cannot take care of themselves: homes for the elderly, psychogeriatric provisions, and care for the mentally handicapped. Processes of choice should, according to the commission, be orchestrated with this principle of necessary care as the first criterion for decision making.[7] Three other criteria are then added: is the provision effective, is it efficient, and could it be left to individual responsibility? The four criteria are then hierarchically positioned in a so-called funnel with four sieves, through which every medical provision has to pass in order to decide which provisions are allowed to be part of basic insurance schedules. If a provision passes the test of necessary care, it then has to be tested on effectiveness, efficiency, and responsibility. The commission then uses examples like in vitro fertilization, homes for the elderly, homeopathic medicines, sports injuries, and dental care to reach the conclusion that even with these criteria it is hard to reach just decisions in accordance with the principles of solidarity. Against this background the commission argues that the furthering of an "appropriate use" should be a crucial goal of public discussions and interventions.[8]

The report ends with a proposal for a public campaign, a so-called communication plan. Here a wide range of organizations are invited to participate in a two-year project, funded with public means. The main goal is to convince the general public that choice is necessary and desirable and that individuals and organizations are capable of making choices at all levels of social life. The aim is to work toward a new awareness of "appropriate use" and new kinds of social consensus that prepare the ground for public decision making. Women's health organizations are asked to participate in the campaign because they have in the recent past developed critiques of medicalization processes and thus have "experience in dealing with choice": women's groups are addressed as the vanguards of autonomy and free choice against medicalization. But prior to this, women are mentioned in the first paragraph of the communication plan in a more general mode. There they are addressed as persons who can influence the care consumption of others and thus as potential "chains" in the furthering of appropriate use:

> Women generally have great influence on the care-consumption of many others. Mothers decide the care-choices for their children, women usually advise their partners on care choices and adult women are often involved in the care choices of their parents. ("Choices in Health Care" 1992, 149)

So while women's health organizations are addressed as the political vanguards of free choice, women as a category are addressed in a rather traditional role: as the central actors in families, where they can influence the "care-consumption" of their near and dear.

LEGAL EQUALITY AND NECESSARY CARE

"Choices in Health Care" has been applauded and criticized for its introduction of a community-oriented approach in the public discussion on health care. A more thorough reflection on the report reveals, however, that its considerations are framed in a peculiar mixture of normative vocabularies, combining arguments from communitarianism with those of a liberal rights discourse and distributive justice. To this mixture are then added fragments of communicative ethics, by the introduction of the idea of a public discussion on the question of whether everything possible should be done. This idea of communicative ethics tends to turn, however, into a top-down moral-pedagogical discourse, when it is supposed to lead to a furthering of "appropriate use," and especially so while women are addressed as social guardians of responsible use of health care services. The normative approach in "Choices in Health Care" can be better characterized as a mixture of fragments of conflicting and sometimes incompatible normative frameworks than as a clear-cut paradigm. In what follows I will take the leading concept of the report, "necessary care," as a starting point for reflection on the normative contradictions of the report. By analyzing these frictions in terms of gender and citizenship I will try to uncover the discursive spaces for bringing feminist theories of care to the public debate about health care.

Let me first look again at what task the concept of "necessary care" is supposed to perform. The commission uses this concept in its endeavor to develop objective criteria about which medical provisions should be legally covered by a schedule of basic insurance. By invoking a community-oriented approach the commission wants to curtail the discursive power of, on the one hand, the individual consumer, who is supposed to have an endless reservoir of needs, and, on the other hand, the medical professionals, who can argue only in biomedical terms. "Normal social participation" must then become the norm for access to public health care provisions. Here resides, of course, a familiar problem for political philosophy: is it possible to derive reasonable or generalizable norms for social participation? After all, societies contain a great variety of moral convictions about what normal social behavior should entail. The crucial question, discussed by philosophers from different viewpoints, is whether it is possible to find a "minimal consensus" on these points that can lead to policy decisions while conforming in a maximal degree to standards of justice and solidarity.

These are questions that belong in the domain of discourse ethics or could be seen as questions of procedural justice. The commission has, however, evaded the philosophical and political complexities of these questions by resorting to a more familiar vocabulary, the constitutional language of equal rights and solidarity. These abstract legal norms are supposed to be of value because they are generally accepted, universal, and enforceable. Although the concepts of necessary care and social participation are derived from a communitarian approach,[9] the commission has selected normative concepts of a liberal ethics of rights and of distributive justice in order to operationalize the demands of community life. This should lead to the question of how the relationship between, on the one hand, "social participation" and, on the other hand, "equality, solidarity and the protection of human life" could be worked out in more detail. Do these norms have the potential of facilitating responsible and reflected processes of selection of health care services that should be guaranteed for all? I will discuss the way the report deals with two examples of women's health care provisions in order to show the selective workings of the normative framework of "Choices in Health Care."

In the first example, the report uses "normal social participation" as an argument to state that in-vitro fertilization (IVF) and cosmetic surgery are not forms of necessary care. IVF would not be necessary because, in the eyes of the majority of the commission, involuntary childlessness does not hinder women's "normal participation." The same would go for cosmetic surgery: this could be considered "luxury" that is not at all necessary for women's social participation. It is striking that any explicit reflection on the meaning of "normal social participation" is absent at this point. The implicit norms for social participation are, however, clearly visible between the lines: they entail participation in the public sphere of paid labor and politics. These are indeed the official goals of Dutch government policies concerning women's emancipation (Outshoorn 1991). The IVF example shows that having children is apparently not considered as "social participation" (Berkel 1994). And the example of cosmetic surgery shows that subjective feelings of identity inhering in bodily images are labeled "extrasocial" phenomena (Davis 1995). Issues of women's reproductive capacities and women's identities are relegated to a private sphere of individual preference and thus individual responsibility. Women's health issues are thus brought under the normative regime of "independence" and "equality," norms that govern the public sphere, conceptualized from the perspective of labor market participation.

A second example resides in the way the report invokes equality norms in order to argue about "necessary care" in the context of the so-called weaker groups in society. The report invokes the constitutional rule of equality first and foremost in order to find normative foundations for solidarity with the elderly and the mentally handicapped and to guarantee them access to the health care system. They are then constructed as "people who cannot take care of themselves." In the first instance this statement invokes moral and political sympathy: solidarity with and care for the weak and vulnerable can indeed be taken as a fundamental moral obligation. This statement can, however, be interpreted from other perspectives as well. It can be seen as a generalizing and potentially stigmatizing way of talking about the elderly, because they are primarily constructed as weak and needy. And it can be interpreted as containing a questionable counternorm about care, because it starts from the idea that "normal" citizens can take care of themselves.

GENDER, CITIZENSHIP, AND CARE

The conception of citizenship and care is not spelled out in detail in the report. It can be traced, however, along the proposed line of investigation of paradigms, by looking for metaphysical suppositions and unquestioned terminology and by tracing implicit meanings or subject positions and institutionalized patterns of interpretation: suppositions that go without saying because they are part of the taken-for-granted or belong to the parameters of hegemonic discourse (Fraser 1989, 146). Thinking in terms of citizenship and care can for several reasons be of help when elaborating this approach, at least if we are prepared to stretch the language of citizenship beyond the liberal vocabulary of individuals, rights, and duties and to include in it normative questions of the adequacy of public speech and discourse and questions about the good life. An approach in terms of a broadened concept of citizenship can place considerations of care firmly in the public domain, the sphere where deliberations about the best social arrangements for care should take place. And it can provide inroads to discuss the suppositions about identity and human nature that inform public policies on health care, provided that we recognize and consciously employ the normative dimensions of both concepts of citizenship and care.

The contours of the conception of citizenship and care in "Choices in Health Care" can then become more visible when we combine its normative idea of the individual who can take care of him/herself with its suppositions about normal social participation. The idea of the independent individual fits into a neoliberal conception of citizenship, where it figures as the central normative ideal for human personhood. Normality is in this conception constructed as self-sufficiency, the ability to lead an independent life in economic, social, and political respects. The image of the self-sufficient individual corresponds to an individual who is not in need of care when engaging in "normal social participation." I qualify this conception of citizenship as neoliberal because it corresponds to the mode of regulation that guides the restructuring of many Western welfare states at this historical juncture. The idea of the self-sufficient individual fits into the program of reprivatization of public provisions and the introduction of market-oriented forms of regulation. "Normal" citizens are then first and foremost constructed as individual participants in the labor market. This individual is supposed to translate his/her needs for care in terms of market-oriented behavior, thus conceiving him/herself as a care consumer in a market of supply and demand of caring services.

This conception of citizenship and care has its origins in the history of Western political thought. It was Aristotle who laid the foundation for this mode of conceptualizing citizenship and politics by the way in which he delineated the polis from the household (Tronto 1994; Spelman 1989). While the household was seen as the place where life-sustaining activities take place in the form of labor by wives and slaves, the polis was constructed as the place where male free citizens came together to engage in common affairs and to deliberate about and live the good life. It was this coming together in the polis that was constructed by Aristotle as the constitutive act of human freedom. Political participation and freedom are, then, closely connected, and they are linked together by drawing a distinction between freedom and necessity. The public sphere is then considered as a domain where free males can transcend not only embodiedness but also the finite and mortal aspects of the human condition. In the polis, free males were coming together in order to do deeds and make works of art that leave their traces on history, providing them thus as citizens with the idea of immortality. The Western tradition is thus left with a mode of theorizing politics, where care is associated with immanence, necessity, and the private sphere, while politics is constructed as a social activity that enhances the freedom of the human subject, by freeing *him* from the burdens of necessity and the fear of finity and death.

These short genealogical remarks can enable us to identify several hidden marks of gender in the political and normative idiom of "Choices in Health Care." The report not only exhibits a gendered mode of thinking about politics; it also leaves us with a paradoxical mode of speaking about care when deliberating about public responsibilities. While citizens are invited to participate in a public discussion about necessary care, care is at the same time situated *outside* the realm of "normal social participation." Care is primarily supposed to have a supportive function, a function of "repairing" citizens for their normal social participation. This exemplifies a thoroughly instrumental vision of health, a vision in which health is a condition for the achievement of other ends and thus something that should be evaluated against the background of individual "life-plans." It is, as Joan Tronto has stated, a model that overemphasizes the autonomous, rational, life-project choosing vision of the (male) individual, who perceives illness as a "foreign invasion" (Tronto 1994, 6). Illness and disease are perceived as deviations from normal social functioning instead of inherent, though often disturbing, parts of human life. Some philosophers perceive illness indeed as a threat, as the object of a fundamental human fear, from which the state should protect its citizens (i.e., Callahan 1994). This concords with a construction of care as a "necessary evil," as something that should be there but also has to be contained, an image that returns in the central proposition of "Choices in Health Care" that individuals, unless corrected by collective decisions about boundaries, want too much care, and will have "endless" needs.

Against this background the most general feminist response to the constructions of normality in "Choices in Health Care" should be that they coincide with gender-laden images. When care is situated outside the sphere of social participation, it is put in the black box of the private realm, where so-called informal arrangements guarantee that care is provided spontaneously. While the report argues for a priority of care for the elderly, it doesn't even touch upon the question of how this care should be provided; nor does it refer to the complex sociopolitical problems around informal care. It just draws upon the silent logic of a "natural" provision of care in the family and kinship networks, where it seems self-evident that women care spontaneously for others whenever there is a need (Sevenhuijsen 1993b; Knijn 1994).[10] The effects of this "gender logic" extend not only to the social arrangements of care, the question of who cares for whom, but also to the institutionalized symbolic meanings of care. Gender is in this respect a powerful factor that gives meaning to care. Images of care still have strong connotations of femininity, privacy, and dependency, while the opposites of these—labor, independence, and public identities—are more easily associated with masculinity. We could indeed speculate that considerations of care get constantly banished from the public sphere and from full political consideration because they are marked by hidden meanings of femininity.[11] An approach that takes public "male" norms as the normal perspective easily adopts the viewpoint of the privileged and the powerful: those who can speak from a position where the receiving of care is taken for granted, without having to fully realize what is involved in processes of providing care, a position that is called by Joan Tronto one of "privileged irresponsibility" (Tronto 1993, 174).

We can conclude, then, that the endeavor to find foundations for "necessary care" in a combination of ideas about "normal social participation" and constitutional norms of equality is bound to lead to a contradictory and selective mode of reasoning. It leads to a discursive track where judgments about medical provisions are brought under the normative regime of labor-market participation as primary norm. This normative regime tends to marginalize care, because it considers care as a precondition for social participation instead of as a social phenomenon and a meaningful social activity in itself. This framework can only deal with feminist issues when they are phrased in the language of individualism, independence, and equality as sameness. Women are then fitted in the regulatory parameters of late modernity by being asked to enter the world of paid labor and independent citizenship and to see the world of care as "traditional," as a barrier to freedom and equality.[12] Seen from this perspective it is not surprising that the main text of "Choices in Health Care" does not explicitly talk about women. Its leading normative framework of distributive justice and legal equality addresses women as gender-neutral citizens for whom sexual difference is supposed to be irrelevant or marginal as a factor of consideration. Differences with regard to men and women would only matter when they could be phrased as differences in health conditions between the sexes.

THE OPPOSITION BETWEEN INDIVIDUAL AND COMMUNITY: HOW TO TALK ABOUT NEEDS?

It could be said, then, that the framework of "Choices in Health Care" is informed by the perspective of the independent citizen, who needs as little care as possible and who is at the same time not engaged in reflection upon the nature of his/her needs for care. A basic problem in this respect resides in the strict delineation of an individual approach from a community-oriented approach in the report. Needs are unequivocally relegated to the domain of the so-called individual approach of health and health care. Needs are depicted as "preferences" and as individual entities that spring from the psychic dispositions of individuals. This confirms the liberal way of conceiving the relation between individual and society and individuals and politics. Liberalism in its most pure form sees individuals as prior to society. When it is argued in the contractual mode it constructs society as a compact between individuals, who arrive with needs and preferences in the public sphere. Since Thomas Hobbes and John Locke, liberal politics is explicitly or implicitly the construction of a social-political contract, necessary to "curb" these individuals in their need-satisfying drives, because they would otherwise harm each other by unmitigated self-interest, violence, theft, or the usurpation of power (Pateman 1988; DiStefano 1991; Jones 1993). "Choices in Health Care" tries to depart from the liberal framework by invoking communitarian solutions or by selectively stating that needs might be socially constructed. Communitarians would, however, go much further: they would deny the image of the "unencumbered individual" and would take individuals with their needs, preferences, values, and moral considerations as part of communities, and thus as the basis for moral and political life. In "Choices in Health Care" the liberal individual remains, however, the prototypical human subject. This individual is held responsible for recognizing needs and for translating them into claims to the health care system. Needs are overridingly constructed as "unlimited," as entities that should be curtailed in order to facilitate an orderly discussion about responsible choices. This individual irresponsibility is then contrasted with a positive image of a responsible community as a sociopolitical norm.

This leads to a mode of reasoning in which the individual and the community are seen as opposites and played out against each other.[13] Instead of seeing individuals with their needs, their feelings of identity, their hopes and fears about illness, and their moral considerations as an inherent part of political life, we are supposed to see "the" individual as a threat to community values. And instead of constructing human communities as entities that ought to respond to the needs of its members, we are asked to imagine a political community that argues about care with abstract legal norms as the main point of reference. The public conversation is thus left with the paradoxical task of inviting citizens to proliferate their views about choices in health care, while at the same time forbidding them to bring their needs for care forward as a legitimate topic of collective deliberation. The only discursive space for needs is the space of individual preference, as when one wants, for example, "luxury" treatments like cosmetic surgery and expensive fertility treatments. Not only does this lead to paradoxical modes of public speech; this discursive strategy can also be seen as ineffective. It is ineffective because people do let their own needs and desires, and their views on those of others, speak when they talk about health and illness and about the complex moral questions in the domain of care. One could even say that it is rather immoral *not* to reserve discursive spaces for different kinds of "needs talk." For how can a community ever care properly about and for its members if there is no space to communicate and deliberate about the way in which people experience needs? Judgments about the necessity of care are, then, by implication evaluations of needs.

In spite of these critical remarks I do not want to suggest that the concept of "necessary care" should be dropped from our political vocabulary; on the contrary, considerations about the necessity of care and social participation might give fruitful inroads for public discussions about health care, provided that we do not start our normative deliberations about care by invoking objective norms and images of human nature that are derived from a liberal ethics of rights and provided that we overcome the manifold ways in which gender-laden binary thinking has invaded the frameworks of public discourse (like for example that between individual and community or that between needs and social participation). "Necessary care" might be a fruitful concept when we acknowledge the contextual and the narrative character of needs for care. It is exactly the search for objectivity, universalizability, and economic rationality that troubles so many moral discourses about care and needs. It is, for example, often presumed that when we want to take needs into account, we have to reach consensus over a list of "basic needs," which would inhere in human nature. Lists like that are usually limited to a most general overview, like the need for shelter, food, and decent health care, so that they cannot grasp the more complex question of which provisions are necessary under specific circumstances. A more important problem, however, is that this approach is again linked to an individualistic perspective on human nature and to implicit or explicit gendered images.

An alternative approach could draw upon social constructionism and narrativism, which have recently informed social and normative theory and have led to creative research and theorizing in women's studies (Walker 1989; Pyne Addelson 1994; Shrage 1994; Davis 1995). These approaches open up spaces for reflection about the way needs are constructed by social experiences and interactions. By taking needs as narrative events we can also see how they are the object of negotiation and contestation. "Gender" should be an integral part of such an approach, since it enables us to see how, for example, the ascription and the experience of gendered identities feed into the way women and men experience their bodies and their health condition and the way they care for and about themselves and others. This approach can also counter the workings of power and privilege in discourses about needs. It can, for example, sensitize us to the ease with which the professionals can claim cognitive authority in interpreting the needs of the "needy" and for the discursive power with which they can indeed construct complete (often gendered) social groups as needy, thus marking them as objects for social regulation and intervention. It is within the power of professionals not only to justify in this way their position as persons who guard the lives of the "needy" but also to bring themselves forward as persons who can speak on their behalf in the public domain (Fraser 1989; Pyne Addelson 1994). There are indeed many historical traditions in which needs are discussed in patronizing and p/maternalistic modes of objectifying and "othering" the needy (Tronto 1993). By constructing "situated knowledges" about needs and about care it becomes possible to empower the subjects who are the bearers of needs and to make their considerations on their condition an integral part of public deliberations. And it would enable us to engage in public disputes about the relevance of gender in concrete situations, instead of forgetting about it altogether, as is the case in the liberal discourse of equality-as-sameness, which informs countless public policy documents.

This is especially relevant when arguments from a feminist perspective are to be validated in political discussions on health care. Until recently, women have predominantly been the *object* of medical science and medical discourse. The medical profession and related experts have extensive forms of power to define and structure what counts as women's needs and indeed of femininity and "true" feminine behavior (Martin 1987; Schiebinger 1989; Jacobus et al. 1990). A recent example resides in the way in which menopause and osteoporosis are constructed as cases of hormonal failure that threaten to undermine the "feminine" aspects of women's lives (Hall 1994; Wingerden 1994). The feminist health movement of the last two decades has, in its critiques of medicalization processes, proliferated a broad spectrum of alternative views of women's needs that could be interpreted as "needs in context." From these activities several "need contests" have arisen that should get a place in public discussion rather than being precluded from it from the start. This calls for what Nancy Fraser has called a "politics of need-interpretation" (Fraser 1989). Public discussions should in this model be orchestrated as forms of open deliberation about the origins of needs and about the question of why and how needs should be met and where we should draw boundaries between private and public responsibilities in this respect.

APPROACHING HEALTH CARE POLICIES FROM THE ETHICS OF CARE

"Choices in Health Care" is all in all rather ambivalent about the nature of the public deliberations that could lead to responsible political choices in the health care system. Although the report opens doors by taking solidarity and social participation as a starting point for decision making, it closes these doors again by resorting to the language of rights and individualism in its search for objective criteria about the necessity of care. Because needs are excluded from the discussion about necessary care and because the report hardly reflects on the conditions under which care is provided, we are left with a fragmented view of care and health, in which care is overridingly conceptualized as and molded into a commodity. This market-oriented pattern is repeated in the communication plan. Citizens are supposed to talk about "appropriate use" and to channel their choice in that direction, not reflect upon their needs. The general public and the decision makers are asked to come to normative judgments about care in terms of the distribution of goods and services, not in terms of needs, social relations, social processes, systems of knowledge, cultural images, and systems of values. Politics about health care is overridingly seen as strengthening the market system, corrected and regulated though by a neocorporatist political system of negotiations and bargaining. Thus the tendency toward the creation of new "care bureaucracies" is strengthened. Because the logic in such a system confines policy issues to choices about insurance schedules and designing uniform standards of behavior, "Choices in Health Care" has missed the chance of better implementing one of its central goals, that of countering the culture of medicine.[14]

In the end the report remains caught in the parameters of the distributive paradigm, a framework that is, in the words of Iris Young, marked by a "tendency to conceive social justice and distribution as coextensive concepts" (Young 1990, 16). Because this framework can deal with issues of gender only in marginal and distorted ways, it cannot incorporate in a satisfying way many considerations brought forward by feminists in the last decade. The assignment to women of a gatekeeper's function in the health care system concords with the market-oriented individualism of the report. The report can be best understood as an endeavor to regulate the demand side of the "market of health care": it is indeed phrased in the language of supply and demand. This is also a sign of the fact that "Choices in Health Care" is predominantly oriented toward the regulation of demand, a conclusion that is supported by the statement in the report that the power structure on the supply side is too resistant to political regulation. Apparently women as house/gatekeepers are easier to regulate. This observation gains in relevance once we realize that women are addressed here in a social role with many responsibilities and (in most cases) little access to power resources, and thus with only few possibilities to stand up for their own needs.

Feminist scholars have in many ways questioned the feasibility of moral theories that start from the assumption of a self-interested, calculating, and exchange-oriented human being. If moral and political deliberations would start instead by following the ethic of care, by confirming the reality and the relevance of human interactions, interdependence, and relationships, we would have to modify a considerable part of the assumptions about the self and about needs and interests that circulate in our political system and its hegemonic normative frameworks. The care ethic has indeed such an innovating potential because it brings us to reformulate the moral domain and moral subjectivity and thus to redefine questions that need our judgment as well as the way judgments could or should proceed. And since judgment is such an intrinsic part of citizenship, the care ethic has the potential of shifting the boundaries between ethics and politics (Sevenhuijsen 1991; Tronto 1993; Tronto 1995a). Joan Tronto has, in cooperation with Berenice Fisher, defined caring as "a species activity that includes everything that we do to maintain, continue and repair 'our' world so that we can live in it as well as possible. That world includes our bodies, our selves and our environment, all of which we seek to interweave in a complex, life-sustaining web" (Tronto 1993, 103). Caring thus conceived is not a marginal activity of life; it is indeed one of the central processes of human existence. Caring is not confined to the family nor to private relations; it is also situated in formalized social and political institutions in our society.

The definition of Tronto and Fisher is quite broad: it could refer to nearly all the activities that we engage in in human life. For the purpose of discussing the politics of health care I would prefer a narrower definition, where needs are conceptualized as the quintessential object of caring, and then to continue to see care as a process, with different phases or dimensions, that entail divergent moral attitudes, values, and activities. Tronto and Fisher have identified four phases of caring as a process, in a way that can help to clarify the way persons and institutions deal with care: caring about (recognizing that there is a need that should be met), caring for (the assuming of responsibility for the meeting of the need), caregiving (the actual practice and work of caring), and care receiving. Each of these phases gives rise to moral dimensions of care, or to specific moral values. These are identified by Fisher and Tronto as (successively) attentiveness, responsibility, competence, and responsiveness. In order to see the political dimensions of these values, it should be stressed that they are not abstract norms that can be invoked when considering a given situation, but rather moral and cognitive attitudes, or as "epistemological virtues" (Code 1991; Rooney 1991).

By implication there cannot be such a thing as an "objective" situation of needs for which politicians can then seek a solution. How we come to know situations of needs and needs for care depends upon our willingness to use care as a "pair of spectacles" or as a viewpoint and to practice its epistemological virtues when talking and deliberating about needs. The question of how to best know a social situation is, then, an indispensable part of moral and normative deliberation (Code 1991). Because caring is defined as an activity or as a practice, it enables us to deal in an integrated way with phenomena like acting, thinking, and judging on care. Defining care this way counters tendencies to narrow it down, as for example when it is approached as an emotional disposition or as a moral intuition or when it is conceptualized primarily in an economic vocabulary of labor. We are invited instead to think about the way social practices give rise to certain attitudes and moral frameworks and vice versa. Seeing care as a practice also enables us to draw upon women's experiences and moral considerations as carers, without linking these to useless speculations about a special "feminine" or "female" disposition toward caring.[15]

Such a political approach to care has also the capacity to perceive and address issues of power and to adapt our judgments about care politics to the fact that power and conflict are implied in every phase of the caring process, as well as in our common deliberations about the way social institutions should care about and for human beings. Power structures deliberations about necessary care, depending upon the position from which one speaks. Needs are often perceived differently from the perspective of the providers and the receivers of care, and their "negotiations" about needs can be indeed informed by a wide range of motives and considerations. Providers of care are, by lack of access to power resources and of control over their work situation, often not in a position to give care in a way that comes up to their standards of quality, as in the case of home helpers for the elderly, who are supposed to do only the cleaning work or the washing of their clients, without engaging in social interaction (Gremmen 1995). As I said earlier, needs are objects of negotiation and contestation and thus of power struggles about who gets what. Power and privilege are important factors that shape structural relations of "giving and receiving" and of "speaking and listening" when it comes down to the social distribution of attentiveness to needs. And these social relations are in many ways stamped by structural factors of gender, race, and class and by the ways in which these factors coincide in individual lives.

When we take it as a goal to counter these power mechanisms in processes of care, several leading concepts in the political discussion on health care should be redefined. It is my claim that a well-reflected ethics of care enables us indeed to do this. I will here consider five such concepts: social participation, autonomy, equality, justice and solidarity. Again I will discuss them as citizenship concepts: my aim is to rethink them from the perspective of a collective discussion about the availability of and access to good health care in modern societies and thus in a sense to "prepare" them as leading normative concepts for public decision making.

Social participation. When we have to reach responsible forms of political judgment about the availability of health care services, how caring arrangements contribute to meaningful social participation might indeed be an important question to ask. It would be better, however, not to answer this question in abstract or generalizing terms, but to talk about meaningful forms of social participation in many forms of social groups and social practices and to do this from the perspective of the individuals concerned. Arguing from the care perspective can prevent us from confining social participation to paid labor, without forgetting of course that a considerable part of caring is done and can be done in professional situations: it opens indeed space for normative deliberation about where to draw boundaries between public and private forms of providing care. It enables us to account for the fact that individuals are, in the course of a life span and in different contexts, frequently circulating along the roles of caregivers and care receivers.

When we want to do justice to care as a crucial element in social life, we should account for the need of including the possibility of caring in the way economic arrangements and social policies are structuring life plans,[16] just as much as we should account for the fact that dealing with health and illness is an integral part of human life situations. Social participation could turn into a just standard of judgment about the availability of health care services, when we account for diversity, vicissitude, fragility, vulnerability, and dependency as basic aspects of the human condition, instead of arguing from a standard life script or from a standard healthy human body. This would, for example, imply that working conditions, the designing of public space and of access to cultural spaces and modes of expressing sexual pleasure, should account for the fact that a considerable part of the population is living lives that are marked by disabilities or chronic diseases.

Autonomy and choice. "Choice" is in fact the central normative concept in "Choices in Health Care." Because it is presented as the leading concept in each and every situation it is used in a rather unidimensional and unreflective mode, as if there is a direct line from the choices we make in individual life situations as patients or consumers to the choices politicians should make when discussing modes of regulation. This disguises the fact that different situations ask for different considerations and different forms of judgment. Choice is also not invoked in an "innocent" mode in the report. Citizens are supposed to make choices so that collective need for caring services can be contained. In other words: choice is conceptualized as a shield against too much need for care. While until recently the Dutch welfare state held itself responsible for good systems of care for its citizens, these citizens are now constructed as the problem, at least when they translate their needs into claims. Choice and autonomy are thus positioned against care.

Here an approach from feminist moral philosophy would first and foremost question the ways in which care and autonomy are positioned as binary, hierarchically ordered opposites. Autonomy is indeed often assigned the task of freeing individuals (and indeed often *the* prototypical human subject) from dependency, contingency, vulnerability, and the disorders of embodiment, as well as the gender connotations of these phenomena. An ethics of care would replace the idea that dependency hinders human beings in their autonomy with the idea of interdependency, and by recognizing the ways in which good care can contribute toward behaviors and choices that enhance feelings of self-respect, individual integrity, and agency. Care should not be reserved for interactions with "needy" persons; it should rather be thought of as a phenomenon that structures and enables human interactions in a great diversity of modes. This acknowledges the moral value of relations, the idea that good relationships are a prerequisite for adequate caring, just as good care should confirm the cared for in their feeling of being unique individuals. The way we configure our human relationships with others is indeed an important moral event in itself, since the possibility of entertaining human relationships is decisive for the way we enable ourselves and others to experience and handle the moral dilemmas we face in our individual and collective lives. If such a relational approach were combined with diverse and balanced forms of accountability of the different actors in the care process, the care-autonomy opposition would fall apart in many moral practices and political deliberations.

These ideas could also contribute toward the quintessential goal of "Choices in Health Care," that of more thorough reflection on the sources of the culture of medicine. When autonomy is onesidedly conceptualized as self-sufficiency, self-governance, and freedom from contingency, it can indeed fuel the promise of medical technology to free the human subject from a wide variety of inconveniences. This discourse is, for example, quite powerful in the bioethical texts that dominate the public discussion on biotechnology and genetic engineering (Sevenhuijsen 1995). Dethroning "autonomous man" from his privileged status in moral reasoning and indeed as the central goal of moral politics (in the sense of engineering the human subject) could lead to more humane, contextualized forms of deliberations about the desirability and thus the social necessity of specific forms of medicalized knowledge and medical technologies. It would lead to a continuous reflection on the suitability of the medical domain and medicoethical vocabularies to deal with questions of human fragility and finitude.

Equality. Equality figures in "Choices in Health Care" on two levels: that of constitutional equal rights and as "equivalence," the injunction to see our fellow citizens as equals. Together with the norm of solidarity these norms are invoked with the aim of protecting weaker parties in social life (the elderly and the mentally handicapped) and to argue for a priority of caring for these groups over the development of expensive life-saving medical technologies (captured in the well-known Dutch policy maxim "care before cure"). This implies that equality is invoked in the parameters of distributive justice, in order to protect those who would be worse off if we would distribute goods and services with equal claims for all. In accordance with the argumentational rules of the distributive paradigm, the report identifies relevant differences between individuals and determines these as differences in the seriousness of illness and the measure in which individuals are (in)capable of taking care of themselves.

As I argued before, this approach has an inherent tendency to blindness for social differences and social relations because it starts from a norm of equality as sameness. This approach tends to see difference as deviance from the dominant norms, or to naturalize difference: if differences cannot be corrected by just patterns of distribution, they are in the end attributed to "natural" differences between individuals (Thornton 1986; Young 1990). When feminist politics is phrased in the terminology of the distributive paradigm, it thus remains caught in a dilemma between equality and difference. When invoking equality the adaptation to "male" norms seems inescapable (as can be perceived in the dominance of paid labor as norm for social participation), but talking in terms of difference can look daunting as well, because it often leads to fruitless speculation about "natural" sex differences, derived from gender-laden images of the body. Thinking in terms of the distributive paradigm has, then, adversarial effects on the way social groups can profile themselves in the public sphere, just as it has adversarial effects on our modes of normative theorizing. The norm of equality as sameness makes us forget about the necessity of reflecting upon how to counter patterns of "othering" and how to value difference.

My negative appraisal of equality as sameness and of the argumentational rules of the distributive paradigm should not be read, however, as an argument that we could dispense with equality norms and (re)distributive politics when trying to reach responsible judgments about health care policies. Instead, we would have to reframe norms of equality and of entrance to public provisions in such a way that they would meet basic standards of social justice. This is also important when we want to counter the deeply entrenched tendency to think in terms of an opposition between an ethics of care and an ethics of justice and to mark these as "female" and "male" forms of moral reasoning, reifying these into gender-divided ethical systems. At least three concepts of equality are crucial in this respect.

First, the norm of *equality in access and voice* in the public space is important, because this is the place where social groups concerned can discuss their experiences and develop their views about health and necessary care (Young 1990). This is not just a question of interest representation but more of the ability to participate in public deliberations where concepts of the self and her needs and interests are shaped. Participation in the public sphere is also important, because this is the domain where ways of thinking and acting are changed and where cultural symbols about bodies, health, and illness or about body-mind relations are (trans)formed. Equality in access and equality in voice are important guarantees against traditional images and paternalism in the medical professions and against tendencies of "othering" social groups by marking them as different and thus making them into deviants. This approach is, for example, relevant for the current Dutch discussion if medical operations to reconstruct the hymen for Islamic girls should be made available by the Dutch health care system. When such a discussion is not receptive toward the views of the women concerned, it easily slips into institutionalized patterns of aversion to "strange habits" or "traditional customs," thus punishing the women concerned instead of trying to understand their dilemmas and their motives. Another example concerns the availability of health care services for HIV-positive women, who are often heroin addicts, ex-addicts, or prostitutes. They need special health care services, specialized forms of medical research and guaranteed access to the health care system, not only in view of their own health condition but also when they are pregnant and raise children. An approach from equality in access and voice ensures that their need for adequate care is taken into account. It counters the tendencies of punishing them by ascribing to them "irresponsible" behavior and thus turning them into "deviants" compared with "normal" persons. The care ethic is of help here, because values like attentiveness and responsiveness have the potential of orchestrating the moral deliberations concerned in an open-ended way and questioning the ways in which patterns of normality are being constructed.

The principle of equality of access and voice is the stepping stone to the second valuable equality-norm, that of *equal opportunities*. By giving different social groups the possibility of raising their voice, we get a richer view of the domains that should be discussed when talking about equal opportunities and of arguments that can justify claims in this respect. This is relevant in the context of choices in health care, because policy strategies are at the moment directed at substituting formal with informal care, often without considering the extended gender effects of these strategic interventions. Public policies about the structuring of paid labor should be evaluated against the idea that men and women should have equal chances of giving and receiving care when needed, not least because the possibility of entertaining intimate relationships is one of the basic values of human life and a crucial condition of human flourishing.

The principle of equal opportunities should also entail that the logic of thinking in terms of heterosexual "couples" should be countered when designing caring arrangements. The "couple paradigm" has unjust effects for lesbians and gay men in the caring process and withholds us from thinking about their needs for care, just as it tends to stigmatize women who raise children without men. It also overlooks the fact that the majority of the elderly are often widowed women who do not have partners to take care of them. Policy proposals of making informal care the kernel of the care system for the elderly have in these situations the effect that daughters and women friends become responsible for primary care, with the effect that care remains women's business.

The third important equality principle is that of *equal rights*, if we can at least shape these in such a way that they can account for differences in needs and values among individuals and social groups. This means, for example, guaranteeing women rights to health care services that adequately support them in sexual problems, pregnancy, and childbirth. The possibility of home deliveries should, for example, be guaranteed, not only because many women want it that way but also because the furthering of home deliveries can counter tendencies toward the medicalization and technologization of human reproduction. Equal entitlements to social services can be a guarantee against processes of marginalization and exclusion and thus a guarantee for equal opportunities and just conditions of human flourishing. This is, again, of crucial importance against the background of immigration and the need to design just multicultural societies. Neoliberal regimes have a tendency to exclude immigrants from social services, and thus from public health care, by arguing that they should first attain full legal citizenship of the receiving country. By implication great numbers of women are threatened to be excluded from maternity care or from health care for their children.

Justice and solidarity. By thus revising ways of arguing about social participation, autonomy, and equality and putting them in a communicative and relational paradigm that accounts for diversity and situated forms of subjectivity, the dichotomy between care and justice loses ground in our arguing about justice.[17] Again, it remains important to remember that the care-justice dichotomy is at its sharpest when justice is framed in the epistemological parameters of the distributive paradigm, in which abstract rationality, impartiality, and sameness are paramount. When starting, instead, our moral arguments from social practices and from an explicit awareness about the workings of power and domination, as well as its discursive and narrative patterns, and when practicing the moral-epistemological activities of caring, we might be able to arrive at enriched notions of justice. Considerations of social justice will remain of crucial importance for public decision making. They should have the capacity to counter practices of arbitrary rule and domination and to accommodate standards of fairness in the treatment of individuals by the law and the establishment and effects of public provisions. They should enable human beings to participate in the *res publica*, the public domain where we come together in order to establish norms of common humanity and good forms of living and acting together.

Justice thus conceived cannot be formulated in a standard set of norms and rules, be they procedural or substantive. It should be rather seen as a process in which procedure and substance are mixed in specific modes or as a common commitment to structure our collective lives in ways that come up to situational considerations about just rules and public provisions. It should build on values like reconciliation, reciprocity, multiplicity, and responsibility and on the willingness and the ability of citizens to accept responsibility for each other's well-being (Flax 1993; Frazer and Lacey 1993, 206). Justice thus conceived explicitly opens discursive spaces for deliberating about injustices or, in other words, to continuously reflect on which forms of "evil" should be countered in our common ways of living together. This sharpens the eye, for example, to the cruelties done to women by male violence and its effects on women's well-being, be it in intimate relations or in larger settings: the streets, workplaces, and situations of war, just as it should feed collective feelings of responsibility to counter violence and deal with its consequences, e.g., by guaranteeing counseling services for refugees and psychotherapy for raped women and survivors of sexual abuse as part of the collective health care system.

This conception of justice also opens avenues for dealing with difference and diversity and for countering the way in which the distributive paradigm tends to turn difference into otherness and deviance. This is relevant for assessing political issues of health care, since respect for difference is a countervailing power against tendencies for governing "the" human subject by engineering bodies into standardized entities. The ethical impulse of respect for diversity can thus enhance democratic values in the way citizenship is conceived, at least if we accept, in the spirit of Hannah Arendt (1958), the idea that the basic task of democratic societies should be to find just ways of dealing with plurality. This would by no means imply that we have to accept every self-stated difference at face value, nor indeed that health care need claims of different individuals and social groups should always be met with public means. Neither would it imply accepting the logic that everybody should always participate in public decision making. The politics of health care could very well be framed in models of representative democracy, provided that positions of power and decision making are open to representatives of all social groups and provided that public spheres are open to different voices and different forms of accountability are developed: guarantees that can counter the forms of "privileged irresponsibility" that still too often inhere in the logic of public administration and in public discussions about care.

Such a renewed way of thinking about justice would also imply the revision of notions of solidarity. The distributive paradigm is attractive for many social groups and political theorists because at first sight it enables standards of solidarity with those who would be worst off without it. I would, however, argue that these forms of solidarity, as laid down in "Choices in Health Care," are overwhelmingly based on rationalistic arguments that push us in the direction of a "calculative" and monologic, often even self-centered, forms of solidarity. This form of subject-centered solidarity employs several norms of sameness and thus constructions of normality. It limits its discourse to solidarity for those who cannot meet hegemonic standards and thus positions "others" as needy or weak persons who are in a position of arrears. When we start from the moral attitudes of caring, this might indeed support forms of solidarity that can deal with radical alterity, the idea that human beings are differently situated and this is exactly the reason why we need forms of public dialogue and collective support. This "caring solidarity" can better deal with the diversity of needs and life-styles, for which we have to find forms of common understanding, than solidarity norms that start from norms of homogeneity and a "standard" human subject.

Seen in this perspective the contradictions in "Choices in Health Care" can be made productive. By the combination of a policy document and a public campaign, the Dutch government has opened the door to ongoing public discussions about the availability and quality of health care. These discussions would proceed better, however, if the ethical model proposed for the public discussion would be revised. An ethic of care, combined with a politics of need interpretation and caring solidarity could be integrated in dialogical open-ended forms of discourse ethics. This points to the necessity of constructing citizenship not exclusively in a liberal rights model but first and foremost as an activity and an attitude which can in the end lead to forms of health care rights and social provisions that come up to standards of social justice.

NOTES

1. I am indebted to many women who have contributed to this project, but especially to Claar Parlevliet, Annemiek Meinen, and the contributors to the books we produced as a result of these campaigns (Parlevliet and Sevenhuijsen 1993; Meinen et al. 1994). Several of the ideas in this essay grew in close conversation with Joan Tronto. Finally I want to thank Joan Tronto, Iris Young, and an anonymous reader of *Hypatia* for their thoughtful comments on an earlier version.

2. I think this is not only relevant from the point of view of Dutch politics or the feminist input in Dutch public discussion. I hope my approach has a broader relevance than the Netherlands, not in the least because the Dutch government offers the concerned policy document and its procedure of decision making, produced under the title "Choices in Health Care," as a model for public policy making to other countries, such as the United States and South Africa. The report was translated into English in 1992. The model of the report and the campaign was brought to the United States by several Dutch policy makers as an example for Hillary Clinton's project to reform the U.S. health care system. After the publication of the report the chairman of the commission, the cardiologist A. J. Dunning, was appointed as a member of a commission of the World Bank that advises the South African government on the future of its health policies.

3. See the installation letter of the commission, published in "Choices in Health Care" (1992, 7–8). An interesting detail for U.S. readers is that the Oregon experiment was put forward as an example in this letter. The commission has, however, decided not to pursue this model, but instead to develop a more explicit normative framework that would structure processes of choice.

4. An analysis of the report is confronted with the problem that there are different versions of it. The best-known version in the Netherlands is an abbreviated one, which

was produced to support the public discussion after the commission had finished its work. The original report is more extended. It contains more examples and is more nuanced in its argumentation, although the basic arguments are similar. I will refer as much as possible to the English translation of the report, which comes closer to the extended version. If necessary I will point to the differences between the two versions, since the bolder statements in the shorter version have guided the public discussion.

5. At this point the report is critical of the Oregon experiment, in which the population was asked to make a list of preferences to be compiled in a document containing priorities. The commission states that lists like these make it impossible to "pass a verdict on the possible result."

6. At this point there are substantial differences between the two versions of the report. While the shorter version clearly argues for the community approach and against the other approaches, the longer version argues for a hierarchy in application of the approaches. The community approach should be applicable to discussions on a macro level, the medical-professional approach on the meso level, while the individual approach could apply to choices of individuals.

7. In this part of the report the commission also asks the question of whether solidarity should be limited by several other principles. It concludes that there are no convincing arguments for limits of age and life-style but favors a limited possibility of weighing costs and benefits of certain provisions and the possibility of allowing for individual preferences in insurance schedules, as for example the possibility of concluding a contract that excludes abortion for those who have moral objections against it, the so-called pro-life contract.

8. Examples of proposals of the report: stimulating discussions about standardization of diagnoses and treatments and about protocols for medical practice; better control over the availability of medicine; stimulating the use of simple medicines; standardized research about effectiveness of, for example, psychotherapy; new systems of accountability of the medical professions, by setting up platforms for negotiations between organizations in the health care sector.

9. The report's main reference at this point is the work of the U.S. philosopher Daniel Callahan (1987, 1990).

10. The importance of recognizing informal care and the designing of just provisions in this field was brought forward by a great majority of the women who participated in the discussion projects following the issuance of "Choices in Health Care." In that respect the campaign has been quite successful in influencing the political agenda.

11. It could thus be seen as an example of what the Australian philosopher Val Plumwood has, in her analysis of the workings of dualisms, recently denoted as "backgrounding": the conflicts generated by relations of dominance by attempts of the master to both make use of the other, organizing, relying on, and benefiting from the other's services, and to deny the dependency which this creates (Plumwood 1993, 48).

12. This approach is present in Susan Moller Okin's work on distributive justice and the family (1989). I have commented on this in Sevenhuijsen 1993a.

13. Several political philosophers have tried to position the ethic of care on the communitarian side of the liberalism-communitarianism controversy. In my view this is a pointless endeavor: it denies the possibility that the ethics of care is a moral perspective of its own and it overlooks the many points of epistemological and political divergence between communitarianism and care ethics. It also tends to block the possibility

of using the ethic of care for developing renewed concepts of justice. "Choices in Health Care" is for me indeed a good proof that the liberalism-communitarianism divide is a fruitless path to pursue for feminist ethics. For a well-developed feminist critique of the liberalism-communitarianism opposition in political theory, see Frazer and Lacey 1993.

14. The course of political decision making after the publication of the report proves this point in several respects. Because the concept of "necessary care" remains empty, it is open to conflicting interpretations. And because there is ample space to discuss these conflicting interpretations, policy makers tend to resort to the more familiar concepts of effectiveness and efficiency, thus confirming an economic-financial point of view.

15. Thus it might also be possible to avoid the recurring tendency toward foundationalism in ethical frameworks, and thus also in thinking about an ethics of care. I have elaborated on this in Sevenhuijsen 1993a.

16. This points, for example, to the necessity of flexible parental leaves and provisions for temporary leave for caring for sick relatives and friends.

17. Joan Tronto has argued recently that care as a virtue has the potential of mediating between justice and democracy, concepts that are hardly linked in the great canons of political theory (Tronto 1995).

REFERENCES

Arendt, H. 1958. *The human condition*. Chicago: University of Chicago Press.

Berkel, D. van. 1994. Kiezen voor minder voortplantingstechnologie? In Meinen et al., 138–157.

Callahan, D. 1987. *Setting limits: Medical goals in an ageing society*. New York: Simon and Schuster.

Callahan, D. 1990. *What kind of life: The limits of medical progress*. New York: Simon and Schuster.

Callahan, D. 1994. *What kind of patients ought we to be?* Unpublished paper.

Choices in health care. 1992. A report by the Government Committee on Choices in Health Care, the Netherlands. The Hague: Ministry of Welfare, Health and Cultural Affairs.

Code, L. 1991. *What can she know? Feminist theory and the construction of knowledge*. Ithaca: Cornell University Press.

Davis, K. 1995. *Re-shaping the female body: The dilemma of cosmetic surgery*. New York: Routledge.

DiStefano, C. 1991. *Configurations of masculinity: A feminist perspective on modern political theory*. Ithaca: Cornell University Press.

Flax, J. 1993. *Disputed subjects: Essays on psychoanalysis, politics and philosophy*. New York: Routledge.

Fraser, N. 1989. *Unruly practices: Power, discourse and gender in contemporary social theory*. Minneapolis: University of Minnesota Press.

Frazer, E., and N. Lacey 1993. *The politics of community: A feminist critique of the liberal-communitarian debate*. New York: Harvester/Wheatsheaf.

Gremmen, I. 1995. *Ethiek in de gezinsverzorging: Gender en de macht van zorg*. Utrecht: Jan van Arkel.

Hall, E. 1994. Hormonale mythologie rond de overgang. In Meinen et al., 124–137.

Harding, S. 1986. *The science question in feminism*. Ithaca: Cornell University Press.

Jacobus, M., et al., eds. 1990. *Body/politics: Women and the discourses of science*. New York: Routledge.

Jones, K. B. 1993. *Compassionate authority: Democracy and the representation of women*. New York: Routledge.

Knijn, T. 1994. Zorg met mondjesmaat: Paradoxen rond de dagelijkse zorg. In Meinen et al., 56–73.

Martin, E. 1987. *The woman in the body: A cultural analysis of reproduction*. Boston: Beacon Press.

Meinen, A., C. Parlevliet, and S. Sevenhuijsen, eds. 1994. *Op haar recept: Vrouwen in politiek debat over de gezondheidszorg*. Amsterdam: De Balie.

Okin, S. Moller 1989. *Justice, gender and the family*. Princeton: Princeton University Press.

Outshoorn, J. 1991. Is this what we wanted? Positive action as issue perversion. In E. Meehan and S. L. Sevenhuijsen, eds., *Equality politics and gender*. London: Sage, 104–121.

Parlevliet, C., and S. L. Sevenhuijsen 1993. *Zorg bekeken door een andere bril: Vrouwen en het debat over 'Keuzen in de zorg.'* Utrecht: Werkgroep Vrouwenstudies Sociale Wetenschappen.

Pateman, C. 1988. *The sexual contract*. Oxford: Polity Press.

Plumwood, V. 1993. *Feminism and the mastery of nature*. London: Routledge.

Pyne Addelson, K. 1994. *Moral passages: Toward a collectivist moral theory*. New York: Routledge.

Rooney, P. 1991. A different 'Different voice': On the feminist challenge in moral theory. *The Philosophical Forum* 22 (4): 335–361.

Schiebinger, L. 1989. *The mind has no sex? Women in the origins of modern science*. Cambridge: Harvard University Press.

Scott, J. W. 1986. Gender: A useful category of historical analysis. *American Historical Review* 91 (5): 1035–1075.

Sevenhuijsen, S. L. 1991. The morality of feminism. *Hypatia* 6 (2): 173–191

Sevenhuijsen, S. L. 1993a. Paradoxes of gender: Ethical and epistemological perspectives on care in feminist political theory. *Acta Politica* 1993 (2): 131–149.

Sevenhuijsen, S. L. 1993b. Hoe krijgen we de onderkant van de zorg weer boven? *Gezondheid en Politiek* 11 (3): 11–14.

Sevenhuijsen, S. L. 1995. De dubbelzinnigheid van autonomie: Reflecties over een feministische bio-ethiek. *Filosofie en Praktijk* 16 (1): 2–22.

Shrage, L. 1994. *Moral dilemmas of feminism: Prostitution, adultery and abortion*. New York: Routledge.

Spelman, E. 1989. *Inessential woman: Problems of exclusion in feminist thought*. Boston: Beacon Press.

Thornton, M. 1986. Sex equality is not enough for feminism. C. Pateman and Gross, eds. *Feminist challenges: Social and political theory*. Sydney: Allen & Unwin, 77–98.

Tronto, J. C. 1993. *Moral boundaries: A political argument for an ethic of care*. New York: Routledge.

Tronto, J. C. 1994. Wrong premises, wrong choices: A feminist perspective on care and health. Unpublished paper.

Tronto, J. C. 1995a. Care as a basis for radical political judgments. *Hypatia* 10 (2): 141–149.

Tronto, J. C. 1995b. *Caring for democracy: A feminist vision.* Utrecht: University of Humanistics.

Walker, M. Urban 1989. Moral understandings: Alternative 'epistemology' for a feminist ethics. *Hypatia* 4 (1): 15–28.

Wingerden, I. van 1994. Vrouwen en de overgang: Valkuilen, verleiding en feministische variatie. *Gezondheid en Politiek* 12 (3): 21–24.

Young, I. M. 1990. *Justice and the politics of difference.* Princeton: Princeton University Press.

4

The Combat Exclusion and the Role of Women in the Military

JUDITH WAGNER DECEW

Many women and feminists have for years been identified with antiwar and antimilitarist efforts, and have been both initiators and staunch supporters of pacifist movements. However, as increasing numbers of women are serving in the military beyond traditional roles such as nursing, administration, and communications, and as the sexism, harassment, and inequity in the military is being more highly publicized, women scholars are beginning to address issues surrounding the role of women within the military.[1]

I begin by describing central themes in the feminist debate about military values and gender, urging that despite the feminist emphasis on antimilitarism and nonviolence, there are important reasons to attend to the desirability of struggling for women's equality in the military. I then turn to the exclusion of women from military combat duty, an exclusion given implicit legal sanction by the Supreme Court in 1981 in *Rostker v. Goldberg*,[2] a decision holding that there was no gender-based discrimination in requiring men but not women to register for the draft. I argue that Rehnquist's majority opinion in *Rostker* endorses, despite his disclaimers, unsubstantiated judgments about the "proper role" of women, relies on an overly narrow interpretation of Congress's stated purpose for draft registration, and accepts the combat exclusion based on a mistaken reading of the history of its adoption, thus undermining his arguments and perpetuating inequality for women in the military.

Hypatia vol. 10, no. 1 (Winter 1995) © by Judith Wagner DeCew

To make the last point I review and assess the history of the adoption of the combat exclusion, showing that the exclusion was never given adequate justification by Congress. Next I examine further arguments that have been given in favor of the combat exclusion, many of which were not reflected in the earlier debates. I argue that there are strong replies to each and that most are based on sociopolitical considerations rather than military need. I then present additional reasons for lifting the combat exclusion.

We might well wonder why, given the wealth of arguments against the exclusion, it continues to be hotly debated and strongly supported by many. I suggest that related case arguments as well as feminist analyses of equality help explain why so many continue to defend the exclusion despite weak justifications and strong counterarguments. In conclusion, I point out why lifting the combat ban to gain equal opportunity for women has implications for treatment of military women in the areas of sexual harassment and abuse.

THE FEMINIST DEBATE ON WOMEN AND THE MILITARY

It is important to note that there is no single feminist position on the exclusion of women from combat. For years feminists committed to equality have been divided over issues concerning the role of women in the military, and it would be a mistake not to recognize this diversity of views.[3] Nevertheless, there is a long tradition of antiwar and antimilitarist sentiment among many women and feminists, which has sometimes precluded discussion of the combat exclusion for women in the military.

Feminist scholars who have examined the relationship between gender, violence, and war have often associated violence with male sexuality and nonviolence with mothering and nurturing. Thus, for example, Catharine MacKinnon (1989) has repeatedly emphasized the relationship between male sexuality and force, particularly violence against women in the form of rape, battery, and sexual harassment, Nancy Hartsock (1989) has traced ways in which virility and violence are commonly linked, and Cynthia Enloe (1983, 13–14) has called attention to respects in which the notion of combat is fundamental to the concepts of manhood and male superiority. Virginia Held writes that Betty Reardon (1985) claims:

> that sexism and the war system arise from the same set of authoritarian constructs. A social order based on competition, authoritarianism, and unequally valued human beings, upheld by coercive force controlled by male elites, gives rise, on her view, to both sexism and the system of war. The profile of men who abuse women is similar to that of soldiers; some view the similarity as "deliberate and necessary." Military combat training uses women hating as part of its method of turning men into soldiers. (Held 1993, 146)

Amy Swerdlow (1989), Judith Stiehm (1983), and Sara Ruddick (1980), among others, have emphasized in addition the relationship between a commitment to nonviolence and the activities of caring for and raising children. Ruddick notes the incompatibility between a mother's aim to preserve life and military destruction, and she traces parallels between peacemaking by mothers and nonviolence techniques advocated by Ghandi and Martin Luther King.

Given this context of feminist discussion and the widespread feminist commitment to peace and pacifism, it may seem incompatible with feminist ideals to be concerned with women's equality in the military and the exclusion of women from combat duty. Indeed, Virginia Held has suggested that many feminists find it bizarre or sick or at least misguided for women even to seek an equal right to fight, to kill, or to participate in the institutions of the military on a par with men. These feminists believe that women should strive for a much more meaningful equality, one that would empower women to prevent war, to make military combat obsolete, and to make military service unnecessary for anyone.[4] In this context it is not surprising that most recent feminist writing on the subject has not even addressed the issue of an equal right for women to participate in military combat.

Feminists may believe that a right to serve in combat in the military exists but that it should take low priority for feminist thinkers, given the many rights denied women around the world. Or, more strongly, they may reject any female participation in U.S. interventionist and military endeavors, particularly under male orders. They may believe an equal right to carry out U.S. military orders, which they find both morally outrageous and internationally illegal, is a right they would prefer not to have. By arguing against the combat exclusion, however, I am not thereby endorsing current military activities. I believe we can and must discuss the egalitarian concerns raised by the exclusion independently of assessments of general military policies, procedures, and objectives.

There are, furthermore, two considerations that make the inequality of the combat exclusion relevant for a wide range of feminists. First, we can idealize the military in such a way that we see it as the kind of institution that will be needed even in a largely peaceful and demilitarized world, to deal with the kinds of peacekeeping efforts that will continue to be necessary in a world without the military institutions and activities with which we are currently familiar. Second, we must realize how nonideal this world is and can be expected to remain. It is arguable that military establishments and military efforts are necessary and even justifiable, when, for example, they are used to prevent atrocities and violations of human rights such as those we have seen in such places as Bosnia and to provide aid in crises like that in Rwanda.[5] If this is correct, there is good reason for feminists to be concerned about the combat exclusion, the importance of women gaining equal treatment in the military, and their ability to be promoted to positions where they can transform military practices. Although my argument provides just one liberal feminist approach, it is, I believe, a compelling one.

THE *ROSTKER* LEGACY

The Military Selective Service Act required registration of males but not females for possible military service. The purpose of such registration, as stipulated by Congress, was to facilitate conscription of military personnel. Rehnquist's majority opinion in *Rostker* sets forth a two-pronged argument justifying the registration of men but not women. Note that I am not arguing for the draft (indeed I have great misgivings about a draft for men and women), but I utilize the *Rostker* case because it has major implications for the combat exclusion.

The majority's primary argument relies on deference to the legislature. Rehnquist claimed that the scope of congressional power is especially broad in the military context. On his view, courts should not in general substitute their own judgments concerning which policies will be desirable, and this customary deference is enhanced in military affairs and national defense contexts where courts are far less competent than Congress to pass judgment. Emphasizing that "deference does not mean abdication" (70), Rehnquist argued that since Congress specifically considered the question of the registration of women for the draft and recommended against it, their decision was not an "accidental byproduct of a traditional way of thinking about females" (74) and hence it was inappropriate to overturn their legislative decision. He claimed, in fact, that the Constitution required this deference to the legislature. Rehnquist also explicitly chided the district court for exceeding its authority and ignoring Congress's conclusions that the need for women in noncombat roles could be met by volunteers and that staffing noncombat positions with women during a mobilization would be "positively detrimental" to the important goal of military flexibility.

Rehnquist's second argument addressed the equal protection issue more specifically. He agreed that Congress's determination that any future draft would be characterized by a need for combat troops was sufficiently justified by testimony at the hearings. Because women were excluded from combat by statute in the navy and air force, and by military policy in the army and marines, he concluded that "men and women are simply not similarly situated for purposes of a draft or registration for the draft" (78). Thus, he continued, excluding women from registration did not violate the due process clause of the Fifth Amendment.[6] Congress was entitled to base the decision on military need over equity.

Note that the district court had rejected the defendant's deference to Congress argument as well as the plaintiff's request that the constitutional standard used be "strict scrutiny" and had instead relied on the midlevel "heightened scrutiny" or "important government interest" test articulated in previous sex discrimination cases (see *Craig v. Boren*, 429 U.S. 190 [1976]). In contrast, Rehnquist distinguished such cases as *Reed v. Reed* (404 U.S. 71 [1971]) and *Frontiero v. Richardson* (411 U.S. 677 [1973]), which involved overbroad classifications, and cited other recent cases such as *Schlesinger v. Ballard* (419 U.S. 498 [1968]), as supportive of his view. *Schlesinger*, which had challenged the navy's policy of allowing females a longer period than males to attain promotions needed for continued service, was cited as a case where the "different treatment of men and women naval officers . . . reflects, not archaic and overbroad generalizations, but, instead, the demonstrable fact that male and female line officers in the Navy are not similarly situated with respect to opportunities for professional service" (66).

Combat restrictions formed the clear basis for Congress's decision to exempt women from the draft registration. Given that women had been excluded from combat through statute and policy, Congress concluded that they would not be needed in the event of a draft, and therefore decided not to register them. Thus, while we think of *Rostker* as the draft case, it is also crucially a combat exclusion case. According to Rehnquist, *Rostker*, like *Schlesinger*, relied appropriately on a Senate report that said in part, "In the Committee's view, the starting point for any discussion of the appropriateness of registering women for the draft is the question of the proper role of women in combat" (S. Rep. No. 96–826, cited by Rehnquist at 67). Rehnquist stressed in his own words that "Congress was fully aware not merely of the many facts and figures presented to it by witnesses who testified before its Committees, but of the current thinking as to the place of women in the Armed Services" (71). Clearly the idea was that women should be protected from combat situations. Furthermore, it is explicit in the opinion that the reason men and women were not "similarly situated" for a draft or registration for one was "because of the combat restrictions on women" (78). Rehnquist added gratuitously that women would not actually be excluded by the decision because they could always volunteer for military service.

It should be clear at this point that despite his disclaimers, Rehnquist repeatedly relied on and reasserted Congress's emphasis on the "proper role" of women in the military. This "proper role" was invoked as the justification for the combat exclusion, which in turn formed the basis for the exclusion of women for registration for the draft. In reply to the district court he also cited further problems associated with registering women which had been raised in hearings: that "training would be needlessly burdened by women recruits who could not be used in combat," and "other administrative problems such as housing and different treatment with regard to dependency, hardship and physical standards" (81). Rehnquist's claims to the contrary, these arguments raise questions of convenience, not military need.

Second, while the case does not judge the combat restriction per se, the exclusion is accepted uncritically by Rehnquist and then given as the basis for the conclusion that men and women are not similarly situated in this instance and thus, as unlike cases, may be treated differently with no equal protection violation. The exclusion thus plays a pivotal role in the argument. Yet we can now see that Rehnquist's interpretation of the stated purpose of the registration, to facilitate preparation for a draft of combat troops, justifies his conclusion only when read far more narrowly than is reasonable. That is, even if the combat exclusion is accepted, preparing for a draft of combat troops does *not* imply that only combat positions will need to be filled. Approximately one-third of the positions were acknowledged to be roles where women could serve effectively. Including women in a draft to gain their skills in communications, radar repair, navigation, jet engine mechanics, drafting, surveying, meteorology, transportation, administrative and medical specialties, and so on, could save the time needed to train men in those fields and could release men from noncombat jobs to move to combat positions, thus facilitating rather than hindering a mobilization.

Third, Rehnquist's primary argument, relying on deference to Congress, is of course a common one. But it leaves the combat exclusion itself unchallenged from a constitutional point of view. It is thus staggering to discover that the combat exclusion for women was, when first enacted, merely an addition not originally part of the bill and not ever adequately justified in congressional testimony (see Gordon and Ludvigson 1991).

HISTORY OF THE ADOPTION OF THE COMBAT EXCLUSION

The original Senate bills establishing a regular corps of women in each of the services were introduced in 1947 and did not contain any provisions that would have excluded women from combat roles. At the Senate Armed Services Committee hearings little attention was paid to the possibility of legislating a mandatory combat exclusion, although some discussion indicated the services' intentions not to use women in combat situations. General Eisenhower, for example, testified concerning the value of women in the military, but his compliments were laced with comments about the roles for which women were well suited (Gordon and Ludvigson 1991, 4). In the House of Representatives, during the air force portion of the hearings there was no discussion of adding a combat exclusion for women. It was only during navy testimony that Representative Vinson proposed a legislative exclusion:

> I propose an amendment, if somebody will draft it. I am just throwing it out for what it is worth. Those are my views. I think it will strengthen the bill to have it positively understood by Congress that ships are not places to which these women are going to be detailed and nobody has authority to detail them to serve on ship.

> Of course, they are not going to be detailed to serve on ships, but you cannot tell what happens, you know, because somebody might say they need a few of them up there to do communications or other kinds of work and I do not think a ship is the proper place for them to serve. Let them serve on shore in the Continental United States and outside of the United States, but keep them off the ships. Of course, they ought to be on hospital ships. (Quoted in Gordon and Ludvigson 1991, 8).

Despite testimony from Captain F. R. Stickney of Navy Personnel that "we do not feel, though, that it was [*sic*] necessary to write that into law, Mr. Vinson" (Gordon and Ludvigson 1991, 8), the proposed amendment appeared later in the hearing. There was further objection to the amendment, but the bill considered the following year included combat exclusions for the navy and the air force. During the House debate, Representative Short commented, "we have put in those safeguards which I think are wise. We do not want our women killed" (Gordon and Ludvigson 1991, 11). There was no other specific discussion on combat exclusions. There seemed merely to be a general understanding that women would fill noncombat roles. The bill passed the House with the exclusion amendment. When submitted to the Senate it was described as essentially the same bill that originally passed by the Senate, with no mention of the addition of the combat exclusion. Moreover, the conference report made no reference to the rationale behind the combat amendment.

Consider, however, related House testimony that displays an attitude toward women in the military that was probably typical of the time:

> All these positions that will be filled by women at the present time are of a so-called housekeeping nature such as your excellent secretaries in many of your offices . . . women that men would have to replace.
>
> For every job ashore filled by a Wave [*sic*] officer you deny a male officer, who, after several years at sea, [has] the right to come ashore and occupy such an assignment.
>
> Enlisted men objected to the idea of having to take orders from a WAVE officer. Put yourself in the position of an enlisted man and I am sure you will agree with them. (Quoted in Gordon and Ludvigson 1991, 12)[7]

Clearly there was a prevailing view that if women were to serve in the military at all, it would be to do "women's work," and this presumably influenced views on the combat exclusion. But in all the congressional discussions on the issue, no military purpose for the exclusion seems to have been articulated. It appears that the only reasons for the exclusion were paternalistic protectionism and stereotypical views about what work women were suited for.

We find corroboration for this conclusion in Judge John Sirica's 1978 opinion in *Owens v. Brown* (455 F. Supp. 291 [D.D.C. 1978]), which held that the absolute ban on assignment of female personnel to sea duty, except in certain ships, violated the equal protection guarantee of the Fifth Amendment:

> The part of Section 6015 being challenged . . . was added casually, over the military's objection and without significant deliberation. . . . The provision was not directed at enhancing military preparedness . . . (n)or was it inserted to take account of the practical considerations associated with integrated shipbound personnel. . . . Instead, the sense of the discussion is that Section 6015's bar against assigning females to shipboard duty was premised on the notion that duty at sea is part of an essentially masculine tradition. ("The Combat Exclusion Laws" 1991, 4)

It is worth remembering that despite all its restrictions,[8] the 1948 act ultimately provided permanent status to women in all the armed forces (both regular and reserve) and so provided for a group of trained women who could be mobilized in an emergency. This was a first step toward moving women from their second-class status as citizens allowed only in auxiliaries.

ARGUMENTS FOR AND AGAINST THE COMBAT EXCLUSION

Subsequently, there has been considerably more discussion of arguments both in favor of and against the combat exclusion for women. We would do well to describe them in categories. One argument, exemplified in the quotation given above from Representative Short, mirrors the early paternalistic and protectionist justifications for the exclusion, namely that women should not be hurt or killed in combat. In General Westmoreland's words, "No man with gumption wants a woman to fight his Nation's battles. I do not believe the American public wants to see a woman . . . do a man's job and that is to fight."[9] The underlying premises are that only certain jobs are appropriate for women and that the public expects and demands that women will be kept out of harm's way so they do not become victims. One obvious reply is that women have often served at substantial risk of injury in noncombat and semicombat positions and have been POWs as well. They are surely exposed to combat when serving as nurses or administrative assistants at the front lines. These women are not out of harm's way and may be doubly vulnerable if they have received little training in self-protection.[10] Note, in addition, the ironic relation between service and risk for women:

> U.S. military history in fact demonstrates that when the nation's level of military activities is reduced, women are no longer needed in service and their military activity is commensurately reduced; however, when military emergencies arise a role for women in service is quickly

> rediscovered. This results in the irony that women have served in the military in greater numbers precisely when the risks were the greatest, but their military participation was less acceptable when the risks were lower.[11]

Furthermore, as the definition of "combat" changes over time or due to different guidelines in the four services, the protection afforded women by the combat exclusion is diminishing. Finally, battle versus homefront lines may be irretrievably blurred in nuclear warfare so that there is no choice about whether or not women "go to war." Some women receive training in nuclear/biological/chemical (NBC) defense; yet if women not "in combat" are subject to the threat of an NBC attack, the combat exclusions are obsolete to the extent they are based on the fear of risk to women.

A second common argument favoring the combat exclusion cites the physical disadvantages of women, such as strength, stamina, and muscle. This diminished physical ability of women is often cited as the reason women cannot meet the physical demands of ground combat, including tasks such as carrying and lifting. Therefore, the argument continues, their presence impairs military efficiency (Tuten 1982, 247). Of course men who lack upper body strength are not for that reason prohibited from combat duty. Moreover, the statutes exclude women from combat ships and aircraft, not land activities. In reply, others point out that physical strength is only one of many attributes necessary to perform successfully as sailors and aviators, and physical conditioning may compensate for much lack of strength for ground troops. In addition, many have emphasized that the small physical stature of the Viet Cong and North Vietnamese did not lead to military success for the American forces whose troops were usually of larger stature. The issue is not one of lowering standards for performance to allow women to participate. Rather, it seems that efficiency should dictate gender-neutral determinations of whether or not an individual (male or female) has the competence, skill, and strength to serve in any given position. Note also that with the growing complexity of modern weapons systems, technical ability and education are becoming far more important than physical strength in determining eligibility and qualifications for many military positions.

Another popular argument used to justify the exclusion of women stresses the purported psychological differences between men and women. It is often claimed that women are less able than men to withstand the stress of combat, that women are too emotional and volatile to perform under combat stress. There are two strong replies to this argument. First, critics note the overall performance record of women in World War II, Korea, Vietnam, and more recently in Panama, Operation Desert Storm, and elsewhere, not only as nurses on the front lines but also as military police, pilots, flight engineers, and so on. Second, they point to the record of women who serve as urban police and firefighters under analogous stress. There does not seem to be documented evidence to establish the claim that women will deal less well than men with combat pressure.

Fourth, pregnancy and child-rearing are cited as reasons women cannot serve effectively in combat. It is claimed that pregnancy hinders military readiness, the ability to deploy rapidly, and the length of women's service careers (see Mitchell 1989; Yarborough 1985, 31, cited in "Combat Exclusion Laws" 1991, 25). These concerns may stem from a social perception of the "proper role" of women. But whatever their origin, they do not seem to acknowledge that women are pregnant only a short part of their lives, that some women never become pregnant at all, and that readiness procedures and policies could well accommodate the 5–10 percent of military women who are pregnant at any given time. Men as well as women have child care responsibilities, and all military personnel are expected to take responsibility for dependent care arrangements in case of a mobilization.

A fifth reason cited for excluding women from combat is the fear that some women will fail to develop a "team spirit" or "bond" with men in combat (see D'Amico 1990, 7). The assumption underlying this argument is that males will bond with males, and females with females, but bonding will not occur across the sexes. This argument mirrors similar claims about group cohesion used against allowing blacks in the military, indicating that fear and prejudice are at least partially at its base. Respondents argue that bonding is important, especially in military emergencies, but that it is more dependent on leadership, trust, organization for a common goal, the pressure of imminent danger, and a willingness to sacrifice than on any considerations relevant to sex differences. Respondents suggest the problem is not that women will not be active participants on the "team," but men's attitudes: men will not accept women with a "team" spirit unless encouraged to do so.

A sixth reason cited against allowing women in combat is that the presence of women will lead to sexual relationships and disruption of discipline. But this argument relies on the dubious assumptions that existing rules against sexual "fraternization" will not be obeyed and that sexual relationships will be more of a threat in combat situations than elsewhere in the military.

Seventh, some have expressed worries that if women participate in combat, the image of the U.S. armed forces will suffer. The simple reply to this is that Canada and Great Britain have now made it a violation of law to bar women from combat or to place restrictions on their number, and Israel conscripts women into the military. These countries, and others that include women in the military, do not appear to have a tarnished image of military strength and preparedness. Preparations to commit women to combat might, in contrast, demonstrate especially strong resolve.

Finally, a somewhat darker and more malevolent interpretation of the combat exclusion is that it is an expression of the belief that women are inherently inferior and therefore should have subordinate status. The nineteenth-century *Dred Scott* case provides an interesting analogy. When Justice Taney sought to explain why the drafters of the Constitution could not have intended to include blacks within the term "citizens," he relied in large part on the long-standing exclusion of blacks from service in the military. Taney understood how law can be used to express and reinforce subordinate status. He also understood the fundamental nature of the activity of defending one's country as an indication of one's worthiness.[12]

It is clear from this summary of justifications and replies that most of the arguments against allowing women in combat are based on sociopolitical considerations, some quite dubious, rather than military need. Not only are there readily available replies to these arguments favoring the combat exclusion, but there are also a variety of additional justifications for abolishing the exclusion. The most often cited is the impact on individual women in the military who face fewer job opportunities and choices (and therefore less access to medical, educational, retirement, and veterans' benefits), less opportunity for promotion and career advancement, as well as less opportunity to gain the experience needed to gain promotion. Sheila Tobias has argued that women's exclusion from combat has been a barrier to their political success as well (Elshtain and Tobias 1990, 163–88). Advocates for the exclusion argue that opening career opportunities for women is not a function of the armed forces.[13] But for years career opportunity has been an argument used to promote the military services for men.

More difficult to document is the morale problem for women who are capable of doing a job but who are nevertheless excluded and who are thus not able to get recognition for the tasks they can perform or the risky service they endure. A flip side of the morale problem is the resentment felt by males who feel they must hold more than their share of some undesirable duties because women trained to do them are precluded from that service. Low morale surely can affect military capability and management. Excluding women from combat can also limit military flexibility. Shifting and disrupting a crew in wartime damages cohesiveness and military readiness, for example. And troop movement can be delayed while military officials try to determine whether or not female personnel can participate. As Senator William Proxmire commented in 1986,

> Barring women from combat has resulted in complex and arbitrary restrictions that limit our military. (Congressional Record, March 21, 1986: S3182–3183, cited in Gordon and Ludvigson 1991, 16)

> The first consideration in any issue of military personnel must always be national security, and, indeed, that is my primary concern. The combat exclusion policies deprive our forward battle areas of available personnel resources and limit our flexibility. . . .
>
> I am not saying that every position should be open to every soldier. Of course no soldier should be assigned to a position for which he or she is not qualified. . . . Gender-neutral physical requirements would address this concern without arbitrarily excluding qualified candidates. . . . We are wasting our personnel resources. . . .
>
> It is important that those women feel that they are a valued part of our armed services and that they be regarded with ample opportunities for advancement. We owe them that. The women in the military serve our country faithfully, and, despite the combat exclusion policy, many women risk their lives every day at dangerous posts like the Mx and Minuteman launch sites. They must not be treated like second-class soldiers. (Gordon and Ludvigson 1991, 16–17)

Finally, there is the serious problem of defining "combat duty." Military definitions differentiate combat missions, close combat, direct combat, combat support, and combat service support, to name a few. The definitions are not always consistent from one branch of the services to another, leading to confusion and inconsistency in determinations of which positions are or are not open to women ("Combat Exclusion Laws" 1991, 11–14). Redefinition of positions in which women can serve results in reassignment, retraining, and career uncertainty, which in turn can affect retention and morale.

EQUALITY AND FEMINIST ANALYSIS

Bernard Williams has said: "Equality is a popular but mysterious political ideal. People can become equal (or at least more equal) in one way with the consequence that they become unequal (or more unequal) in others. . . . It does not follow that equality is worthless as an ideal" (Williams 1981, 185). Differentiating types of equality does not lessen the importance of equality.

Equal opportunity and equal treatment are two of the most distinctive conceptions of equality, and both are at issue for women in the military. During the 1970s there were many gains in these areas, achieved through the federal courts. Women won the right to the same benefits for dependents as males, the right to remain in the military after bearing children, the right to attend military academies, and the right to a lengthier discharge time frame than men, given that women had fewer promotional opportunities. Despite these successes the combat exclusion has remained in effect, and despite the numerous arguments and replies defending elimination of the exclusion, it is still widely supported both within and outside the military. Why is this? Why has the combat exclusion remained so entrenched? Why does the legacy of *Rostker* remain, leading many to deny the equality issues at stake?

Let me suggest two reasons. First, equality for women in the military has been precluded by subtle arguments that reappear. In 1979 in *Personnel Administration v.Feeney* (442 U.S. 256 [1979]) the Supreme Court upheld Massachusetts's absolute hiring preference for veterans, notwithstanding its obvious negative impact on women. The Court concluded that the legislature had no intention of discriminating against women, only the intention of helping veterans who just happened to be overwhelmingly male. *Feeney* is particularly relevant in two ways. It illustrates the economic subordination that comes with the military's exclusion of women. In addition, the opinion uses a two-step reasoning process similar to the *Rostker* analysis. In *Feeney* the Court assumed the legality of the previous exclusion of women from the military and focused only on the hiring preference. As explained above, in *Rostker* the Court assumed the legality of the combat exclusion and focused only on the draft exclusion. This sort of sequential reasoning is useful for condoning inequality and subordination. The inequality can be made to disappear if one assumes away its antecedent.

Second, feminist analysis applied to equal protection of the law can help us understand why the combat exclusion persists, and that understanding can in turn help us determine strategies to gain further equality for women through its abolition. Martha Minow has recently discussed ways of applying feminist analysis to the legal doctrine of equal protection of the law. She calls attention in particular to three assumptions underlying that doctrine:

> Feminist theorists stress and challenge three assumptions that usually remain unstated in analyses of equality and discrimination. The first is that the perspective of the excluded or subjugated person or group is irrelevant or untrustworthy in evaluating claims of discrimination: the perspective presumed relevant is that of those with the power to structure social institutions and to rule on charges of discrimination. The second assumption is that the equality inquiry does and should use as the norm for whether likes are treated alike those who have been privileged in the past: generally, white, male, Christian, English-speaking, able-bodied persons. The third assumption is that the status quo in social and economic institutions is sufficiently fair and uncoerced, and resists change.
>
> In making these assumptions explicit, feminists suggest that the assumptions are themselves contestable and that alternative starting points should be used. (Minow 1991, 639)

Consider the first assumption that the only relevant perspective for evaluating equal opportunity claims is that of those in power, not the perspectives of the complainants. We see this clearly at play in *Rostker* as well as in later arguments. Rehnquist, for example, does not see *Rostker* as a legitimate equal protection case. But the history of the adoption of the combat exclusion shows that deference to the legislature is very suspect in that case. First, almost no women in the military were questioned during the original hearings on the 1948 bill and the exclusion amendment. One male representative suggested its addition, and it was tacked on in a haphazard manner. Second, even in 1981, deference to the legislature basically meant deferring to the white males in power. It allowed virtually no input from women in general or women in the military. Even if not explicit or intended, women were treated from the early hearings to the *Rostker* decision as if they had no valuable or relevant input on the question. This is emphasized throughout later hearings when most testimony is from men who repeatedly refer to "them" or "those women." Clearly the perspective advanced is not that of women in the military.

Consider next the second assumption cited by Minow concerning who makes the determination when cases are "alike" or "similar" enough to require equal treatment. There is continued focus, from *Rostker* on, on the "proper role" for women, the need to protect women from harm, on physical strength, psychological ability to handle stress, on male bonding, and problems of pregnancy. That these are used repeatedly to differentiate men and women gives strong indication that the determination is being made by individuals who are reinforcing stereotypical views about women as fragile, emotional, and weak, who should be home tending their children, and who are thus not similar enough to men to be treated like them. The tendency to disregard the many counterarguments and contrary evidence on women's interest in serving in the military even under severe risks, on their effectiveness in military and civilian positions under combat-like stress, on their physical conditioning in the military, and on their qualifications for positions relying on education more than physical strength, points out that the norm being applied is one of a physically strong and unemotional male needed for ground combat. Given the contrast between the norm used and the stereotype of women appealed to, it is hardly surprising that women are judged not to be similarly situated to men, and are thus automatically excluded.

The refusal of advocates of the combat exclusion to allow career advancement to be considered a relevant or important military goal for women, despite repeated emphasis on it as a legitimate goal for men in service, shows as well that the female perspective is being ignored and that the norm being used necessarily excludes women. But it also illustrates reliance on the third assumption, that the status quo in social and economic institutions is viewed as sufficiently fair by those making decisions about women's role in the military. According to those defending the exclusion, men need the jobs, and there is no need to provide for or guarantee positions or promotions for women. The military is doing just fine as it is.

In sum, the arguments favoring the combat exclusion repeatedly ignore the perspective of women, rely on stereotypical views of their needs and abilities, and assume there is no difficulty with the status quo of the military, thereby ensuring that women cannot and will not be deemed similar enough to men to be treated alike. Using Minow's analysis, therefore, we can see that the question of whether or not to allow women in combat generates a paradigm equal protection case.

If this is correct, then there may be hope for change as more women are able to speak up and be heard in positions of authority and power. Since Sheila Widnall has been appointed Secretary of the Air Force, we can expect to have more military women called into hearings to voice their views on the qualifications and need for women in the services. Similarly, more military men and congressional leaders are taking views like that of Senator Proxmire. For example, former President Bush's Navy Secretary, Sean O'Keefe, urged (before he left office) that the navy should permit women to fly combat aircraft and serve on all navy ships and amphibious vessels (*Boston Globe*, January 7, 1993). Although his comments are not binding, they do signal a new attitude. We can also look forward to more women joining Representative Pat Schroeder on the Senate Armed Forces Committee. And we now have the new voice of Ruth Bader Ginsberg on the Supreme Court as a justice who is already articulately defending the strengths and abilities of women. These show, I believe, that we can expect and should demand future testimony and arguments to expose and reject the common assumptions made in the past.

CONCLUSION

Military policy has changed to allow women to serve in more positions, though this has often had less to do with logic and argumentation than with powerful events such as the navy's Tailhook scandal. However, combat restrictions still remain. Maintaining the exclusion for special flight operations units and for ground troops, for example, continues to reinforce stereotypes and perpetuate inequality for women. A blanket ground combat exclusion is unacceptable. The relevant question must be who is qualified to do the job. What is required is full acknowledgment that the issue of women in the military *is* a question of equal opportunity and that assumptions and arguments supporting the exclusion from the past to the present are deeply flawed.

Over the last twenty years arguments against women's combat service have changed to de-emphasize claims about the instability of women, but concerns about unit cohesion are still featured, and considerations of strength keep reappearing, particularly for the army and the marines. Future discussion must focus instead on the relevant considerations, equity and military need, both of which provide strong justifications for abolishing the combat exclusion.

One final point. I have focused until now on the combat exclusion, merely alluding to the sexual abuse and harassment now well documented in the armed services. (Tailhook is only one case. There are also reports of rape and sexual assault in the Persian Gulf during Operation Desert Storm and reports of various levels of sexual harassment including demeaning sexual jokes and demands for sex.) But combat exclusion and sexual harassment are closely connected.

Harassment and abuse are made worse by the exclusion. Wherever women are barred, their absence leads to a culture that breeds sexism and domination. It is arguable that integrating woman and giving them equal opportunity can lead to gains in equal treatment and can decrease sexism more effectively than instruction for men about sexual harassment. While harassment may initially increase with more inclusion of women, over the long term it will ease. Consider, for example, the experience in the air force where 97 percent of the jobs are open to women as opposed to only 59 percent of the jobs in the navy. The women in the air force who understand the technology are rarely harassed (*Time*, July 13, 1992). Until women can compete based on the same standards as men, they are likely to remain vulnerable to harassment and mistreatment. If they are not allowed to use their full abilities, it will continue to be easy for them to be treated as if they do not have the skills and to be stereotyped as unable, unqualified, and unneeded, as "detriments" to military effectiveness rather than the assets they are. Thus, another major argument for the elimination of the combat exclusion is its effectiveness in minimizing sexual harassment and abuse in the military.

NOTES

An earlier version of this paper was presented at a conference on Feminist Ethics and Social Policy at the University of Pittsburgh Graduate School of Public and International Affairs, November 6, 1993. Portions of this paper are reprinted in Bushnell (1995). I am grateful to participants at the conference as well as to Cynthia Enloe, Virginia Held, Susan Brison, James Sterba, and the referees from *Hypatia* for helpful material and comments, though they may not all agree with my conclusions.

1. Recent books addressing the role of women in the military include Muir (1993) and Stiehm (1989). See Katzenstein (1993) for a review of both books.

2. *Rostker, Director of Selective Service v. Goldberg et al.*, 453 U.S. 57 (1981). Quotations from this case are noted in the text by page numbers. Note that *Rostker* involved a male plaintiff and the executive branch at the time supported registering women for the draft, but Congress disagreed.

3. The National Organization for Women, for example, submitted an amicus brief in *Rostker* supporting the draft of women as well as men. Other feminist groups disagreed. Similarly, with respect to the combat exclusion, women both within and outside the military hold different views.

4. From comments presented at a conference on Feminist Ethics and Social Policy at the University of Pittsburgh Graduate School of Public and International Affairs, November 6, 1993.

5. I am indebted to Virginia Held for these points.

6. The guarantee of equal protection is found in two amendments to the U.S. Constitution. The Fourteenth Amendment applies to actions of state governments, whereas the prohibitions of the Fifth Amendment apply to actions of the federal government and so are at stake here. Although the text of the Fifth Amendment does not expressly guarantee equal protection of the law, the U.S. Supreme Court has held that this guarantee is included within the due process clause of the Fifth Amendment in *Bolling v. Sharpe*, 347 U.S. 497 (1954).

7. Comments from Representative Andrews followed by two comments from Representative van Zandt. Cong. Rec. 2 June 1948: 6969 and 6869–70. Beginning in 1943, women serving in the Naval Reserve had been known as Women Accepted for Voluntary Emergency Services (WAVES).

8. Other restrictions included a separate rank and promotion structure for women and men, different minimum age restrictions on enlistment for women and men, a limitation on total female enlisted strength of 2 percent of personnel on duty in each service, a 10 percent ceiling on female officers who could serve as permanent regular lieutenant colonels and navy commanders, and a 20 percent ceiling in the navy for the number of lieutenant commanders. Many of these restrictions on rank and percentage limits were reversed in 1967 ("Combat Exclusion Laws" 1991, 3–5).

9. Hearings on Women in the Military, 1979 at 75 ("Combat Exclusion Laws" 1991, 9).

10. Susan Brison has pointed out to me that combat training provides important self-defense skills useful in nonmilitary contexts, and is arguably of equal or even greater value for women than for men.

11. "Combat Exclusion Laws" (1991, 22). See also Enloe (1983) for a description of how the government campaigned hard during the war to recruit women for military service and factory jobs (to replace the men who went off to war), and then after the war engaged in a full scale propaganda blitz to send women back to their homes so men could have their civilian jobs back.

12. I am grateful to a referee from this journal for this point.

13. For example, see opposing statements by J. Philip Anderegg and Nicholas Kamillatos, in "Combat Exclusion Laws" (1991, 49, 51).

REFERENCES

D'Amico, Francine. 1990. Women at arms: The combat controversy. *Minerva: Quarterly Report on Women and the Military* 8(2): 1–35.

Elshtain, Jean Bethke and Sheila Tobias. 1990. *Women, militarism, and war: Essays in history, politics, and social history*. Lanhan, MD: Rowman and Littlefield.

Enloe, Cynthia. 1983. *Does khaki become you? The militarization of women's lives*. Boston: South End Press.

Gordon, Marilyn A. and Mary Jo Ludvigson. 1991. A constitutional analysis of the combat exclusion for air force women. *Minerva: Quarterly Report on Women and the Military* 9(2): 1–34. First published in different form in *U.S. Air Force Journal of Legal Studies* 1(1990), and *The Naval Law Review* 1(1990).

Harris, Adrienne and Ynestra King, eds. 1989. *Rocking the ship of state*. Boulder, CO: Westview.

Hartsock, Nancy. 1989. Masculinity, heroism, and the making of war. In *Rocking the ship of state*. See Harris and King 1989.

Held, Virginia. 1993. *Feminist morality*. Chicago: University of Chicago Press.

Katzenstein, Mary Fainsod. 1993. The right to fight. *The Women's Review of Books* 11(2): 30–31.

MacKinnon, Catharine. 1989. *Toward a feminist theory of the state*. Cambridge: Harvard University Press.

Minow, Martha. 1991. Equalities. *The Journal of Philosophy* 88(11): 635–644.

Mitchell, B. 1989. *Weak link: Feminization of the American military*. Washington, DC: Regnery Gateway.

Muir, Kate. 1993. *Arms and the woman*. London: Hodder and Stroughton.

Reardon, Betty. 1985. *Sexism and the war system*. New York: Teachers College Press.

Ruddick, Sara. 1980. Maternal thinking. *Feminist Studies* 6: 342–67.

Stiehm, Judith. 1983. The protected, the protector, the defender. In *Women's and men's wars*. New York: Pergamon Press.

Stiehm, Judith Hicks. 1989. *Arms and the enlisted woman*. Philadelphia: Temple University Press.

Swerdlow, Amy. 1989. Pure milk, not poison: Women strike for peace and the test ban treaty of 1963. In *Rocking the ship of state*. See Harris and King 1989.

The combat exclusion laws: An idea whose time has gone. 1991. The Association of the Bar of the City of New York Committee on Military Affairs and Justice. *Minerva: Quarterly Report on Women and the Military* 9(4): 1–55.

Tuten, Jeff M. 1982. The argument against female combatants. In *Female soldiers—combatants or noncombatants: Historical and contemporary perspectives*, ed. Nancy Loring Goldman. Westport, CT: Greenwood.

Williams, Bernard. 1981. What is equality? Pt. 1 of Equality of welfare. *Philosophy and Public Affairs* 10(3): 185–224.

Yarborough, J. 1985. Sex and the military: The feminist mistake. *Current*, 27–32.

5

Fathers' Rights, Mothers' Wrongs?

Reflections on Unwed Fathers' Rights and Sex Equality

MARY L. SHANLEY

The recent case of *Baby Girl Clausen*, involving a custody dispute between the biological parents, Cara Clausen and Daniel Schmidt of Iowa, and the adoptive parents, Roberta and Jan DeBoer of Michigan, over who should be recognized as the legal parents of baby Jessica, focused national attention on the issue of what rights biological unwed fathers may have to custody of their infant offspring. When Cara Clausen, at the time unmarried, gave birth to a baby girl, she gave her irrevocable consent to the child's adoption two days after its birth, as did the man she named as the child's father on the birth certificate. Within weeks, however, Clausen regretted her decision and informed Daniel Schmidt that he was the baby's father. Schmidt responded by filing a petition to establish paternity, and initiating legal action to block the adoption. Schmidt contended that a biological father has a right to custody of his child unless it is shown that he is "unfit" to be a parent. After some two years of litigation, Michigan declared it did not have jurisdiction in the matter and Iowa proceeded to enforce its decree that Schmidt's parental rights had never properly been terminated and the child had to be returned to his physical custody.[1]

Many of those who commented on the case asked whether Daniel Schmidt's alleged rights should be enforced in the face of the trauma Jessica, now a toddler, would suffer in being removed from the only family she had known. While this matter merits serious attention, I focus on a different issue raised by the

Hypatia vol. 10, no. 1 (Winter 1995) © by Mary L. Shanley

case, namely the basis and nature of an unwed biological father's right to veto an adoption decision of an unwed mother. This question was obscured in the case of *Baby Girl Clausen* because Daniel Schmidt initiated his action with the full cooperation of Cara Clausen, who had come to regret her decision. But it was *his* rights that the Iowa courts upheld, holding that an unwed biological father had a right to preclude an adoption initiated by the biological mother or the state.

There have been a significant number of cases in which an unwed biological father has sought to reverse the biological mother's decision to allow a child to be adopted, statutory provisions stipulating under what conditions an unwed biological father's consent is necessary vary greatly from state to state, and legal thinking on the matter is quite unsettled.[2] Many courts continue to apply the traditional rule that they must consider the "best interest" of the child in making any decision about custody. Supporters of biological fathers' rights, by contrast, argue that when the biological mother does not wish to retain custody, the biological father's claim automatically takes precedence over that of some "stranger" or potential adoptive parent (Boyd 1990; Buchanan 1984; Eveleigh 1989; Hamilton 1987–88; Raab 1984; Serviss 1991; Steward 1990; Zinman 1992).[3] Interestingly, some advocates of women's rights have also criticized the best interest standard as too subject to the biases of individual judges but have argued that women's unique role in human gestation and childbirth, as well as various aspects of their social and economic vulnerability, dictate that an unwed biological mother must be able to make the decision to have her child adopted without interference by the father or the state (Becker 1989; Erickson 1984; Erickson 1990, 39 n. 22; Rothman 1989). According to this view, neither the biological mother nor the state has an obligation to seek the biological father's consent to the adoption decision, or even to inform him of his paternity. From such a perspective, statutes that require biological mothers, but not biological fathers, to consent to the adoption of their newborn infant do not deny men equal protection. The debate between advocates of these two perspectives takes us to the difficult issue of what, indeed, should be the grounding of *anyone's* claim to parental rights.

From my perspective, neither the "fathers' rights" nor the "maternal autonomy" position provides a fully satisfactory basis for thinking about the custodial claims of unwed biological parents. I am persuaded by considerations advanced by advocates in both camps that the best interest standard is unsuitable for cases involving newborns surrendered by their mothers for adoption, in part because that standard does not adequately recognize the claims of biological paternity, and in part because it is difficult to guard adequately against the biases of individual judges. But almost all arguments for unwed fathers' rights are based on a notion of gender-neutrality that is misleading, not only because of women's biological experience of pregnancy but also because of the inequality inherent in the social structures in which sexual and reproductive activity currently take place. Many arguments in favor of a mother's right to decide on the custody of her child, by contrast, expose the ways in which gender-neutral rules applied to situations of social and economic inequality may in practice perpetuate male privilege. These insights might suggest that one good way to compensate for the present social and economic inequalities would be to give women complete or at least preponderant decision-making authority about reproductive matters until present social and economic inequalities based on sex diminish, but such a policy would run the risk of reinforcing the gender stereotype that women, not men, are the natural and proper nurturers of children. Law and social policy in the area of parental rights must walk a very fine line between adopting false gender-neutrality by treating men and women identically on the one hand, and reinforcing gender stereotypes on the other (on this dilemma more generally, see Eisenstein 1988).

The theoretical question of who should have parental rights and on what grounds is complicated by the practical consideration of what will prove to be the best means of moving toward both greater sexual equality and acceptance of diverse family forms. (I am, for example, concerned that any principles I develop here be compatible with enabling lesbian life-partners to parent a child free from threats by a known sperm donor to seek parental rights after agreeing prior to conception not to do so.)[4] I am also influenced by my belief in the desirability of sexual equality in both the public and private spheres, which requires not only access to jobs and public activity for women, but also the assumption of concrete, day-to-day, "hands on" responsibility for child-rearing by men (see Johnson 1994).

I argue here that a liberal polity interested in protecting the possibility for intimate association and family life for all its members should articulate norms that ground parental claims in a mixture of genetic relationship, assumption of responsibility, and provision of care to the child (including gestation). In the case of a newborn, this means that the biological father must take concrete steps to demonstrate his commitment to the child prior to the biological mother's relinquishment of the child for adoption, and courts must have the authority to judge both his efforts and the mother's objections to his claim. Only some such standard, I believe, recognizes the complexity of the sexual, genetic, biological, economic, and social relationships between adults and among adults and children that are involved in human reproductive activity.

Beyond the legal issues raised by unwed biological fathers' claims to custody, considering the rights of unwed biological parents also raises issues about individual rights in situations dealing with family relationships. By looking behind abstract assertions of individual rights to examine the dependency, reciprocity, and responsibility involved in family relationships, I suggest that the traditional liberal understanding of autonomous individuals must be revised to take account of the fact that persons are not fundamentally isolated and discrete but constructed in and by their relationships to others.[5]

UNWED PARENTS' CUSTODY RIGHTS IN COMMON LAW AND CONSTITUTIONAL LAW

THE PATRIARCHAL CONSTRUCTION OF THE COMMON LAW REGARDING CUSTODY

A frequent theme in much of the literature advocating unwed fathers' rights is that unmarried fathers have been treated unfairly as a result of widespread social hostility toward them. Arguing that an unwed biological father has a right to be informed of the birth of his child under any circumstances, John Hamilton complains that "until a few years ago, unwed fathers were ignored or received virtually no protection from either the United States Constitution or the statutes of most states. Indeed, courts and legislatures traditionally have been openly hostile to the recognition of parental rights of unwed fathers" (Hamilton 1987–88, 949–50). Elizabeth Stanton argues that "custody was vested in the mother because the law presumed that she was better suited to raise children," a presumption Stanton regards as both unwarranted and hurtful to men.[6] Commentaries that assume that laws placing custody of nonmarital children in their biological mothers' hands reflected hostility to biological fathers display a profound misunderstanding of the patriarchal roots of family law, as well as a stunning indifference to the devastating social and economic consequences of unwed motherhood for women.

The common law, which largely regulated legal aspects of family relationships in America well into the nineteenth century was profoundly patriarchal; legal definitions of who is a father and the extent of paternal responsibilities governed not only a man's relationships with his children but also with women both inside and outside his family. Under the common law a man had complete custodial authority over any children born of his wife, and no legal relationship at all to children he sired out of wedlock. The child of his wife took his surname; the nonmarital child did not. The marital child had a right to financial support from him; the nonmarital child did not. The marital child had the right to inherit from him if he died without a will; the nonmarital child did not (Becker 1989, 498).

The husband's authority over the marital child was an extension of his authority over his wife. Under the common law doctrine of coverture, a wife's legal personality was subsumed in that of her husband during marriage. A wife could not enter into contracts, sue or be sued, or engage in other legal transactions without being joined by her husband. He owned outright her movable property and had control of (although he could not alienate) her real estate. Torts she committed in his presence were chargeable to him, not to her. A married woman also had no right to refuse her husband sexual access—marital rape was not recognized as an offense. So complete was the husband's custodial authority that during his lifetime he had the power to convey his parental rights to a third person without the mother's consent, and he could name someone other than the mother to be the child's guardian after his death.[7]

Thus, under the common law, a man's legal relationship to his offspring was governed by his relationship to their mother. If the woman was his wife, a child was "his," so much so that he exercised exclusive custodial authority. If the mother was not his wife, however, the child was "filius nullius," the child of no one. Obviously, these rules affected both lineage and property. They allowed a man to lay claim to legitimate heirs (for without marriage, who would know for certain who the father of a child might be?) and to avoid squandering his estate supporting other children. While the father was shielded from financial responsibility for his "spurious" offspring, a woman who bore children outside of marriage was "ruined"; unmarried mothers' desperate attempts at suicide and infanticide dot the pages of social histories and nineteenth-century novels. Although the nonmarital child could inherit from no one, Poor Laws assigned mothers financial responsibility for their offspring and gave them custodial rights as long as they kept their children off public support. A woman's responsibility for her nonmarital children punished her for sex outside of marriage and increased women's incentives to join themselves to men through marriage.

It is no wonder that women's rights advocates from the mid-nineteenth century on protested against the patriarchal assumptions and the sexual double-standard implicit in this configuration of rules governing marital and nonmarital procreation. During the nineteenth century, in part due to women's rights advocacy, legislatures began to replace common law rules with statutes that granted wives equal custodial rights with their husbands. By the early twentieth century, when parents divorced, judges began to prefer mothers as custodians of marital children of "tender years" (usually under seven or ten years of age).[8] Eventually the standard of the "best interest of the child"—which did not automatically prefer either spouse and which purported to recognize the needs of the child as paramount—replaced any presumption explicitly favoring the custodial claim of either married parent if they divorced.

With respect to the custody of nonmarital children the law changed more slowly, and the impetus came mainly from children's rights advocates who wanted to get rid of the legal disabilities of "illegitimacy," such as the inability to collect survivors' benefits, receive child support, and inherit from the father (*Weber v. Aetna Casualty & Surety Co.*, 406 U.S. 164 [1972]; *Gomez v. Perez*, 409 U.S. 535 [1973]; and *Trimble v. Gordon*, 430 U.S. 762 [1977]). Thus the common law protections of fathers against the claims of nonmarital children and their mothers have been largely dissolved, and paternal responsibility for out-of-wedlock children established. But the common law history provides no basis for paternal *rights* to such children. Some advocates of unwed biological fathers' rights have argued, however, that while unrecognized in the common law, the ability to raise one's biological child is a fundamental interest protected by the United States Constitution, and that under the Constitution men and women must have equal rights to claim custody of their nonmarital offspring.

THE EMERGENCE OF UNWED FATHERS' CONSTITUTIONAL RIGHTS

Over the past twenty years, five decisions of the Supreme Court—*Stanley v. Illinois*, *Quilloin v. Wolcott*, *Caban v. Mohammed*, *Lehr v. Robertson*, and *Michael H. v. Gerald D.*—laid down some guidelines for thinking about unwed fathers' rights. These decisions have established that at least in those instances where an unmarried biological father has established a relationship with his child by an unmarried woman, the father's right to continue the relationship may be constitutionally protected. Although these decisions do not by any means resolve all the dilemmas surrounding the custody of infants born to unmarried biological parents, they provide a useful starting point for thinking about those issues.

The Court first considered the custodial rights of unmarried biological fathers in 1972 in *Stanley v. Illinois* (405 U.S. 645 [1972]). Mr. Stanley had lived with his three biological children and their mother, to whom he was not married, intermittently for eighteen years. When the mother died, the state of Illinois declared the children wards of the state and placed them with court-appointed guardians. This was done without a hearing as to Stanley's fitness as a parent. Stanley protested, arguing that Illinois law denied him equal protection of the laws since neither unwed mothers nor married fathers or mothers could be deprived of custody of their children unless they were shown to be unfit. The state argued that Stanley's fitness or unfitness was irrelevant, because an unwed father was not a "parent" whose existing relationship with his children must be considered; an unwed father was presumed unfit because he had not married the mother. The Supreme Court rejected Illinois's argument, and stated that "the private interest here, that of a man in the children he has sired and raised, undeniably warrants deference and, absent a powerful countervailing interest, protection" (*Stanley v. Illinois*, 405 U.S. 645 [1972] at 651). Failure to provide a hearing on parental fitness for an unwed father violated both the due process and the equal protection clauses of the Fourteenth Amendment.

In cases after *Stanley* the Court drew distinctions between biological fathers who, like Stanley, had been involved in raising their biological children and those who had not assumed day-to-day practical responsibility for them. In *Quilloin v. Walcott* (434 U.S. 246 [1978]), Leon Quilloin sought to prevent the adoption of his eleven-year-old biological child by the child's stepfather, Mr. Wolcott. The Court upheld a Georgia statute that stipulated that a biological mother alone could consent to the adoption of her child; the consent of the unwed biological father was required only if he had legitimated the child. The Court said that no due process violation occurred when contact between the biological father and child had been only sporadic.

The next year, hearkening back to *Stanley*, the Court said in *Caban v. Mohammed* (441 U.S. 380 [1979]) that a New York statute that required unwed biological mothers, but not biological fathers, to consent to the adoption of their children was unconstitutional when an unwed biological father's relationship to his child was "fully comparable" to that of the mother. Caban, like Stanley, had been involved with raising the children, having lived with their mother and supported them for several years. The case arose when the mother's new husband sought to adopt her children. Mr. Caban, who had previously lived with the children and their mother for several years, argued that the law which required only the biological mother's consent to adoption violated the equal protection clause. Caban also claimed that biological fathers had a due process right or liberty interest "to maintain a parental relationship with their children absent a finding they are unfit as parents" (*Caban v. Mohammed*, 441 U.S. 380 [1979] at 385). New York argued that the distinction between biological mother and biological father was justified because of the fundamental difference between maternal and paternal relationships with their children. The Supreme Court agreed with Caban, holding that "maternal and paternal roles are not invariably different in importance," but it explicitly reserved any opinion about whether a distinction such as New York had made would be valid with regard to newborn adoptions (441 U.S. 380 at 392, n. 11).

Lehr v. Robertson (463 U.S. 248 [1983]) also concerned a biological father's effort to block the adoption of his child by her stepfather, but unlike Mr. Stanley and Mr. Caban, and like Mr. Quilloin, Jonathan Lehr had almost no contact with his biological daughter, Jessica. Lehr claimed, however, that he had a liberty interest in an actual *or potential* relationship with Jessica and that the State's failure to provide him notice of her pending adoption violated due process. He also asserted that the New York statute violated equal protection because it required the consent of the biological mother, but not the biological father, for an adoption. The case was complicated by the fact that the majority and minority disagreed over whether Lehr had ignored the child until recently, or, as he claimed, had repeatedly attempted to establish contact with her from the time of her birth but was thwarted by her mother. The majority held that Lehr had not made sufficient contact to establish a parental right, declaring that a biological father's constitutional rights are a function of the tangible and affirmative responsibilities he accepts toward his offspring. The biological connection alone, the Court held, is not sufficient to *guarantee* an unwed father a voice in the adoption decision, although it affords him an *opportunity* to be heard: The "biological connection . . . offers the natural father an opportunity that no other male possesses to develop a relationship with his offspring. If he grasps that opportunity and accepts some measure of responsibility for the child's future, he may enjoy the blessings of the parent-child relationship," but if he fails to grasp the opportunity, "the Equal Protection Clause does not prevent a State from according the two parents different legal rights" (*Lehr v. Robertson*, 463 U.S. 248 [1983] at 268). In a dissent, Justice White, joined by Justices Marshall and Blackmun, disagreed not only about the factual question of whether Lehr had attempted to contact Jessica but also with the framework used by the majority to determine the existence of the unwed biological father's liberty interest. Justice White asserted that "the 'biological connection' is itself a relationship that creates a protected interest" (463 U.S. 248 at 272). In Justice White's view, the majority decision is more demanding than the Constitution requires and fails to recognize that the biological tie gives an unwed biological father a constitutionally protected interest that warrants, in this case, that Lehr be afforded a hearing to establish legal paternity and to be heard with regard to Jessica's adoption.

The rule that the Supreme Court seemed to be developing in these cases, namely, that an unwed biological father who had established a substantial relationship with his child had a constitutionally protected interest in maintaining that relationship, was sidelined in the Court's most recent decision dealing with an unwed biological father's rights. In *Michael H. v. Gerald D.* (491 U.S. 110 [1989]), the Court found that a California statute creating an irrebuttable presumption that a woman's husband was the father of a child she bore was constitutional. A biological father, Michael H., who had lived intermittently with and provided care to his biological daughter and her mother even though the mother was married to and intermittently lived with her husband as well, argued that he had a right to a hearing to establish his paternity when the husband and wife sought to cut off his contact with the child.

The case produced no fewer than five opinions from a deeply fractured Court. The plurality decision, written by Justice Scalia and joined in full only by Chief Justice Rehnquist, rejected Michael's claim (491 U.S. 110 at 113–32). Justice Scalia contended both that the state had an interest in preserving the "unitary family" and that neither Michael nor his genetic daughter had a constitutionally protected liberty interest in maintaining their relationship.[9] Justices O'Connor and Kennedy agreed with Justice Scalia's conclusion but not his reasoning.[10] In a concurring opinion, Justice Stevens asserted, without much apparent basis, that Michael could have obtained visitation rights as an "other person having an interest in the welfare of the child" and so did not need further protection (491 U.S. 110 at 133). Two dissenting opinions supported Michael's right to a hearing but used quite different grounds to do so. Justice White, joined by Justice Brennan, reiterated the view he expressed in *Lehr* that biology itself creates a presumptive parental right. Justice Brennan, joined by Justices Marshall and Blackmun, argued that the *combination* of biology and nurture establishes the liberty interest Michael claimed (491 U.S. 110 at 142–43).

It is important to note that despite the fact that they arrived at opposite conclusions, both Justice Scalia's and Justice White's opinions adopted male-centered models of the basis of parental rights. Justice Scalia looked to the law to protect the paternal rights of married men by basing those rights on a man's legal relationship with the child's mother. Justice White grounded paternal rights in a biological tie established by blood tests, regardless of a man's legal ties to the mother. Both opinions made it unnecessary for the law to ascertain the *mother's* wishes or intentions with respect to paternal claims to her child. By contrast, and although they too reached opposite conclusions, both Justice Stevens and Justice Brennan considered the interests and actions of the mother to be relevant to establishing paternal claims. For Justice Stevens, the inherent biological and sociological differences between care of the fetus by a woman and a man justified different treatment of parental rights at the time of birth. Justice Brennan suggested that once a relationship between father and child exists, the mother cannot then exclude an otherwise fit father from being heard with respect to his paternal rights. Justice Brennan's opinion left open the question of to what extent Michael's situation was like or unlike that of an unwed biological father of a child born to an unmarried woman.

These decisions do not tell us whether under the Constitution an unwed biological father has a right to veto the adoption of a newborn even if he has had no opportunity to establish the kind of relationship and provide the kind of care that the Court has declared protects parental rights.[11] Must the law provide an unmarried biological father an opportunity to demonstrate his commitment if the biological mother does not allow him access to the child? Advocates of fathers' rights insist that unwed biological fathers do have such a constitutional right and that when the biological mother has decided to relinquish her parental rights, a biological father, unless shown to be "unfit," is entitled to assume custody of his offspring without a hearing on the best interest of the child.

FIT FATHERS AND COMPETENT MOTHERS: WHO SHALL DECIDE WHEN BIOLOGICAL PARENTS DISAGREE?

AN UNWED FATHER'S RIGHT TO "GRASP THE OPPORTUNITY" TO BECOME A PARENT: THE PURSUIT OF ABSTRACT EQUALITY

In recent years some biological fathers have claimed that, because of the mother's lack of cooperation, they have not found any way to meet the Court's demand, articulated in *Lehr*, that a biological father who wants to retain his parental rights and "enjoy the blessings of the parent-child relationship" act to "grasp the opportunity" to develop a relationship with his offspring by assuming some "responsibility for the child's future" (463 U.S. 248 at 262). Should a biological father have the opportunity to veto an adoption regardless of the wishes of the mother? Should adoption proceedings be precluded until the father has been heard? What considerations should guide us as we try to evaluate such issues? To answer these questions we need to think about both the basis of claims for custodial rights and the relative claims of biological mothers and fathers outside of marriage.

The argument that the biological father must be given custody when the biological mother chooses not to raise the child is grounded first of all in the conviction that parenthood is a significant good in the lives of men as well as women. Fathers might wish to raise their children for the same reasons mothers do—sharing intimacy and love, nurturing a child to adulthood, seeing one's genetic inheritance survive into the next generation, and passing on ethnic and religious traditions. A commitment to gender neutrality led most states to abandon an automatic maternal preference if mother and father, married or unmarried, each sought custody, and the same commitment would suggest that the law presume that the law must require the consent of *both* parents before the child can be adopted.

Various commentators support an unwed biological father's right to veto the adoption of his child on the grounds that fathers have a fully comparable interest to that of mothers in exercising parental rights and responsibilities. Claudia Serviss says all parents have "a constitutionally-protected opportunity interest in developing a parent-child relationship" (Serviss 1991, 788). John Hamilton argues that all unwed fathers have a right to be notified by the state of the existence of their offspring and be heard before any adoption can proceed, and that the state may therefore require the biological mother to identify the biological father (Hamilton 1987–88), while Daniel Zinman insists that the state must allow a biological father to take custody of his child when the biological mother has relinquished her rights, unless he is shown to be unfit (Zinman 1992). In a recent California case, *In the Matter of Kelsey S.*, the California Supreme Court appeared to agree that a gender-neutral standard should prevail. It held unconstitutional a statute that gave unwed mothers and legally recognized or "presumed" fathers a greater say in preadoption proceedings to terminate parental rights than it gave to unwed biological fathers. The court declared that the statute rested on a "sex-based distinction" that bore no relationship to any legitimate state interest once the child was outside the mother's body and she had decided to relinquish custody.[12]

The presumption of fitness for biological parents also avoids the dangers of subjective judgment and cultural prejudice that seem unavoidable in attempts to determine the child's best interest (Bartlett 1988, 303). One supporter of an unwed father's right to custody argues that a best interest determination "is subject to abuse and may lead to paternalistic infringement on the parent-child relationship in the name of the child's welfare. Given the long waiting list of adoptive parents that exists today and the traditional preference for rearing a child in a two-parent home, a best interest test is a no-win situation for the unwed father of a newborn with whom he has not yet had the opportunity to develop an emotional tie."[13] In 1987, the Georgia Supreme Court explicitly rejected the best interest test in favor of a fitness standard on the grounds that it was presumptively unfair to compare the putative father with adoptive parents with whom the child had never lived. It held that "If [the father] has not abandoned his opportunity interest, the standard which must be used to determine his rights to legitimate the child is his fitness as a parent to have custody of the child. If he is fit he must prevail" (*In re Baby Girl Eason*, 257 Ga. 292 at 297, 358 S.E. 2d 459 at 463 [1987], qtd. in Zinman 1992, 993–94).

Use of the best interest test in cases of an infant who has lived with no adult care-giver for any appreciable period of time should be changed not only in the interests of sex equality but of family diversity as well. The best interest standard invites the court to make judgments about the relative merit of a whole array of "lifestyle" issues that are not subject to scrutiny when an unwed biological father does not contest a biological mother's wish to retain custody of her child. A "fitness" standard applied to unwed biological fathers would avoid the possibility that an adoption decision might rest on a judge's preference that a child be raised in a two-parent household rather than by a single male, or a judge's prediction that middle-class professionals will give a child more "advantages" than the child would receive in a working-class home. If no action (or failure to act) by the biological father shows that he should not be entrusted with custody, then value judgments concerning different lifestyles and household arrangements should be precluded from inappropriately influencing the custody decision concerning the placement of a newborn infant.

To argue that the courts should abandon the best interest standard when an unwed biological father wishes to raise an infant does not, however, imply that the only relevant consideration is the biological father's "fitness." The question of whether an unwed biological father shall have a right to custody of his newborn infant is not about paternal rights *tout court*, but also or alternatively about an unmarried woman's authority to decide who shall take custody of her newborn child. For the biological father to assume custody, the biological mother's expressed wishes concerning the child's placement will of necessity be overridden. Arguments that a biological father should be able to veto the adoption decision of the biological mother and assume custody unless proven to be unfit run up against counter arguments that the courts should defer to an unwed biological mother with respect to placement of her child. It is to these considerations that I now turn.

AN UNWED MOTHER'S CLAIM TO DECISIONAL AUTONOMY: TAKING CONTEXT SERIOUSLY

Arguments in favor of the "fitness" standard for unwed biological fathers falsely assume that once a biological mother has surrendered the child for adoption she has no further relevant wishes with respect to custody. Defenders of an unwed biological father's right to veto an adoption often contrast what they portray as his laudable desire to assume custody and to care for the child with the biological mother's uncaring decision not to raise the child herself. The image of the "bad mother," and the assumption that if the mother chooses not to raise the child, she must be indifferent to its fate, hover just beneath the surface of such depictions. The notion that once a mother decides to relinquish her child for adoption she can have no further relevant concerns distorts and denigrates both her experience of pregnancy and the nature of her decision.[14] But relinquishment of the newborn for adoption may reflect any of a wide array of circumstances: lack of money or job prospects, youth or immaturity, feelings of inadequacy or isolation. While some women may be indifferent to the placement of their children, in most cases relinquishment is not a sign that the biological mother does not care for the child; in most cases women agonize over the adoption decision and try to make certain to do what is best for their offspring (Sweeney 1990, Erickson 1984, 459 and n. 65; Erickson 1990, 38 n. 44).

A woman's decision to place her biological child for adoption also does not mean that she is indifferent about the question of who raises the child. The argument that an unwed biological father should be preferred to adoptive parents because they are "strangers" to the child inappropriately ignores the biological mother's preference that the child be adopted through an agency or private placement rather than placed with a guardian or in the father's custody. If the mother has had very little contact with the father beyond the act of intercourse that led to her pregnancy, the father may be as much a *social* "stranger" to her and the child as the adoptive parents, and his claim rests on genetics alone. Contrasting the biological father's rights to those of strangers obscures the fact that the fundamental or precipitating disagreement about custody is not between the adoptive parents and the biological father, but between the two biological parents. And if the mother has known the father over a considerable period of time, her unwillingness to make him the custodial parent needs to be examined to see why she feels as she does, just as it would be if the parents were married.

Are there any reasons to weigh the biological mother's wishes about who shall (or shall not) take custody of the child more heavily than those of the biological father? At the time of birth the relationship of biological father and mother to the child is neither biologically nor socially symmetrical. She has borne the child for nine months, activity for which there is no precise male analog; indeed, no one else can perform functions analogous to those of gestation.[15] The biological mother's "expectant" state has affected both her own physiological experience and the ways in which others view and interact with her.[16] The Supreme Court has recognized the significance of this asymmetry between mother and father during pregnancy by holding that a wife is not required to notify her husband or obtain his consent before getting an abortion (*Planned Parenthood of Southeastern Pennsylvania v. Casey*, 112 S. Ct. 2791 [1992]). To what extent should asymmetry of biological function during gestation affect the right to make custodial decisions concerning a newborn?

Some theorists argue that the fact that only the woman is engaged in the physical gestation of the human fetus should make a decisive difference in the rights to be accorded unwed mothers and fathers in deciding on the custody of their offspring. According to sociologist Barbara Katz Rothman, parenting is a social relationship and parental rights are established by care-giving. In her view, the biological difference between mother and father is crucial and conclusive in establishing their respective claims for custody of newborns: "Infants belong to their mothers at birth because of the unique nurturant relationship that has existed between them up to that moment. That is, birth mothers have full parental rights, including rights of custody, of the babies they bore" (Rothman 1989, 254). By the same token, other persons with a genetic tie to the child do not have such rights: "We will not recognize genetic claims to parenthood, neither as traditional 'paternity' claims nor as genetic maternity in cases of ovum donation" (254). Rothman would have the gestational mother's absolute claim last for six weeks after giving birth, and so the adoption decision would rest solely in the mother's hands during that period. After six weeks, "Custody would go to the nurturing parent in case of dispute" (255). Rothman emphasizes that her preference for the gestational mother rests on her understanding of pregnancy as "a social as well as a physical relationship," and that "*any* mother is engaged in a social interaction with her fetus as the pregnancy progresses" (97). Neither the physical interdependence nor the social relationship between mother and fetus can be fully shared by any other adult, no matter how attentive. Actual care-giving, not genetic connection, creates familial bonds and, in this case, Rothman argues, custodial rights.

Others also have argued that parental rights usually are not symmetrical and that the social or biological bonds (or both) between mothers and children should give mothers the authority to decide who should have custody of their offspring. Nancy Erickson argues that the liberty interest that a parent has "to control the care, custody, and upbringing of the child" pertains only to the mother (not the father) of a newborn. At birth the mother is "not only the 'primary caretaker parent,' she is the only caretaker parent" because of her role during pregnancy (Erickson 1984, 461–62). Thinking about custody of older children of parents who divorce, Mary Becker argues that mothers are so frequently the primary care-givers of their children that it makes sense to adopt an automatic "maternal deference" standard rather than hold a hearing to try to determine what arrangement would be in the child's best interest: "When the parents cannot agree on a custody outcome, the judge should defer to the mother's decision on custody provided that she is fit, using the 'fitness' standard applicable when the state is arguing for temporary or permanent separation of parents and children in intact families" (Becker 1992, 971). Becker is not terribly worried that giving primacy to the mother's wishes might in some instances permit a woman to deprive a caring father of custody: "A maternal deference standard would recognize that mothers, as a group, have greater competence and standing to decide what is best for their children . . . than judges, fathers, or adversarial experts. . . . Mothers will sometimes make wrong decisions, but in the aggregate they are likely to make better decisions than the other possible decision makers" (972). Becker's reasoning applied to custodial decisions affecting newborns suggests that courts should defer to a biological mother, both because the woman has provided direct nurture to the fetus during pregnancy, and because, on average, biological mothers' decisions are likely to be as good as or better than those of anyone else.

Martha Fineman, similarly very critical of the best interest standard, would replace it with a "primary care-giver" standard (Fineman 1991). Fineman argues that the best interest of the child standard frequently disadvantages mothers by looking to the likely future financial resources of father and mother. It would be more appropriate (both in terms of fairness to the parents and of the child's emotional well-being), Fineman asserts, to look instead at who has actually given the child physical and emotional care up to the present. In most, but not all, instances, this will be the mother. Although Fineman does not discuss custody of newborns, if courts were to apply the primary care-giver standard to the kinds of disputes I am discussing, it would suggest that the mother who has borne and given birth should make the custody decision concerning the infant.

Many arguments for giving an unwed biological father custody of an infant child whom a biological mother wishes to have adopted not only ignore the physical and social experiences of pregnancy but also invite no inquiry at all into the conditions under which the woman became pregnant. Just as inquiry into the biological father's actions during the mother's pregnancy is permissible to encourage paternal nurturance and to counter notions of male ownership of children, so attention to the circumstances under which conception took place is reasonable to ensure that the child was not conceived as the result of abusive behavior toward the mother.[17] In trying to determine which parent's wishes concerning adoption should prevail, it would not be unreasonable for the law to regard an unmarried biological father who had been in a long-term relationship with the mother or shared living expenses with her and their offspring differently than one who engaged in casual or coercive sex (perhaps a "date rape" that the woman did not prosecute) or deceived the woman (perhaps saying he was single when he was in fact married) or willfully ignored the fact that the girl was under the age of consent.

While they refute the patriarchal premise of many fathers' rights arguments that a father has a right to custody of his biological offspring unless he is proven to be "unfit," many arguments that mothers should have the exclusive right to decide to place their offspring for adoption run the risk of treating some men unjustly and of locking both women and men into traditional gender roles. If parental claims are properly grounded in the first instance in a *combination* of biological ties and nurturance, then while a father's genetic link per se does not give him parental rights, it becomes a reason *to look to see* if he has attempted to assume responsibility for the child, and has done so without interfering with the mother's well-being. If, and only if, he has acted accordingly, should a court recognize his claim to custody.

RETHINKING THE BASES OF PARENTAL RIGHTS: RESPONSIBILITY, RELATIONSHIP, AND CARE

If unwed biological fathers should have some custodial claim to their children but not the extreme claim qualified only by "fitness," what standards should define the extent of their rights? The law needs to adopt stringent criteria for assessing the biological father's intention to take responsibility for and act as a parent to his child even prior to birth. Such criteria will require us to shift our thinking and mode of argumentation away from an emphasis on parents as owners to parents as stewards, from parental rights to parental responsibilities, and from parents viewed as individuals to parents as persons-in-relationship with a child.[18]

Many discussions of the "rights" of biological mothers and fathers reveal the inherent tension in liberal theory and legal practice between protecting individuals and their freedoms and protecting and fostering those relationships which in fundamental ways constitute every individual.[19] The language of parental rights emphasizes the parent's status as an autonomous rights-bearer, and invoking individual rights has proved useful in minimizing the role of the state in people's procreative and child-rearing decisions. For example, begetting, bearing, and raising children are for many people part of the good or fulfilling life that the liberal state is obligated to protect. No one seriously proposes that children should simply be assigned at birth to the best possible or next available parents without regard to who begot and bore them. Courts have recognized the importance of intergenerational ties for many people and protected the liberty to procreate and parent a child not only in custody cases like *Stanley* and *Caban*, but in decisions prohibiting forced sterilization, such as *Skinner v. Oklahoma* (316 U.S. 535 [1942]).[20] And since biological parents have a variety of incentives to care for their children to the best of their ability, assigning custody to them simultaneously protects children's rights as well as those of adults and sets important bounds to the exercise of state power.[21]

Yet in other contexts, use of the language of parental rights inappropriately focuses on the individual parent rather than on the relationships that are inherent in being a "parent." Katharine Bartlett has advocated recasting many legal disputes that involve parents and children in such a way that the language used does not pit one "right" against another, but emphasizes the view that parenthood implies deep and sustained human connection and must be grounded in adult responsibility for children: "The law should force parents to state their claims . . . not from the competing, individual perspectives of either parent or even of the child, but from the perspective of each parent-child relationship. And in evaluating (and thereby giving meaning to) that relationship, the law should focus on parental responsibility rather than reciprocal 'rights.'" Bartlett suggests that language based more explicitly on open-ended responsibility toward children would capture the nature of the parent-child relationship better than discussions framed in terms of parental rights (Bartlett 1988, 295).[22]

When someone is considered in the role of parent, he or she cannot be viewed apart from the child that makes him or her a parent; an "autonomous" (in the sense of unfettered or atomistic) individual is precisely what a parent is *not*. A "parental right" should not be viewed as pertaining to an individual per se, but only to an individual-in-relationship with a dependent child. It is therefore entirely appropriate for the law to require that efforts be made to establish a relationship before a parental right can be recognized.

Asking a court to determine whether a man or woman has made efforts to establish a parental relationship with a newborn is, however, fraught with difficulties that involve the different physical relationship of biological father and mother to the fetus during pregnancy, the social relationships between biological father and mother, and the need to minimize both intrusiveness by the courts and subjectivity in their judgments. Indeed, part of the attraction of both the paternal fitness test and the maternal deference standard is that each of these provides a fixed criterion for determining an unwed biological father's custodial claim. Unfortunately, however, the efficiency and clarity of each of these criteria are purchased at the cost of reducing legal discourse about family relationships to an assertion of either fathers' or mothers' rights.

My proposal that an unwed biological father have an opportunity to establish through his behavior his intention to parent his offspring tries to minimize the legal effects of biological asymmetry without ignoring altogether the relevance of sexual difference. I assume that an unwed biological mother has demonstrated a parental relationship with her newborn by virtue of having carried the fetus to term, while an unwed biological father may be required to show actual involvement with prenatal life if he wishes to have custody of the child. The model or norm of "parent" in this case, therefore, is established not by the male who awaits the appearance of the child after birth, but by the pregnant woman (Eisenstein 1988, 79–116).

Some people might object that assuming maternal care simply by the fact of pregnancy is invalid, especially in cases in which the mother has taken drugs or engaged in other behavior that might have a harmful effect on the fetus. As Cynthia Daniels has pointed out, the image of the pregnant drug addict is deeply disturbing, "representing as it does the paradox of a woman simultaneously engaged in the destruction of life (addiction) and the perpetuation of life (pregnancy)" (Daniels 1993, 98). In such cases, should the mother forfeit either her claim to custody or her claim to make the decision to place the child for adoption?[23]

It is tempting to blame, and to seek to punish, the pregnant addict when confronted by the needs of children who are physically or mentally impaired as a result of their exposure to harmful substances during gestation. It is important, however, to ascertain just what the drug-dependent mother is guilty of, and whether punishment or taking away her right to be heard concerning custody of her child is an appropriate response to her behavior.[24] In cases of maternal drug use, it is sometimes difficult to distinguish whether damage to a newborn resulted from drugs taken by the mother or from other factors such as drugs taken by the father, environmental pollutants (particularly high in poor neighborhoods), and malnutrition.[25] What is the degree of a woman's culpability if, like many drug-addicted pregnant women, she sought treatment for her addiction, but was turned away?[26] Even if in a particular case it could be ascertained that fetal damage was uniquely caused by drugs the mother took, it does not follow that she was so indifferent to the well-being of her child that she should be deprived of her right to be heard with respect to placing the child for adoption. The care the pregnant woman has given the fetus through bearing it to term and the harm her actions have caused it cannot be separated; both involve the biology and chemistry of gestation, the passage of materials across the placenta through the bloodstream. To see the pregnant drug addict as a child abuser rather than a person who is herself in need of medical treatment is to ignore the inseparability of mother and fetus during pregnancy (see Young 1994). The mother's decision to place the child for adoption will often be made in an effort to protect the child from harm now that it can be cared for outside her body.

The different biological roles of men and women in human reproduction make it imperative that law and public policy "recognize that a father and mother must be permitted to demonstrate commitment to their child in different ways."[27] What actions might a court accept as indications that an unwed biological father had made every effort to act as a parent to the child? Recent legislative efforts in New York State show that this question is not easily answered. In 1990, in *In re Raquel Marie X.* (76 NY 2d387 [1990]), the New York Court of Appeals struck down a statute that stipulated that only a father who had established a home with the mother for six months prior to her relinquishment of the child for adoption could veto the mother's adoption decision. The court held that the provision imposed "an absolute condition . . . only tangentially related to the parental relationship" and allowed a woman who would not live with a man the power unilaterally to cut off his constitutionally protected interest in parenting his child (76 NY2d at 405, 559 N.E. 2d at 426, 559 N.Y.S. 2d at 863). It instructed the legislature to find some other way to gauge a father's commitment to his unborn child's welfare, and set forth certain standards that lower courts were to follow in the meantime when judging an unwed father's parental commitment. "The father must be willing to assume full custody, not merely attempt to prevent the adoption, and he must promptly manifest parental responsibility both before and after the child's birth."[28] In assessing the father's demonstration of responsibility, judges should look at such matters as "public acknowledgment of paternity, payment of pregnancy and birth expenses, steps taken to establish legal responsibility for the child, and other factors evincing a commitment to the child" (76 NY2d at 428, 559 N.E. 2d at 428, 559 N.Y.S. 2d at 865).

Although courts in New York have used these guidelines in resolving a number of cases involving unwed fathers' efforts to block mothers' adoption decisions in the years since *In re Raquel Marie X.*,[29] four years have gone by without the New York legislature passing a new statute governing an unwed father's right to veto an adoption. Three recent bills introduced in the legislature (two in the Assembly, one in the Senate) have differed strikingly in their underlying approaches to unwed fathers' rights. Both the variety of provisions in these bills and the fact that none has been enacted into law reflect a widely shared uncertainty over what considerations should be brought to bear to determine the nature and extent of an unwed biological father's custodial rights. I discuss these bills in the order of what each requires for a father to establish his right to consent to the adoption of his offspring, from the weakest to the strongest stipulations.

The first of two bills (A. 8028) introduced in the Assembly during the 1993 and 1994 legislative sessions, listed a number of actions an unwed father of an infant under six months might take to establish his right to consent to the adoption. The bill would make his consent necessary if he openly lived with the child or the child's mother prior to the placement of the child for adoption; *or* held himself out to be the father of such child during such period; *or* paid or offered to pay a reasonable sum, consistent with his means, for the medical expenses of pregnancy and childbirth; *or* initiated judicial proceedings to obtain custody of the child; *or* married the child's mother.[30] Since the father needs to have taken only one of these actions and may have initiated judicial proceedings after the child was born, this bill applies a simple "fitness" test and requires no showing of interest prior to the child's birth.

By contrast with the minimal expectations put on unwed fathers by A. 8028, the Senate bill (S. 3776) introduced in the Senate during the 1991 and 1992 legislative sessions requires that a father have demonstrated his commitment to his offspring in a number of ways both prior to and after the birth of the child.[31] It does so by replacing most "or"s in the Assembly bill with the conjunctive "and," thus insisting that a biological father have supported the mother or baby financially, held himself out as the father, and taken steps to initiate legal proceedings to assume custody of the child.

The second Assembly bill (A. 8319) introduced during the 1993 and 1994 legislative sessions would exact an even stronger commitment from the father. It stipulates that the father have paid or offered to pay a reasonable part of the medical expenses of pregnancy and childbirth and the child's living expenses, and that he have initiated judicial proceedings to establish paternity and to obtain sole custody of the child within clearly specified time limits. The bill further stipulates that "'ability to assume sole custody' shall mean ability to assume guardianship and custody of the child and become the primary caretaker of the child for the foreseeable future."[32] This bill clearly means to grant the right to consent to an adoption only to unwed fathers who demonstrate that they have been and will be actively engaged in the care and upbringing of their offspring; the stipulations rest on an image of father as caretaker and nurturer, not simply as progenitor.

A. 8319 goes a long way to enact the spirit of the principles set forth in this essay, but a fully adequate statute would go further. A court should be required to hear a mother's objections, if she has any, to a father's assuming custody of the child, both because the birth of a child has resulted from a web of social interactions and relationships, and because the mother's relinquishment of the child for adoption should be viewed as the last in a series of actions meant to provide care for the child, not as an act of abandonment that gives her no interest in the child's placement. In cases in which the mother objects to the father's assumption of custody, a court should listen to the *reasons* the mother opposes placing the child in the biological father's custody. Because parental rights must be grounded in the provision of care and the assumption of responsibility, if an unwed mother could demonstrate that her pregnancy was a result of force, coercion, or deception, or that she had been under the age of consent when intercourse occurred, the father would be held to be "unfit." This still might not meet the possibility that a man who desired children might impregnate a woman whom he knew would neither abort nor raise a child, provide care and financial support throughout the pregnancy, and petition for paternity and custody—a kind of inexpensive "surrogacy." I am convinced that such intentional instrumental use of any woman's body is morally abhorrent, but I am not certain how to ensure that such a man could not assume custody of his offspring under such circumstances.

Finally, a statute should provide that a pregnant woman who wishes to make plans for her child should be able to ascertain early in the pregnancy whether or not the father will step forward later to oppose the adoption. The law should provide that she be able to notify him in writing of the pregnancy and preclude him from a veto if he fails to act soon after receipt of such notification. Similarly, if a father is found to be entitled to veto an adoption, a mother should be able to negate her consent to the child's adoption and be put back in the same position she was in prior to her consent, that is, as one of two unwed parents each of whom seeks custody (Erickson 1991).

One purpose of spelling out what actions the father needs to take to establish his claim would be to ascertain as early as possible during the pregnancy or after birth whether or not he wished custody, so that infants could be definitively freed for adoption. Where the mother objected to the father's assuming custody, a hearing would be necessary. A hearing would, of course, take more time than assigning custody based on a rule that any "fit" biological father prevail or that a mother be able to make the decision to place her child for adoption unimpeded by the biological father. But a hearing to ascertain whether an unwed biological father has grasped the opportunity to parent his newborn should not cause more delay than a best interest hearing. Such a hearing would be to ascertain facts about the unwed father's behavior and the mother's considered opinion concerning custody, not to try to project what custodial arrangement might be in the child's best interest.

These considerations leave unresolved the thorny issue of how the law should deal with cases in which a biological mother lies to the biological father about his paternity or otherwise hides her pregnancy, making it impossible for him to take any action to signal his willingness to take care of his offspring. In 1992 the New York Court of Appeals addressed the question of what effect a lack of knowledge of a woman's pregnancy should have on a biological father's right to seek custody after learning of the child's existence. In *Matter of Robert O. v. Russell K.*, an unwed biological father sought to overturn the adoption of his son on the grounds that either the mother or the State had a duty to ensure that he knew of the child's birth, and that their failure to inform him denied him his constitutional rights. The New York court acknowledged that "the unwed father of an infant placed for adoption immediately at birth faces a unique dilemma should he desire to establish his parental rights." His opportunity to "shoulder the responsibility of parenthood may disappear before he has a chance to grasp it." But although the father, Robert O., acted as soon as he knew of the child's existence, the adoption had been finalized ten months previously. "Promptness," said the court, "is measured in terms of the child's life, not by the onset of the father's awareness." Robert O., having failed to determine in a timely fashion whether the woman with whom he had lived was pregnant, lost the right he would have had to an opportunity to manifest his "willingness to be a parent" (*Matter of Robert O. v. Russell K.*, 80 NY2d 252 [1992] at 262). The responsibility to know of a child's existence should fall on the man who would assume responsibility for raising the child. By contrast, one defender of unwed fathers' rights proposes a jail sentence of up to two years for a woman who refuses to name the father of her child when surrendering the infant for adoption! (Hamilton 1987–88, 1103 n. 406).[33] A biological father aware of a woman's pregnancy should be required to act prior to birth and soon after he suspects his paternity; a biological father who is actively kept ignorant might be allowed to step forward for some specified period after birth (probably not less than eight weeks nor longer than six months), but thereafter the importance of establishing a firm parent-child relationship would preclude his advancing a parental claim. The child's need for such a relationship should also lead to requirements that courts hear and decide disputes concerning the adoption of infants expeditiously.

Although the reflections set forth in this essay suggest various reforms in the laws governing the custody of nonmarital children, they do not in and of themselves answer the question of whether the case of *Baby Girl Clausen* was decided correctly. I find that very hard to do because neither side grounded its position in the kinds of principles I have put forward here. The Iowa statute that Daniel Schmidt invoked to claim that the adoption could not be finalized required the biological father's consent, but no showing that he demonstrate his commitment to the child prior to (or even subsequent to) birth. The father's mere opposition to the adoption was a sufficient basis upon which to grant him custody. The DeBoers, for their part, based their claim that they should be allowed to adopt Jessica on the best interest standard. Placing the child with the Schmidts reinforced the notion that a biological tie between man and child automatically creates a custodial claim. On the other hand, favoring the DeBoers would not only have reinforced the best interest standard but might have been viewed as rewarding them for prolonging legal proceedings after Schmidt raised his claim.

The outcome consonant with the principles advanced here would have granted a hearing to Schmidt, recognizing that while his biological tie alone did not guarantee him custodial rights, the fact that he acted immediately after learning that he was Jessica's biological father and within four weeks after her birth established grounds for a hearing and, provided that Cara Clausen did not object, for custody. Had Clausen objected, the hearing would not have attempted to determine whether the child's best interest would be better served by granting custody to Schmidt or the DeBoers, but whether Schmidt's actions were sufficient to establish a claim to custody. To establish his right to consent to the adoption, he would have to demonstrate that he had good reason to believe that the child Cara Clausen was carrying was not his offspring, that he acted immediately and decisively to assume full custody after learning that he was Jessica's biological father, and that he had done so within the statutory limit for advancing such a claim. It seems to me likely both that Schmidt's claim would have been recognized and that the likelihood of a ruling in his favor would have been much clearer to the DeBoers and their lawyer than was the case under the law then in effect.

The main lesson to be drawn from cases like *Baby Girl Clausen* is that it is imperative that states formulate adoption laws that will reflect the principle that parental rights are established in the first instance by a combination of biology and the provision of care, a principle already articulated by the Supreme Court. Another lesson may be that in certain instances it would make sense to allow some form of legal recognition to the fact that a child may have multiple "parents": genetic parents (sperm and egg donors), biological parents (the gestational mother and genetic father), stepparents, adoptive parents, social parents (that is, those who actually provide care), and legal guardians.[34] The possibility of some such recognition might avoid some cases in which unwed biological fathers who have not married the mothers of their offspring seek to block the adoption of the infant. Some of these cases seem motivated not so much by the man's desire to raise the child as by his fear of losing all opportunity to know a child he has sired. There may be ways of dealing with this fear short of blocking the adoption. Adoption registries that allow adopted children and birth parents to contact one another by mutual consent when the child has reached his or her majority seem to have been helpful to biological parents, adoptive parents, and children alike. They allow for the simultaneous recognition of the importance of both biological and social parenting, and in doing so undercut the suggestion that something about adoption is shameful and best kept hidden. Such registries also take into account the perspective of children who want to know their biological forebears, without weakening either the legal rights and responsibilities of the social (adoptive) parents or the primacy of the emotional bonds between adoptive parents and children.

Beyond these legal changes, cases such as *Matter of Robert O. v. Russell K.* and *Baby Girl Clausen* should also lead us to try to understand the circumstances that might lead an unwed mother to lie about or conceal the paternity of her child, such as fear of violence or harassment, or shame over an unwanted sexual relationship. Working toward justice in family relationships requires struggling to eliminate the social conditions that give rise to such fear and shame, and also requires making sure that all citizens have access to the resources that allow family relationships to survive and flourish, so that no biological parent will be forced by economic factors to relinquish custody of children they would prefer to raise themselves had they the resources to do so.

CONCLUSION

This analysis of disputes over paternal custody of nonmarital newborns makes it abundantly clear that the language of individual rights, so central to liberal political theory, and to the due process and equal protection guarantees of the U.S. Constitution, is not well-suited to dealing with complex issues of parent-child relationships. Although notions of maternal or paternal rights are not useless (for example, they allow us to think about limits to state intervention), they tend to focus attention on an adult *individual*, whereas parental issues involve two adults and a child, and the relationships among them.[35] Legal and social discourse alike must put the lived relationship between parents and between parent and child, not the rights of individuals alone, at the center of the analysis of parental claims. In particular the language of a father's "right" to custody of his infant child based on his genetic tie obscures the complexity of the relationships involved in human reproductive activity.

Because parenting involves being in a relationship with another dependent person, a parental "right" cannot properly be conceived of as something independent of the relationship. An individual can exercise a parental right, but the existence or the nature of the right cannot be explained by reference to that individual alone. Only by taking account of the interpersonal dependency, reciprocity, and responsibility involved in family relationships will we be able to approach a world dedicated to achieving both lived equality between men and women and committed parents for every child.

NOTES

I thank Julie Bartkowiak, Joan Callahan, Ann Congleton, Stephen Ellmann, Nancy Erickson, Leslie Goldstein, Mona Harrington, Alice Hearst, Wolfgang Hirczy, Martha Minow, Uma Narayan, Susan Okin, and Joan Posner for helping me think about the issues raised in this essay. I began work on this article while a Fellow at the Center for Human Values at Princeton University, for whose support I am very grateful.

This essay was originally presented as a paper at the Conference on Feminist Ethics and Social Policy, University of Pittsburgh, November 5–7, 1993. It appears in somewhat different form in Callahan (1995). An expanded and revised version appears with the title "Unwed Fathers' Rights, Adoption, and Sex Equality: Gender-Neutrality and the Perpetuation of Patriarchy" (Shanley 1995).

1. *In the Interest of* B.G.C., Supreme Court of Iowa, No. 207/91–476, 92–49, September 23, 1992, and *In the Matter of Baby Girl Clausen*, Michigan Court of Appeals, No. 161102, March 29, 1993.

2. A summary of the different statutory provisions in all fifty states regarding who must give consent to an adoption and under what conditions is found in *Adoption Laws: Answers to the Most-Asked Questions* (Rockville, MD: National Adoption Information Clearinghouse, n.d.).

3. Hirczy (1992) and Hamilton (1987–88) argue that the law should insist that the paternity of every child be established at birth, a necessary prerequisite for an unwed father's assertion of paternal rights.

4. New York City Family Court denied parental rights to a man who donated sperm to a lesbian couple in *Thomas S. v. Robin Y.* (599 N.Y.S. 377 [1993]), on the grounds that the child's mothers were her "parents" and that the sperm donor's genetic tie and occasional visits with the child did not in themselves establish a parental relationship. Denial of parental rights to sperm donors does not address the question of whether a child has a right to know who his or her biological parents are.

In this article I leave aside cases of contract parenthood, artificial insemination by donor, and embryo transfer. All of these practices raise issues that involve the distinctions between genetic, biological, and "intentional" parents, and all involve more than two adults who claim the status of "parent." I discuss the claims of a married sperm donor who together with his wife tries to become a parent by hiring a gestational ("surrogate") mother in Shanley (1993). I argue there that the enforcement of pregnancy contracts against the gestational mother's will would dismiss the relevance of a woman's biological and social experiences of relationship to a fetus during pregnancy and undermine the principle that parental rights are rooted in the assumption of concrete responsibility for a fetus or child.

5. On reconceptualizing the liberal individual, see Held (1993, esp. 192–214). On the concept of autonomy in liberal theory, see Nedelsky (1989, 7–36) and (1990, 162–89). On the limitations of the legal concept of individual rights see Glendon (1991).

6. Stanton (1987, 92). Stanton quotes Note, "Custody Rights of Unwed Fathers" (*Pacific Law Journal* 4 [1973]: 923): "Various reasons have been proposed for considering the unwed mother a more natural guardian than the father. These include: (1) the mother is more easily identified than the father; (2) she is biologically better suited to care for and nurture the child; and (3) the natural bonds of love and affection for the child are stronger in the mother than in any other person."

7. Blackstone ([1783] 1978, 1: 453). On coverture in general see Shanley (1989). On laws governing custody in the early United States, see Grossberg (1985) and Hartog (1993).

8. Also important was the rise in both social and judicial attention to childhood and its particular needs. See Zainaldin (1979, 1038–89); Grossberg (1985); and Hartog (1993).

9. Scalia argued that the proper methodology of discerning what interests are protected by the due process clause is to look at "the most specific level at which a relevant tradition protecting, or denying protection to, the asserted right can be identified" (491 U.S. 110 at 127–28, n. 6).

10. O'Connor and Kennedy disagreed with Scalia's attempt to identify "the most specific level" of a "tradition" to discover what interests are protected by the due process clause (491 U.S. 110 at 132).

11. Jonathan Lehr raised this issue but it was not definitively answered in *Lehr v. Robertson*, since the majority of the Supreme Court rejected evidence Lehr offered to support his contention that his early efforts to know his daughter had been rebuffed by her mother.

The Supreme Court may be asked to decide whether an unwed biological father has a right to veto the adoption of a newborn if he has had no opportunity to establish a relationship during its early days if it hears an appeal from the decision of the Illinois Supreme Court, *In re Petition of John Doe and Jane Doe, Husband and Wife, to Adopt Baby Boy Janikova* ([No. 76063] 1994 WestLaw 265086 [Ill.]).

12. See Goldberg (1992).

13. "Recent Developments: Family Law—Unwed Fathers' Rights—New York Court of Appeals Mandates Veto Power over Newborn's Adoption for Unwed Father Who Demonstrates Parental Responsibility—*In re Raquel Marie X.*" *Harvard Law Review* 104 (January 1991): 807. Fineman (1988, 770) and Eveleigh (1989) also express strong reservations about the best interest test in custody adjudication.

14. For a discussion of the many ways legal and social discourses label women as "bad mothers" see Roberts (1992). By contrast, Eveleigh (1989) writes as if the biological mother who has relinquished custody has no further relevant interest in her child; when a biological father seeks custody of his newborn offspring, the relevant interests, she says, are those of the state, the father, and the child.

15. The uniqueness of pregnancy has implications for the custodial claims not only of unwed fathers but also for those of a lesbian partner who had planned to co-parent a child, as well as those of a genetic mother who might turn to a "surrogate" to bear a child on her behalf.

16. On the social construction of the experience of pregnancy and childbirth see Martin (1987) and Rothman (1982).

17. It is not necessary to accept Catharine MacKinnon's view that fully consensual sexual relations between men and women are virtually impossible to achieve in our society in order to acknowledge that the context in which sexual relations take place—including great disparities of social and economic resources—can make sexual relationships more or less consensual or coercive. See MacKinnon (1989, 174) and (1987, 88). For an opposing view see Roiphe (1993), which sees many feminist challenges to social structures of inequality that affect relationships between men and women as contributions to an ideology not of female empowerment but of female weakness and need for protection.

18. Smith (1983) argues against the "property model" of parenting and family relationships.

19. Excellent discussions of the ways in which classical liberal theory pays insufficient attention to the ways in which individuals are constituted in and by their relationships to others are found in Held (1993); Nedelsky (1989) and (1990); Ruddick (1989); and Tronto (1993).

Issues involving children raise in a particularly acute manner the tension between protecting people as individuals and protecting family associations or family ties. On the dilemmas inherent in using privacy language to afford protection to both individuals and families see Karst (1980).

20. Although see also cases that permitted sterilization of the mentally retarded, *Buck v. Bell*, 274 U.S. 200 (1927) and *Sterilization of Moore*, 289 N.C. 95, 221 S.E. 2d 307 (1976).

21. See Okin (1989) and Olsen (1985) for a clear analysis of the impossibility of complete state neutrality toward the family.

22. For an interesting critique of Bartlett that is flawed by its failure to recognize the deeply individualistic as well as the patriarchal characteristics of contemporary family law, see Dolgin (1990).

The idea that parental rights depend on the fulfillment of parental duties receives one of its classic expressions in John Locke's argument against the patriarchal ideas of Sir Robert Filmer. Filmer held that the very act of begetting a child gave a father sovereignty over his offspring. By contrast, Locke asserts that not procreation but only providing care for a child bestows parental authority and that by nature (although not necessarily by law) mothers share such authority. But despite Locke's rejection of patriarchal reasoning with respect to both polity and family, patriarchal notions crept back into much liberal political theory and law because these used the language of the rights of autonomous individuals to talk about or characterize the relationship between parent and child. To some extent, when nineteenth-century feminists began their assault on the common law doctrine of coverture, they used Lockean notions of individual freedom and equality to argue that mothers should have equal rights over marital children. Even these reforms, however, did not subvert the notion of parental autonomy or of parental rights to custody. See Locke ([1690] 1980, 2.6.58). On patriarchalism see Schochet (1975); on Locke's antipatriarchalism see Shanley (1979).

23. I leave aside the question of whether the mother should be subject to prosecution for fetal abuse, although I do not think she should be.

24. This is not to deny responsibility to drug-dependent pregnant women. As Cynthia Daniels writes, "Clearly, race, class, and gender inequality limit an individual's access to a full range of options, but they do not negate all choice. The behavior of poor addicted women may be 'determined' in the historical sense that they are born into conditions which they did not create and cannot control, and which set strict limits on their lives, but this does not mean that they lose all power to shape their own destinies" (Daniels 1993, 125).

Dorothy Roberts has written with great insight about the ways in which issues of equality and privacy arise in prosecutions of drug-addicted women of color who have babies (Roberts 1991).

25. Studies have shown that the consequences for offspring of poor women who used alcohol and drugs during pregnancy were much more severe than for offspring of upper-income women, chiefly because of differences in nutrition (Nesrin Bingol et al. 1987. "The Influence of Socioeconomic Factors on the Occurrence of Fetal Alcohol Syndrome" *Advances in Alcohol and Substance Abuse* 6(4): 117; cited in Daniels 1993, 125).

26. Two-thirds of the major hospitals in fifteen cities surveyed by the House Select Committee on Children, Youth, and Families in 1989 reported that they had no place to which to refer drug-addicted pregnant women for treatment (Karol L. Kumpfer. 1991. "Treatment Programs for Drug-Abusing Women" *The Future of Children* 1[1]: 52; cited in Daniels 1993, 126). In the same year, there were 135 treatment beds available for the more than four thousand pregnant drug-dependent women in the state of Florida (*Johnson v. State of Florida*, Petitioners' Initial Brief, Appeal from the District Court of Appeal, Fifth District 77, 831 Sup. Ct. of Fla. [1990], p. 31; cited in Daniels 1993, 126). Many drug treatment programs do not accept pregnant women for fear that they will be sued if the woman loses the pregnancy as a result of treatment (Chavkin 1991, 1556).

27. "Recent Developments: Family Law—Unwed Fathers' Rights— . . . *In re Raquel Marie X* . . . ," p. 805 (footnote omitted).

28. "Recent Developments: Family Law . . . —*In re Raquel Marie X* . . . ," p. 803.

29. For example, *Matter of Kiran Chandini S.*, 166 A.D. 2d 599, 560 N.Y.S. 2d 886 (1990); In the *Matter of John E. v. John Doe*, 564 N.Y.S. 2d 439 (1990); *Matter of Stephen C.*, 566 N.Y.S. 2d 178 (1991); *Matter of Robert O. v. Russell K.*, 80 NY2d 252 (1992).

30. New York State Legislature, Assembly, A. 8028, May 17, 1993; introduced by Member of the Assembly Vito Lopez and referred to the Committee on the Judiciary.

31. New York State Legislature, Senate, S. 3776–B, March 11, 1991; introduced by Senator Mary Goodhue.

32. New York State Legislature, Assembly, A. 8319A, June 4, 1993; introduced by Member of the Assembly Vito Lopez (at the request of the Governor) and referred to the Committee on Children and Families.

If the father needs to work to support the child, he clearly cannot provide uninterrupted childcare. The stipulation that he be the primary caretaker of the child is meant to preclude men who intend to turn the care of their offspring over to other family members from blocking adoptions. This raises very hard issues about how the law might recognize the roles of members of extended families in raising children, and this aspect of any proposed bill needs further deliberation.

33. Less drastically, Justice Titone, concurring in *Robert O. v. Russell K.*, also felt it unreasonable to require that a man who wishes to assert paternal rights know of the pregnancy of his sexual partner.

34. See interesting suggestions for ways in which the law might recognize more than two parents in Bartlett (1984). See also Bartholet (1993).

35. I leave aside cases of contract parenthood, artificial insemination by donor, and embryo transfer, for example, in all of which issues involving distinctions between genetic, biological, and "intentional" parents arise, and in all of which there may be more than two adults claiming the status of "parent." See above note 4.

REFERENCES

Adoption laws: Answers to the most-asked questions. N.d. Rockville, MD: National Adoption Information Clearinghouse.

Bartholet, Elizabeth. 1993. *Family bonds: Adoption and the politics of parenting.* Boston: Houghton Mifflin.

Bartlett, Katharine. 1984. Rethinking parenthood as an exclusive status: The need for legal alternatives when the premise of the nuclear family has failed. *Virginia Law Review* 70(5): 879–963.

———. 1988. Re-expressing parenthood. *Yale Law Journal* 98(2): 293–340.

Becker, Mary. 1989. The rights of unwed parents: Feminist approaches. *Social Service Review* 63(4): 496–518.

———. 1992. Maternal feelings: Myth, taboo, and child custody. *Review of Law and Women's Studies* 1: 901–92.

Blackstone, William. [1783] 1978. *Commentaries on the laws of England.* 4 vols. 9th ed. Ed. Berkowitz and Throne. Oxford: Clarendon Press.

Boyd, Jeffrey S. 1990. The unwed father's custody claim in California: When does the parental preference doctrine apply? *Pepperdine Law Review* 17: 969–1010.

Buchanan, Elizabeth. 1984. The constitutional rights of unwed fathers before and after *Lehr v. Robertson. Ohio State Law Journal* 45: 311–82.

Buck v. Bell. 1927. 274 U.S. 200.

Caban v. Mohammed. 1979. 441 U.S. 380.

Callahan, Joan C., ed. 1995. *Reproduction, ethics and the law: Feminist perspectives*. Bloomington: Indiana University Press.

Chavkin, Wendy. 1991. Mandatory treatment for drug use during pregnancy. *Journal of the American Medical Association* 266(11): 1556–61.

Daniels, Cynthia R. 1993. *At women's expense: State power and the politics of fetal rights*. Cambridge: Harvard University Press.

Dolgin, Janet L. 1990. Status and contract in feminist legal theory of the family: A reply to Bartlett. *Women's Rights Law Reporter* 12: 103–13.

Eisenstein, Zillah. 1988. *The female body and the law*. Berkeley: University of California Press.

Erickson, Nancy S. 1984. The feminist dilemma over unwed parents' custody rights: The mother's rights must take priority. *Journal of Law and Inequality* 2: 447–72.

———. 1990. Neither abortion nor adoption: Women without options. Paper presented at the American Association of Law Schools (AALS), San Francisco, 6 January.

———. 1991. Proposal for a model law on unwed fathers' adoption rights. Unpublished paper. Brooklyn, N.Y.

Eveleigh, Laurel J. 1989. Certainly not child's play: A serious game of hide and seek with the rights of unwed fathers. *Syracuse Law Review* 40: 1055–88.

Fineman, Martha Albertson. 1988. Dominant discourse, professional language, and legal change in child custody decisionmaking. *Harvard Law Review* 101(4): 727–74.

———. 1991. *The illusion of equality: The rhetoric and reality of divorce reform*. Chicago: University of Chicago Press.

Glendon, Mary Ann. 1991. *Rights talk: The impoverishment of political discourse*. New York: Free Press.

Goldberg, Stephanie B. 1992. Having my baby. *ABA Journal* 78: 84–86.

Gomez v. Perez. 1973. 409 U.S. 535.

Grossberg, Michael. 1985. *Governing the hearth: Law and the family in nineteenth-century America*. Chapel Hill: University of North Carolina Press.

Hamilton, John R. 1987–88. The unwed father and the right to know of his child's existence. *Kentucky Law Journal* 76: 949–1009.

Hartog, Hendrick. 1993. Breaking the marital bond. Princeton University. Unpublished manuscript.

Held, Virginia. 1993. *Feminist morality: Transforming culture, society, and politics*. Chicago: University of Chicago Press.

Hirczy, Wolfgang. 1992. The politics of illegitimacy: A cross-national comparison. Paper presented at the Annual Meeting of the American Political Science Association, Chicago, 3–6 September.

In the Interest of B.G.C. September 23, 1992. Supreme Court of Iowa, No. 207/91–476, 92–49.

In the Matter of Baby Girl Clausen. March 29, 1993. Michigan Court of Appeals, No. 161102.

In re Baby Girl Eason. 1987. 257 Ga. 292, 358 S.E. 2d 459.

In re Raquel Marie X. 1990. 76 NY2d 387.

Johnson, Sally. 1994. Helping fathers become parents. *New York Times*, 24 February, metropolitan edition, C1.

Karst, Kenneth L. 1980. The freedom of intimate association. *Yale Law Journal* 89(4): 624–92.

Lehr v. Robertson. 1983. 463 U.S. 248.
Locke, John. [1690] 1980. *Second treatise of government*. Ed. C. B. Macpherson. Indianapolis: Hackett.
MacKinnon, Catharine A. 1987. *Feminism unmodified: Discourses on life and law*. Cambridge: Harvard University Press.
———. 1989. *Toward a feminist theory of the state*. Cambridge: Harvard University Press.
Martin, Emily. 1987. *The woman in the body: A cultural analysis of reproduction*. Boston: Beacon Press.
Matter of Robert O. v. Russell K. 1992. 80 NY2d 252.
Michael H. v. Gerald D. 1989. 491 U.S. 110.
Nedelsky, Jennifer. 1989. Reconceiving autonomy: Sources, thoughts, and possibilities. *Yale Journal of Law and Feminism* 1(1): 7–36.
———. 1990. Law, boundaries, and the bounded self. *Representations* 30: 162–189.
New York State Assembly. A. 8028. May 17, 1993.
New York State Assembly. A. 8319A, June 4, 1993.
New York State Senate. S. 3776–B. March 11, 1991.
Okin, Susan M. 1989. *Justice, gender, and the family*. New York: Basic Books.
Olsen, Frances. 1985. The myth of state intervention in the family. *University of Michigan Journal of Law Reform* 18(4): 835–64.
Planned Parenthood of Southeastern Pennsylvania v. Casey. 1992. 112 S. Ct. 2791.
Raab, Jennifer J. 1984. *Lehr v. Robertson*: Unwed fathers and adoption—How much process is due? *Harvard Women's Law Journal* 7: 265–87.
Recent developments: Family law—Unwed fathers' rights—New York Court of Appeals mandates veto power over newborn's adoption for unwed father who demonstrates parental responsibility—In re Raquel Marie X. . . . 1991. *Harvard Law Review* 104(3): 800–807.
Roberts, Dorothy E. 1991. Punishing drug addicts who have babies: Women of color, equality, and the right of privacy. *Harvard Law Review* 104(7): 1419–82.
———. 1992. Racism and patriarchy in the meaning of motherhood. Paper presented at the Feminism and Legal Theory Project Workshop on Motherhood, Columbia Law School, New York, 4–5 December.
Roiphe, Katie. 1993. *The morning after: Sex, fear, and feminism on campus*. Boston: Little Brown and Co.
Rothman, Barbara Katz. 1982. *In labor: Women and power in the birthplace*. New York: Norton.
———. 1989. *Recreating motherhood: Ideology and technology in a patriarchal society*. New York: Norton.
Ruddick, Sara. 1989. *Maternal thinking: Towards a politics of peace*. Boston: Beacon.
Schochet, Gordon. 1975. *Patriarchalism in political thought*. New York: Basic Books.
Serviss, Claudia. 1991. *Lehr v. Robertson*'s "Grasp the opportunity": For California's natural fathers, custody may be beyond their grasp. *Western State University Law Review* 18: 771–90.
Shanley, Mary L. 1979. Marriage contract and social contract in seventeenth-century English political thought. *Western Political Quarterly* 32(1): 79–91.
———. 1989. *Feminism, marriage, and the law in Victorian England*. Princeton: Princeton University Press.
———. 1993. "Surrogate mothering" and women's freedom: A critique of contracts for human reproduction. *Signs* 18(3): 618–39.

———. 1995. Unwed fathers' rights, adoption, and sex equality: Gender-neutrality and the perpetuation of patriarchy. *Columbia Law Review* 95(1). Forthcoming.

Smith, Janet Farrell. 1983. Parenting and property. In *Mothering: Essays in feminist theory*, ed. Joyce Trebilcot. Totowa, N.J.: Rowman & Allanheld.

Stanley v. Illinois. 1972. 405 U.S. 645.

Stanton, Elizabeth Rose. 1990. The rights of the biological father: From adoption and custody to surrogate motherhood. *Vermont Law Review* 12: 87–121.

Sterilization of Moore. 1976. 289 N.C. 95, 221 S.E. 2d 307.

Steward, Rebecca L. 1990. Constitutional rights of unwed fathers: Is equal protection equal for unwed fathers? *Southwestern University Law Review* 19: 1087–1111.

Sweeney, Maureen A. 1990. Between sorrow and happy endings: A new paradigm of adoption. *Yale Journal of Law and Feminism*, 329–70.

Thomas S. v. Robin Y. 1993. 599 N.Y.S. 377.

Trimble v. Gordon. 1977. 430 U.S. 762.

Tronto, Joan C. 1993. *Moral boundaries: A political argument for an ethic of care*. New York: Routledge.

Weber v. Aetna Casualty & Surety Co. 1972. 406 U.S. 164.

Young, Iris Marion. 1994. Punishment, treatment, empowerment: Three approaches to policy for pregnant addicts. *Feminist Studies* 20(1): 33–58.

Zainaldin, Jamil S. 1979. The emergence of a modern American family law: Child custody, adoption, and the courts, 1796–1851. *Northwestern University Law Review* 73: 1038–1089.

Zinman, Daniel C. 1992. Father knows best: The unwed father's right to raise his infant surrendered for adoption. *Fordham Law Review* 60: 971–1001.

6

Does Comparable Worth Have Radical Potential?

CAROLYN H. MAGID

Since the late 1970s, comparable worth has been of great interest to feminist activists as a reform with radical potential. As a reform, it offered the possibility that it would remedy discrimination and improve the material circumstances of large numbers of working women. Comparable worth had radical potential because advocacy, activism, and victories of the comparable worth movement could contribute to radical social transformation (Feldberg 1984, 311–328).

In recent years, experience with comparable worth implementation and studies of that experience by feminist academics (Acker 1989; Evans and Nelson 1989; Blum 1991), as well as ongoing discussions among feminist activists (Brenner 1987, 447–465; Steinberg 1987, 466–475), have led to questions both about how comparable worth is to be understood and about whether comparable worth implementation and organizing can aid radical objectives. Looking back on a now widely implemented proposal, can we say that comparable worth has radical potential?

Although I am posing a question about radical potential at a time when radical activism or even adherence is in decline in the United States and the political climate is not auspicious for achieving radical objectives, this discussion still matters to those of us who think that justice requires radical social transformation. Comparable worth is proceeding. Some supporters have come to believe that comparable worth can only succeed as a limited reform (Evans and Nelson 1989, 162–173). I argue in this essay that successful comparable worth organizing can retain its radical potential, although much depends on how comparable worth is understood and on the kind of organizing which wins it.

In Part I, I provide brief background on comparable worth. Part II looks at claims and counterclaims about its radical potential. Part III distinguishes two different ways of understanding the place of comparable worth in proposals about social justice. On one, comparable worth is a (distributive) principle of justice. On the other, comparable worth is a temporary and partial remedy for discrimination. I argue that only the latter is consistent with and conducive to furthering radical objectives. Part IV considers how political practice can bring out the radical potential of comparable worth. I use the recent history of implementation to argue that it can happen and to consider what kinds of comparable worth organizing best serve that purpose.

I see my task in this essay as in the spirit of what Iris Young has called "reflective discourse about justice" which would "clarify the meaning of concepts and issues, describing and explaining social relations, and articulating and defending ideals and principles" (Young 1990, 5). Young calls for such reflective discourse to aid social movements in achieving their goals. I hope this essay will be helpful to the comparable worth movement.

I: BACKGROUND

In the last fifteen to twenty years, comparable worth has gone from a demand of the women's and labor movements to policy widely implemented in the United States, especially for public employees. Supporters expected comparable worth to be "the women's issue of the 80s."[1] Although it never achieved that prominence on the movement's agenda, comparable worth did take hold in the public sector and in some unionized private sector workplaces, including unionized clerical work forces at academic institutions. The movement's initial strategies for achieving comparable worth through civil rights litigation have been largely unsuccessful due to the unwillingness of the courts to find for comparable worth, but political strategies (legislative and using collective bargaining) have been very successful. As of 1989, comparable worth activism had won $450 million in wage adjustments in the public sector (National Committee on Pay Equity 1989, 1). By 1991, more than 1,700 cities, counties, school districts, and academic institutions were involved in comparable worth activity (National Committee on Pay Equity 1990, 9). Twenty states had made some wage adjustments and six had made "broad-based adjustments to correct sex and/or race-based wage inequalities" (National Committee on Pay Equity 1991, 8).

Comparable worth, as typically implemented, uses the longstanding management technique of job evaluation to uncover and to correct discriminatory underpayment of work typically done by women. Job evaluation treats job requirements as a composite of skill, effort, responsibility, and working conditions—jobs are ranked in worth based on a combined assessment of level of requirements in these areas. Although job evaluation had been around for years as a method for employer comparison and justification of pay differentials, many employers, including many who used job evaluation, were paying women's jobs substantially less than men's when their jobs were of comparable value. So comparable worth supporters were able to use the same methodology to argue that women's work was unjustly underpaid and to advocate equal pay for work of comparable worth.

Comparable worth can also be understood as a pay equity claim about jobs typically done by people of color. Although some campaigns and settlements in the public sector have resulted in wage adjustments for men of color,[2] most comparable worth campaigns have focused on gender and not race. The published studies I draw on in this essay deal with gender and not race-based comparable worth campaigns (Acker 1989; Evans and Nelson 1989; Blum 1991). There is evidence that gender-based implementation does increase the wages of African American women and men in "women's" jobs (Malveaux 1984). In this essay I focus on gender because my sources do—although I think the case I ultimately make would work as well for race as it does for gender, and will give some reasons to think that as I proceed.

Comparable worth has been seen as an important reform because of its potential to have impact on the low wages earned by most women. Most working women in the United States continue to work in jobs which are predominantly (more than seventy percent) female. Across the board these jobs have been paid substantially less than men's jobs of comparable worth. If the wages for these jobs could be raised to the level of comparably evaluated men's jobs, comparable worth implementation could significantly improve the material circumstances of most working women.

II. RADICAL HOPES: CLAIMS AND COUNTERCLAIMS

Radical supporters of comparable worth organizing believed it could also play an important role in radical social transformation. To understand this position, one needs to understand radical goals, the model of social change underlying radical hopes for comparable worth, and the specific prospects radical supporters saw in comparable worth organizing. I will briefly take up each of these topics in turn. (Given the size of the topics, the complexity of issues, and the divergences in specific feminist radical viewpoints, my remarks can at best sketch some ideas important to many feminist radicals.)

Feminist radicals (socialist-feminist and others) have human liberation as a goal and believe that achieving liberation would require radical transformation of U.S. and other current societies. The transformation would include ending the domination of women by men and of people of color by white people and ending the cultural devaluation of women and people of color. It would require eliminating or vastly decreasing inequalities in social position and resources, including inequalities in pay for work. Many feminist radicals also believe that liberation must include democratic control by all people over all the institutions in which they participate.[3]

The feminist radicals who supported comparable worth believed that people could work toward achieving these radical goals through support of specific reform campaigns which could empower participants, build and connect grassroots movements, challenge dominant ideology, and present radical alternatives. Comparable worth campaigns were seen as having the potential to empower participants and to build the women's and labor movements. They could challenge the cultural devaluation of women and promote egalitarian pay proposals.[4] I will elaborate briefly on each of these prospects.

Comparable worth organizing offered the prospect of empowering participants in many ways. Many women who had not questioned the undervaluation of their skills would see that they had been treated unjustly because they were women. These discoveries would empower and activate these mostly working-class women—drawing them into collective struggle with a sense that they had a contribution to make. By becoming active, they would be taking charge of their work lives. If collective action gives them a role in the comparable worth decision-making process, they will be taking power which belonged to management.

Comparable worth could also empower all who benefit from comparable worth wage adjustments. If wage adjustments provide working women with a living wage, this could initiate an end to women's "economic dependency" (Feldberg 1984, 328), allowing large numbers of women to have more control over their lives.

Feminist radicals were working to build democratic, broad-based, diverse grassroots movements and to bring them together around a radical agenda. This project requires empowerment and activation of working women and men, broadening the base and the agendas of movements, and coalition building. Comparable worth looked very promising on all these requirements. Women empowered (as described above) might participate in and so broaden the base (and agenda) of the women's and labor movements. Comparable worth campaigns also appeared to provide excellent opportunities to build alliances between the women's and labor movements.

Many feminists saw in comparable worth the possibility of challenging the cultural devaluation of women's work. Betsy Wright, of Women for Economic Justice, writes:

> what is considered to be "work" and what kinds of work are valued and compensated have got to change. . . . Pay equity is one crucial piece in a much needed global effort to make behind-the-scenes nurturing work and maintenance work visible and valued. (Wright 1989, 9)

Wright is concerned about the undervaluation of women and the cultural/global invisibility and undervaluing of women's work of caring and support. Although the comparable worth movement began with management-based job evaluation systems, feminist supporters quickly discovered that both the factors measured and the weight accorded to them undervalued women's skills and contribution. This discovery prompted demands for bias-free systems. Radical supporters hoped the comparable worth movement would go on to initiate a broader public discussion of the value of women's work and contribute to a "revolution of values" (Wright 1989, 9).

Socialist feminists saw in comparable worth organizing a springboard to advocate for egalitarian wage proposals. Comparable worth organizing "questions the market basis of wages" (Feldberg 1984, 313) and could generate a public debate about how all work should be paid and who should determine it. This debate could provide a political opening to advocate for proposals to increase wages in low-wage jobs and to decrease or eliminate wage differentials altogether.

Even if one grants that support of specific reforms can be important to achieving radical objectives, there are still fair questions about whether comparable worth is suited to play that role. These questions, concerning equality, values, and movement building, have always been of concern to feminist radicals (Feldberg 1984) but are resurfacing now as supporters look back on the experience of implementation.

Comparable worth proposes to correct an existing inegalitarian pay hierarchy (and class structure) by repositioning women within that hierarchy, not by abolishing it altogether. Radical supporters have always been concerned that support for comparable worth would not help and might impede a movement for greater equality of pay and social position.

Johanna Brenner has developed this line of reasoning. She argues that comparable worth campaigns tend to be "situated within a liberal political discourse on equality" (Brenner 1987, 447), which centers on "the ideal of meritocracy" (448).

> Liberal political thought accepts the notion of inequality and hierarchy: some will have more, some less; some will command, others follow; some will create, others only implement. Equality is defined as equal opportunity, and thus from a liberal perspective, fairness exists when the distribution of individuals within unequal positions reflects their individual qualities—their different motivation, talents, intelligence, and effort—and not their gender, race, religion, or family background. . . . The goal of twentieth century policy is still a just distribution of individuals within a hierarchy of rewards and power. (448–449)

According to Brenner, comparable worth campaigns accept and reinforce ideology on which hierarchies of rewards and power are necessary and right, and our goal is "a just distribution of individuals" within those hierarchies (449). They advocate for equal opportunity (to have one's job paid based on its worth) at the expense of greater economic equality (448).

Another set of concerns focuses on whether comparable worth really offers an opportunity to revalue women's work. Comparable worth begins with a management tool, job evaluation, in its effort to determine worth. This tool was developed using market pay rates in determining value of factors and had as its original purpose rationalizing inequalities in employer pay scales. At this point job evaluation systems are a management industry run by technocrats. If comparable worth organizing utilizes such job evaluation systems, it is far removed from the challenges of value and grassroots activism and empowerment feminist radicals have hoped for. Is it possible to go from one to the other? Or do the theory and practice of comparable worth legitimate and entrench the values and hierarchies that we want ultimately to eliminate (Feldberg 1984), creating an obstacle to recognizing the value in women's work?

Some experienced practitioners of comparable worth suggest that comparable worth campaigns are more likely to be successful at improving wages of women if they use previously implemented management job evaluation systems (Evans and Nelson 1989, 172). If this is right, comparable worth supporters may have to choose between wage adjustments and any hope of revaluation of women's work.

Brenner argues that the process and results of redistributing workers in a hierarchy will divide workers (1987, 461). Evans and Nelson suggest that successful campaigns are ones with a quiet elite bureaucratic process (1989, 171). If these claims are right, supporters of comparable worth might also need to choose between winning an improvement in women's wages and building a movement—or at least comparable worth will not be a good vehicle for movement building.

The issues raised in these objections are serious ones. In what follows I will respond to them, offering a defense of comparable worth's radical potential against the challenge they pose. I will focus primarily on the first two sets of objections, addressing two related questions: (1) Can support of comparable worth lead to more egalitarian ideology, activism, and outcomes? (2) Can comparable worth prompt a reappraisal of the way our society values women's work? Answers to these questions involve both understanding the place of comparable worth in theories of justice and assessment of comparable worth practice.

III: COMPARABLE WORTH AND SOCIAL JUSTICE

We need to distinguish two ways of understanding the place of comparable worth in proposals about social justice. Although both versions look at worth as a function of job content/job requirements, one version (CW1) sees comparable worth as a (distributive) principle of justice—i.e., in a just society jobs would be paid in accordance with their "worth." The other version (CW2) sees comparable worth as part of remedial justice—it is a temporary and partial remedy for discrimination. I see comparable worth as a discrimination remedy. While apparently the more modest proposal, CW2 offers a way to preserve comparable worth's radical potential; CW1 is incompatible with egalitarian objectives (and problematic in other ways).

In elaborating a distinction between CW1 and CW2, I believe I am developing the justice issues for comparable worth in ways not previously done. Comparable worth supporters have not clearly and consistently distinguished these different versions, and the comparable worth literature typically blurs the distinctions and/or suggests both.

According to CW1, comparable worth is a distributive principle of a just society. Whatever else this claim means, it is saying at least that (a) jobs have "intrinsic" worth; (b) jobs are worth more or less depending on what it requires to do them, and can be rank ordered on the basis of their worth; and (c) a just society will pay people in accordance with their place in a job worth hierarchy—so that higher worth jobs pay more.

How does U.S. society fare as assessed from the vantage point of CW1? It is clear we underpay jobs typically done by women and people of color. CW1 would require that we pay these jobs their true worth. Failure to do so is an injustice. CW1 would also require other pay adjustments if other jobs were not paid in accordance with their intrinsic worth.

CW1 can be understood as part of liberal meritocratic discourse criticized by Brenner. Paying according to worth would reposition undervalued jobs in wage hierarchies and give women/minorities their due while retaining the hierarchies themselves and the commitment to reward more highly valued jobs with higher pay. CW1 would be a permanent policy in a just society.

How would CW1 fit with labor market determination of wages? I believe that this question can't be answered in abstraction from a specific set of value assessments and a specific analysis of the workings of the labor market or markets, all very controversial topics. It is theoretically possible (though I believe *highly* implausible) that one-time adjustments of pay to meet the CW1 standard would result in wages that would be sustained by the market after that, requiring no further intervention. (This would require the inequities to be relatively limited and the market easily correctable.) It is also possible that the policy would need to stay in place permanently as a market modification like the Equal Pay Act or the minimum wage.

Can CW1 fulfill radical hopes for comparable worth? CW1 may be consistent with one way of revaluing "women's" work—revaluation would create a new meritocratic hierarchy of pay which could conceivably aid in ending cultural devaluing of women. But CW1 is explicitly counterposed to radical objectives about pay equality—it is inconsistent with the radical claim that just societies require equality in pay. To support CW1 is to support an alternative to this or similar egalitarian pay scales and objectives. And such support in practice legitimates inequalities and makes it harder for radicals to advocate or achieve more equality.[5]

CW1 could in fact lead to justification for increased inequality. Although supporters of comparable worth usually see it as reducing inequality by raising the wages for "women's" work and narrowing the male/female pay gap, adoption of CW1 could lead to increased pay inequality in societies or employment contexts which currently have small pay differentials. In the Oregon comparable worth experience, a task force proposal which was not eventually implemented would have created pay differentials for some social work positions where none had previously existed (Acker 1989, 116–117).

I am suggesting that CW1 is inconsistent with radical egalitarian pay objectives. I also believe that CW1 rests on untenable claims about intrinsic worth and its possible reflection in job evaluation systems. I will sketch my objections here, although I can't fully do justice to this major topic.

Saying that jobs have intrinsic worth must mean in part that there is an absolute or at least objective standard for worth. But there is no societal agreement about the worth of jobs. People disagree, e.g., on whether caring for people is worth more than caring for people's investment portfolios. If there is a set of intrinsic worths, how would we find them given profound disagreements?

Will the scientific methodology of job evaluation systems revised to eliminate perceived biases give us intrinsic worth of work? Every dimension of job evaluation involves choices which incorporate values and may reflect the social position of those choosing. Even if we grant (and should we?) that the factors relevant to worth of work are skill, effort, responsibility, and working conditions, there is tremendous disagreement about how much each of these should weigh in relation to others, and these disagreements have major impact on outcomes. Often systems give much less weight to working conditions than skills, e.g., with the result that blue-collar jobs are seen as worth less than white-collar jobs. If a system gave more weight to working conditions, blue-collar jobs would experience increased worth. Which is the objective worth? Neither. Both involve subjective value judgments.

After extensive study, the National Research Council of the National Academy of Sciences claims:

> Acceptance of a comparable worth approach—the attempt to measure the worth of jobs directly on the basis of their content—does not require an absolute standard by which the value or worth of all jobs can be measured. In the judgment of the committee, no such standard exists, nor, in our society, is likely to exist. The relative worth of jobs reflects value judgments as to what features of jobs ought to be com-

> pensated, and such judgments vary from industry to industry, even from firm to firm. Paying jobs according to their worth requires only that whatever characteristics of jobs are regarded as worthy of compensation by an employer should be equally so regarded irrespective of the sex, race, or ethnicity of job incumbents. (Tong 1988, 378)

I would add that as employers might disagree with each other about the worth of jobs in their workplaces, so too employees might and do disagree with their employer. Whose assessment would be the objective one? Is there an objective standard which transcends the different class positions and reflects "true" worth?

I am suggesting that there is not now an objective unitary standard of worth based on job requirements and we have no reason to expect that we could have one. If CW1 makes claims for justice based on the existence of such a standard, it is implausible.

With CW2, comparable worth isn't a distributive principle for a just society but a temporary means to remedy injustice now in the United States (and some other) societies. The injustice is the discriminatory denial of real equality of opportunity now and in the past in the workplace and other institutions of our society. This discrimination has resulted in underpayment of women's work—i.e., lower wages for most women than they would have received without the discrimination.[6] Comparable worth as a (partial) remedy is "a wage setting process that gives all employees wages that reflect the choices available to the workers who have historically had the widest range of choices" (Evans and Nelson 1989, 67). When comparable worth plays its part to remedy that discrimination, it can be replaced by other approaches to wage determination. Comparable worth is a temporary measure—something we can go on from.

The idea that we could accept comparable worth but move beyond it has always been in discussion in comparable worth literature (Feldberg 1984, 311–328), although undeveloped. I develop it here by arguing that comparable worth should be seen as conceptually analogous to affirmative action. Like affirmative action, comparable worth is a remedy for both overt and longstanding systemic institutional discrimination, discrimination which denies the victims real equality of opportunity. To end the discrimination and achieve equal opportunity in the future, it is necessary to intervene in the institutions which perpetuate it. While making changes may not be quick or easy, it is possible to articulate goals which, once met, would lead to ending the intervention.

It should be clear that there is no contradiction between support of CW2 now and support of more equality of wages later—it is probably less clear how support of CW2 could be helpful in that larger objective. I will return to that issue after I answer some basic questions about CW2: What is the discrimination CW2 is designed to correct? Why this remedy? And how do we measure the worth of work? (In the space allotted, I will do less than justice to each of these.)

What is the discrimination? Discrimination here is understood as both overt and institutional. Most women work in "women's" jobs because their access to a full range of options has been restricted. Access and choices have been restricted by deliberate exclusions and by institutional structures and practices which result from and perpetuate them. These include "crowding" of women into a narrow range of occupations, segmented labor markets, and internal labor markets.[7] But choice is also restricted by women's responsibilities for child care, by hostile workplace climates, and by socialization of both choosers and their potential colleagues. (This is of course not a complete list). Current wages paid to the vast majority of women in "women's" jobs reflect (and are lower because of) the above-mentioned and other long-term systemwide denials of equal opportunity. Raising the wages of "women's" jobs is a partial remedy for those denials. Even if one could now root out all the contributing factors to denial of equal opportunity (both overt and institutional), the pay scales which were the result of past exclusions would continue to be unjustly low without a comparable worth correction. (Note that it isn't sufficient to adopt comparable worth alone either—both real equal opportunity and comparable worth are needed. I will return to this point shortly.)

It is important to be clear just why we need to look at remedies and criteria for worth in connection with CW2. Consider the following line of reasoning: CW2 doesn't make comparable worth a distributive principle of a just society, and it doesn't assume that work has intrinsic worth. These assumptions are problematic, but they do give us an easy way to explain that comparable worth is just. If instead the problem is systemic institutional discrimination, we can accept the problem and still question whether comparable worth is the right remedy. And if we are not relying on a belief in the intrinsic worth of work, how will we develop and defend our criteria for deciding on wage adjustments?

Similar questions are often asked about affirmative action policy as a response to systemic institutional discrimination. Supporters of affirmative action are asked why, if the problems are systemic, the burden of the solution should fall on workplaces and educational institutions. They are asked how setting goals and timetables is not artificial and arbitrary. As I attempt to answer these questions for CW2, I will look at the answers some supporters have given for affirmative action as a guide. (These rationales for affirmative action are of course controversial. While I agree with them, I do not defend them here. Instead, I suggest that those who agree should also be comfortable with the claims of CW2.)

For affirmative action, use of this remedy was decided as an empirical question about what would work to remedy the effects of systemic discrimination, given specific features of this discrimination and the broader social (and legislative/juridical) context. Can we carry the same reasoning over to comparable worth?

Will raising the wages for women's work *help* remedy the effects of systemic discrimination given the nature of that discrimination and the broader social context? I believe that it will, for the following reasons: (1) as already suggested, it will raise wages devalued by discrimination, and without it, those effects will not be corrected at any time in the foreseeable future; (2) as ongoing implementation efforts suggest, the current social context offers good prospects for public support and implementation of comparable worth. We need to keep in mind that support of CW2 is not an alternative to other important discrimination remedies, e.g., affirmative action, changes in the culture of the workplace, etc. It is a supplement.

How do we determine worth? I consider this question to be analogous to issues for affirmative action about setting goals and timetables. I will look briefly at the issues for affirmative action as a guide to answers for comparable worth. Any affirmative action practitioner knows that there is no simple, single, or uncontroversial way to set goals and timetables. Affirmative action is a partial remedy to a systemic problem. What should our criteria and expectations for this remedy be? There are many possible ways to answer here. Do we set goals with reference to the percentage of the relevant group in the community (and how do we define the community)? Or do we look at the percentage in the pool of people with specific training (and how do we determine the required training)? Choices about how to set goals have impact on the speed and extent of possible change; different choices may imply different beliefs about what justice requires.[8]

How does affirmative action implementation deal with setting goals and timetables? Goals and timetables are tailored to the specific context. They make choices which can be defended, although not conclusively, against alternatives. (Obviously affirmative action has been very controversial, but that has not prevented massive implementation.)

How does the affirmative action analogy help us in understanding which criteria we should choose in determining worth? There are important disanalogies here, including that federal affirmative action monitors have the power to determine goals and timetables and this power is in contention for comparable worth. The relevant analogy is that there is no single and uncontroversial standard of worth. The lack of any such objective standard did not prevent affirmative action from going forward, and it should not do so for comparable worth. We need to recognize that values are implicit in all systems, including those which seem neutral and scientific. This understanding should lead supporters to insist (1) that workers be included in the process of deciding on the study and choice of evaluation systems, and (2) that the evaluation process be open to scrutiny. Workers should try to advocate for and win a system which avoids perceived bias against contributions of women and more highly values the contributions made in "women's" jobs. It should of course also avoid perceived bias against and devaluing of the contributions of people of color. Ideally it should also be seen to be defensible by different groups of employees.

I have argued that support of CW2 is consistent with support of greater equality in pay scales as a long-term goal. To show that CW2 has radical potential, I need to show that it could be helpful in achieving the goals with which I began. Can support of CW2 promote egalitarian ideas? Can it help in building a movement which could win these and other radical goals? Can it help in a revaluation of values?

The issues raised by Brenner and others don't automatically disappear when we talk about comparable worth as a remedy. Even temporary and remedial uses of comparable worth ask people to accept job evaluation systems which legitimize inequalities of pay. The concept also promotes equality of opportunity, which Brenner (and others) counterpose to promoting equality, since it seems to value equal treatment in a given social context and not to challenge contextual inequalities.

I want to argue that CW2 rests on claims about equal opportunity and worth which feminist radicals can support, and that advocacy and implementation of comparable worth can help us achieve other egalitarian and radical goals.

I want to begin with the justification of comparable worth as a corrective for inequality of opportunity. What does "equality of opportunity" mean here? Conservatives use a minimalist concept of equality of opportunity (take the most qualified person to come through the door, without regard to why some don't come or don't have qualifications). Radicals recognize that given societal inequalities, real equal opportunity requires more than the conservative's version. When the environment includes barriers to some groups and not others, equal opportunity requires changing what is "curable" about the environmental inequalities (Williams 1977, 79–92). When CW2 supporters argue, e.g., that overt exclusions or hostile work environments or gender role socialization creates barriers for women which lead to crowding of women into "women's" jobs, depressing wage rates in those jobs, they are saying that equal opportunity requires "curing" these problems as well as their effects on wages. There is no opposition here between support of equality of opportunity and support of greater societal equality. (In fact the discussion of the requirements of real equality of opportunity is an opening to consider whether this requires equal pay.) Advocacy of CW2 with this rationale can help promote more societal equality.[9]

Much of the excitement of comparable worth has always come from its directing our attention to questions about the worth or value of work. By denying that there is an "objective" and value-free basis for determinations of worth, CW2 debunks the pretensions of job evaluation as a neutral management methodology. And it opens the possibility of advocacy, struggle and dialogue about what we do and should value and how those judgments ought to be reflected in pay scales. Worth as understood for CW2 provides both reason and occasion to think about "a revolution of values" (Wright 1989, 9).

I have been suggesting that the concepts of equal opportunity and worth used by CW2 can be used in support of greater societal equality and a revolution of values. But of course these concepts don't exist in a vacuum—how we proceed politically will allow or prevent these issues from coming forward. What political practice will make these developments possible? And can we expect to achieve it for comparable worth? I conclude my essay with answers to these questions.

IV: COMPARABLE WORTH AND POLITICAL PRACTICE

The concepts I have been describing require a context in which activism and justifications and discussion can have impact on political consciousness and political action. What contexts fit these requirements? At the least this must mean that comparable worth—its methodology and rationales—must become a subject of discussion and concern to the general public and/or to grassroots activists in a comparable worth campaign. And if worth is going to be understood as a matter for political struggle and not simply a matter of management science, campaigns need to reach those understandings and challenge management control and systems.

Is it possible to do this?

We can point to cases where comparable worth was won without doing these things. Sara M. Evans and Barbara J. Nelson describe an implementation process for state employees in Minnesota in which preexisting job evaluation systems were used by state bureaucrats to calculate and pay substantial comparable worth adjustments to typically female job categories. Although the enabling legislation was passed as a result of efforts by feminist and labor leaders, the implementation did not challenge existing values or empower women—in fact the process was so quiet that many beneficiaries did not know that they had comparable worth pay increases (Evans and Nelson 1989, chap. 7).

After surveying implementation efforts in Minnesota and elsewhere, Evans and Nelson express the concern that achieving comparable worth might require both acceptance of traditional job evaluation systems which ratify existing values and a quiet and elite bureaucratic process—they say that "effective political advocacy has tended to remain in the hands of a relatively small political elite, and implementation appears highly subject to technocratic control" (Evans and Nelson 1989, 171).

We can also point to cases where feminists challenged traditional job evaluation systems without a clear comparable worth victory. Joan Acker describes a process in Oregon in which both feminist leaders and union officials were involved in adopting, modifying, and implementing an evaluation system for state employees. In this process feminists were able to raise issues and challenges about values. But the discussions went on among a small elite committee and did not generate broad-based discussions or grassroots activism. And the committee did not succeed in getting comparable worth adjustments based on their proposals. Ultimately the state funded a much more modest scheme in which the pay of the lowest paid workers was increased (Acker 1989, chaps. 3–5).

Can we do better than this? That is, can we run a publicized grassroots campaign which makes a space for developing egalitarian ideas, challenges management control and evaluation systems, and wins?

In an extremely important book, *Between Feminism and Labor: The Significance of the Comparable Worth Movement*, Linda Blum presents the results of her research on the comparable worth movements and their successes in San Jose and Contra Costa County, California. In both cases, Blum attributes the successes of the movements to their grassroots mobilization of working women. In San Jose, women workers mobilized and won comparable worth adjustments after a highly publicized strike when the city refused to give pay adjustments to match the outcomes of job evaluation studies. In both cases, women workers challenged management control and management approaches to evaluation. In both cases in different ways, activism resulted in comparable worth adjustments. The full stories in all their complexities are extremely well presented by Blum—I urge all interested readers to read her account (1991).

Like most women who discover comparable worth, the women workers in San Jose and Contra Costa began to challenge values by challenging the legitimacy of existing pay scales. One nurse asked, "Why should pharmacists be paid twice as much as me? . . . Pharmacists tend to be viewed as professionals, with prestige. Nurses have no prestige, and are viewed as handmaidens. If we had ten times more education, still we would be paid less . . . " (Blum 1991, 106).

Workers in San Jose went on to discover that management job evaluation systems were not simply scientific or neutral and to engage in political struggles over how their work should be valued. Grassroots activists and their union pushed for a new job evaluation study, researched the methodology of the management team doing the study, and used those results to find ways to intervene in the process—through education of workers about how to answer management questionnaires in ways that would capture often unrecognized skills and responsibilities in their work and through participation on the evaluation committee (72–83). This process demystified job evaluation and gave those many women involved a clear sense of the subjective nature of choices about value.

For example, although management succeeded in getting workers to agree that wages would be raised to near the median salary level of *all* jobs with the same job evaluation score-range, workers saw that there was another seemingly preferable alternative—one which figured the median salary level of *men's* jobs (82–83). One worker comments: "We don't want to be equal to a depressed salary. We want to be equal to a reasonable salary, which we figure is an average of *men's* salaries. . . . " (83).

I have been describing ways that women in these campaigns came to see questions of value as political choices rather than management science. Women involved in these campaigns were also led by their experiences to put the burden of proof on those who sought to justify salary differentials. Blum reports on interviews with two women workers involved in the campaigns. One argues that

> comparable worth means paying for what you had to have learned for a job. You take the qualifications and rate them somehow. But there's the rub—who does the rating?
>
> Comparable worth is *not* socialistic. It's not everybody getting the same thing. I'm not for *that*. But [pondered the issue]—then I do hear of doctors getting $70,000 a year. Are they *worth* it? . . . (177)

The other woman argues:

> I think comparable worth is really very socialistic. You revalue everything you've got in society. It's a real threat. . . . It undercuts the people who traditionally have been thought to be more valuable—a manager over a social worker, or a policeman over a teacher, or seeing clericals as now doing critical work. It makes you think: What *are* the difficult jobs? What are we willing to pay for? What *is* most important to us as a society? (177).

While neither of these women directly embraces an egalitarian approach, their comparable worth experience has made them receptive to such possibilities, rather than reinforcing their beliefs in hierarchies, old or new.

I asked whether a publicized grassroots comparable worth campaign could win while at the same time challenging management control and valuation systems and making space for egalitarian ideas. These comments by participants in the process allow us a glimpse of the space comparable worth can provide for this kind of egalitarian discourse.

There is of course much more to accomplish in such contexts. For example, in these California experiences we do not see successful efforts to give substantially more value (and more pay) to unrecognized or undervalued skills usually associated with women and "women's" work—"human relations" skills such as negotiation, organizing for collective action, and caring. The movement did not advocate egalitarian pay scales, nor did it critique the existence of hierarchies of pay and status. But these grassroots comparable worth campaigns provide space for these ideas and openness to considering these outcomes.

I have argued that we can understand, advocate, and hope to implement comparable worth in ways consistent with and conducive to specific radical objectives. Following Blum, I am also suggesting that the model of organizing which makes success on this basis possible is a publicized and vocal grassroots campaign which challenges management control and management values. This finding should not surprise feminist radicals. Feminist radicals typically claim that working people can do better for themselves than an elite (adversarial or sympathetic) will do on their behalf. But it is still good to find that the implementation experiences which offer the best opportunity to achieve radical objectives also confirm radicals' confidence in human capacities.[10]

NOTES

1. This formulation was publicized by San Jose Mayor Janet Grey Hayes. Cited in Bureau of National Affairs 1981, 35.

2. Ronnie Steinberg reports, "In some cases, including Florida and New York City, pay-equity study results point to much higher adjustments on the basis of race than on gender" (Steinberg 1987, 468).

3. These ideas were the common currency of many feminist activists in the 1980s. See, for example, Solidarity: A Socialist-Feminist Network 1981.

4. These ideas were widely shared informally within the women's movement.

5. There might seem to be another way to understand this version of comparable worth which would at least reconcile it with egalitarian goals. In presenting one version of comparable worth, Rosemary Tong argues:

> Comparable worth policy would replace the labor market dynamic of supply and demand with compensation according to the relative worth of jobs, as measured by job content. It would logically lead to a radical restructuring of the labor market, in which virtually all jobs were seen as equally valuable to society and worth equal compensation. (Tong 1988, 381)

Tong's claim might be seen as a variation on the idea of comparable worth as a distributive principle of a just society. Instead of being a permanent policy with an expectation of permanent inequalities in income (as I have been presenting it), comparable worth would be a permanent policy which shifts to equality of income as people shift their conception of the value of work (as Tong suggests). It is perhaps conceivable that people could start by acceptance of comparable worth as a principle of justice on current concepts of value and move to accepting it with radically different concepts of value. But there is surely no "logical" connection here. Comparable worth implementation has not had this outcome. It would be misguided optimism to support a permanent policy with an inegalitarian thrust in the assurance that it will transform in a completely egalitarian direction (Tong 1988, 374–382).

6. Of course people of color, male and female, face discriminatory denial of real opportunity past and present, and this is reflected in concentrations of people in jobs based on race and lower wages for those jobs. Comparable worth can function as a partial remedy for race-based discrimination on the same reasoning which makes it suitable for gender-based discrimination.

7. These concepts are familiar in economics. For their use in connection to comparable worth, see Gold 1983 (on crowding, 45; on segmented labor markets, 14–18; on internal labor markets, 19–20).

8. There are at least two very different ways to understand the purposes of affirmative action: (1) that it is aiming at a redistribution of people in occupations based on their group's proportion in some population, and (2) that it is aiming to intervene in ongoing systemic discrimination sufficiently to allow real equality of opportunity at some future point, with no conclusions about what distributions equal opportunity would produce. I support the latter version. Whichever version one supports, however, there are still alternative and incompatible ways of setting goals and timetables.

9. As is perhaps obvious, the same line of argument can be used for inequalities which are a function of race.

10. I owe my interest in comparable worth to my experience working with clerical workers organizing for comparable worth in the early 1980s under the auspices of District 65—United Auto Workers. I am very grateful to have worked with a great group of women at an exciting time. Thanks to Marlene Fried, Nancy Fraser, and Roslyn Feldberg for good discussions early in this project and to Diane Raymond, Jon Mandle, Iris Young, and Patrice DiQuinzio for useful comments and criticism of recent drafts. My research on comparable worth has been supported by a sabbatical from Bentley College and an appointment as a Bunting Fellow.

REFERENCES

Acker, Joan. 1989. *Doing comparable worth: gender, class and pay equity*. Philadelphia: Temple University Press.

Blum, Linda M. 1991. *Between feminism and labor: The significance of the comparable worth movement*. Berkeley: University of California Press.

Brenner, Johanna. 1987. Feminist political discourses: Radical versus liberal approaches to the feminization of poverty and comparable worth. *Gender and Society* 1(4): 447–465.

Bureau of National Affairs. 1981. *The comparable worth issue: A BNA special report*. Washington, D.C.: Bureau of National Affairs.

Evans, Sara M., and Barbara J. Nelson. 1989. *Wage justice: comparable worth and the paradox of technocratic reform*. Chicago: University of Chicago Press.

Feldberg, Roslyn L. 1984. Comparable worth: toward theory and practice in the U.S. *Signs* 10(2): 311–328.

Gold, Michael Evan. 1983. *A dialogue on comparable worth*. Ithaca: ILR Press/Cornell University.

Malveaux, Julianne. 1984. Low wage black women: Occupational descriptions, strategies for change. NAACP Legal Defense and Education Fund paper, January 1984. (Cited in Evans and Nelson.)

National Committee on Pay Equity. 1989. *Newsnotes 10*. Washington, D.C.: National Committee on Pay Equity.

National Committee on Pay Equity. 1990. *Newsnotes 11*. Washington, D.C.: National Committee on Pay Equity.

National Committee on Pay Equity. 1991. *Newsnotes 12*. Washington, D.C.: National Committee on Pay Equity.

Solidarity: A Socialist-Feminist Network. 1981. *Discussion bulletin on socialist feminism*. Somerville, Mass.: Solidarity: A Socialist-Feminist Network.

Steinberg, Ronnie. 1987. Radical challenges in a liberal world: The mixed success of comparable worth. *Gender and Society* 1(4): 466–475.

Tong, Rosemary. 1988. Three incomparable perspectives on comparable worth. In *Ethical theory and business*, 3rd ed., ed. Tom L. Beauchamp and Norman E. Bowie. Englewood Cliffs, N.J.: Prentice Hall, 374–382.

Williams, Bernard. 1977. The idea of equality. In *Sex equality*, ed. Jane English. Englewood Cliffs, N.J.: Prentice Hall, 79–92.

Wright, Betsy. 1989. We need a revolution of values. *Sojourner: The Women's Forum*, January.

Young, Iris Marion. 1990. *Justice and the politics of difference*. Princeton, N.J.: Princeton University Press.

7

"Male-Order" Brides

Immigrant Women, Domestic Violence, and Immigration Law

UMA NARAYAN

Despite increased awareness of the need to attend to the experiences of women who are on the margins of society because of their class, race, ethnicity, and sexual orientation, little attention has been paid by feminist philosophers to problems that particularly affect *immigrant* women, many of whom are women from Third World countries. The experience of immigration is often a difficult one for both men and women, involving moving great distances from the familiar contexts of one's homeland to the rigors of life in a foreign country, where they face not only the disempowering unfamiliarities of the new context, but also prejudice and discrimination. For many women immigrants in particular, the shift to a new context only exacerbates their gender-linked vulnerabilities and powerlessness.

This paper analyzes one set of problems that confront many immigrant women to the United States. The majority of immigrants to the United States today are women (Housten et al. 1984). Although some of these women immigrate in their own right, others enter the United States with an immigration status dependent on marriage to a man who is either a U.S. citizen or a Legal Permanent Resident (LPR). Their ability to acquire citizenship or LPR status is dependent on the goodwill of their husbands and on the survival of their marriages. I wish to focus on the problems faced by women with such "dependent immigration status" if they face abuse and violence within their marriage.[1]

Hypatia vol. 10, no. 1 (Winter 1995) © by Uma Narayan

Although recent events have given issues of domestic violence extensive media coverage, there has been little attention to battered immigrant women, who are not only disempowered by all the factors that affect battered women who are citizens, but who also confront legal prohibitions against seeking employment and the threat of deportation if they leave abusive marriages.

For many immigrants, moving to a new country often precedes acquiring the legal status of a citizen or of a permanent resident of that country by several years. In a context of increasing global immigration, we need to attend to the implications of citizenship as a status that, for many immigrants, is obtained via the mediation of complex legal rules, which are often insensitive to predicaments faced by immigrant women. When immigration rules render women legally dependent on their husbands in a manner that is oblivious to problems of domestic violence or make legal provisions to help battered immigrant women that assume immigrant women to have the knowledge, resources, and choices of the sort enjoyed by mainstream male citizens, these rules *exacerbate* immigrant women's lack of autonomy instead of helping to enhance their autonomy. Such immigration rules seem more concerned with "policing the borders" between noncitizens and citizens than with helping to make empowered citizens of immigrant women who are in the process of legally negotiating these borders in order to acquire citizenship.

This essay consists of two sections. In the first section I consider the factors that make many immigrant women particularly vulnerable to domestic violence, and I critically address the conjunction of social and political forces that impede drawing public attention to immigrant women's heightened vulnerability to battering. I argue that the racism and the gender-related forms of powerlessness that these women face in foreign contexts often combine with the sexism and cultural chauvinism they encounter in their own immigrant communities to form a constellation of forces that render these women highly vulnerable to domestic violence and that disempower them in terms of taking action to end or escape the violence. In the second section I analyze aspects of current U.S. immigration law that are detrimental to the welfare of immigrant women who face violence within their marriages, and criticize the normative assumptions and priorities that underlie these policies. I then suggest a number of changes in our immigration laws that would ameliorate these problems, and set out the normative vision that should inform and structure our immigration policies.

IMMIGRANT WOMEN AND INCREASED VULNERABILITIES TO BATTERING

Although data on battered women are difficult to obtain and evaluate, empirical evidence suggests that women whose immigration status depends on their husbands are more at risk for battery than women in general. There are wide variations in the studies that seek to ascertain the percentage of all married women who experience some form of violence within their marriages. Estimates range from 12 percent to 50 percent (see Sigler 1989, 12–13). A recent report by the American Medical Association reported that one in three women will be assaulted by a domestic partner in her lifetime.[2] The estimated rates of battery for immigrant women seem considerably higher. One study reports that 77 percent of women with dependent immigrant status are battered. Of the victims of domestic violence at the Victim's Services Agency in Jackson Heights, Queens, 90 percent were immigrants (see Anderson 1993, n. 9).

What factors contribute to such heightened vulnerability to abuse? Women with dependent immigration status are often more economically, psychologically and linguistically dependent on their spouses than wives in general. Dependent immigration status legally prohibits them from seeking employment. Many lack fluency in English, a factor that impedes their ability to negotiate the routines of everyday life without their husbands' assistance. The language barrier impedes social relationships except with those who share their linguistic background, but members of their linguistic community are often people connected to the husband, unlikely to assist against the husband's abusive conduct (Hogeland and Rosen 1990). Contact with members of one's linguistic community can be entirely lacking for foreign wives whose husbands are Americans who do not share their ethnic background. Community norms within immigrant communities also work to disempower battered women. Citing the director of Everywoman's Shelter in Los Angeles who points out that in many Asian communities saving the honor of the family from shame is a priority that deters immigrant women from reporting domestic violence (Rimonte 1991), Kimberlè Crenshaw remarks, "Unfortunately, this priority tends to be interpreted as obliging women not to scream rather than obliging men not to hit" (Crenshaw, N.d.).

There are additional factors that heighten vulnerability to domestic violence for *particular groups* of women with dependent immigration status. Due to U.S. military presence overseas, since World War II more than 200,000 women, mostly Asian, have married U.S. servicemen and immigrated to the United States as "military brides" (Anderson 1993, 1406). Studies reveal that *rates* as well as the *severity* of domestic violence are greater in military families than in civilian families. One study indicated that military men used weapons on their wives twice as often as civilians, and that three-fourths of the cases were life-threatening, compared to one-third of cases involving civilians (Anderson 1993, 1406). Researchers conclude that "the worst of the civilian cases were the norm for military cases" (Shupe et al. 1987, 67–70). A number of factors account for this heightened degree of violence. Periods of extended separation when soldiers are stationed away from home and the social isolation due to the transient nature of military postings are thought to increase the stresses on military family life; but the most significant factor is believed to be the aggressive values indoctrinated into soldiers that carry over into domestic contexts (Anderson 1993, 1406). If military wives are at greater risk for domestic violence than civilian wives, and if women who are dependent immigrants are at greater risk than other women, the possibility that dependent immigrants who are military brides face substantial risks of violence is frighteningly high indeed.

A number of women immigrate to the United States to marry virtual strangers. Approximately 2,000 to 3,500 American men annually marry "mail-order wives," according to current estimates (Kadohata 1990). The typical man who seeks a "mail-order bride" is described as an older, politically conservative, college-educated white man, with higher than average income, who has had bitter experiences with divorce or breakups.[3] The vast majority of women who are available as "mail-order brides" are young Asian women from poorer Southeast Asian countries. However, women from Eastern European countries and from areas that were formerly part of the Soviet Union seem to have recently joined these lists in significant numbers (Henneberger 1992). Many of these women come from backgrounds marked by grinding poverty, unemployment, and political turmoil. Men who seek these women as marriage partners have motivations in which sexist and racist stereotypes play significant roles. Men who marry "mail-order brides" want women who will be totally dependent on them; they are disenchanted with changing gender roles and often blame the women's movement for their inability to find locally the sort of woman they wish to marry (Joseph 1984). They hope to find "beautiful, traditional, faithful" Asian wives, who will not seek to work outside the home, in contrast to local women whom they deem "overly liberated," and not devoted enough to their husbands and families (Villipando 1989, 321). The "mail-order bride" businesses exploit stereotypes of Asian women, tapping into existing views of Asian women as Lotus Blossoms and Geisha Girls, devoted and deferential to men, the "feminine" and "delicate" counterparts of their loud, independent western sisters (Tajima 1989).

The "mail-order bride" phenomenon illuminates interesting details of the nexus between race and gender stereotypes prevalent in the United States. Economically vulnerable women from African countries, for instance, are not in demand as wives. Submissiveness and deference do not seem to be stereotypical qualities attributed to women of African descent. White "mail-order brides" have increased in number as a result of the recent economic and political upheavals in the former Soviet bloc, and have become quickly "popular," judging by the catalogues. This suggests that many men prefer white "mail-order brides" over Asian women, when available. I was unable to find any full-scale study of such "mail-order" marriages, but newspaper reports suggest that "mail-order brides" are frequently subject to violent assault and abandonment.[4]

Many immigrant men settled in the United States marry women from their countries of origin. I focus, for reasons of familiarity, on marriages between Indian men settled abroad and women from India. There are similarities between the situations of "mail-order brides" and the situations confronted by these Indian women, since both are entering into arranged marriages to relative strangers and are vulnerable to domestic abuse for many of the reasons previously discussed. Some immigrant Indian women confront particular problems in leaving an abusive marriage, problems that might affect women in other immigrant communities as well. Leaving an abusive marriage to return home, even if economically feasible (which it frequently is not), often results in social stigma for the woman and her family, and leaves her with few hopes for remarriage. In India, men who are U.S. citizens or LPRs are regarded as very attractive matrimonial prospects, which puts them in a position to demand very high dowries from the families of the women they marry. Paying a large dowry constitutes a tremendous economic sacrifice on the part of a woman's family, resulting in great pressure on daughters to "make the marriage work" (see Narayan 1993, 159–70).

Quite a few expatriate Indian men seek to marry women raised in India because of a conviction that such women will make better wives, be more "traditional," "family oriented," and less independent or assertive than their Indian counterparts "corrupted" by being raised in western contexts. The stereotypes held by Indian men looking for "really Indian" wives have an astonishing resemblance to those held by western men looking for Asian "mail-order brides." The same insidious and stereotypical contrast between traditional, home-loving, faithful, self-sacrificing nonwestern women and independent, aggressive, sexually promiscuous "Westernized" women operates in both sorts of marriages. The gender stereotypes that are culturally chauvinistic oddly mirror those that are racist. The qualities that constitute a "good wife" seem to cut across a plurality of cultural landscapes. What all these men are looking for is not only a wife with the appropriately subservient attitudes toward her husband, but a wife who is materially and socially disempowered in ways that will prevent her from challenging their authority. They are looking for a genuine "male-order" bride, in fact. The very dependencies that make these women "attractive wives" ensure their relative powerlessness to confront violence within their marriages.

Even many women who are citizens endure domestic violence within their marriages because of economic dependence, fear of losing custody of their children, social isolation, and ignorance about institutions that might offer shelter or assistance. If marriage is not an empowering institution for many women who are citizens, the disempowering nature of the institution is only exacerbated when a woman's ability to remain in the country depends on the continuation of the marriage. Dependent immigration status is often exploited by husbands, who use the threat of deportation to ensure that their wives do not leave or seek assistance when abused. Since many western and nonwestern men who marry immigrant women are explicitly looking for dependent and subservient wives, they are unlikely to have qualms about using the conjunction of violence and threat of deportation to control their wives.

It is not surprising that women whose dependence on their marriage is high and who have few resources with which to negotiate changes in their husbands' behavior are more susceptible to prolonged physical abuse. While women from all categories and walks of life are susceptible to domestic violence, the *degree* of this susceptibility is clearly affected by material and social structures that disempower particular groups of women. Unfortunately, a variety of factors collude against calling attention to the fact that particular groups of marginalized women are often more vulnerable to domestic violence than their more privileged sisters. These factors contribute to a lack of awareness about the specific problems that confront battered immigrant women. I will discuss some of these factors.

Sexism and cultural chauvinism often collaborate to create tremendous resistance to acknowledging the extent of domestic violence within immigrant communities. I have encountered resistance, among expatriate Indians as well as Indians back in India, to confronting the degree of abuse women face within arranged marriages. Attempts by Indian feminists to call attention to issues of violence against women, such as rape, harassment, dowry-murder and dowry-related marital abuse were often condemned by sections of the Indian intelligentsia as an imposition of irrelevant "Western" agendas (Katzenstein 1991–92, 7). Among Indian immigrants as well, there is a sexist and culturally chauvinistic insistence that "our traditions" guarantee respectful treatment of women and that "our families" do not suffer from problems perceived as endemic to "Western" marriages. Lower rates of divorce among Indians are often uncritically offered as proof that women do not suffer abuse within the institution of arranged marriage. Variants of these attitudes might be prevalent in other immigrant communities as well.

While such attitudes constitute a willful denial of domestic violence within these immigrant communities, other elements also impede acknowledgment of factors that may heighten vulnerability to domestic violence on the part of women of color and immigrant women. Kimberlè Crenshaw points out an odd and detrimental collaboration between the politics of U.S. feminist groups addressing domestic violence and the cultural politics of many minority and immigrant communities. Crenshaw reveals that the Los Angeles Police Department would not release statistics that would show the correlation between arrests for domestic violence and racial group, because of conjoint pressures from domestic violence activists who feared the statistics would be used to dismiss domestic violence as a "minority problem" and by representatives from minority communities who worried that the data would reinforce racist stereotypes. Crenshaw concludes, "This account sharply illustrates how women of color can be erased by the strategic silences of antiracism and feminism" (Crenshaw, N.d.), making it difficult to address the specific problems confronting victims of domestic violence who are women of color.

A genuinely feminist and antiracist approach to domestic violence should recognize that such "strategic silences" betray the interests of women of color, and instead advocate sensitivity to the ways in which different groups of battered women are differently impeded in their abilities to secure assistance. Immigrant women are more vulnerable to domestic violence because of economic, social, and legal factors—such as lacking legal standing to work, and the threat of deportation if they leave their marriage—that do not burden women who are citizens. Worries that acknowledging immigrant women's heightened susceptibility to domestic violence will reflect badly on immigrant communities or immigrant men can, I argue, be countered by emphasizing that immigrant women who marry mainstream U.S. citizens (as is the case with most "military brides" and "mail-order brides") also face greater obstacles to leaving abusive marriages.

The "strategic silences" Crenshaw discusses contribute to policies that are blind to the specific problems that confront battered immigrant women. When immigrant community leaders, who are most often men, deny the domestic abuse prevalent in their communities, they make it harder to create, publicize, and maintain accessible community-based sources of assistance that would most effectively help battered immigrant women. Such "strategic silences" deflect attention from the *particular* problems that affect battered immigrant women since they contribute to public unawareness of the extent to which the policies of domestic-violence support services and shelters themselves often disempower immigrant or minority women. Crenshaw discusses the case of a non-English-speaking battered Latina woman fleeing murder threats from her husband, who was denied accommodation at a shelter with only English-speaking staff, on grounds that the shelter's policies required the battered woman to call the shelter *herself* for screening, and to take part in support group sessions which a woman lacking English proficiency could not participate in (Crenshaw, N.d.). Lack of attention to the special vulnerabilities of battered immigrant women also results in inadequate immigration policies, whose specific inadequacies I discuss in the next section.

IMMIGRATION LAW AND BATTERED WOMEN IMMIGRANTS

The history of immigration laws and policies in a number of western countries reveals a great deal of racism and sexism (see Bhabha, Klug and Shutter 1985), a discussion of which is beyond the scope of this paper. The most explicit forms of race and gender discrimination formerly rampant in U.S. immigration law seem to have been dismantled. However, current U.S. immigration policies still lack sensitivity to the plight of women with dependent immigration status who are victims of domestic violence. I would argue that aspects of our current immigration policies are good examples of regulations that are *formally gender-neutral*, but which work to the detriment and disempowerment of many immigrant *women* in practice. I shall set out these aspects of current U.S. immigration policy, and explain the problems it poses for battered women who are dependent residents.

Before 1986, when a citizen or LPR married a foreigner and petitioned for the spouse, the spouse was granted permanent residency fairly quickly, and more or less as a matter of course. In 1986, as a result of alleged concerns about "marriage fraud," Congress passed the Immigration Marriage Fraud Amendments (IMFA), which changed the legal process (see Rae 1988, 182–190). Thereafter, the U.S. citizen or LPR had to petition for what was called "conditional resident status" for the spouse. The couple then had to wait for two years after conditional resident status was obtained (during which time they had to remain married), and then jointly petition the Immigration and Naturalization Service (INS) to adjust the conditional residency status to that of permanent residency. Both spouses had to undergo a personal interview with the INS, to prove that the marriage was a bona fide one, before permanent resident status was conferred on the foreign spouse (Anderson 1993, 1412–13).

The two-year waiting period to apply for permanent residency required by IMFA begins on the date the spouse *obtains* conditional resident status, not on the day of *application*, let alone at the time of marriage (Anderson 1993, 1412). Administrative delays in visa processing, which seem to depend on the size of the immigration "quota" for particular countries, means that for many spouses conditional status can continue for four years or more (Tucker 1989, 35). Spouses cannot petition for their *own* immigrant status, (either for conditional residency or for the change to permanent resident status), leaving wives completely dependent on the goodwill of the husband and the continuing viability of the marriage. If the marriage dissolves anytime in the conditional residency period, the foreign spouse stands to lose conditional immigrant status and to become a deportable illegal alien (Anderson 1993, 1404). Since citizens and LPRs are not *obliged* to secure either conditional or permanent resident status for a foreign spouse, many immigrant women may have their legal right to remain in the country *permanently* dependent on the survival of their marriage.

Under initial IMFA provisions, a battered woman with dependent immigration status who wished to leave her marriage during the period of conditional residency could avoid deportation only by showing that she had entered the marriage in good faith and that she had initiated divorce proceedings for "good cause." It was not legally clear however whether spousal abuse constituted a "good cause." In addition, divorce proceedings in "no-fault" divorce states yielded little evidence that could be used to support "good cause" (Tucker

1989, 38). Besides, few battered conditional residents were likely to use this provision, since it required that they possess the psychological, economic, and legal resources to initiate and conclude successful divorce proceedings. The very conditions that render these women vulnerable to battering are unlikely to make initiating divorce proceedings a real option for them. Even those few conditional resident women able to secure a divorce could not *count* on evidence of their abuse constituting a "good cause"; they thereby risked deportation as a consequence of divorce.

In 1989, the House Judiciary Committee on Immigration, Refugees and International Law held a hearing on domestic violence in marriages between American citizens and foreigners. Representative Louise M. Slaughter testified that many battered conditional residents had no viable legal options. She introduced a bill, passed in 1990[5] which provided that battery and extreme cruelty if alleged and proven, could qualify a conditional resident for a waiver during the waiting period. Initiation and termination of divorce proceedings was not required, if abuse could be proven. This legislation also terminated the condition that the divorce had to be for a "good cause." It held that the termination of a "good faith" marriage involving a conditional resident could itself constitute a waiver, without regard to the reasons for the divorce.[6]

Although the 1990 immigration legislation was a significant improvement, the manner in which the INS construed regulations to implement this legislation is seriously problematic, and considerably dilutes its usefulness. The INS regulations have very stringent requirements of *evidence* regarding spousal battery. To prove physical battery, the woman needs "expert testimony in the form of reports and affidavits from police, judges, medical personnel, school officials and social service agencies," and the INS must be satisfied with their credibility.[7] The conditions for proving extreme mental cruelty are even harder to meet, since that requires the evaluation of a professional "recognized by the Service as an expert in the field."[8] Agencies serving battered immigrant women criticized these evidentiary requirements as significantly curtailing the intended practical benefits of the battered-spouse waiver legislation. Representative Slaughter herself described the INS regulations as "obscene," given that her legislation was intended to help a class of women who "almost by definition" lack access to professional help (Anderson 1993, 1420).

I will set out and critique some assumptions that seem to underlie these U.S. immigration policies. The IMFA was passed as a check on what was perceived to be a growing tide of "sham marriages" designed to beat the immigration system (see Rae 1988, 181–83). The INS claimed that the rate of marriage fraud is 8 percent, rising to 15 percent in the Los Angeles area, which it estimates is the highest in the United States (Anderson 1993, n. 60). However, these figures seem of questionable reliability for three reasons. An *extremely* small statistical sample, one-twentieth of one percent of immigration petitions filed in 1984, was used to support these claims. The INS did not use cases in which fraud was *demonstrated*, but estimates derived from the "personal judgment" of investigators. Though purportedly a random sample, INS selections seemed to have skewed the findings toward higher incidences of fraud (see Tucker 1989, 28–29). It can thus be argued that IMFA was based on highly speculative assertions of a "rising tide of illegals."

IMFA policies may well be the result of immigration policy makers pandering to public anxieties about increasing illegal immigration. Policies designed to curb the number of immigrants, legal or illegal, are likely to win public popularity, given recent data that show that one in five U.S. citizens would be in favor of sending immigrants who had arrived in the last decade "back where they came from."[9] The punitive implications of these stricter policies on battered immigrant women are unlikely to affect the popularity of policy makers, since they are neither well known nor likely to elicit extensive public outrage. In its concern to distinguish "good faith" marriages from "sham" marriages, IMFA policies fail to focus adequately on the fact that many "good faith" marriages are highly abusive contexts for immigrant women. As a result, our immigration policies give greater priority to keeping out "illegals" than to protecting the welfare of many women *legally* attempting to immigrate to the U.S., arguably a case of misplaced priorities. Oddly enough, though INS data showed levels of fraud in *occupational* immigration to be as high as those through "sham marriages," occupational immigration applicants were not restricted by IMFA (Tucker 1989, 34). One can only wonder why illegal entry as a *worker* is considered less serious than illegal entry as a *spouse*. It has been suggested that public concerns about "sham marriages" tend to focus on cases of *immigrant men* marrying U.S. women as an expedient to obtaining citizenship or LPR status, and then divorcing these women, rather than on *immigrant women* marrying U.S. citizens or LPRs.[10] If this is true, and it is certainly plausible (see Brooks 1985), it would suggest that IMFA policies are motivated by a desire to protect "our" women from exploitation and illegal conduct by immigrant men, with little consideration given to their effects on law-abiding immigrant women married to U.S. men. Lack of serious INS policy initiatives directed at fraud in occupational immigration might then be explained by the fact that such fraud does not raise concerns about the sexual exploitation of U.S. women by immigrant men.

I would argue that both the earlier IMFA requirement that a battered spouse demonstrate that she had initiated divorce proceedings for "good cause" and the later INS regulations of stringent evidence of spousal battery reveal a seriously inadequate understanding of the life-situations of battered immigrant women. They are instances both of *formally gender-neutral policies* that have a disproportionately adverse impact on women, and instances of policy makers failing to see the *implicit gender-implications of* seemingly gender-neutral policies. Although the policies result in both men and women who immigrate by virtue of marriage to a U.S. citizen or LPR having their immigration status dependent on the goodwill of their spouse and the survival of their marriage, few immigrant men seem likely to suffer from heightened vulnerability to domestic violence as a result, given the gendered nature of domestic violence. Furthermore, few immigrant men married to U.S. citizens or LPRs are likely to share the special vulnerabilities of immigrant women who are married to military men or deliberately chosen as partners because of qualities that make them more amenable to the control and domination of their husbands.

The INS's evidentiary requirements regarding abuse are no more sensitive to the concrete constraints on immigrant women's agency than IMFA's prior requirement that they prove their divorce was secured for "good cause." The INS's underlying picture of a battered immigrant woman seems to be that of an agent who has the knowledge, resources, and confidence to avail herself of the services of legal and medical experts and of social service agencies, to secure her immigration status without her spouse's cooperation, a picture of agency and autonomy that few immigrant women are likely to match. These inflated ascriptions of autonomy are then inscribed in legal policies that circumscribe further the limited autonomy of battered immigrant women. The INS evidentiary requirements reflect a frightening lack of attention to the specific vulnerabilities of battered immigrant women *even in a context of policy changes specifically designed to address their plight.*

I have argued in a previous article that there are many instances where legal policies assume a tacit normative notion of a "standard person," a notion that works to eclipse the special vulnerabilities that afflict members of various marginalized groups in a variety of contexts (Narayan 1993, 377–78). I would argue that both the earlier IMFA provision requiring divorce and the INS's evidentiary requirements regarding spousal battery constitute clear and terrible examples of this phenomenon. I would argue that those who design policies and regulations should start with a concrete awareness of the contexts, resources, and vulnerabilities of various groups of people likely to be affected by their rules. If immigrant women's heightened vulnerability to domestic violence were central to the awareness and concerns of makers of immigration polices, a number of changes in these policies would appear eminently reasonable. I shall proceed to set out what I think some of these changes should be and to delineate the awareness and priorities that should ground them.

Immigration policy makers should begin with a vivid sense of who many women with dependent immigration status are and what vulnerabilities their life-situations involve. Women with dependent immigration status should also be perceived as *potential citizens*—women who have made often difficult choices to relocate their lives, trusting to the security of marriages made in good faith and planning to reside permanently in the country to which they move. They enter the country legally and have not broken any of its laws. Immigration policy makers also need to recognize that formally gender-neutral policies may have particular adverse effects on women immigrants. They should have a serious commitment to reducing or eliminating these effects. Immigration policy makers should be concerned to empower immigrant women so that deportation is not the only terrible alternative to their remaining in abusive marriages. What changes in immigration policies would follow if these concerns and priorities were given their due importance?

Currently, battered wives whose husbands do not undertake the first stage of the process, where they petition for the wife's conditional residency, are left in the most terrible position of all, with only the option of interminably enduring the battery or facing the possibility of deportation if they leave the marriage. I am inclined to argue that the entire step of having the husband petition for the wife's conditional residency status should be eliminated. When a foreigner marries a U.S. citizen or LPR, her proof of marriage and her documentation of legal entry should suffice to confer conditional resident status automatically, and to start the two year clock running with regards to the application for permanent residency. This change would not only reduce bureaucratic paperwork, but also eliminate the power currently available to abusive husbands to keep their wives' ability to remain legally in this country *permanently* dependent on the marriage. My recommendation goes beyond Janet M. Calvo's suggestion that women should be allowed to self-petition for conditional residency, in that it makes this step virtually automatic (see Calvo 1991, 625).

I would also endorse Calvo's recommendation to make it possible for immigrant women to *self-petition* to change their status from conditional residency to permanent residency when the waiting period is past (Calvo 1991, 625). The two or more years of conditional residency allow ample time for the INS to determine if a particular marriage is a "sham." As long as the INS has no reason to believe that a marriage is not a bona fide one, women should not be subject to a form of coverture, where they need their husband's consent and cooperation to change their legal status. Furthermore, IMFA stipulates that once conditional status is granted on the basis of marriage, the alien spouse *may not* seek adjustment to permanent resident status on any other statutory ground, *even if one becomes available* (Tucker 1989, 29). This provision puts an insurmountable obstacle in the way of those battered women who might otherwise be able to gain permanent resident status by acquiring employment of a sort that would qualify them in their *own right* for permanent resident status. This provision too is arguably a form of coverture and needs to be eliminated.

For women who wish to leave abusive marriages during the period of conditional residency and who lack other statutory grounds for seeking permanent residency, the INS should modify its battered spouse waiver in ways that reduce the stringent evidentiary requirements that are virtually impossible for immigrant women to meet. Immigrant women should not be required to provide legal and medical testimony as to their abuse. Testimony about their abuse obtained from relatives, friends, family members, and religious workers should be granted significant weight when available, since immigrant women are more likely to turn to them, rather than to mainstream professionals, for help. I would further suggest that the woman's word about abuse should suffice for a waiver to be granted as a matter of course, unless the INS has some evidence to suggest that she is involved in a marriage scam. As long as there is no reason to doubt a "good faith marriage" on her part, there seems to be no pressing reason for the INS to doubt the woman's word as to abuse. Women who are genuinely involved in "sham marriages" seem unlikely to call attention to themselves by petitioning for battered spouse waivers during the period of conditional residency.

That many women with dependent immigration status confront economic and social problems as the price of leaving their marriage should *itself* constitute strong evidence for the INS to believe their testimony about abuse. Leaving abusive marriages is hardly a convenient decision for many immigrant women, since it confronts them with the hard task of making a life for themselves, and sometimes for their children, in a difficult foreign context. INS evidentiary requirements as to abuse are insensitive to these facts, and seem tantamount to an assumption that these women are lying, even when there is no reason whatsoever to believe that they are. These stringent evidentiary requirements cannot be justified on the grounds of safe-guarding the husband's rights. Unlike criminal prosecution where the burden of proof is justifiably set high, the INS's acceptance of immigrant women's word as to abuse would not involve the imposition of legal penalties on the other spouse. The spouse's rights are not affected if the woman's testimony about battery is accepted as sufficient for obtaining a waiver during the period of conditional residency. Besides, the INS accepts credible personal statements from foreign nationals seeking political asylum as proof of a "well-founded fear of persecution" in their country (Anderson 1993, n. 109). It seems odd and arguably sexist to accept a credible person's word as to political persecution, but not as to domestic violence.

Exaggerated worries about "sham marriages" cannot justify policies that jeopardize the welfare and human rights of battered women with dependent immigration status. Protecting the welfare of legal women immigrants should have at least as much priority as detecting illegal immigrants involved in "sham marriages," especially when there seem to be no grounds for believing that the policies that would empower battered immigrant women would facilitate the perpetration of "sham marriages." Immigration policies that add unnecessary obstacles to immigrant women escaping domestic violence, however unintentionally, collude with abusive husbands.

Such policies changes should, if made, be highly publicized. Otherwise, immigrant women will continue to believe that leaving an abusive marriage will entail their deportation, a belief that will be exploited by their husbands. I advocate that foreigners who marry citizens or LPRs should be given a clear and concise account of their immigration rights by the INS, but I suspect this is too utopian to expect. Immigrant communities, and agencies that work within them, would be best situated to put such information together in the appropriate languages and ensure that immigrant women obtain this information. In order for this to happen, immigrant communities need to deal with their denial of domestic violence, and to support actively a range of programs and institutions to assist battered immigrant women.

Although writing on citizenship has often been concerned with a just and equal distribution of the privileges and benefits of membership to members of groups marginalized *within* a national community, the focus has tended to be on inequalities affecting those who are *already members* of the body of citizens and not on those involved in the process of acquiring such membership (see Phillips 1993 and Shklar 1991). It often continues to be an uphill battle to get laws and policies generally to be nonracist and nonsexist, in ways that ensure equitable rights to all citizens. However, immigration laws and policies also raise issues of *what states owe to non-citizens who are in the process of becoming citizens*. A nation that supposedly prides itself on being a nation of immigrants ought to take pride in protecting persons who are involved in the process of acquiring permanent immigration status and in becoming its citizens. An immigration policy that was truly sensitive to issues of domestic violence would structure its regulations and priorities in a manner that afforded the maximum of protection to the interests of battered immigrant women. The sorts of changes in immigration policy I have advocated would be fairly easy to implement and would considerably reduce the constraints that keep women with dependent immigration status locked into violent marriages.

NOTES

I would like to thank Radhika Balakrishnan, Jennifer Church, Elizabeth A. Kelly, and Susan Zlotnick for generous assistance with earlier drafts of this paper. Thanks to Iris Young, Patrice di Quinzio, and the editors of *Hypatia* for the many ways they have helped to make this paper better.

1. That "undocumented women" suffer similar problems with respect to domestic violence is borne out by Hogeland and Rosen, (1990). However, I limit the scope of my discussion to women who enter the United States legally, and not on women who are illegal immigrants.

2. When violence hits home, *Time Magazine*, 4 July 1994, 12–13.

3. This profile is based on a 1983 survey of 265 American men "actively seeking a partner from the Orient," Mates by mail: This couple catalogues affairs of the heart, *Chicago Sun Times*, 12 August 1984.

4. See Deanna Hodgin, 'Mail-order' brides marry pain to get green cards, *Washington Times*, 16 April 1991, E1; James Leung, Many mail-order brides find intimidation, abuse: Marriages made in China for U.S. citizenship, *San Francisco Chronicle*, 4 September 1990, A9; and Kalinga Seneylatne, Australia: Filipino mail-order brides end up being murdered, *Inter Press Service*, 20 July 1991.

5. Pub. L. No. 101–649, 104 Stat. 4978, Section 701 of the Immigration Act of 1990.

6. 8 U.S.C. 1186 (a) (c) (4) (B) (1990 Supp. II).

7. 8 C.F.R. 216.5(e) (3) (iii) (1992).

8. 8 C.F.R. 216.5 (e) (3) (vii) (1992).

9. A "60 Minutes" segment entitled "Go Back Where You Came From" that aired on Sunday, 22 May 1994, cited a recent CBS survey that came up with this finding.

10. I am indebted to Laurie Shrage for this suggestion.

REFERENCES

Anderson, Michelle J. 1993. License to abuse: The impact of conditional status on female immigrants. *Yale Law Journal* 102 (6): 1401–30.

Bhabha, Jacqueline, Francesca Klug, and Sue Shutter. 1985. *Worlds apart: Women and immigration and nationality law*. London: Pluto Press.

Brooks, Andree. 1985. Single mothers are the targets in marriage fraud, *New York Times*, 13 June 1985, C1.

Calvo, Janet M. 1991. Spouse-based immigration laws: The legacies of coverture. *San Diego Law Review* 28(3): 590–628.

Crenshaw, Kimberlè. N.d. Mapping the margins: Intersectionality, identity politics and violence against women of color. *Stanford Law Review*. Forthcoming.

Henneberger, Melinda. 1992. Well, the Ukraine girls really knock them out. *New York Times*, 15 November 1992, E6.

Hogeland, Chris and Karen Rosen. 1990. *Dreams lost, dreams found: Undocumented women in the land of opportunity*. Booklet published by the Coalition for Immigrant and Refugee Rights and Services, Immigrant Women's Task Force.

Housten, Marion F. 1984. Female predominance in immigration to the United States since 1930: A first look. *International Migration Review* 18(1): 902–25.

Joseph, Raymond A. 1984. American men find Asian brides fill the unliberated bill: Mail-order firms help them look for the ideal woman they didn't find at home. *Wall Street Journal*, 25 January 1984.

Kadohata, Cynthia. 1990. More than he bargained for. *New York Times*, 7 January 1990, 15, book reviews.

Katzenstein, Mary F. 1991–92. Getting women's issues onto the public agenda: Body politics in India. *Samya Shakti* 6: 1–16.

Narayan, Uma. 1993. Paying the price of change: Women, modernization, and arranged marriages in India. In *Women's lives and public policy: The international experience*, ed. Meredeth Turshen and Briavel Holcomb. Westport, CT: Greenwood Press.

Narayan, Uma. 1993. "Standard persons" and "non-standard" vulnerabilities: The legal protection of non-standard interests. In *Justice, law and the state*, ed. Mikael M. Karlsson, Olafur P. Jonsson and Eyja M. Brynjarsdottir. Berlin, Germany: Duncker and Humblot.

Phillips, Anne. 1993. *Democracy and difference*. University Park: Penn State University Press.

Rae, Karen L. 1988. Alienating sham marriages for tougher immigration penalties: Congress enacts the Marriage Fraud Act. *Pepperdine Law Review* 15(1): 181–205.

Rimonte, Nilda. 1991. A question of culture: Cultural approval of violence against women in the Pacific-Asian community and the cultural defense. *Stanford Law Review* 43(6): 1311–26.

Shupe, Anson D., William A. Stacey, and Lonnie R. Hazlewood. 1987. *Violent men, violent couples: The dynamics of domestic violence*. Lexington, MA: Lexington Books.

Sigler, Robert T. 1989. *Domestic violence in context: An assessment of community attitudes*. Lexington, MA: Lexington Books.

Shklar, Judith N. 1991. *American citizenship: The quest for inclusion*. Cambridge: Harvard University Press.

Tajima, Renee E. 1989. Lotus blossoms don't bleed: Images of Asian women. In *Making waves: An anthology of writing by and about Asian-American women*, ed. Asian Women United of California. Boston: Beacon Press.

Tucker, Joe A. 1989. Assimilation to the United States: A study of the adjustment of status and the Immigration Marriage Fraud Statutes. *Yale Law and Policy Review* 7(2): 20–100.

Villipando, Venny. 1989. The business of selling mail-order brides. In *Making waves: An anthology of writing by and about Asian-American women*, ed. Asian Women United of California. Boston: Beacon Press.

8

Intimate Danger

The Case for Preemptive Self-Defense

SHARON E. HARTLINE

STRANGER VIOLENCE—AN EASY CASE

Edwin juggled his groceries down Broadway and turned onto 26th Street. He set his bags down on the stoop of his apartment building and fumbled through his bunch of keys.

When he felt someone walk by him, Edwin realized that he was standing in the middle of the sidewalk. He slid over a step and impatiently continued to fumble through his keys. He glanced up and saw the flash of a switchblade before his face. Edwin stepped back.

"Where's your money? Give it to me, or I'll carve your face."

"I just bought groceries. I have fifty cents on me."

"Sure."

Edwin's attacker slowly walked toward him, waving the blade in front of him. Instantaneously, Edwin pulled a gun from his jacket and shot his assailant in the chest. He ran around the corner to a store and called the police.

The rules of the criminal justice system purport to be "objective" and "neutral." They define crimes and defenses and specify the types of evidence that may be presented. In theory all defendants are treated equally. Circumstances of one individual's case are not unfairly privileged over those in another's.

Let us assume that a prosecutor considers bringing charges against Edwin. The prosecutor would examine Edwin's actions in relation to the legal definitions of murder and the rules of traditional self-defense.[1] Let's take a look at these aspects of the law.

Traditionally, murder has been defined as "the unlawful killing of another 'living human being' with 'malice aforethought'" (LaFave and Scott 1986, 605). More recently murder has been defined in a more discriminating way, distinguishing various degrees of murder with respect to the state of mind of the defendant. Thus first-degree murder is typically defined in terms of the intention to kill, second-degree murder in terms of the intention to cause serious bodily harm or injury, and so forth (605). For a charge of murder to be valid, the following conditions must obtain: the conduct of the defendant must be the "legal cause" of the death of a human victim within a day and a year of defendant's conduct and be accompanied by a "malicious" state of mind (one of those listed above)(611).

A defendant can mount a defense in two basic ways: one can attempt to make an *excuse* for one's action or one can attempt to show that the action is *justified*. Insanity and self-defense are the two most common defenses to a charge of murder.[2] Insanity does not appear to be relevant to Edwin's case. The former is an example of excuse, the latter of justification. Rather, a prosecutor would consider whether or not Edwin's act of homicide was justifiable and consider the guidelines for traditional self-defense.

In pleading self-defense to the charge of murder, one admits causal responsibility for the act of homicide but claims that the act was justified. A successful plea of self-defense necessarily involves three elements: proportional force, reasonable belief of necessity, and imminent danger.[3] Let us examine each element.

Under the requirement of proportional force, the amount of force one uses must be "appropriate" to the attack one faces. Generally, nondeadly force may be used if one reasonably believes that another is about to inflict unlawful bodily harm upon one's person and if it is necessary to use such force to prevent it. Deadly force may only be used when one reasonably believes that another is about to inflict unlawful death or serious bodily harm upon one and that it is necessary to use deadly force to prevent it. This requirement is generally interpreted as ruling out the use of a deadly weapon upon an unarmed assailant (LaFave and Scott 1986, 456).

The requirement of reasonable belief further defines the situation in which the use of force is justifiable. It requires that an individual's belief "in the necessity of using force be reasonable" (457). The "reasonable person" defines the standard of reasonable belief. That is, a belief is said to be reasonable if the average person in the same circumstances would have formed the same beliefs as the defendant. It is important to note that this requirement allows for mistaken beliefs (457). If one's belief was reasonable but mistaken, one's defense is to be upheld.

The third requirement of self-defense is imminent danger. This requirement narrows the situations in which deadly force may be used to those in which one believes that an attack by an assailant will "be almost immediately forthcoming" (458). The logic behind this requirement is that if the attack is not immediate there may be other ways for the individual to avoid it, e.g., by leaving the area or calling the police. However, there are cases where this requirement of imminence may be inappropriate. Consider the case of a kidnapper who says he will kill his hostage in one week. Taken literally, the imminence requirement would require that the hostage wait a week until the kidnapper directly attempted to kill her. However, it seems wrong to expect the kidnapped individual to wait a week to defend herself when she may have opportunities to strike out at the kidnapper prior to an imminent attack. Also, if she were to wait until an attack were imminent, she might be unable to defend herself at that moment.[4] "The proper inquiry is not the immediacy of the threat but the immediacy of the response necessary in defense" (458). Thus it may be necessary to respond outside the situation of an immediate threat.

How would Edwin fare if his actions were scrutinized with respect to traditional self-defense codes? Other things being equal, it is likely that Edwin would not be charged with a crime, for his actions clearly meet all the requirements of traditional self-defense.[5] The proportional force requirement is fulfilled by the fact that Edwin used deadly force in the face of a deadly weapon in the hand of his assailant. The reasonable belief requirement is clearly met in light of the words and actions of the assailant. The imminence requirement is also clearly fulfilled. Edwin saw a knife coming toward him. No one can question the immediacy of this attack.

The requirements of self-defense fit Edwin's case to a tee, and his actions would likely be interpreted as justifiable homicide. In fact, his case is so clear, one wonders if the requirements were not written for cases like Edwin's. Let's turn to a case in which the requirements do not fit.

INTIMATE VIOLENCE—A HARD CASE

Jim had been beating Patty for fourteen years. The beatings began three weeks after they were married. That night a drunken Jim accused Patty of having an affair and landed a blow to her jaw. When Patty regained consciousness, Jim was gone. She staggered into the living room and cried as she rocked in a chair. She tried to call her parents, but how could she expect them to believe something that she didn't even believe herself? Jim had hit her. Later Jim came home and apologized profusely. He said he loved her; he promised he would change; he would stop drinking; he would never hit her again. Patty forgave him. The next day she found a bottle of rosewater on her dresser.

That was fourteen years ago. Before the regular beatings began.

Before Jim kicked, and punched, and pummeled her. Before they moved to yet another town, to yet another of Jim's job sites. Before Jim dragged her across the floor and raped her on the kitchen table. Before she visited the emergency room. Before the police were called. Before she was kicked in the abdomen while she was pregnant with Kelly and then again with Shaun. Before she left and came back and left again. Before she realized she couldn't raise her children on welfare. Before she realized she couldn't raise her children by working because she couldn't afford child care. Before she went back for the last time. Before the bottles of rosewater got smaller and smaller and finally stopped showing up on her dresser. Before the last beating.

The kids were already asleep when Jim finally got home. He had lost his job—again. He smelled like beer and had that look in his eye. "I'm hungry," he growled. Patty tried all her tricks—she whipped up some biscuits and threw steaks on the grill outside. She turned on the radio and tried to soothe herself with Duke Ellington's melodies as she prepared a salad. Jim flew into the kitchen and threw the radio across the room. He was trying to watch the news in the living room and the radio was too goddamn loud. Why did she always have to start a fight? Why? Patty said that she didn't want to fight, and Jim slapped her across the face. She had an answer for everything, didn't she? He slammed her into the stove and repeatedly shoved her head into the wall. He hurled her out the back door and then picked her up and held her arm over the coals. She wailed so loudly that a neighbor came out to see what was happening. Jim pulled her inside, and for hours he pummeled her through the house. The entire time Jim beat her he told her she was ugly and worthless—everybody would be better off if she would just die. Finally, he threw her into the walk-in closet in their room and went into the living room to watch TV. Exhausted, he dozed off.

Patty crawled out of the closet and drew herself up onto the bed. "I can't live through this again." She reached into Jim's nightstand drawer where he kept his revolver. She crept into the living room, and as Jim lay sleeping in the chair, she shot him twice in the chest. Suddenly the doorbell was ringing. She lay the gun down and answered the door. Before her stood two police officers, responding to the neighbor's phone call. "Call an ambulance. My husband needs an ambulance."

If one considers what Patty has to look forward to as she faces the criminal justice system, one quickly realizes that she will traverse a different course than Edwin. Edwin's case would probably not bring a charge from the state's prosecutor, but Patty would almost definitely be charged with a crime. In all likelihood she would be charged with murder, for she shot her partner while he lay sleeping. Patty's actions (getting the gun, walking to the next room and then shooting Jim) would probably be interpreted as showing an intent to kill. In turn, Patty would be charged with first-degree murder. Let's assume that Patty doesn't plea bargain, that is, she doesn't plead guilty to a lesser crime in order to receive a reduced sentence. Let's assume she claims that her actions were justified, and she enters a self-defense plea to the charge of murder. What do traditional self-defense codes mean for individuals like Patty?

The traditional requirements of self-defense are not fulfilled in Patty's case. The most obvious problem in her case is the imminence requirement: there was no immediate and direct threat to her. A sleeping partner cannot present an imminent danger to one's life. It is very likely that Patty would not even be allowed to plead self-defense.[6] She may be forced to use another legal strategy, such as the excuse of insanity. But is it that Patty's act is really unjustifiable? Or are self-defense codes unfairly biased against women in her situation?

Self-defense requirements appear to be neutral; they define a justification for homicide. An examination of cases like Patty's reveals these codes to be anything but neutral.

Under these codes, individuals are portrayed as if their legally relevant interactions with one another can be confined to a "snapshot." That is, self-defense requirements are concerned with what a person believes and does in a single moment. In turn, they carve out a slice of a person's life and ask the individual to define herself with respect to a narrow window of time that constitutes but a moment of her existence. Thus self-defense codes draw attention away from the "movie version" of a defendant, which includes her psychosocial makeup, the dynamics of a long-term relationship with her assailant, and her evolving values. Self-defense codes define these aspects of an individual as legally irrelevant to the act of homicide. Evidence that covers a broader time-frame is admitted on a case by case basis at the discretion of a judge. Traditional self-defense codes demand very little information about the defendant, yet serve as the basis for making important decisions about her. This raises the question of whether such codes are unfairly biased in the assumption they make about persons and situations. Below I will argue that the narrow time-frame assumptions of traditional self-defense are unfairly biased against those who suffer long-term victimization in intimate relationships.[7]

I begin with the imminence requirement, as it is this requirement that binds the rules of self-defense together. That is, if an attack is not imminent, generally one cannot plead self-defense. Therefore, under traditional self-defense, one only speaks of proportional force and reasonable belief when imminence of an attack is apparent.

I also begin with the imminence requirement because the narrow time-frame embodied by self-defense codes is most apparent here. Imminence requires that an individual believe that death or severe bodily harm "be almost immediately forthcoming" (LaFave and Scott 1986, 458). Deadly or nondeadly force used *after* a serious attack does not constitute traditional self-defense; rather it is often interpreted as revenge. Also, traditional self-defense is generally not viewed as including the use of force well *before* an attack, regardless of the probability that the attack will occur sometime in the future. Nonimminent threats that existed in the past or that may come in the not-so-immediate future do not bring into play traditional self-defense.

However, if self-defense codes do not recognize past or future threats as legally significant, how do these codes really portray threats? The narrow time-frame really means that when a threat is not imminent, it no longer exists in any legally significant way; the threat disappears. If one follows the logic of this requirement and considers when "real" threats end, it would seem that there are generally no lingering threats of death.[8] "Real" threats are represented as short-term confrontations by assailants and so are ephemeral.

The types of confrontation this requirement most readily applies to are those in which a defendant and assailant are strangers to one another (see Gillespie 1989, Castel 1990). Here the relation between the assailant and the defendant is momentary or brief. The lines are relatively clear. If the assailant is present and demanding money as in the scenario about Edwin, an imminent threat is present; if one escapes or the assailant leaves, the imminent threat is over. One may be shaken or wonder if the assailant will return. However, an impinging sense that one may be killed in the very near future has ended.

The imminence guideline marginalizes cases of violence within intimate relations. In such relations violent interactions take place over extended periods, and a victim may live with her assailant. If one attempts to interpret a case of violence between intimates with codes that embody a narrow time-frame, one naturally draws the conclusion that if the threat of death or severe bodily harm is not immediate, then there is no threat.

However, this is unfair to battered women. Within violent, intimate relations, even if the threat of death or severe bodily harm is not immediate, the danger for the battered women is still serious, constant, and very real. Just as it seems unreasonable to hold a hostage to an imminence standard in the face of confinement by a terrorist, it is unreasonable to bar a battered woman like Patty from using force and then pleading self-defense. In using the imminence requirement to interpret cases like Patty's, the law ignores the real danger that battered women experience and so commits an injustice against those women.[9]

As discussed earlier, the requirement of proportional force generally rules out using a weapon to defend oneself against an unarmed assailant. The logic underlying this requirement seems to be that it is unfair to have an extreme advantage over your assailant. A "fair fight" ensues when neither the defendant nor the assailant is armed, or when both are armed. A principle of equality is thus implied by the requirement of proportional force. And the assumption is made that unarmed individuals are about the same in size, strength, and fighting prowess. Does this notion of equality favor certain individuals? If so, which individuals does it marginalize?

This notion of equality applies best to a case of a barroom brawl where (generally) men enter into fights. In a brawl a fight proceeds blow for blow until one man falls, or the police are called and the fight is broken up. What underlies this vision of equality, then, is a fight scene among individuals who are more or less equally matched (Gillespie 1989, 6).

What is not envisioned by this requirement is a scene in a household in which a man of greater weight, strength, and fighting prowess slugs his female partner. The requirement of proportional force typically does not take into account the physical differences that often exist between the sexes. It also does not take into account how abusers may gain a psychological advantage over their partners through patterns of repeated abuse. Battered women's knowledge of the level of their abusers' brutality and the deep fear that they experience before, during, and after attacks put them at a serious psychological disadvantage.

The requirement of reasonable belief focuses on the person's belief in the moment that she uses force against an assailant. However, this standard is defined by the law in an insufficiently discriminating way in terms of the beliefs of the "average person." Such a definition means that if under similar circumstances the average person would form the same beliefs as the defendant, then the defendant's belief is reasonable.

However, the average person is not an individual who has experienced long-term violence and the type of victimization suffered by battered women. Nor does the average person understand such victimization. The average person partakes in intimate relationships that are relatively tranquil in comparison to battering relationships.[10] She or he transposes this understanding of a "normal" relationship with a battered woman's experience and concludes that an individual poses no threat to his partner unless he presents an imminent threat.

The law's definition of reasonable belief is biased in two ways. First, it reinforces the imminence requirement and, in turn, entrenches the narrow-time frame of traditional self-defense codes even more deeply. Second, it discounts the actual threats to battered women which may not be imminent but are constant and real.

More appropriate than the law's "average person" standard would be an "average battered woman" standard.[11] An average battered woman standard would treat battered women more fairly by reflecting the kind of knowledge battered women possess but the average person lacks. In the next section I develop a new form of self-defense plea incorporating a reasonable belief standard that is responsive to the special understanding battered women have of their relationships.

PREEMPTIVE SELF-DEFENSE—A NONTRADITIONAL CASE

Traditional self-defense codes require that women like Patty force the description of their actions into a narrow time-frame that is biased in favor of stranger violence. In view of this bias, how is it possible for the criminal justice system to fairly adjudicate cases like Patty's? My answer is that the system can be fair only if it incorporates a new type of self-defense plea which I call preemptive self-defense.

Three strategies define preemptive self-defense. First, preemptive self-defense would abolish the imminence requirement in cases where individuals are repeatedly and seriously assaulted by the same person. Second, the requirement of reasonable belief would be reinterpreted. Third, the requirement of proportionality would be retained, although certain assumptions made under traditional self-defense would be rejected. This proposal would have the effect of opening up the time-frame under which a person could legally use deadly force in self-defense by allowing for the use of such force in the face of death or severe bodily harm that is reasonably believed to be forthcoming, even if not immediately.

The first element of preemptive self-defense is the rejection of the imminence requirement. However much the imminence requirement is appropriate to cases involving violence between strangers, it is inadequate within intimate relationships that involve patterns of violence and severe power inequalities. Owing to the power imbalance between the battered woman and her abuser, if a battered woman waits until a threat of death or severe bodily harm is imminent, it is too late for her; she will be overpowered by the abuser. Just as an imminence requirement does not make sense in the case of a hostage, it does not make sense in the case of a battered woman. By eliminating the imminence requirement, preemptive self-defense gives a woman who is powerless in the face of a conscious batterer a fair chance to defend herself.

The second element of preemptive self-defense doctrine is a reinterpretation of the requirement of reasonable belief. Under traditional self-defense, reasonable belief is understood as the belief of the average person. Yet there are severe restrictions on what the average person can understand and appreciate. As the average person has not experienced long-term victimization at the hand of an intimate, there is a tendency in the average person to discount long-term victimization and the severity of threats contained therein. In the understanding of the average person a reasonable belief of death or severe bodily harm requires an imminent threat from the assailant.

Given these tendencies of the average person, it seems that a more appropriate standard of reasonable belief would be one that is tailored to women in battering relationships. In such a relationship a woman could reasonably believe that a preemptive strike is necessary. That is, a woman could reasonably believe that if she waited until a threat was imminent, she would be unable to effectively defend herself due to the power inequality between her partner and herself. In turn, the requirement of reasonable belief in the case of preemptive self-defense is defined via the "reasonable battered woman" standard. That is, a woman's belief in the necessity of killing her batterer in a nonconfrontational situation is reasonable if the average woman when put in the situation of long-term abuse would believe that the only effective way to defend herself is to kill in a preemptive fashion. Two main considerations help to dictate whether the killing was necessary: whether her batterer posed a real threat to cause her death or grave bodily harm and whether the woman had a viable option of safely exiting the relationship. Aspects of the woman's experience that may help a jury define whether a particular woman's belief in the necessity of using lethal force was reasonable could include the severity of the battering and her attempts to use the helping professions, including the police.

The third element of preemptive self-defense, the proportional force requirement, remains similar to its counterpart in traditional self-defense. The only difference is that preemptive self-defense would reject the assumption that has often been used in applying the principle of proportional force, namely, that one can only use a weapon in the event that one's assailant also bears a weapon. Even with respect to traditional self-defense, courts are beginning to recognize that there are exceptions in which that assumption does not apply. The existence of substantial inequalities in size and strength as well as the presence of multiple assailants constitute such exceptions (LaFave and Scott 1987, 456). In these exceptions inequalities between individuals are recognized in applying the principle of proportional force. In preemptive self-defense, no assumption is made concerning the equality of the parties, and accordingly, it would allow a battered woman to use a weapon against her batterer even if he were unarmed.

I want to stress here that preemptive self-defense is not a special protection only for battered women like Patty. First, it is not a model of self-defense exclusively for heterosexual women. Although I use a heterosexual woman as my model, preemptive self-defense could be used by any victim of battering regardless of gender or sexual persuasion. If this is the case, then other victims of battering, besides heterosexual women, could also use this defense. Second, I do not view preemptive self-defense only as a defense for victims who suffer abuse at the hands of their partners. Preemptive self-defense could be used by other victims of long-term violence, such as victims of child abuse or elderly people suffering abuse at the hands of their family members. These applications of preemptive self-defense are possible, for this defense uses intimate but coercive relationships as a model rather than relying on the model of violence between strangers.

A doctrine of preemptive self-defense would no doubt raise considerable controversy. In the remainder of this essay, I discuss some of the objections that may be raised against it and respond to the objections.

The first objection questions why preemptive self-defense should be allowed in cases in which a woman remains in an abusive relationship. Someone may argue that because the woman stayed in the battering relationship, she is partly responsible for the danger in which she found herself. The woman could have removed herself from the abusive situation, thereby averting the need to use preemptive deadly force against her abuser.

While it is true that battered women often make a voluntary choice to stay in the relationship up to a certain point, those who kill their abusers typically have decided that the relationship cannot be salvaged. External impediments, however, restrict their exit options, so that in many cases killing their abusers is the only feasible way they have of severing the relationship and preserving their own lives.

The agency of a battered woman is limited by external factors in ways that undercut the charge that she is responsible for the danger in which she finds herself. Batterers will often track down their partners and use violence to coerce them into remaining in the relationship. At times batterers will even threaten the lives of their children in their efforts to prevent the woman from effectively exercising her exit option.

Moreover, another external limitation involves the scarcity of public resources provided for battered women by state and local organizations. Battered women cannot always count on family support, and shelter space is limited.[12] Battered women are often faced with homelessness if they decide to flee their batterers.[13] Again, battered women's exit options are severely limited by factors beyond their control.

In light of these external limitations on their agency, it does not make sense to blame all battered women for failing to safely and nonviolently sever their relationships; they are not responsible for the lack of feasible exit options. Nor is it fair for the law to deny them the only mode of self-defense, preemptive self-defense, with which they can effectively protect themselves.[14] In any given case, the question of a woman's feasible exit options should be a matter to be decided by the court. The point is that battered women should not automatically be denied the plea of self-defense if they kill their batterers in nonconfrontational situations.

The second objection invokes the fear of a slippery slope. Some may be concerned that preemptive self-defense could be abused by people who are not in abusive relationships. For example, wives may be encouraged to kill their husbands for their life insurance policies and then plead self-defense. Or children may be tempted to kill their parents for an inheritance. The result would be many more truly unjustified homicides in which the perpetrator goes free.

This objection would have validity if preemptive self-defense eliminated all the traditional requirements of self-defense. However, requirements of reasonableness and proportional force would still be in place, and the defendant still needs to prove that these requirements were met. Undoubtedly, some people will seek to abuse preemptive self-defense, but all defenses are subject to such abuse and that is not a peculiar liability of preemptive self-defense.

The third objection maintains that a doctrine of preemptive self-defense would foster more killings in another way. Some may argue that the doctrine would encourage battered women to kill their husbands sooner, before some effective intervention might occur. The result would be an increase in the number of killings.

One must remember that while battered women fear their abusers, they are also in love with them and committed to their relationships with their batterers. Especially in the early stages but even in later stages of battering relationships, love is often one of the reasons that women remain with their batterer or return to the batterer after they have fled (Hoff 1990, 44; Gelles and Straus 1988, 154). For battered women, violence is a last resort. By the time they even contemplate such violence the possibility of effective intervention to repair the relationship is virtually nonexistent. Their care for the batterer is ultimately what will keep them from killing their husbands indiscriminately within earlier stages of their relationships.

CONCLUSION

In this essay I have shown how traditional self-defense doctrine is tailored for relationships between strangers and unfairly biased against women in long-term abusive relationships. I have proposed a new form of self-defense called preemptive self-defense in order to counteract this bias and give women a fair chance of protecting themselves against their abusers. It is my hope that those in the criminal justice system will seriously consider the adoption of preemptive self-defense.[15]

NOTES

1. Murder and self-defense codes vary from state to state. What follows is a general conception of these codes derived from the text of Wayne R. LaFave and Austin W. Scott (1986).

2. In using an insanity plea, a defendant claims that due to a defect in her ability to reason, she is generally or was temporarily unable to determine right from wrong. In effect, she claims that she was not responsible for her actions and, therefore, is not guilty of the crime (LaFave and Scott 1986, 304).

3. Duty to retreat is also a requirement of self-defense and raises interesting questions about intimate violence and battered women. Generally it is agreed that one need not retreat from one's own home in order to evade an attack. However, some argue that one must retreat if the individual against whom you use force is a cohabitator of the domicile. Others argue that an attacker's status within the domicile ought not to require retreat, as the defendant has no safer place to which to retreat (LaFave and Scott 1986, 461). Within the use of traditional self-defense, these arguments have important implications for the ability of battered women to use deadly force against men with whom they live. However, for the purposes of this paper I will discuss the other requirements of self-defense.

4. LaFave and Scott (1986) borrow this case from Paul H. Robinson (1984).

5. In claiming that this is an "easy case," I do not mean to imply that race, ethnicity, and class are not relevant to prosecution decisions. The disparity in arrest, prosecution, and sentencing with respect to race, ethnicity, and class is well documented. See Mann (1993), Lynch and Patterson (1991), and Reiman (1979). For the purposes of this paper I focus on the stranger bias implicit within traditional conceptions of self-defense. A fuller account of biases of the system would examine the intersection of race, class, and gender as they enter into the system.

6. Although most battered women kill in the presence of an imminent threat, those who kill outside the context of an imminent threat are precluded from pleading self-defense. See "Developments" (1993) and Kinports (1988).

7. I borrow the term *narrow time frame* from Mark Kelman (1981).

8. Susan Estrich (1987) speaks of a similar problem with respect to what she calls "real" rape. Estrich argues that society, particularly individuals working in the criminal justice system, generally view rape by a stranger as "real" rape.

9. Boyle (1990) argues that the imminence requirement has traditionally focused on sudden emergencies and ignored "on-going, developing emergencies" that are more prevalent in intimate relationships.

10. It is estimated that in the United States approximately 1.8 million women are severely beaten each year. Approximately 25 percent of all emergency room visits by women are related to battering. Although these statistics call attention to a severe problem in this country, they do not suggest that a majority of women (or men) in this country suffer from repeated abuse at the hands of their partners. See Hotaling et al. (1988) and Goldberg and Tomlanovich (1984).

11. For discussions concerning standards of reasonable belief and attempts to incorporate a more subjective standard of reasonableness into traditional self-defense codes, see Maguigan (1991), Ogle (1989), Schneider (1986), and Blackman (1986).

12. For a discussion of the lack of resources available to battered women, see Frieze and Browne (1989), Schechter (1982), and Dobash and Dobash (1979).

13. A high percentage of homeless women report being battered. In one study approximately three-fourths of women report battering as the leading cause of their homelessness. See Hagen (1987), D'Ercole and Stuening (1990), and "Homeless Women" (1991).

14. Members of our society could mitigate external limitations on battered women's agency by opening more shelters and pressuring batterers to change their behavior, e.g. by demanding that they be prosecuted. However, many members of our society remain unwilling to expend the resources that would bring about these changes.

15. I would like to thank Anita Allen, Andrew Altman, Amy Baehr, Eva Feder Kittay, and Peter Williams for providing me with critical comments on earlier drafts of this essay.

REFERENCES

Blackman, Julie. 1986. Potential uses for expert testimony: Ideas toward the representation of battered women who kill. *Women's Rights Law Reporter* 9: 227–238.

Boyle, Christine. 1990. The battered wife syndrome and self-defense: Lavalle V.R. *Canadian Journal of Family Law* 9: 171–179.

Castel, Jacqueline. 1990. Discerning justice for battered women who kill. *University of Toronto Faculty Law Review* 48: 229–258.

D'Ercole, A., and E. Stuening. 1990. Victimization among homeless women: Implications for service delivery. *Journal of Community Psychology* 18: 141–152.

Developments—Domestic violence. 1993. *Harvard Law Review* 106: 1498–1597.

Dobash, R. Emerson, and Russell Dobash. 1979. *Violence against wives: A case against patriarchy*. New York: Free Press.

Estrich, Susan. 1987. *Real rape*. Cambridge: Harvard University Press.

Frieze, Irene Hanson, and Angela Browne. 1989. Violence in marriage. In *Family violence*, ed. Lloyd Ohlin and Michael Tonry. Chicago: University of Chicago Press, 163–218.

Gelles, Richard, and Murray Straus. 1988. *Intimate violence*. New York: Simon and Schuster.

Gillespie, Cynthia. 1989. *Justifiable homicide*. Columbus: Ohio State University Press.

Goldberg, W. G., and M. C. Tomlanovich. 1984. Domestic violence victims in the emergency department. *Journal of the American Medical Association* 251: 3259–3264.

Hagen, J. L. Gender and hopelessness. 1987. *Social Work* 32: 312–316.

Hoff, Lee Ann. 1990. *Battered women as survivors*. New York: Routledge.

Homeless women: Moving toward a comprehensive model. 1991. *American Psychologist* 46:1161–1169.

Hotaling G., D. Finkelhor, J. Kirkpatrick, and M. Straus, eds. 1988. *Family abuse and its consequences*. Newbury Park: Sage.

Kelman, Mark. 1981. Interpretive constructions in the substantive criminal law. *Stanford Law Review* 33: 591–673.

Kinports, Kit. 1988. Defending battered women's self-defense claims. *Oregon Law Review* 67: 397–423.

LaFave, Wayne R., and Austin W. Scott. 1986. *Substantive criminal law*. 2nd ed. St. Paul: West.

Lynch, Michael, and E. Britt Patterson, eds. 1991. *Race and criminal justice*. New York: Harrow and Heston.

Maguigan, Holly. 1991. Battered women and self-defense: myths and misconceptions in current reform proposals. *University of Pennsylvania Law Review* 140: 379–486.

Mann, Coramae Richey. 1993. *Unequal justice: A question of color*. Bloomington: Indiana University Press.

Ogle, Nancy. 1989. Murder, self-defense, and the battered woman syndrome in Kansas [State v. Stewart, 243 Kan. 639, 763 P.2d 572 (1988)]. *Washburn Law Journal* 28: 400–412.

Reiman, Jeffrey. 1979. *The rich get richer and the poor get prison*. New York: Wiley.
Robinson, Paul H. 1984. *Criminal law defenses*. Vol. 1. St. Paul: West.
Schechter, Susan. 1982. *Women and male violence: The visions and struggles of the battered women's movement*. Boston: South End Press.
Schneider, Elizabeth. 1986. Describing and changing: Women's self-defense work and the problem of expert testimony on battered women's syndrome. *Women's Rights Law Reporter* 9: 196–222.

9

Mixed Black and White Race and Public Policy

NAOMI ZACK

There is so much myth involved in the classification of Americans into black and white racial categories that the facts about race are part of the subject of Racial Theory. Racial Theory is the intellectual structure within which it is possible to develop an understanding of how *race* is socially constructed. In that theoretical context, the ordinary concept of race in the United States, which purports to be about something hereditary and physical, has no scientific foundation; neither does this concept have an ethical rationale that ensures just treatment for individuals or a maximization of benefits for all concerned groups. In this essay, I mean to sketch the historical, empirical, and emancipatory context for permitting American individuals of mixed black and white race to identify themselves racially. Such permission would be a matter of future public policy in many different political, intellectual, scientific, and educational contexts—it would reflect a massive paradigm shift in emancipatory black and white racial thought and action, just as the historical denial of permission has reflected white racism and racial oppression. Because the case of black and white racial mixture has always been the site of the most stringent impositions of racial purity in American culture, argument for self-identification in that case is an important beginning for unraveling racial mythology in general.

Hypatia vol. 10, no. 1 (Winter 1995) © by Naomi Zack

THE ONE-DROP RULE

The racial categories of black and white race form a rigid, asymmetrical classification system in the United States. On a folk level, it is assumed that an individual is either black or white, but not both.[1] However, there have been individuals acknowledged as having both black and white ancestors since seventeenth-century colonial days, so something besides the facts of heredity as they are understood in other cases of ancestral diversity must be at work here.[2] At work is the one-drop rule, which has been reflected in the United States census since 1920. According to the one-drop rule, an individual is racially black if he or she has one black ancestor anywhere in her genealogical line of descent, and this holds regardless of whether, or how many, white, Asian, or Native American ancestors were also present. By contrast, a person is white only if she has no nonwhite ancestors. That is the logic behind American racial designations, and its only basis is the public policy that was associated with black chattel slavery. Nevertheless, Americans assume that there are biological foundations for racial classifications. That there are no such foundations is worth a few minutes to review.

THE BIOLOGY OF RACE

First of all, the drop in the one-drop rule refers to a drop of blood. It used to be believed that ancestors literally passed their blood on to their descendants and that this blood mixed with the blood of other ancestors whenever a child was conceived. We now know that this is nonsense: maternal and fetal blood circulate separately; blood is not passed on, but its type is copied genetically; there are no general racial blood types—human blood types are distinguished for transfusion purposes, and full siblings may have incompatible blood types.[3]

According to biological anthropologists, the racial unit is not an individual but a population that has more of some physical traits than other populations. There probably never have been pure races because racial populations have rarely been isolated from members of other racial populations. Social taboos may substitute for geographical isolation in breeding populations, but no such taboo has ever been completely effective; and even if such a taboo were effective, the physical traits that would be designated as racial traits would be a matter of cultural choice and not biology.[4] Biologically, there is no *general* genetic marker for race. There are genes associated with particular physical traits that have been socially designated as racial traits, but no gene for white race, black race, Asian race, or any other race has been scientifically identified during the centuries in which the modern idea of race has been in circulation.[5] It is important, in this regard, to note the contrast with sex. Although all individuals do not neatly divide into XX or XY on a chromosomal level because of borderline and more complex combinations of X and Y, nevertheless, X and Y are identifiable as general sexual markers that determine more specific sexual characteristics.[6] Even after all social constructions of sex and gender are filtered out, the overwhelming majority of individuals are XX or XY. This general XX-ness or XY-ness causes or explains less general physical characteristics, which themselves have underlying genes. For example, the presence of XX predicts the presence of the gene for ovaries. If it were the case that all of the specific physical sexual characteristics varied along continua and that XX and XY did not exist, then there would be no general genetic basis for sex. That is the situation with race. The specific physical characteristics that different cultures have designated as racial in different ways, vary, without any underlying general genetic marker that causes them or that can be used to explain their presence. Once one realizes this, it becomes clear that *race* is what cultures take it to be. As a *general* biological characteristic, which is how racist cultures construct race, race does not exist. But given racist constructions, race has a powerful social reality, and it is therefore an extraordinarily complex subject to both refer to and dissolve at the same time.

Due to the one-drop rule, an American classified as black may have more genes that cause physical characteristics considered to be white than an American classified as white. The presence of a black ancestor does not ensure the presence of any of the genes of that ancestor beyond the second generation. This is because individuals get one-half of their genes from each parent, and there is no guarantee that they have genes from all four grandparents—the "racial" genes, that is, the genes underlying perceptible traits that the culture has designated as "racial" traits, might be just as likely to drop out as the non-racial ones. Lest it seem contradictory to speak—even in quotes—of racial genes in the same breath as a claim that there are no genes for race, it should be remembered that a racial gene is a gene for a trait that has been *culturally* determined to be a racial trait. There is nothing specifically racial in a biological sense about a "racial" gene. "Racial" genes are genes that underlie skin color, hair texture, and other physical characteristics of human beings. They otherwise have nothing extra, physically or genetically, to distinguish them from other "nonracial" genetic differences, except that these "racial" genes have been designated, picked out, identified, as "racial." Finally, it should also be noted that so-called racial genes do not get inherited in clumps. Most genes are subject to dispersal and recombination at conception, and the genes behind the physical traits that society has picked out as racial are no more likely to get passed on together than are genes for traits to which society attaches no racial significance.[7] This is why individuals who are otherwise presumed to be of the same race do not all have the same racial traits.

Groups of individuals from the same geographical area, such as a part of precolonial Africa, may share some biological traits among their members, such as dark brown skin and curly hair. But the designation of these traits as racial is a purely cultural construction. Ever since the colonial period racial designation has accompanied the oppression and exploitation, or domination, of the groups so designated. During the seventeenth, eighteenth, and nineteenth centuries, the domination of what are now called third world populations was practiced by Europeans on a global scale. The physical differences from Europeans of these third world peoples and the assumed difference in geographical origins of their ancestors became the basis of modern European concepts of race. Until the 1920s, social scientists also assumed that cultural differences among racially designated groups were physically inherited.[8]

THE AMERICAN HISTORY OF THE ONE-DROP RULE

In colonial America, prisoners from Africa were worked as slaves, along with Europeans and Native Americans. By the end of the eighteenth century, these African slaves were known as "n"egroes—the 'n' was always lowercase until the Harlem Renaissance—and only "n"egroes could be enslaved in the United States.[9] By that time, those individuals who were then called "negroes" and who historians after the 1930s refer to as "Negroes," but who should probably be referred to as American slaves, had been conceptualized as a distinct race from whites, lower in biological hierarchy and intellectually and morally inferior to whites (Zack 1993, 116–122). So, first African prisoners were made slaves and then they were defined as a "race" of "negroes." Every member of this "race" of "negroes" was posited as having the characteristics of a population that was essentially different from the "white" population. (Unfortunately, the limitations of this essay preclude investigation of the development of cultural constructions of racial whiteness, not to mention the racialization of the indigenous American population.) Why was it necessary to posit that difference as a matter of public policy? Because the white population, as a matter of public policy, based on Enlightenment political theory, was constructed as having a human birthright of freedom (Immerwahr and Burke 1993, 26–7). The next conceptual step in the American racializing program, insofar as it was connected with the institution of slavery, entailed an identification of enslavement itself as a determinant of race.

The common assumption among contemporary historians is that in English North America, "Negroes" were enslaved because they were "n"egroes.[10] In fact, the situation was worse than that: African prisoners and their descendants were enslaved and kept in slavery for the simple reason that they or their ancestors were first enslaved. This was accomplished through the mediating concept of race, specifically the concept of "negro race."

The final North American public policy regarding the children of female slaves was beneficial to the economic interests of the owners of female slaves. As owners of living things, these owners wanted to have secure ownership of the offspring of what they already owned. Since only "n"egroes could be owned as slaves, the only way that they could own the children of their slaves were if those children were "n"egroes. As everyone has always known, the fathers of many children of women slaves were not slaves or "n"egroes. Therefore, to protect the economic interests of slave owners in English North America, the institution of slavery gave birth to the one-drop rule, as a matter of public policy. By contrast, in Louisiana under French rule and throughout Latin America, manumission of children with slave mothers and free white fathers was common all through the period of slavery. Those children were recognized as mixed black and white race.[11]

It became illegal to import slaves into the United States in the 1830s. Then the cotton gin increased the speed with which cotton could be processed, and the need for slave labor to grow cotton increased. The large-scale miscegenation of the slave population due to generations of sexual exploitation of female slaves by free whites, as well as intraracial miscegenation within the "n"egro population, resulted in an otherwise embarrassing number of "whiter" slave offspring, who, if they were not automatically designated "n"egroes, because only negroes could be enslaved, would have presented a disastrous loss of capital for the slave economy. After Louisiana came under the rule of Anglo-Americans, and throughout slavery in the United States after the 1850s, all the children of slave mothers, regardless of their paternity, were assumed to have the racial status of their mothers. This was of course contrary to English custom and law, which supported patriarchal descent in all other matters of lineage and property (Zack 1993, 57–61).

Even though, originally, the economics of slavery determined the public policy of the one-drop rule, the abolition of slavery did not mitigate the application of this rule. Between the Civil War and 1915 the one-drop rule became the law in most states, where it was expressed in so-called antimiscegenation laws that proscribed interracial marriage (Zack 1993, 79–82).[12] Ironically, this policy was locked in place among African Americans during the Harlem Renaissance, when many prominent mixed-race black spokespersons explicitly took up Negro identities to the conceptual obliteration of their white ancestors. At the time, there was no choice in the matter because the United States census no longer recognized a category of mixed race; so anyone who was "black" according to the one-drop rule was not accepted as white in American society (Zack 1993, 95–112). Even though the antimiscegenation laws were struck down by the United States Supreme Court in 1967, the one-drop rule has never been successfully challenged as a basis for racial classification. Officially, and according to custom, an American is black given one black ancestor, no matter how many white ancestors she has and regardless of her social experiences.

MIXED BLACK AND WHITE RACE AND PRESENT PUBLIC POLICY: IN PRINCIPLE

The American history of racial categorization was unjust. Against the widespread understanding that the United States has a long history of racial injustice, this might occasion a yawn. However, we are still trapped in the rigidity of notions of biological racial difference that presuppose pseudoscientific ideas of race. And the one-drop rule is still public policy. Whites assume that this is how blacks want it, and blacks continue to reproduce it socially for a variety of reasons, including the preservation of hard-won affirmative action benefits that reinforce "pure" racial identities, family and community loyalty, and the continuing devaluation and oppression of individuals with African ancestry by individuals without African ancestry.

Nonetheless, many individuals of mixed black and white race, especially of first generation "mixture," experience the one-drop rule not only as racist in itself, against them, but as fundamentally supportive of the false categories of race. The whole idea of race requires an assumption of a population stable in certain physical characteristics, which will "breed true." That is, the idea of race rests on fantasies of racial purity.

The question is not whether it is better for an individual with black and white ancestors to be designated white, or partly black and partly white, than all black, because addressing the question in those terms accepts a foundation of the unjust treatment of blacks by whites. Rather, these are the pertinent questions: Since there is no such thing as race and our present legacy of racial categories is shot through with pseudoscience and racist habits and beliefs, how should "race" be determined? Who should decide what race I am to myself? How should anyone determine the "race" of another person? Notice that there are two levels to these questions. If race is a fiction, then the person of pure race is in the same position regarding these questions as the person of mixed race. But, if race is accepted or recognized as a social reality, then, in the context of the nonsense of the one-drop rule, the person of mixed black and white race presents a special problem to herself and others.

I would like to stay on the level that all notions of race are fictions, but I don't think that is yet feasible at this time in American culture. Therefore, I am provisionally going to go along with the fiction that there are such things as black and white race, as a basis on which to consider the ongoing one-drop rule from the standpoint of an individual of mixed black and white race. How should mixed black and white individuals identify themselves and be racially identified by others at this time?

I think that the only emancipatory answer to that question has to be provided by the individuals themselves. It has been estimated that between 75 percent and 90 percent of all African Americans have some white ancestry. Within this group, the group likely to self-identify as mixed race is probably no more than 10 percent or 15 percent (Williamson 1980, 9–16, 125). If, however, there is no scientific foundation to the concept of race, that is, if races do not exist, then neither do mixed races exist. The facts of racial mixture, namely the existence of individuals of mixed race, undermine the very notion of race, which presupposes racial "purity." Since there never have been pure races, it is impossible to calculate degrees of racial mixture. Still, despite these puzzles, on a folk level, Americans take race very seriously, and it is only fair that those individuals who do not fit into any one of the recognized racial categories have an opportunity to identify themselves, that is, to choose their own racial identities.

As it stands now, most people "choose" a racial identity after they have learned how others identity them. This is a passive process of choice, closer to socially approved assent than free choice. Children with a black parent and a white parent, and even greater degrees of racial diversity, are now obligated to "choose" which box to check as they move through the various institutional processes of racial identification in the culture. They choose the box that "best" applies to them, but nothing in official or social reality permits them a choice of *everything* that applies to them in racial terms.

Broadly speaking, even given the racial fictions in place, every person defines for herself what it means to be what she is racially by learning about her family history. Using present energy and making commitments for the future, she invents her racial identity at the same time that she tells herself she is discovering it. This is an existential point. The person of mixed race is as entitled to this existential process, with its self-defining illusion of invention masquerading as discovery, as is the person of presumptively pure race. In the present case, she has a right to be mixed race rather than black race or white race. At present, she can be white only if she lies about the presence of a black ancestor. And she can only eschew all racial identity, should she choose to invent herself on the ground of her discovery that race is a fiction, if she refuses to participate in many cultural contexts that might otherwise benefit her. This right for a mixed race person to be mixed race seems to be a fundamental requirement for psychological and social health, but it is as difficult to create a general justification for it as it is to justify the right of human beings to selfhood. In fact, the generality of the justification can only be anchored by something beyond American law and culture, as I will try to do in a moment. United States federal racial classification systems presently allow for only four racial categories—black, white, Asian and Native American, with an added ethnic rider of Hispanic or non-Hispanic. Where categories of "other" have been added to state forms, according to "Directive 15," the components of "other" in individual cases are reassessed, and if an individual has a black ancestor, the individual is reclassified as black (see Fernández 1995; Graham 1995).

In June 1993 the United States House of Representatives Subcommittee on Census, Statistics, and Postal Personnel heard public testimony concerning the inclusion of a multiracial category in the U.S. census. As of this writing, the outcome of those hearings is inconclusive. It is not merely that even liberal public record keeping is constrained by outmoded concepts of race in the population at large. The inconclusiveness is further diffused by the expressed concern of African American interest groups that if part of their presently designated constituency of African Americans redesignates itself as multiracial, the remaining constituency will lose affirmative action gains (see Wright 1994). Nonetheless, many black and white mixed-race Americans continue to wonder whether one-drop black racial identification, based on biological fiction, should be supported at the expense of more accurate description and record keeping. It is difficult to see how anyone except the mixed-race individuals themselves would have a right to decide that matter.

According to international moral-political rights theories, as stated in the United Nations Charter, the right of Americans of mixed race to identify themselves and be identified, that is, recognized, as a distinct racial category would seem to be related to other social and political rights of self-determination. The analogue to national self-determination in this political sense, for mixed black and white Americans, is racial self-identification. As with emerging nations, united within themselves by geography, self-identification precedes identification and recognition by others.

Mixed-race people do not constitute geographically continuous, potentially sovereign entities as groups, so there is no issue of political independence at stake. But, neither do racially pure groups present a basis for national sovereignty—except within separatist movements, which in the United States, at least, have been motivated by extremist and supremacist ideologies. There has been, of course, some geographically based political districting of black racial interests in the United States in recent years for the presumed benefit of blacks. If some of the people in those districts revise their identification as racially mixed and not-black, there is concern that the remaining blacks would not benefit as much as when the group was larger (Wright 1994). But, the resulting groups could form coalitions. And the racism against blacks that presupposes nonexistent general differences among all members of racially designated populations will have been undermined to the extent that everyone publicly acknowledges that some American blacks have white ancestors and are therefore not, strictly speaking, "black." If all blacks are not black because some of them are also white, then the rigid differences that people mistakenly assume have a biological foundation would begin to soften in American folk thought. This would in turn undermine racism as a psychological attitude based on an assumption of strong physical difference.

Furthermore, the United Nations Charter expresses an international moral-political consensus that all individuals are entitled to the same rights, regardless of race and color (Article 2). If blacks and whites have a right to identify themselves as such, then so do mixed black and white individuals. The United Nations Charter also stipulates that no one may be compelled to belong to an association (Article 20, #2). If the one-drop rule does not have the biological foundation it has been assumed to have in American history, then no one should be compelled to be black. And, if race itself is a fiction, then no one should be compelled to identify herself or be identified by others in any way at all racially, if she so chooses. Failure to identify in some specific way racially, or in any way racially, ought not to put anyone at a disadvantage compared to those who do so identify.

In the context of freedom of association as stipulated by the United Nations Charter, racial identification has not yet been addressed because it has been assumed up to now that racial identification has a neutral, factual foundation. Indeed, the international theoretical work on race has primarily focused on the promulgation of the findings of the social and biological sciences of the first half of the twentieth century, which concluded that cultural differences among racial groups are matters of historical contingency rather than physical heredity.[13] But, since there is no empirical, factual foundation for the American one-drop rule of black racial classification, in many cases of mixed race, there are no neutral, factual determinants for racial identification. Given this absence of an assumed biological foundation for racial identification, if it is, for whatever reason, necessary that mixed-race individuals be identified by race, those individuals have a right to choose their racial identifications, based on the United Nations Charter right to freedom of association.

In situations where an individual's chosen racial designation is at odds with how others classify her, care should be taken by those others to refine the empirical basis on which they make their identifications. And in many cases, the reliance on socially coerced self-identification, that is, the one-drop rule, is so strong that experts will have to dispense with racial categories altogether. An interesting example of this is found in recent American Medical Association policy recommendations for the detection of sickle-cell anemia in infants. It was formally believed that infants of nonwhite racial groups were at higher risk for this disease; however, medical practitioners have come to realize that they have no reliable criteria for identifying all infants racially, so the recommended procedure for detection is to test all infants for sickle-cell anemia, regardless of the racial group to which they seem to belong or are said to belong (Clinton 1991, 2158).

Mixed-race individuals would also have a right to reject all racial identification, just as a full right to freedom in religious affiliation would include the choice of no religious affiliation, or the choice of atheism. I have so far been suggesting that black and white mixed-race Americans would chose to identify as mixed race or nonracial. But even that is too stringent a projection once the false categories begin to crumble. Some people who are mixed black and white race will choose to be black. Others will choose to be white. And still others will choose to identify based on Asian or Native American ancestry.

MIXED BLACK AND WHITE RACE AND PRESENT PUBLIC POLICY: IN FACT

Parallel to the foregoing theoretical justification for self-identification for individuals of mixed race, there is a demographic and grass-roots basis for such self-identification that public policy theorists and planners need to allow into their awareness as specific contexts make relevant. Statistically, mixed-race births in the United States have increased 26 times as much as pure-race births over recent decades.[14] And now, for the first time in American history, due to the success of the Civil Rights movement, albeit incomplete and begrudged, there is a generation of mixed black and white individuals who are not ashamed of their racial origins, and whose parents do not experience a need to apologize for having brought them into the world.

Project RACE (Reclassify All Children Equally), an organization originating from efforts to change racial designations of school children in Georgia, has been lobbying legislatures in recent years to include multiracial categories on the U.S. census and in local record keeping. The membership of the Association of MultiEthnic Americans consists of mixed-race families and their children; they actively support one another through social and cultural events and newsletters in which they share their experiences in the larger society that does not recognize their existence as mixed race.[15]

When people from different racial categories have children, as they always have done despite the existence of social or legal strictures, and whether they do so as a result of exploitation, accident, ignorance, or love, fairness in a racial society requires that those children receive the same degree of racial respect as presumptively racially pure children, especially since it is widely assumed that racial identities are constructed in childhood in ways closely connected with self-esteem on deep motivational levels. It is not known to what extent the importance of a child's positive feelings about race is a result of racism in the culture. Neither is it known whether it would be consistent with other aspects of mental health and social adjustment for individuals to eschew all racial identity—even in a racist society. Before the studies can be conducted that will provide empirical answers to these questions, however, the conceptual framework or theoretical assumptions that would otherwise underlie such studies must be reexamined. There is no reason to believe that social scientists are not as burdened by racial mythology as other people.

At this time, for the first time in American academic letters, a small, rapidly increasing number of scholars from varied disciplines are beginning to discuss these issues of microdiversity, and the subject of mixed race is becoming a recognized addition to curricula that address diversity and multiculturalism: Paul Spickard (1989), F. James Davis (1991), Maria P.P. Root (1992), and I (1993, 1995) have recently published book-length works on the topic of mixed race in the United States; and further work is in press as of this writing. (The popular print media and commercial publishing houses are not far behind, or ahead, as the case may be.) The general scholarly topic is *Racial Theory*, the specialization at issue is *Mixed Race* (or *Multirace*), but in practical policy-making contexts, the facts that need to be addressed are the facts of *microdiversity*. The term "microdiversity" points to the reality that many individuals are racially diverse within themselves and not merely diverse as members of groups that are believed, in often erroneous ways, to be racially different from other groups.

The map of the emancipatory scholarship of microdiversity is now on the drawing board: it may be filled in by tracing out the complex varieties of microdiversity which exist in reality; or it may blaze a route to a neo-universalist rejection of the concept of race in both scholarly and popular culture. In historical analyses, microdiversity intersects with critiques of patriarchy because the one-drop rule is a legacy of white male slave owners; and in feminist analyses of contemporary culture, microdiversity intersects with gender because mixed-race women are still stereotyped as exotic, erotic, and morally defective.

In terms of present practice and policy, microdiversity has indeterminate connections with affirmative action. Since the aim of both affirmative action and the scholarship of microdiversity is to improve the institutional situations of individuals who would otherwise be overlooked or abused, both become redundant if they succeed. In the meantime, if affirmative action is just and effective, the facts of microdiversity strengthen its mandate because people of mixed race have never before been positively acknowledged to exist. So long as Americans believe in races, they will believe in racial whiteness, and whites will probably continue to be generally better off than nonwhites. And if affirmative action programs continue to be the chosen strategy for achieving equality, then mixed-race individuals, insofar as they do not belong to the white, privileged, dominant group, would continue to qualify as affirmative action clients (or "patients").

I want to close with a word of caution. Tigers have to be dismounted with great care. It's one thing to understand within a safe forum that race is a biological fiction. In American culture at large, the fiction of race continues to operate as fact, and in situations of backlash against emancipatory progress, the victims of racial oppression, nonwhites, are insulted and injured further for their progress against oppression. If those who practice such second-order oppression begin to employ the truth that race is a fiction, gains already secured against first-order oppression (or in redress of it) could be jeopardized. This is a risk many will find daunting, but the answer is not to back off from the truth but to realize that it will take a while to replace the fictitious cultural realities. If the truth about mixed black and white race and race in general were to be (affirmatively) taught throughout the American educational system, it would take about two generations to have a real effect on the culture—the first generation would learn it in school and teach it to their children.

NOTES

1. For more comprehensive discussions of the inadequacy of the American folk concepts of black and white race, see Zack (1993, 1994).

2. For a book-length treatment of the history of mixed black and white race in the United States, conducted within the traditional racial paradigm, see Williamson (1980).

3. For the facts on blood and race, see Zack (1993, chap. 2 and references).

4. For a discussion of race and breeding, see Zack (1993, chap. 4).

5. For an argument about the *modernity* of contemporary concepts of race, see Bernal (1987, 439–45, 454–5). See also Zack (1996, chap. 12).

6. For a discussion of the development of X and Y as chromosomal markers of sex, see Kevles (1985, 238–50).

7. For discussions of variations in racial genes, see Dubinin (1965, 68–83) and Dunn (1965, 61–67).

8. For accounts and discussions of the history of the concept of race in the social sciences see Leiris (1965) and Wacker (1983).

9. For descriptions of nineteenth century-racial hierarchies and source references, see Zack (1993, 58–61, 78–79).

10. For example, Immerwahr and Burke write, "Only blacks were slaves and slaves were slaves *because* they were black" (1993, 27).

11. The classic comparison of North and South America on this issue is Degler (1971).

12. For further details on the history of antimiscegenation laws, see Sickels (1972).

13. For the United Nations positions on race, culture, and heredity, see "Four Statements on the Race Question" (drafted at Unesco House, Paris) in Kuper (1965, 344–364).

14. For the statistics on the increase of mixed-race marriages and births, see Special Reports (1993, 20–21).

15. See Project Race Newsletter, April 1993 (Roswell, Georgia).

REFERENCES

Bernal, Martin. 1987. *Black Athena*. New Brunswick: Rutgers University Press.

Clinton, Jarrett J. 1991. From the agency for health care policy and research. *Journal of the American Medical Association* 70 (18): 2158.

Davis, F. James. 1991. *Who is black?* University Park: Penn State Press.

Degler, Carl N. 1971. *Neither black nor white: Slavery and race relations in Brazil and the United States*. New York: Macmillan.

Dubinin, N. P. 1965. Race and contemporary genetics. In *Race, science and society*. See Kuper 1965.

Dunn, L. C. 1965. Race and biology. In *Race, science and society*. See Kuper 1965.

Fernández, Carlos A. 1995. Testimony of the Association of MultiEthnic Americans. In *American mixed race: The culture of microdiversity*. See Zack 1995.

Graham, Susan. 1995. The grass roots advocacy. In *American mixed race: Exploring microdiversity*. See Zack 1995.

Immerwahr, John and Michael Burke. 1993. Race and the modern philosophy course. *Teaching Philosophy* 16 (1): 26–27.

Kevles, Daniel J. 1985. *In the name of eugenics*. Berkeley: University of California Press.

Kuper, Leo, ed. 1965. *Race, science, and society*. New York: Columbia University Press.

Leiris, Michael. 1965. Race and culture. In *Race, science and society*. See Kuper 1965.

Root, Maria P.P. 1992. *Racially mixed people in America*. Newbury Park: Sage.

Sickels, Robert J. 1972. *Race, marriage and the law*. Albuquerque: University of New Mexico Press.

Special Reports. 1993. *I-Pride Newsletter* 15(January): 20–21.

Spickard, Paul. 1989. *Mixed blood: Inter-marriage and ethnic identity in twentieth-century America*. Madison: University of Wisconsin Press.

Wacker, R. Fred. 1983. *Ethnicity, pluralism and race*. Westport: Greenwood.

Williamson, Joel. 1980. *New people*. New York: Free Press.

Wright, Lawrence. 1994. One drop of blood. *New Yorker*, 25 July, 46–55.

Zack, Naomi. 1993. *Race and mixed race*. Philadelphia: Temple University Press.

———. 1994. Race and philosophic meaning. *APA Newsletter on Philosophy and the Black Experience* 93: 2.

———. 1995. *American mixed race: The culture of microdiversity*. Lanham: Roman and Littlefield.

———. 1996. *Bachelors of science: Seventeenth century identity then and now*. Philadelphia: Temple University Press.

10

Agency and Alliance in Public Discourses about Sexualities

JANET R. JAKOBSEN

Calls for alliance politics have become prevalent in contemporary feminist ethics and politics, particularly with regard to feminist public sphere actions directed at affecting public policy.[1] Alliances, however, have not always proven easy, nor have they always been effected without significant contradictions. Complexities arising from the contradictions of alliance politics have been particularly notable in the formation of alliances around questions of U.S. public policy and sexuality. In order to analyze some of these complexities I consider a series of alliances and splits enacted in public discourses about sexualities.

The first alliance, the one that initially drew me into this project, was enacted, if only momentarily, among feminist antiviolence advocates, conservative Christians, and the state in the formation of the 1986 *Final Report* of the Attorney General's Commission on Pornography (Meese Commission).[2] How is it that Andrea Dworkin, the author of the political critique, *Right-Wing Women* (1978), came to be testifying on the same "side," against pornography, with conservative Christians such as Ardeth Kapp and June Griffin? Moreover, how do we make sense of the fact that the discourses formed through this alliance ultimately have proven dangerous to lesbians and feminists and queers,[3] for example, in the disputes over National Endowment for the Arts funding for lesbian writers Audre Lorde, Chrystos, and Minnie Bruce Pratt?[4]

Hypatia vol. 10, no. 1 (Winter 1995) © by Janet R. Jakobsen

Two related public moments represent splits or failures in solidarity where alliance might otherwise have been expected. How is it that, in the 1980s, discourses about sexualities within lesbian and feminist communities developed into a series of splits and debates known as the "sex wars"?[5] With regard to a related public moment, How do we account for the failure in solidarity related to the public alliance enacted in 1991 by white feminist media commentators in relation to Anita Hill during the "second round" of hearings on the confirmation of Clarence Thomas to the Supreme Court? This alliance failed to work on behalf of Anita Hill because it failed to articulate the complexity of her experience of sexual harassment in relation to her position as an African American woman.[6]

While these alliances or splits, in some respects, may have been the result of the power politics of the moment, they may also be symptomatic of deeper problems of alliance politics, particularly since they appeared at a variety of sites and among actors who were otherwise committed to diversity and complexity in alliance. For example, the "sex wars" were enacted among activists, as well as within the overly simplified constraints of testimony before the Meese Commission.[7] Thus, I will argue that in addition to the simplifications of U.S. politics, the actors could not fulfill their own commitments to diversity and complexity in public because in each case the outcome was overdetermined by the demands of modern public sphere discourse.

The demand that on entering public sphere discourse actors constitute themselves as moral agents according to a modern model—as internally coherent, rational, and autonomous—works to control diversity and flatten complexity.[8] In particular, the demand for coherence requires the exclusion of any elements—such as ambiguity, conflict, and contradiction—which threaten that coherence. This demand tends to structure conflict or ambiguity as mutually constitutive oppositions, and alliances of strange bedfellows occur as complex relationships are flattened into one side or the other of an opposition. Conversely, the demands of coherence may undercut alliances among actors with similar political interests as the denial of internal diversity and complexity—such as the diversity of women who face sexual harassment—enables a divide-and-conquer strategy on behalf of dominant interests to prevail.

The strictures of modern agency are, however, difficult to resist because they are based on demands that appear necessary for the very possibility of self-constitution as a moral agent. Moral agency in its modern, coherent form may appear to be particularly effective because it clarifies the ambiguities and conflicts of agency, thus clearing a path for action.[9] The morally self-legislating (self-policing) agent is, thus, induced to constrain her representations of diverse and complex sexualities for the sake of what appears to be effective agency. These moments of public discourse about sexualities show, however, that modern agency may actually be more constraining than empowering for lesbian and feminist and queer actors (in fact, for anyone who is marginalized by modernity). Thus, I will also consider some moments of public discourse about sexualities which resist the demands of modern agency in order to investigate whether nonmodern agency may better enable alliances that recognize diversity and complexity.

AGENCY AND ALLIANCE

I turn first to the testimony of feminist antiviolence advocates before the Attorney General's Commission on Pornography, otherwise known as the Meese Commission. The effects of modern public discourse which enabled the alliance of the moment between feminists opposed to sexual violence and conservative Christians dedicated to sexual purity are perhaps most apparent in the feminists' dependence on criteria to establish agency. For antiviolence advocates criteria such as the "subordination" and "degradation" of women serve to clearly establish categories for action by distinguishing those sexually explicit materials that are pornographic and, therefore, actionable by law, from those materials that are not harmful to women and, therefore, not actionable. In claiming to act only in relation to clearly distinguishable categories—regulating only clearly problematic sexual images—feminist antiviolence advocates create a clear means of action and, hence, a clear agency.

Appeals to modern criteria may initially appear to be effective when entering the framework of public policy because they make feminist arguments fit into the already established framework. For example, by using "subordination" as a criterion, arguing that certain sexually explicit images contribute to the subordination of women, antiviolence advocates attempted to base legal action against these images in civil rights claims to equality, rather than in the traditional regulation of "obscenity."[10] Modern criteria, however, are supposed to operate free of context, providing the tools necessary to distinguish categories in any context in which they appear. Thus, codification of subordination as an effective means of categorizing sexually explicit images can just as easily be used in traditional regulation of obscenity and indecency as in support of equality for women.[11] Because the criterion of subordination can be broadly applied to any social group, Jesse Helms could later appropriate it against nondominant art by adding "religion" to the list of protected social groups and then claiming that art that criticized or challenged the dominant culture subordinated Christianity.[12]

This slippage in application across contexts is compounded by slippages internal to the meaning of criteria. For antiviolence advocates the criterion of "degradation" distinguishes those materials that treat women as objects and sanction violence against women from those sexually explicit materials that are not harmful to women. When used before the Commission, however, the meaning of degradation "slipped" as it was appropriated into a discursive alliance that effectively shifted the grounds of feminist claims. For conservative Christians and for the commission, "degradation" can be broadly applied to virtually all sexually explicit materials (particularly queer images) because nonsanctioned sexualities and public displays of any sexuality are thought to degrade the moral fiber of the individual and society as a whole.[13] Thus, in the *Final Report* feminist claims were appropriated into a policy statement that reinforced the traditional legal framework of regulating pornography according to "obscenity" law.[14]

It is problematic for feminist antiviolence advocates constituted as modern agents to guard against this appropriation, however, because to admit to slippage or contradiction in meaning is to undercut themselves and their discourses as effective, in other words to undercut their agency.[15] Subordination and degradation cannot be appealed to as criteria, if they are in any way ambiguous, because they cannot serve their function as creating clear distinctions out of confusion. Thus, although appeals to modern criteria may initially appear to provide effective agency, they may also open agents to appropriations which undercut that effectiveness. The attempts of feminist antiviolence advocates to act effectively in relation to the state were appropriated by the Meese Commission and by Jesse Helms so as to narrow the public meaning of the feminist antiviolence movement. Public discursive enactments were pushed away from critiques of social and cultural sites of patriarchal dominance (including critiques of Reagan administration policy and of the nuclear family) and toward the reinstatement of obscenity regulation that was later used against lesbians and feminists and queers.[16]

Feminist antiviolence testimony before the Meese Commission was just one moment in the series of debates over pornography, sex work, and sexual practices through the 1970s and 1980s which came to be known as the "sex wars." These debates tended to split rather than enable alliances among lesbians/feminists/queers as reified oppositions between antiviolence and pro-sex advocates were repeatedly reasserted despite attempts to subvert the coherent categories on which these oppositions depended.[17] One of the most dramatic moments of opposition was at the 1982 "Toward a Politics of Sexuality Conference" held at Barnard College,[18] where the articulation of women's contradictory relationship to sexuality through the conjunction of "pleasure and danger" (Vance 1992), (in recognition of the ways in which women's sexualities are constituted within a space delineated by both these axes) was broken down into a binary opposition.[19]

The question becomes, How is it that actors who are otherwise committed to recognizing diversity and complexity are repeatedly induced into oppositional stances and actions? One answer to this question is that the exclusionary correlative of coherence induces agents into a reified opposition because it implies that the recognition of any aspect of the "other side's" claims within one's own position threatens the effectivity of agency.[20] Thus, discursive constitution within modernity establishes agency by projecting an oppositional "other" that is then negated.

Given these constitutive constraints, it is not surprising that the contradictions of women's position in relation to sexuality are elided, resulting in the constitution of antiviolence and pro-sex projects as oppositional rather than interdependent. For example, even as antiviolence advocates constituted themselves as coherent agents through the use of criteria, so also, when acting in relation to the state, pro-sex advocates invoked criteria, particularly "consent," in order to establish a coherent category of protected sexually explicit materials and acts. Once again, the meaning of consent "slipped" as it moved from its development in particular erotic communities to public sphere invocations of the protections of the liberal state. The complex meaning of "consent," as developed in lesbian/feminist/queer communities vis-à-vis sexual practices, a meaning that recognizes the continuing implication of sexual acts and images in power relations, is flattened into a liberal category that removes sexual acts and images from their implication in power and, hence, undermines a language of critique.[21] In its application as a modern criterion, consent becomes the only relevant factor and the complexity of any act or image—its constitution in relation to sex/gender/race/class hierarchies and the coexistence of consensuality and nonconsensuality—becomes inarticulable.[22]

As the structure of modern public discourse continually pushes public sphere actors toward a coherent agency, where the boundaries necessary for coherence are established through binary opposition, lesbian/feminist/queer discourses about sexualities are vulnerable to recuperation into dominant ideologies. Thus, the testimony of antiviolence advocates supports the position of the Meese Commission, while antiviolence advocates have argued that the liberal invocation of consent allows a problematic alliance between pro-sex advocates and male-dominated interests, particularly commercial pornography (see, e.g., Leidholdt and Raymond 1990). Even as unexpected alliances with dominant interests are formed, the possibility for alliances across the complex interrelations of lesbians/feminists/queers with respect to sexuality are broken apart into the reified oppositions of pro-sex and antiviolence.

The problematic effects of this reified opposition have contributed, for example, to problems for lesbians/feminists/queers in forming alliances across race and class differences. In "Queen for 307 Days: Looking B(l)ack at Vanessa Williams and the Sex Wars," Jackie Goldsby (1993) argues that the discourses developed specifically in the "sex wars" are inadequate to the articulation of black women's sexuality.[23] The two "sides" of the "sex wars"—sides established in white, middle-class ideologies—tend simply to induct analyses of race and class into one side or the other of the debate, thus, eliding the ways in which race and class differences may challenge the constructions of sexuality on which the debate depends. For example, because of the genealogy of categories marked by degradation and subordination in relation to white, middle-class standards of purity and disembodiedness in sexuality, the use of these criteria as distinguishing features of problematic sexualities tends to elide race and class differences. Similarly, appeals to consent may elide the implication of sexual images or practices in race and class hierarchies. Thus, it is not a simple accident that some of the splits over sexualities which are marked by these categories are interrelated with splits over race and class positions.[24]

The inadequacy of contemporary public discourse about sexualities is further apparent in the problematic alliances that were enacted by white feminists—most dramatically by white feminist media consultants including Catharine MacKinnon—in relation to Anita Hill during the second set of hearings on the appointment of Clarence Thomas to the Supreme Court. The problem of white feminist discourse with regard to Anita Hill, as documented in the volume edited by Toni Morrison, *Race-ing Justice, En-gendering Power* (1992) and the 1992 "Frontline" documentary on the hearings, was its inability to articulate the complexities of Hill's position as an African American woman (see esp. Crenshaw 1992). White feminists discussed the hearings as if they were only (singularly) about a case of sexual harassment and sexism by the Senate Judiciary Committee, ignoring the conjunction of sexism and racism. Thus, an alliance was formed with Hill by subsuming her in a "side" already established by white feminists.

The complex interplay of gender, race, class, and sexuality was repeatedly elided by both the Judiciary Committee and the media commentary. The Judiciary Committee initially failed to take Hill's charges seriously, thus, excluding the issue of sexual harassment from the first round of hearings and setting the stage for the spectacle of hearings focused only on sexuality. Moreover, the Judiciary Committee used Anita Hill as an African American woman to do their work for them even as they undermined her credibility. Only through Hill's testimony were they willing to question Thomas's appropriateness as an appointee to the Supreme Court and, yet, the senators failed to take a stand on behalf of Hill or against sexual harassment. The Judiciary Committee virtually refused to challenge Thomas on the basis of his qualifications or his statements in the first round of hearings. Through this refusal, in conjunction with the staging of the second spectacle, the senators enacted a drama in which it appeared that Thomas was on trial only for his sex, and, hence, his claim of a high-tech lynching spectacle resonated with the racism enacted by the Judiciary Committee. In effect, Thomas's claim delineated a bifurcated analysis where the issue in the hearings was either a case of racism or of sexism, thus eliding Hill's position at the conjunction of these two oppressions. Both the Judiciary Committee and white feminist media commentators contributed to bifurcation by failing to show awareness of the historical position of African American women in relation to lynching or by speaking only of Hill's sex/gender oppression.

This bifurcated analysis further contributed to the construction of Thomas as representative of the African American race, a representation used by the Bush administration, which was extended by Thomas so as to establish his credibility. This representation undergirded Thomas's claims that his class status as a successful professional represented both the success of African American struggle and of the male, individualist American dream of mobility, a claim based in part on his distance from the female members of his family, particularly his portrayal of his sister as a welfare dependent (see Painter 1992; Lubiano 1992). Thus, Thomas's construction as an African American who took part in American class mobility recuperated the dominant gender, race, and class systems by implying that the opportunity for individual, male, class mobility undercut social group oppression. In contrast, without claims to male individualism and once her position as an African American was elided, Hill's similar class position as a successful professional was implicated in conservative senators' claims that she was self-promoting and socially inappropriate. Hill's willingness to cross the boundaries that were expected to limit her class mobility because of her race and gender locations marked her with the implication that she would also fail to accept the boundaries of sexual respectability—either by attempting to date her boss in the "woman spurned" scenario or by not keeping silent and publicly speaking of "unmentionable" sexuality. Ideologies of race- and class-dominance were rarely mentioned by white feminist commentators, despite the fact that the conjunction of these ideologies with gender- and sexual-dominance contributed to the ultimate confirmation of Thomas to the Supreme Court.

In order to recognize the complexity of the situation, the singularity of the focus on Hill as oppressed by sex/gender discrimination would have to be subverted by an analysis of multiple identifications/oppressions. Modern constructions of agency and alliance, particularly when constituted within a legal or public policy framework, seem strikingly unable to articulate this type of complexity, however. So, legal theorist Kimberlè Crenshaw (1989) has shown that while legal claims on behalf of gender, or race, or class may succeed, claims based on the intersections of these oppressions, such as those made by African American women, are unlikely to succeed. Similarly, in public discourses about sexualities, agents are induced to constitute coherent "sides" along a single axis of oppression which undercut potential commitments to diversity and complexity and, thus, undermine effective agency and alliance politics.

AMBI-VALENCE AND THE POSSIBILITIES FOR ALTERNATIVE AGENCY

I now turn to an alternative example, an alliance that articulates precisely the type of complexity that was missing in relation to Anita Hill. Through this example, I construct an alternative model of agency which resists the coherent and unifying aspects of modern agency by employing the very multiplicity and complexity which has proven problematic for alliance formation within modern public discourse. Kobena Mercer formed this type of alliance in his reading and rereading of Robert Mapplethorpe's photographs, particularly the series of black male nudes collected in *Black Males* (1982) and the *Black Book* (1986).[25] Mercer reads and then rereads his own processes of identification as a black, gay, male reader of the photographs. In order to question his own implication in the racialized and sexualized discourses in which the photos also participate, Mercer reads these identifications not as predetermined essences, but as acts themselves, as processes. His first reading as a viewer who wants to look at the photos, but who fails to find what he "wants to see," pushes him toward an identification with the black men in the photos as objects, as objectified through the production of the photographs, abstracted and split from their subjectivity and, thereby, fetishized. Mercer is led to a new reading, however, after Mapplethorpe's death from AIDS and after the public controversy over the exhibition of the photos, a controversy in which Jesse Helms was able to draw on the modern criterion of subordination to incite action against the "obscenity" of the photos. This rereading for multiple meanings—for ambi-valence—allows him to articulate the multiplicities and ambiguities of his identifications not just with the black men of the photos on the object side of the subject-object split but also with Mapplethorpe. Mercer recognizes his identification with Mapplethorpe as a gay man and his own implication along with Mapplethorpe on the subject side of this split—Mercer as viewer, Mapplethorpe as author. Moreover, he recognizes (beyond simple objectification) the subjectivity of the men in the photos and the interaction between these men and Mapplethorpe. Thus, the oppositions which informed his first reading are undermined by a number of complexities.[26] This rereading does not, however, simply do away with the first reading, nor does it "save" the photographs from implication in racialized and racist discourses.

The recognition of the multiple meanings of the images does, however, open a space of possibility, a space *between* readings, which can be used as the ground for new alliances. The structure of binary opposition in the first reading creates a gap between two sides which is so wide as to be unbridgeable and, at the same time, flattens the two sides together in their mutual constitution. Mercer, in rereading the photographs, moves from being stuck on one side—the object side—of an unbridgeable chasm—the chasm between subject and object and the racialized chasm between Mercer and Mapplethorpe—to a space in between where he identifies as both subject and object in relation to the photographs. He uses this space to form an alliance with Mapplethorpe in resistance to Helms's reading of the photos as images of degradation in need of regulation. This alliance does not erase the distance or the racial "difference" between Mercer and Mapplethorpe, but rather problematizes Mapplethorpe's white male subject position by acknowledging that it is also a white *gay* male subject position, a move that does not erase race, but rather acknowledges the complexity of identifications. Mercer works in the space between himself (his identifications) and Mapplethorpe('s) not just because they share a point of identification as gay men but also because of the ways in which whiteness is produced in relation to blackness. In so doing, he subverts the opposition between whiteness and blackness showing the space between them to be both more confused (more ambi-valent) and more negotiable.

Mercer's questioning of the production of whiteness extends (while it also in some ways resists) Trinh T. Minh-Ha's critique of the Mapplethorpe controversy in "The Other Censorship" (1991). Trinh questions the ways in which the controversy itself was structured by Mapplethorpe's position and action as a privileged white man, in particular the ways in which "free speech" is most likely to be mobilized on behalf of "white male artists" (231). Mercer's reading complicates Trinh's reading of Mapplethorpe as simply a "white male artist,"[27] while at the same time joining her in enacting a critical questioning of whiteness, maleness, and privilege in relation to the production of art.[28] This questioning provides a grounding for interrogating what is actually protected when the rallying cry of "freedom of expression" is invoked, given that speech is not constructed in a space of complete "freedom" outside the constraints and privileges of racist, classist, sexist, colonialist/imperialist, and/or heterosexist discourses. Thus, questioning the "other censorship" articulates the conditions that constrain the possibilities for production of alternative subjectivities, including gay/queer subjectivities.

Given the complex sets of power relations within which Mapplethorpe's photographs have been produced and read, Mercer acknowledges that the recognition of multiplicity does not in itself undo the possibility that the photos (and the context of their production and viewing) may lend themselves to racist reading.[29] The articulation of the space in between allows Mercer to consider interracial alliances and also to raise questions in relation to those alliances, for example questions about how sexuality and eroticism are implicated in alliances: "Under what conditions does eroticism mingle with political solidarity? When does it produce an effect of empowerment? And when does it produce an effect of disempowerment? When does identification imply objectification, and when does it imply equality?" (210). Thus, working in the space in between identifications opens possibilities for a new language of critique without foreclosing possible alliances. In this case, reading Mapplethorpe's photos for the ambi-valence of meanings, opens a space for political struggle to resist both the implication of the photos in racist discourses—that is, to resist the implication that the photos tell *the* singular truth of black men—*and* to resist the Helmsian reading of the photos as degrading and obscene.

Reading Mercer's constitution of alternative grounds for agency and alliance allows a rereading of the possibilities for action in other public discourses about sexualities. For example, when read for ambi-valence, the sexually explicit images or contested sexual practices that became the sites of the "sex wars" do not tell a simple story of the subordination of women—of abuse as abuse; neither do they tell a simple story of sexual liberation—of sex as sex—where consent clearly distinguishes sex from abuse. Multiplicity subverts reified oppositions as the two "sides" are broken up and scattered across a field of meanings and contradictions. There is no simple or singular way to negotiate this field. The option of creating a clear path, an agency, by pushing all the blocks to agency to one side and, thus, freeing the other side for moral action, is no longer available. While such a shift may seem to undercut agency by undercutting its clarity, it also creates possibilities because it is no longer necessary to establish agency by projecting an oppositional other which is then negated.

The alternative conceptualization of agency, independent of oppositional coherence, also highlights new possibilities for lesbians and feminists and queers to resist alliances with dominant interests by not acceding to apparently seamless shifts in meaning in public sphere discourses. New resistances to appropriation become possible because agency is no longer dependent on contextless criteria or categories. Thus, for Mercer, the process of rereading the Mapplethorpe photos in order to better articulate the context of his critique specifically enabled him to resist an appropriation of his critique by Jesse Helms. Analogously, reading for ambi-valences and multiple meanings highlights dangers that are hidden by modern constructions—for example, the possible racist reading of Mapplethorpe's photographs, a reading that is hidden by a singular agency enacted to protect either Mapplethorpe's queer representations or his "free expression." Multiplicity alone does not resist these dangers, precisely because there is ambi-valence (possible contradiction). Reading for multiplicity may, however, highlight where to resist and may aid in articulating the complexities faced by those who do resist.

Formulating agency as resistance to the implication of sexuality in discourses of race, gender, class, and sexual dominance, rather than as the search for a singular right act, allows for new possibilities of cross-racial alliance and simultaneously highlights the continuing dangers which such alliances must negotiate. For example, the problem of white feminist discourse in forming an alliance with Anita Hill was the inability of white feminists to work in the space in between, specifically in the space between their identifications with Hill as a woman and the racial difference/distance between their position and hers. Unable to work in the space in between, white feminists formed an alliance with Anita Hill by pulling her across the chasm of difference into their coherent "side." Within their coherent structuring, Hill was constituted only as a female claimant of sexual harassment and Thomas only as a male perpetrator. This moment of sexuality as public spectacle replicated the way in which race and class analyses were inducted into one side or the other of the "sex wars" within lesbian and feminist discourses.[30] Hence, when white feminists attempted to ally with Anita Hill, the alliance failed in that it did not articulate Hill's position as much as it extended the claims of white feminist analysis of sexual harassment. If the space in between identifications and differences is a space of complexity, then it is the space that would allow for the simultaneous articulation of crisscrossed relations of power created by structural oppressions based on gender, race, class, and sexuality—an articulation that would have made white feminists' attempts to form an alliance with Anita Hill look much less like an appropriation.

Alliance politics demands more than the ability to work across any singular difference. Rather, the singular articulation of difference, or even the joint articulation of differences along lines of gender and sexuality, which has been common in so much lesbian/feminist/queer discourse, runs the risk of extending the articulation of sexuality which "originates in, stays with, the dominative mode of culture" in the United States (Spillers 1992, 78). I am not simply inciting a discourse which somehow focuses on all differences simultaneously, a move with universalizing tendencies that can reinstate a singular discourse by subsuming multiple sites of struggle; rather, I am suggesting that by reading for multiplicity and ambi-valence it might be possible to articulate the "intersectionality" (Crenshaw 1989) of differences—the points at which multiple processes of social differentiation come together to form nexuses of oppressions, as well as the spaces in between the chasms of differentiation. Even as modernity is structured so as to layer oppressions while simultaneously promoting "the colonialist creed 'Divide and Conquer'" (Trinh 1991), it also creates gaps—openings that can be exploited in developing agency that recognizes complexity articulated through multiplicity.

Is it possible to resist the modern demand for coherence and still speak and act effectively—still have agency—in the contemporary U.S. public sphere? There is no simple (singular? coherent?) answer to this question, in that at any given moment, public speaking and acting is unlikely to be wholly resistant to modernity or dominating discourses—ambi-valence remains.[31] I focus on resistance to the demands of modern agency simply as one possible point of leverage for creating new alliances in the public sphere. There have in recent years been some striking examples of public activity that has developed a resistance to modern, coherent agency through an articulation of diversity and complexity. One such example is the AIDS Coalition to Unleash Power (ACT UP) as it developed from its initial singular focus on "Drugs into Bodies" into a set of alliances that recognize the multiplicity (diversity and complexity) of the bodies affected by AIDS (Saalfield and Navarro 1991).[32]

A brief analysis of the development of agency within ACT UP shows some of the possibilities, as well as the continuing dangers for new forms of alliance politics. Moreover, the media effectiveness of ACT UP shows that a commitment to diversity and complexity need not undercut, and may actually enable, public effectiveness. ACT UP began in March 1987 as a movement of predominantly white, middle-class gay men whose main focus for "the first six months or more" was "drugs into bodies" (Crimp and Rolston 1990, 37). This focus assumed a singular and coherent site of struggle, the HIV-infected body, which had a clear and primary need: drugs to fight the virus and abate the onset of AIDS. Thus, the main target of early actions was the corporate and government bureaucracy that controlled the apparatus for testing, producing, and selling pharmaceuticals.[33] As organizing proceeded and the constitution of ACT UP diversified, it became apparent that the HIV-infected body was not a singular site of struggle with a singular, primary need, but rather a series of sites, articulated by a series of complex issues; nor, given the nature of the AIDS pandemic, could the HIV-infected body alone define the limits of struggle.

The recognition that the struggle against AIDS implies a complex subjectivity developed from a recognition of diverse bodies with, or at risk for, HIV infection, exemplified by the need for participation in drug trials and other AIDS research by bodies that are not marked by normative white, male, middle-class status, the need for prevention education that reaches diverse persons and communities, and the need to expand the definition of the AIDS itself.[34] For example, various actions over more than three years constituted a crucial struggle, which was victorious in 1992, for a change in the Centers for Disease Control (CDC) definition of AIDS to include opportunistic infections which occur in women and which had been overlooked in the existing definition.[35] The new definition is crucial for many women who are dependent on an AIDS diagnosis to receive the coverage required for access to health care. Sarah Schulman (1994) calls the changing of the CDC definition "in terms of real impact on people's lives . . . perhaps the most significant victory in the AIDS crisis" (215). Once the subject of AIDS activism had been diversified to recognize the complexity of bodies affected by HIV, the agenda of ACT UP changed to focus on the intersections among multiple social issues. For example, for HIV-infected persons who are homeless, the availability of drugs through the regular U.S. health care delivery system was unlikely to provide treatment or to address primary concerns. Thus, issues like housing, access to the health care system, drug treatment programs, along with fighting poverty, racism, sexism, and homophobia became sites of struggle for AIDS activism as well.

Another aspect of ACT UP organizing which has contributed to its work in the spaces in between clear identifications is a willingness to subvert coherence through internal fragmentation. Local chapters, affinity groups, and committees organized around personal identities, issues, and/or skills such as the

Women's Committee and the Majority Actions Committee (both formed in 1988), the PWA Housing Committee, art collective Gran Fury, and video collective DIVA TV operate with autonomy. The autonomy of groups within ACT UP establishes an internally coalitional agency that also formed the basis for coalitions with other organizations, such as the Women's Health Mobilization (WHAM!).[36] The subversion of coherence effected by such internal fragmentation is frequently thought to undercut effectiveness, and yet some of ACT UP's largest successes are the result of this recognition of differences internal to the struggle against AIDS. The media success of "Seize Control of the FDA" (Food and Drug Administration), a crucial moment in educating the public about the limitations of the U.S. apparatus for drug testing and distribution, was dependent on recognition of gender, racial/ethnic, and regional diversity, which gave the story import across various communities.[37]

For ACT UP, the space at the intersections of issues and identifications is a space defined by anger.[38] The definition of this space contrasts with Mercer's focus on the erotic, showing that there is no single definition of the space in between. None of these spaces are without dangers, however. Working in the intersections between various issues and identifications does not necessarily remove either the conflicts or oppressions created by structural dominations. For example, Douglas Crimp and Adam Rolston admit that the initial work toward realizing the diversity and complexity of struggle against HIV infection and AIDS was the responsibility of the women in ACT UP, thus showing that the space at the intersections is not a space free of oppressions or structural dominations. Rather, it is an opening to the possibility of change and difference where the clear oppositions induced by structural dominations are confused enough to allow for new negotiations and alliances across those differences. For example, the opposition between "gays" (assumed primarily to be white men) and "people of color" (assumed to be primarily heterosexual men) is broken down in relation to HIV-infection. The struggle against that infection brought together persons who were assumed to be "opposed" and those, such as women and lesbians, who were elided by such a structurally induced opposition.[39] Nonetheless, conflicts persist. Sarah Schulman (1994, 194) reports continuing sexism in AIDS activism,[40] and Douglas Crimp reports the persistence of a number of conflicts within ACT UP that concern "competing identities and contradictory identifications *across* identities."[41] Articulating and working within the space in between oppositions, at the intersections of issues, is merely an initial step toward working through these conflicts. We have yet to see what form work in between and through these conflicts will take in the future of ACT UP, or of newer groups such as Queer Nation and Lesbian Avengers.

The need for lesbians and feminists and queers to develop alternative forms of agency, forms that enable new alliances in and through public discourses about sexualities, has become critical given the continuing use of divide-and-conquer strategies by those who would extend the dominance of sexist, racist, and heterosexist social structures.[42] Reconstituting agency by reading for multiplicity and ambi-valence is one possible means of laying the groundwork for new alliances. Proliferation, multiplicity, excess, and undecidability are not, however, in themselves sufficient for an agency that is alternative to modern agency; rather, proliferation, undecidability, and ambi-valence open social spaces/sites of struggle where we may be able to build alternative forms of agency and alliance which enable and empower our lives in all of their diversity and complexity.

NOTES

I would like to thank Juliana Kubala, Lesbian Avenger and Brittain Fellow at the Georgia Institute of Technology, and Carrie Jane Singleton, coordinator of the Community AIDS Network of Metropolitan Atlanta (1990–1992), without whose insights this article would not have been possible.

1. For useful explorations of alliance building and women working together across differences see Reagon (1983), Narayan (1988), Albrecht and Brewer (1990), and Hirsch and Keller (1990), particularly Childers and hooks's contribution.

2. All the communities to which I refer—lesbian, feminist, queer, conservative Christian—are amalgamations of more or (frequently) less easy sets of alliances. Thus, within the constraints of this article the terms refer broadly to those communities that might recognize themselves under these signs.

3. I use the conjunction between lesbian, feminist, and queer in order to indicate multiple and complex communities that may overlap but that are not co-extensive. Thus, there is slippage in the set of relations among communities, indicating, for example, communities that are lesbian, feminist, and queer, as well as lesbian communities that may not intersect with feminist or queer communities.

4. See Pratt (1991) for a description of this particular conflict.

5. For summaries of feminist debates over sexualities, particularly over pornography in the late seventies and through the eighties see Rich (1986), Califia ([1981] 1987), Vance's new introduction to the second edition of *Pleasure and Danger* (1992) and Leidholdt's introduction to *The Sexual Liberals and the Attack on Feminism* (1991).

6. See Morrison (1992) for this critique. See also "Frontline" (1992) for an analysis of the hearings, which includes clips of the white feminist media consultants.

7. For a description of one controversy that shows how the oppositions of the "sex wars" undermine commitments to diversity and complexity, see Margaret Hunt's description in *Coming to Power* (Samois 1987) of the 1985 "Feminism, Sexuality, and Power" symposium at Mount Holyoke College:

> Originally, it seems, the conference organizers had in mind a quite broad-based approach to the problem of sexuality and power. They planned a program which included a substantial amount of material on the ways class and race interacted with gender in the organization of sexuality, and they took special care to represent a variety of erotic lifestyles and to avoid the prevalent Western bias of so

> much scholarship on sexuality. What they got was a pitched battle over the question of lesbian S/M, an issue which so dominated the conference as to make all other matters fade into the polished neo-gothic Mount Holyoke woodwork. (81)

My concern is not so much with the intensity of these conflicts as with the ways in which complex discussions of multiple issues vis-à-vis sexualities, including race and class issues, are elided by debate structured as opposition.

8. In this essay, I only obliquely address the conflict in feminist ethics between advocates of "modern" and "postmodern" agencies. See, for example, the useful three-way exchange among Benhabib, Butler, and Fraser in *Praxis International* (1991). In this essay, I assume a position that I argue for at length elsewhere (Jakobsen 1991)—that neither modern nor postmodern agencies provide any guarantee or immunity from implication in dominant or hegemonic cultural formations. Thus, the contemporary project of lesbian/feminist/queer agency is an ongoing project of creating new forms of agency which constitute and empower our lives in all their diversity and complexity, while continually articulating and enacting resistances to changing forms of domination.

9. For an analysis of some of the implications of "clarity" see Lugones (1994).

10. The legislation sponsored by Andrea Dworkin and Catharine MacKinnon would allow women who had been harmed in connection with pornographic representations legal redress based on the violation of their civil rights. For the version passed in Indianapolis and later declared unconstitutional, see Indianapolis, Ind., code section 16–3 (q) (1984). See also Dworkin (1985) and Downs (1989). For the circuit court decision declaring the Indianapolis law unconstitutional see *American Booksellers Association Inc. v. Hudnut.* 771 F.2d (7th Cir. 1985). See MacKinnon (1993) for her most recent analysis of this decision.

11. Moreover, as a legal theorist, MacKinnon remains tied to liberal norms implying that sexual equality represents a sexuality that is removed from its implication in power. See, for example, her critique of Foucault (MacKinnon 1992, 128).

12. In 1989, following controversies over National Endowment for the Arts (NEA) funding for queer artists Robert Mapplethorpe and Andreas Serrano, Senator Jesse Helms proposed an amendment to the new guidelines for the NEA which would prohibit the use of NEA funds for the "dissemination, promotion, or production of obscene or indecent materials or materials denigrating a particular religion." Although the Helms Amendment was eventually defeated, the final bill did include a prohibition on funding for projects considered legally obscene. For statements by various parties to this conflict and a chronological summary see Bolton (1992, 73–118, 346–48).

13. Conservative Christians faced some similar stakes in this alliance, insofar as they, like lesbian and feminist antiviolence advocates, represent a (non-/anti-/post-)modern subculture that is forced to negotiate contradictions vis-à-vis modernity. Moreover, "sexuality" as the truth of the modern self and "woman" as a constitutive "other" of modernity have been two of the major sites for conservative Christian negotiation of these contradictions. David Watt (1991) argues that evangelical Christianity has made a number of "concessions" to feminism over the last several decades. Yet, these "concessions" also represent appropriations that affect, not just the meaning of Christianity, but also the meaning of feminism. Because the positioning of the two sets of advocates (feminist antiviolence and conservative Christian) in relation to the Meese Commission was not precisely analogous, the *Final Report* represented the opportunity to turn these appropriations into public policy. Conservative Christians not only gave testi-

mony but were also represented on the Attorney General's Commission. The makeup of the commission was undoubtedly a representation of the coalition that elected Ronald Reagan and made Ed Meese attorney general. Thus, in acceding to modern public discourse, conservative Christians made some unlikely allies, but because of their position in relation to the particular formation of state power, whatever "concessions" to feminism they may have made effectively became appropriations.

14. See Vance (1993, 36). For the recuperation of the civil rights approach into the already existing framework of obscenity prosecution see *Final Report* (sec. 6.5, 391–96). While the Commission lauds Dworkin's and MacKinnon's efforts in supporting an antipornography civil rights ordinance, particularly the "motivations behind the ordinance" (393), it ratifies the decision rendering the Indianapolis law unconstitutional and argues that the sexually violent and degrading material targeted by the Indianapolis ordinance can only be reached "when it is legally obscene" (394).

15. For example, Carole Vance (1993) reports: "Only one feminist anti-pornography group, Feminists Against Pornography from Washington, D.C., refused to tailor its testimony to please conservative members and attacked the Reagan administration for its savage cutbacks on programs and services for women" (36).

16. In 1990, Jesse Helms wrote a letter to the General Accounting Office requesting an investigation into NEA grants to three lesbian writers, Audre Lorde, Chrystos, and Minnie Bruce Pratt (Pratt 1991, 231). This request took place under the auspices of the amendment attached to the NEA FY 1990 appropriations bill (Public Law 101–121) which included a description of materials considered legally obscene, and therefore prohibited for funding, "including but not limited to, depictions of sadomasochism, homoeroticism, the sexual exploitation of children, or individuals engaged in sex acts and which, when taken as a whole, do not have serious literary, artistic, political or scientific value." This prohibition was later declared unconstitutional in *Bella Lewitzky Dance Foundation v. John E. Frohnmayer et al.*, U.S. District Court, Central District of California, Case No. CV 90–3616 JGD, CV 90–5142 JGD, filed Jan. 9, 1991.

17. I use the term "antiviolence" rather than simply "antipornography" because it indicates the breadth of the values promoted by this movement. The contemporary term "pro-sex" (used for example in the literature of Lesbian Avengers, New York) is another in a list of terms including "anti-anti-pornography," "sex-positive," and "sex radical." Note that although the anti- and pro- of these terms are not complementary—antiviolence is not antisex and pro-sex is not proviolence—the schematic accusation of such complementarity demonstrates how an oppositional structure of debate tends to flatten complexities.

18. For a description of the Barnard controversy see Wilson (1983). See also, Vance ([1984] 1992, epilogue) and the conversation among Joan Nestle, Amber Hollibaugh, and Madeline Davis presented in "The Femme Tapes," Nestle (1991, 254–67).

19. The construction of feminist anthologies as either antiviolence or pro-sex is indicative of the recuperation into opposition of much of the debate. Some anthologies in the early 1980s were constructed to represent one "side" or the "other"; see, for example, Lederer (1980), Samois ([1981] 1987), and Linden (1982). It should be noted that these early anthologies often represent an initial laying out of positions. Anthologies from the period directly after this initial construction, such as Vance ([1984] 1992) and Snitow et al. (1983), can be read as offering more complexity, but they are often read as representative of one "side." MacKinnon (1992), for example, reads these anthologies as one-sided (134), and because of that one-sidedness declares Kate Millett's

analysis of sexual violence against children in *Pleasure and Danger* (Vance [1984] 1992) to be "in the wrong book" (117 n. 2). While there are some signs that the contemporary field is more open (see, for example, Stanton (1992), the anthology in which MacKinnon's declaration occurs), many 1990s anthologies continue to be constructed as representing one "side" or the "other." See Leidholdt and Raymond (1990), Segal and McIntosh (1993), and Reti (1993).

20. For the antiviolence position, coherence is established by bringing all women together through resistance to a shared oppression effected through sexual violence. The appeal of this position is its promise of effective agency for a movement coherently constituted around oppression and liberation. The danger is that any form of diversity tends to threaten this coherence. The coherence of the pro-sex, or sex-positive, position is that there is some coherent entity called "sex" about which we are "pro" or about which we can be "positive." The appeal of this position is that it values both sex and sexual diversity. In the age of HIV/AIDS, this position is particularly appealing as a resistance to the dominant view that to be sex-positive is to be HIV-positive, yet, it too depends on a coherent category "sex," which is not so monolithic after all.

21. Even at these sites, which are somewhat (although never completely) removed from the demands of the state, the liberal meaning of consent can exert its influence, for example, in the appeal to consent by members of the lesbian s/m community in response to critiques of the use of racist imagery. See, for example, Califia's appeal to the First Amendment (1987, 257).

22. Similarly, defense of sexual diversity can devolve into a liberal project that obviates critique. For example, Vance presents a "one-third theory" describing responses to sexually explicit images: "Show any personally favored erotic image to a group of women, and one-third will find it disgusting, one-third will find it ridiculous, and one-third will find it hot" (Vance [1984] 1992, 433). Speaking in defense of sexual diversity, Vance does not raise the question of how these "thirds" are produced, or how responses might be multiple or mobile. Thus, the diversity that is protected is a static diversity, more easily reified than further explored.

23. Goldsby makes this point in response to the failure of these discourses to articulate Vanessa Williams's position in the scandal over her sexuality and the Miss America title. For an analogous analysis of class in relation to dominant discourses of sexuality see Hamilton (1993).

24. For example, Faderman (1993) and Kennedy and Davis (1993) have traced the historical movement away from butch-femme roles of the 1940s and 1950s in relation to upward mobility.

25. For the original reading see Mercer (1987). For the version of the rereading upon which I draw see Mercer (1991). The rereading has also been republished in slightly different forms in Segal and McIntosh (1993) and Abelove, Barale, and Halperin (1993).

26. This recognition allows him to reread the implication of the photographs in certain modernist discourses. Specifically, the juxtaposition of the black male body with the signifiers of modernist high art can be read as undermining both modernist canons of art and of racialized discourse (Mercer 1991, 197).

27. In her reading of Mapplethorpe's position Trinh T. Minh-Ha parenthetically raises the question of "gay artists of color" (1991, 231), but never refers to and, thus, effectively elides Mapplethorpe's sexuality.

28. For a further analysis of these questions in relation to disputes over National Endowment for the Arts funding, see Schulman (1994, 199–203).

29. Mercer (1991, 201–204) argues that Mapplethorpe's representations of Black males are not by themselves sufficient to resist racist reading and, thus, offers the example of Rotimi Fani-Kayode's (1987) Black male nudes as representations that further resist racist discourses.

30. In the production of lesbian and feminist anthologies of the "sex wars" critiques of racism and classism were frequently understood as critiques of the "other side," rather than as critiques of the structure of the debates themselves. See, for example, Califia's response to Alice Walker's critique of the use of racist imagery in a particular representation of s/m practice. Califia points to the ethnic identity of one of the participants in question as obviating Walker's critique, thus removing individual sexual practice from its implication in hierarchical discourses and obviating the importance of racism in debates over sexuality (1987, 270).

31. Although no social spaces of communication and interaction are completely outside the bounds of the modern "public," there are some spaces that are more open to alternative social and cultural formations. For example, Patton (1991) has analyzed the development of "sexual vernaculars" as local discourses in resistance to dominant cultural discourses. A focus on developing discourses that can articulate diversity and complexity in social spaces which are not overdetermined by modernity can be one part of a strategy for bringing complexity and diversity more fully into the public sphere.

32. Another interesting example that bears further analysis is the set of alliances which successfully, if narrowly, defeated heterosexist Proposition 9 in Oregon in the 1992 elections. According to Suzanne Pharr (1993), two separate campaigns developed in Oregon: the No On 9 Campaign focused on modern, coherent, and universalist claims against discrimination and didn't present a specifically lesbian and gay focus; a series of grassroots campaigns, organized through the Oregon Democracy Project and the Rural Organizing Project, focused on already existing organizations such as battered women's shelters, antiracist organizations, and professional groups such as librarians and highlighted a commitment to lesbian and gay rights within broader agendas. The multiple strategies and the ability to hold together and articulate a multiple agenda—for example, at once antiracist and antiheterosexist—resisted attempts by proponents of "Prop 9" to pursue a divide-and-conquer strategy. I thank Melanie Kaye/Kantrowitz for bringing this example to my attention at "Making Worlds: Metaphor and Materiality in the Construction of Feminist Texts," 13–16 October, 1993, University of Arizona.

33. Early actions included one on Wall Street, chosen because it is a representative site of the profits made by Burroughs Wellcome, the producer of AZT (at the time the only Food and Drug Administration [FDA] approved drug to treat HIV infection and the most expensive drug in history, costing each person treated approximately $10,000 annually), an action on the Post Office on tax day advocating the use of tax dollars for AIDS research, and an action on the FDA itself (Crimp and Rolston 1990, 26–51).

34. Another action that exemplified the growing recognition of the diverse sites of struggle against AIDS was the "Nine Days of Protest" in May 1988, which addressed multiple sites of struggle in New York and New Jersey including University Hospital in Newark, black and Hispanic churches in New York City, drug prevention centers, the New York State Office of Corrections, New York City high schools, Shea Stadium (focusing on straight men taking responsibility for safe sex), the International Building at Rockefeller Center, and FAO Schwartz (focusing on inequitable treatment of children with AIDS) (Crimp and Rolston 1990, 52–70).

35. Beginning in 1989 with a teach-in, "Women and AIDS," sponsored by the

Women's Committee of ACT UP, New York, this campaign included two actions in Atlanta in December 1990, a "Women and AIDS" Unity March and Rally for World AIDS Day with keynote speaker Rev. Joseph Lowery, President of the Southern Christian Leadership Conference (SCLC), sponsored by the Community AIDS Network of Metropolitan Atlanta in conjunction with ACT UP members from around the country, and an ACT UP/WHAM action at the CDC two days later.

36. Two major actions that were the result of coalitions between ACT UP and WHAM! were "Stop the Church" in 1989, a demonstration at St. Patrick's Cathedral in New York under the banner, "Stop the Church; Fight Its Opposition to Abortion; Fight Its Murderous AIDS Policy; Take Direct Action; Take Control of Your Body" (Crimp and Rolston 1990, 132), and the December 1990 demonstration, in conjunction with ACT UP, Atlanta, at the Centers for Disease Control.

37. A coalition across the Women's Caucus and Majority Actions Committee, "WIC/MAC" was built for this action to address connections among the two groups in relation to exclusions from AIDS treatment and drug testing (Saalfield and Navarro 1991, 354). Signorile (1994, 5) credits Urvashi Vaid with recognizing the importance of regional diversity to the media effectiveness of this national action. For a further description of "Seize Control of the FDA" and its importance, see Crimp and Rolston (1990, 76–83).

38. The initial self-definition of ACT UP was, "a diverse nonpartisan group united in anger and committed to direct action to end the AIDS crisis" (Crimp and Rolston 1990, 12).

39. For example, the Women's Committee, formed in January 1988, brought together diverse groups of women interested in a number of issues, a diversity demonstrated by the "Women and AIDS" handbook, first developed in 1989 and later published by South End Press as *Women, AIDS & Activism* (ACT UP/NY Women & AIDS Books Group, 1990).

40. Schulman describes the complexities raised by this persistent sexism as follows:

> One question that came up over and over again is, "If the shoe were on the other foot and this were happening to lesbians, don't you think the guys wouldn't help *us?*" And of course I had to answer *yes*, but, at the same time not give in to the homophobic stereotype that gay men hate women and assert, instead, that this lack of reciprocity exists between all men and all women. Straight men are noticeably absent from the battle to win full abortion rights for straight women—and they're *married* to them. It's more about being raised male in this culture which insists that the male experience is the objective, neutral experience from which all other experiences can be generalized. This is why we see so little awareness or advocacy by gay men on women's behalf. Not only with regard to AIDS but also with regard to sexual assault, economic oppression, cancer, and abortion. However, I know at the same time that gay men have been allowed to die because they are *gay* not because they are men. And I also know, from two years of involvement in ACT UP, New York, that there is a general understanding in that organization that sexism is not only wrong—it is politically inefficient. (1994, 196)

41. Crimp enumerates the following conflicts that "suggest something of the complexity of issues raised by the epidemic and of the make-up of the AIDS activist movement."

> There are conflicts between men and women, between lesbians and straight women, between white people and people of color, between those who are HIV-

> positive or have AIDS and those who are HIV-negative. There are also conflicts between those who think we should devote all our energies to militant direct action and those who favor meeting with government officials and pharmaceutical executives as well; between those who want to concentrate on a narrowly defined AIDS agenda and those who feel we must confront the wider systemic ills that AIDS exacerbates; between those who see ACT UP as the vanguard in the struggle against AIDS and those who see direct action as only one of many forms of AIDS activism, which also includes advocacy, fundraising, legal action, and providing services. Negotiating these conflicts is painful and perilous; it has even resulted in splits or dissolutions of ACT UP chapters in some cities. (1993, 315–16)

42. For example, the Traditional Values Coalition has developed a new videotape, "Gay Rights, Special Rights," directed specifically at African American communities contrasting "special rights" for "homosexuals" with the Civil Rights struggles of African Americans. Just as the outcome of the Hill-Thomas hearings was in part dependent on a failure of cross-racial alliance, the effectiveness of this campaign is, in part, dependent on failures of cross-racial alliances within lesbian/gay/queer communities, and particularly among these communities and African American Christian churches.

REFERENCES

Abelove, Henry, Michèle Aina Barale, and David M. Halperin, eds. 1993. *The lesbian and gay studies reader*. New York: Routledge.

ACT UP/NY Women & AIDS Book Group. 1990. *Women, AIDS and activism*. Boston: South End Press.

Albrecht, Lisa, and Rose M. Brewer, eds. 1990. *Bridges of power: Women's multicultural alliances*. Philadelphia: New Society Publishers.

Attorney General's Commission on Pornography. 1986. *Final report*. 2 vols. Washington, D.C.: U.S. Government Printing Office.

Bad Object-Choices, ed. 1991. *How do I look?: Queer film and video*. Seattle: Bay Press.

Bolton, Richard, ed. 1992. *Culture wars: Documents from the recent controversies in the arts*. New York: New Press.

Benhabib, Seyla, Judith Butler, and Nancy Fraser. 1991. An exchange on feminism and postmodernism. *Praxis International* 11(2): 137–77.

Califia, Pat. [1981] 1987. A personal view of the history of the lesbian s/m community and movement in San Francisco. In *Coming to power: Writings and graphics on lesbian s/m*. See Samois [1981] 1987.

Crenshaw, Kimberlè. 1989. Demarginalizing the intersection of race and sex: A black feminist critique of antidiscrimination doctrine, feminist theory, and antiracist politics. *University of Chicago Legal Forum*, 139–68.

———. 1992. Whose story is it anyway? Feminist and antiracist appropriations of Anita Hill. In *Race-ing justice, en-gendering power: Essays on Anita Hill, Clarence Thomas, and the construction of social reality*. See Morrison 1992.

Crimp, Douglas. 1993. Right on, girlfriend! In *Fear of a queer planet: Queer politics and social theory*, ed. Michael Warner. Minneapolis: University of Minnesota Press.

Crimp, Douglas, with Adam Rolston. 1990. *AIDS demographics*. Seattle: Bay Press.

Downs, Donald Alexander. 1989. *The new politics of pornography*. Chicago: University of Chicago Press.

Dworkin, Andrea. 1978. *Right-wing women*. New York: Coward-McCann.

———. 1985. Against the male flood: Censorship, pornography, and equality. *Harvard Women's Law Journal* 9: 1–19.

Faderman, Lillian. 1993. The return of butch and femme: A phenomenon of lesbian sexuality of the 1980s and 1990s. In *American sexual politics: Sex, gender, and race since the Civil War*, ed. John C. Fout and Maura Shaw Tantillo. Chicago: University of Chicago Press.

Fani-Kayode, Rotimi. 1987. *Black male/White male*. London: Gay Men's Press.

"Frontline." 1992. *Clarence Thomas and Anita Hill: Public hearing, private pain*. 50 min. PBS Video Documentary Consortium, videocassette.

Goldsby, Jackie. 1993. Queen for 307 days: Looking b(l)ack at Vanessa Williams and the sex wars. In *Sisters, sexperts, queers: Beyond the lesbian nation*, ed. Arlene Stein. New York: Plume.

Hamilton, Marybeth. 1993. 'A little bit spicy, but not too raw': Mae West, pornography and popular culture. In *Sex exposed: Sexuality and the pornography debate*. See Segal and McIntosh 1993.

Hirsch, Marianne, and Evelyn Fox Keller, eds. 1990. *Conflicts in feminism*. New York: Routledge.

Jakobsen, Janet. 1991. Reason made me do it: The parameters of ethical justification and acceptable alibis. International Association of Philosophy and Literature Annual Meeting.

Kennedy, Elizabeth Lapovsky, and Madeline Davis. 1993. *Boots of leather, slippers of gold: The history of a lesbian community*. New York: Routledge.

Lederer, Laura, ed. 1980. *Take back the night: Women on pornography*. New York: William Morrow.

Leidholdt, Dorchen, and Janice G. Raymond, eds. 1990. *The sexual liberals and the attack on feminism*. New York: Pergamon.

Linden, Robin Ruth, et al., eds. 1982. *Against sadomasochism: A radical feminist analysis*. San Francisco: Frog in the Well.

Lubiano, Wahneema. 1992. Black ladies, welfare queens, and state minstrels: Ideological war by narrative means. In *Race-ing justice, en-gendering power: Essays on Anita Hill, Clarence Thomas, and the construction of social reality*. See Morrison 1992.

Lugones, María. 1994. Purity, impurity, and separation. *Signs*. 19(2): 458–79.

MacKinnon, Catharine. 1992. Does sexuality have a history? In *Discourses of sexuality: From Aristotle to AIDS*. See Stanton 1992.

———. 1993. *Only words*. Cambridge: Harvard University Press.

Mapplethorpe, Robert. 1982. *Black males*. With an introduction by Edmund White. Amsterdam: Gallerie Jurka.

———. 1986. *Black book*. With a foreword by Ntozake Shange. New York: St. Martin's Press.

Mercer, Kobena. 1991. Skin head sex thing: Racial difference and the homoerotic imaginary. In *How do I look? Queer film and video*. See Bad Object-Choices 1991.

Morrison, Toni, ed. 1992. *Race-ing justice, en-gendering power: Essays on Anita Hill, Clarence Thomas, and the construction of social reality*. New York: Pantheon Books.

Narayan, Uma. 1988. Working together across difference: Some considerations on emotions and political practice. *Hypatia* 3(2): 31–48.

Nestle, Joan. 1987. Lesbians and prostitutes: A historical sisterhood. In *Sex work: Writings by women in the sex industry*, ed. Frédérique Delacoste and Priscilla Alexander. Pittsburgh: Cleis Press.

———, ed. 1992. *The persistent desire: A femme-butch reader*. Boston: Alyson Publications.

Painter, Nell Irvin. 1992. Hill, Thomas, and the use of racial stereotype. In *Race-ing justice, en-gendering power: Essays on Anita Hill, Clarence Thomas, and the construction of social reality*. See Morrison 1992.

Patton, Cindy. 1991. Safe sex and the pornographic vernacular. In *How do I look?: Queer film and video*. See Bad Object-Choices 1991.

Pharr, Suzanne. 1993. Community organizing and the religious right: Lessons from Oregon's measure nine campaign. *Radical America* 24(4): 67–75.

Pratt, Minnie Bruce. 1991. Poetry in time of war. In *Rebellion: Essays, 1980–1991*. Ithaca: Firebrand Books.

Reagon, Bernice Johnson. 1983. Coalition politics: Turning the century. In *Home girls: A black feminist anthology*, ed. Barbara Smith. New York: Kitchen Table: Women of Color Press.

Reti, Irene, ed. 1993. *Unleashing feminism: Sadomasochism in the gay 90s*. Santa Cruz: HerBooks.

Rich, B. Ruby. 1986. Review essay: Feminism and sexuality in the 1980s. *Feminist Studies* 12: 525–61.

Saalfield, Catherine, and Ray Navarro. 1991. Shocking pink praxis: Race and gender on the ACT UP frontlines. In *Inside/out: Lesbian theories, gay theories*, ed. Diana Fuss. New York: Routledge.

Samois. [1981] 1987. *Coming to power: Writings and graphics on lesbian s/m*. 3d ed. Boston: Alyson Publications.

Schulman, Sarah. 1994. *My American history: Lesbian and gay life during the Reagan/Bush years*. New York: Routledge.

Segal, Lynne, and Mary McIntosh, eds. 1993. *Sex exposed: Sexuality and the pornography debate*. New Brunswick: Rutgers University Press.

Signorile, Michelangelo. 1994. *Queer in America: Sex, the media, and the closets of power*. New York: Anchor Books.

Snitow, Ann, et al., eds. 1983. *Powers of desire: The politics of sexuality*. New York: Monthly Review Press.

Spillers, Hortense J. [1984] 1992. Interstices: A Small Drama of Words. In *Pleasure and danger: Exploring female sexuality*. See Vance [1984] 1992.

Stanton, Domna C., ed. 1992. *Discourses of sexuality: From Aristotle to AIDS*. Ann Arbor: University of Michigan Press.

Trinh T. Minh-Ha. 1991. The other censorship. Chap. 14 in *When the moon waxes red: Representation and cultural politics*. New York: Routledge.

Vance, Carole. 1993. Negotiating sex and gender in the attorney general's commission on pornography. In *Sex Exposed: Sexuality and the pornography debate*. See Segal and McIntosh 1993.

Vance, Carole, ed. [1984] 1992. *Pleasure and danger: Exploring female sexuality*. 2d ed. London: Pandora Press.

Watt, David Harrington. 1991. *A transforming faith: Explorations of twentieth-century American evangelicalism*. New Brunswick: Rutgers University Press.

Wilson, Elizabeth. 1983. The context of 'Between pleasure and danger': The Barnard conference on sexuality. *Feminist Review* 13: 35–41.

11

"Undemocratic Afflictions"

A Feminist Response to the AIDS Epidemic

KATE MEHURON

Mainstream media representations and public policy discourses since the 1980s have appropriated the AIDS (acquired immune deficiency syndrome) epidemic in the United States as a homophobic public spectacle. This media-driven spectacle has featured moralistic narratives about the overwhelming suffering, deaths, and mourning experienced by the urban North American gay community.[1] AIDS activists have publicly criticized and continue to criticize these mainstream media and policy discourses, mobilizing counter-hegemonic media representations to do so.[2] However, moralistic divisions between those who are "innocent" victims of the epidemic and those who are "guilty" victims continue to be perpetrated by mainstream discourses.

Feminist assessments of this epidemic show that the explicitly homophobic politics of the U.S. AIDS epidemic rely on the ongoing mainstream deployment of traditional gender-oppressive and racist stereotypes of masculinity and femininity.[3] Feminist and gay evaluations also demonstrate that homophobic, racist, and gender-oppressive public policy discourses and institutional practices insulate the general public from a full understanding of the specific routes of transmission of HIV (human immunodeficiency virus) and thus of preventive strategies that are available or that could be invented.[4] Additionally, feminist analyses such as Gena Corea's *Invisible Epidemic* (1992) demonstrate that homophobic, racist, and gender-oppressive public policy discourses and research agendas have perpetuated the invisibility of specific groups of women whose lives have been and continue to be devastated by the epidemic.

This body of gay and feminist institutional criticism has established that in

United States, AIDS is a chronic crisis that is managed by racist, sexist, and homophobic public policies, medical institutions, and federal research agendas (Perrow and Guillén 1990, 152–80). Socioeconomic class differences and racial discrimination, in addition to homophobia and sexism, confounded coalitional efforts in the 1970s and 1980s between the civil rights movement, the gay liberation movement, and the feminist movement. These tensions, as well as the racialized gulf within the feminist movement between dominant white middle-class women's interests and the interests of working-class white women and women of color, are exacerbated in the 1990s by the distortions perpetrated by mainstream institutions about the nature and extent of the AIDS epidemic.

Demographic trends identified by the Centers for Disease Control (CDC), the U.S. Public Health Service, and the National Research Council, forecast, in the council's words, the "undemocratic afflictions" of AIDS with its concentration within urban communities assaulted by poverty, intravenous drug use, and their associated social and medical afflictions. The council's report describes these afflictions: homelessness; rising rates of sexually transmitted diseases and tuberculosis; rising rates of homicide and suicide; poverty-level, single-parent, female-headed households; discriminatory public policies; and the lack of adequate preventive and crisis-oriented medical care in these urban neighborhoods (Jonsen and Stryker 1993). These interrelated hardships are exacerbated by the impact of AIDS in minority communities, and these hardships have coupled with discriminatory public policy, media, and institutional discourses that stigmatize and moralize against people with AIDS. These interrelated structures of gender, race, and sexual oppression have fertilized the growth of conspiracy theories in urban gay communities and African American communities, and they have fostered in mainstream discourses the public image of "gay genocide" (Erni 1994, 89–106).

In the following sections, I briefly review some of the AIDS-related conspiracy theories that have arisen in urban gay communities and African American communities, emphasizing the explicit accusation of genocide which these theories contain. I treat these versions of conspiracy as situated, subjugated knowledges that offer, in the words of Patricia Hill Collins, "partial perspectives on domination" (Collins 1991, 236). I argue that feminist genealogical practices, by assessing AIDS-related conspiracy theories as subjugated knowledges, can seriously address these partial perspectives and generate from them empowering forms of knowledge about and coalitional activism toward the "matrix of domination" that manages the chronic U.S. AIDS crisis.

APPRAISING GENOCIDE

Feminist genealogical practices draw on Foucault's analysis of biopower and his concept of subjugated knowledges, and apply this analysis toward critiques of and oppositional strategies toward structures of masculinist oppression. To the extent that feminist genealogical practices incorporate an analysis of the racist and heterosexist dimensions of masculinist biopower as it is exercised in the AIDS epidemic, they demonstrate important and desirable political affinities with the recent U.S. movement of queer theory and coalitional activism.[5] Specific initiatives by feminists in the New York AIDS Coalition to Unleash Power (ACT UP/NY) during the 1980s and 1990s illustrate such feminist genealogical practices and their political affinities with queer activism.

Foucault's analysis of biopower in *The History of Sexuality* understands biopower's capacities to exercise technological discourses and public policies with genocidal force: a force that *disallows* life to the point of death by the regulatory mechanisms which administer and foster life in Western societies (Foucault 1980[A], 138). Genocidal practices, he claims, are conducted by bureaucratic and governmentally mandated agencies that function as the corporate "managers of life and survival, bodies and race." They have at stake the biological control of populations, and they exercise the power to disallow life to those who are "a biological danger to others" (Foucault 1980[A], 137–39). Foucault's analysis distinguishes between biopower's contemporary corporate deployments of power and the historically older juridical deployments of power which legislate masculinist domination by blood lineage and familial alliance.

Although the corporate and government management of populations is the most recent force field of biopower's operations, genealogical feminists argue that the juridical deployments of blood lineage and familial alliance are significant masculinist forces with which women and minorities must contend in the present. Foucault's distinctions within his analysis of biopower are significant to genealogical feminism when the corporate management of the life and death of populations is examined as a contemporary force that is interlocked with racist and heterosexist legal deployments of blood lineage and familial alliances. Examples include racist and sexist eugenic research agendas and media campaigns, and the heterosexist and elitist "family values" rhetoric which propagandized the Reagan-Bush administration's juridical assault on the civil rights of women and people of color in the 1980s and 1990s.[6] Feminist genealogical practices oppose these assaults by situated, local, and activist forms of resistance to masculinist biopower's technological and legal initiatives. These coercive initiatives would perpetuate or deepen the disenfranchisement and invisibility of specific groups of people. Of particular relevance to feminist genealogical practice is Foucault's understanding of subjugated knowledges as those standpoints which are disqualified by whatever regime of truth is legitimized by biopower's force field of self-authorizing, universalist claims.[7]

The public policy and political discourses of the U.S. AIDS epidemic can be evaluated as constituted by the multiple uses of both deployments of power. Linda Singer, in *Erotic Welfare*, applies a feminist Foucauldian analysis to the aggression of the New Right's national "family values" campaign against the civil rights of lesbian and gay people. Singer calls the rhetoric of the New Right's grassroots neoconservative movement the "logic of epidemic" (Singer 1993, 34–61). This moralizing rhetoric, she argues, draws on the general public's fears of contagion and broader socioeconomic insecurities, mobilizing to overturn antidiscrimination ordinances and laws protecting lesbian and gay people, abortion rights, and women's other reproductive freedoms, and to block safer sex education in the schools. The moralizing rhetoric of the New Right capitalizes on a historically older juridical discourse of patrilineal sovereignty and its vested interests in the patriarchal family. The New Right propagandizes its homophobic "family values" message on a massive scale and obfuscates the socioeconomic sources of the panic logic which it manipulates. While public debate is focused on media-driven "family values" trend stories, other technological and corporate deployments of power are involved in selectively disallowing life.

Media analyst Simon Watney has shown that since the mid-1980s, in compliance with the neoconservative agenda, our popular media have premiered the spectacle of infected gay men as carriers of a depravity of moral will which is potentially contagious to those who are morally well: heterosexual white America. As a public media spectacle, HIV infection and its transmission is dramatized by a "moral etiology" of AIDS: a nonepidemiological account of origins which miraculously spares those who are heterosexual, Christian, married, monogamous, European American, and white. Meanwhile, as what Watney calls the "public masque" of the moralization of this disease continues, the complex material realities of AIDS are rendered invisible by this media-hyped deployment of alliance (Watney 1993, 202–11).

An example of feminist genealogical practice that counters this media hype is the 1990 ACT UP/New York Women and AIDS Book Group collaborative publication *Women, AIDS and Activism*. This book compiles bibliographies of alternative safer-sex video projects and alternative health and safer-sex educational resources for HIV-positive women. It includes the testimony of HIV-positive women who have formed activist communities in the Bedford Hills Correctional Facility. Their HIV-preventive efforts continue to inform local community initiatives in Brooklyn and the Lower East Side of Manhattan for women who are sex workers or who have partners implicated in intravenous drug use or bisexual activity.

Other essays in *Women, AIDS and Activism* demonstrate the strategic compatibilities between feminist reproductive rights initiatives and feminists who are educating against HIV transmission in their local communities. The compatibility of both struggles is fostered by the common scourge of misogynist and racist fetal rights litigation that arose in the 1980s and which most frequently penalizes and criminalizes pregnant women for the bad effects of their poverty, drug use, or ill health on their fetus.[8] This effort by the ACT UP/Women's Book Group and efforts by other emergent resources are examples of the recuperation of types of knowledge which are vital to women who are fighting HIV transmission and the gendered and sexual inequities blocking their access to health care or clinical drug trials (Treichler 1991). The genealogical retrieval of types of knowledge which are disqualified by politically legitimized systems of scientific research or public policy discourses is vital to feminist responses to the AIDS epidemic.

The paradigm of AIDS-related genocide that is generated from feminist revisions of Foucault's analysis of power relations is distinguishable from, yet in important respects is compatible with, the legal definition of genocide provided by the United Nations Convention on the Prevention and Punishment of the Crime of Genocide. The convention asserts that genocide is a crime under international law and defines victims of genocide as those members of a national, ethnic, racial, or religious group who are either killed outright or are the recipients of any of four other sufficient conditions: causing serious bodily or mental harm to members of the group; deliberately inflicting on the group conditions of life calculated to bring about its physical destruction in whole or in part; imposing measures intended to prevent births within the group; and forcibly transferring children of the group to another group (Lang 1990, 6–7).[9]

Feminist interventions in the U.N. paradigm of genocide demand the inclusion of women and sexual minorities in the U.N. definition of potential victims of genocide (MacKinnon 1993, 83–109). Additionally, feminist revisions of Foucault's distinction between corporate and government-juridical deployments of power provide a paradigm of genocide that can identify, through genealogical practices, the specific agencies and institutions that are perpetuating the conditions of genocide which the U.N. convention has laid out. It is unlikely that AIDS activists will be able to legally prosecute the United States government for its genocidal policies of neglect toward people with AIDS, although cogent arguments have been made in defense of the notion of state criminality (Barak 1989). More urgently, feminist revisions and applications of this paradigm can articulate the concrete needs of women and the local strategies of survival and the qualitative enhancement of lives which become explicit as a result of these genealogical practices.

Some of these needs which AIDS-related feminist theory has identified are (1) the enforcement of women's regulatory inclusion in AIDS-related research and clinical trials; (2) women-only AIDS-related research and clinical trials to offset the paucity of data on the effect of HIV infection on women resultant from a decade of exclusively male trials;[10] (3) a national health care system which provides gynocentric health care for women across socioeconomic strata; (4) scientific research on and aggressive corporate investment in the development and marketing of female-controlled prophylaxes against HIV (Stein and

Gollub 1993); (5) federally mandated educational initiatives which nonmoralistically and specifically use the sexual vernaculars of diverse communities of women in national AIDS-preventive education; (6) advocacy for the health care needs and protection of female sex workers from discriminatory civil and police actions in their local neighborhoods; (7) subsidized housing for homeless people with AIDS that are safe shelters from sexual assault and violence (Guillén 1990; 106–26, 152–84; Barak 1991); and (8) the systematic reform of the National Cancer Institute's policies and priorities with respect to both breast cancer research and research regarding HIV-infected women (Solomon 1992).

With respect to (3), the need for comprehensive gynocentric health care for women across socioeconomic strata, feminists are assessing the recent history of the obstacles to such health care. Corea elaborates the history of the CDC's lassitude toward researching women as a risk group in HIV transmission. Over a decade passed before the CDC widened its official definition of AIDS to include invasive cervical cancer and other HIV-associated conditions in women. She explains that most physicians look to the CDC for information, and if they are not alerted to the special symptomatology of HIV infection which women exhibit, then many cases will go undiagnosed. Undiagnosed HIV-positive women also are not eligible for disability benefits from the Social Security Administration. When the CDC revised its definition in 1993 to include invasive cervical cancer, pulmonary tuberculosis, and recurrent pneumonia, new case reports were expected to double. It is spurious to pit breast cancer activism against HIV activism on the comparative grounds of actual diagnosed cases, because HIV positivity in women was virtually invisible during the U.S. AIDS epidemic between 1981 and 1992.

One of the official recalcitrances toward HIV-positive women's health care needs which ACT UP feminist activists have challenged involves the CDC's proposed guidelines for standard of care for the diagnosis, treatment, and prophylaxis of HIV and associated opportunistic infections. These guidelines call for a pap smear at baseline, a follow-up pap smear at six months, and then a pap smear yearly for those women showing no abnormalities. Activists contend that these guidelines will jeopardize women's lives, for HIV-infected women have 45–60 percent incidence of a cervical abnormality called intraepithelial neoplasia, which is an indicator of cervical cancer. Pap smears do not detect this abnormality in 25 percent of cases. Feminist AIDS activists assert that the CDC is again putting women at unnecessary risk, owing to the steeper cost of colposcopies, which detect cervical abnormalities in 60 percent of the cases. Medicaid and private insurers look to CDC standards to determine which medical procedures they will subsidize (Lobbia 1993).

My list of eight major needs which have been identified by AIDS-related feminist theory is far from exhaustive, yet to actually implement any or all of these recommendations is a radical task which requires the politicization of the actual needs and civil rights of street sex workers, intravenous drug users, and homeless women. This is the kind of radical feminist activism exemplified by Dr. Joyce Wallace in her research and health care efforts in New York (Corea 1992, 234–40). Feminist activists need to become involved in what Nancy Fraser describes as the necessary translation from socially marginalized women's discourses to officially recognized discourses. The most crucial work of translation ought to be focused on the actual sexual behaviors and the actual ways of communicating the sexual needs and preferences of women and men of color from low-income urban neighborhoods (Fraser 1989, 171–79).

AIDS public policy analyst Cindy Patton identifies the broad cultural narratives about gender which have been and continue to be disabling to women's health care needs: the racialized dichotomization of women into virgins or whores and their stigmatization as vectors or passive vehicles of sexually transmitted disease. These dominant cultural narratives intertwine with cost-benefit ideologies of limited resources that mobilize the needs of infected gay men against women of color, men who are intravenous drug users against women who are intravenous drug users and their sexual partners, middle-class white women against socioeconomically disadvantaged people, and so on. The history of the CDC's divisive and prejudicial classifications of people into high-risk and low-risk groups has compounded the racist, class-based, and heterosexist character of U.S. public policies. The concrete result has been profound limitations on access to health care and to clinical trials for women and people of color (Patton 1994). Patton calls for public policies to contextually situate the needs of women by conducting the in-depth ethnographic research and qualitative interviewing strategies necessary to yield realistic models of women's sexual practices and to identify the specific cultural issues within local communities which condition HIV preventive efforts. These recommendations name aspects of feminist genealogical practice which, in the long run, can mitigate the collective sense of hopelessness that is fostered by material conditions of deprivation and suffering. Such practices can also alleviate the collective political paralysis that is encouraged by legends of conspiracy circulating in the African American and gay communities.

CONSPIRACY THEORIES

I often hear AIDS-related conspiracy theories dismissed as if their claims were too preposterous to seriously consider. I contend, on the contrary, that some AIDS-related conspiracy theories contain many partially warranted beliefs and that they do function as a form of folk knowledge that sustains a necessary, self-protective boundary of distrust toward medical, military, and research institutional agendas in the United States. My discussion is not designed to prove the truth of any one version of conspiracy. Rather, I briefly summarize some versions of AIDS-related conspiracy theories and suggest that feminist genealogical practices can assuage a community's collective paralysis in the face of well-founded collective patterns of fear and distrust. The preceding discussion has highlighted how feminist genealogical practice locates strategies of resistance which result in self-determinative practices of self-care and self-protection.

Conspiracy theories in African American communities, according to Patricia Turner, are types of contemporary legends that carry the basic theme of the historical conflict between black and white people. Contemporary legends combine rumors (short nonnarrative expressions of belief) and legends (more traditionally grounded narratives of belief). Turner asserts that AIDS-related conspiracy theories in the African American community use contamination motifs, which "refer to any item in which the physical well-being of individual black bodies is being manipulated for racist reasons" (Turner 1993, 138).

In her interviews with many African American informants, Turner finds a general pattern of distrust toward governmental and policy-making agencies. The FBI (Federal Bureau of Investigation), the CIA (Central Intelligence Agency), and the CDC are often named as antiblack conspirators. The historical background for such widespread patterns of collective distrust derives from the folk knowledge passed down from earlier times of crisis. Some of these crisis-oriented times include slavery practices in the antebellum South, the organized antiblack conspiracy of the Ku Klux Klan during the Reconstruction era up to the present, the overt racist discrimination against blacks during World War I and World II, the urban legacy of race riots, the assassination of Martin Luther King and John F. Kennedy with anticivil rights overtones, coercive sterilization and birth-control policies, the Tuskegee Institute's syphilis experiments on nonconsenting and uninformed black men by the U.S. Public Health Service (Jones 1981).

These types of historical precedents are the grounds which have nourished what Turner describes as the "pervasiveness of metaphors linking the fate of the black race to the fates of black bodies, metaphors in use since the very first contact between whites and blacks" (Turner 1993, 3). These historical precedents, coupled with the extreme disparities in health status experienced by African Americans and other minorities in comparison with whites in the United States, have created widespread suspicions that the AIDS virus is either "(a) the aftermath of a biological warfare experiment that was tried out on Africans or Haitians or (b) an intentional use of biological warfare *intended to* diminish the African or Haitian population" (Turner 1993, 158).

Harlon L. Dalton, in "AIDS in Blackface," confirms Turner's observations and isolates two assumptions implicit to the strong claim of genocide carried by these conspiracy rumors:

> The first is that the hostility of white America toward black America is so powerful, or the disregard so profound, that no depredation is unthinkable. This view is rooted in racial strife and feeds on the storehouse of sins visited upon blacks by whites. The second assumption is that under the right circumstances, the government is not above compromising the lives of innocent citizens. (Dalton 1990, 253)

Unfortunately, as both Dalton and Turner note, there is strong supportive evidence for both assumptions. In these times, AIDS is one of the ten leading causes of death for the African American population, and AIDS has become the leading cause of death for black women between the ages of twenty-four and thirty-six. These are devastating statistics, taken with the fact that blacks have, as epidemiologist Samuel Duh writes, "higher morbidity and mortality rates than whites in virtually every disease category, in every age group and in both sexes" (Duh 1991, 8). These facts alone strongly support the suggestion that U.S. public health and social welfare policies have seriously compromised the lives of African American citizens (Barbee and Little 1993, White 1994).

The intentionality of the U.S. government's genocidal neglect and its putative involvement in biological experiments conducted against U.S. citizens arise in gay activist versions of AIDS-related conspiracy theories. Current gay activist criticism is sharply divided between two theories of genocide which I call the chemical-biological warfare version and the corporate failure version. Both of these conspiracy theories circulate as controversial urban legends within and between gay activist networks. These theories, which I briefly summarize below, are supported by a substantive history of antigay discrimination in the United States, discrimination that necessitates a continuing project of documentation by gay-affirmative historians. The institutional collusions between homophobic psychiatric practices, the U.S. military, and governmental McCarthyism provide the compelling historical precedents for any gay or lesbian individual's distrust toward sex-related scientific research, the FBI, CIA, and U.S. military institutions (Shilts 1993).

With this background in mind, the chemical-biological warfare version defends the manmade, Defense Department–sponsored origin of the U.S. AIDS epidemic in chemical-biological warfare research that either accidentally or purposefully infected the politicized gay white men's community in the government-sponsored hepatitis B experiments in San Francisco, Denver, and New York City in 1978–1979 with a synthetic retrovirus manufactured from chimpanzees in federally funded military laboratories. These arguments document the simultaneous experimental inoculation programs sponsored by the World Health Organization (WHO) in collaboration with the U.S. federal government conducted in south central Africa during the same period and the international connections to the infection of Haitians working in Africa and the transmission of AIDS to Haiti.[11] This theory concludes that a federally supported racist and homophobic conspiracy against socially stigmatized groups for the purposes of militarist experimentation is a plausible explanation for the genocidal character of the AIDS epidemic.

The corporate failure version of genocide argues that the selective annihilation of specific sexual and racial minority groups by AIDS is the result of a massive "systems failure" of public policy and health organizations, whose inadequate responses are due to the "negative synergy" produced by the destructive interaction of all of the following and more: (1) popular media distortions; (2) the Reagan, Bush, and Clinton administrations' moralistic indifference to people with AIDS and censorship of public education programs; (3) corporate pharmaceutical opportunism; (4) scientific competitiveness in key federal research agencies such as the National Cancer Institute, the Food and Drug Administration, the National Institute of Allergies and Infectious Diseases, and the Centers for Disease Control; and (5) the lack of resources and the social stigmatization which organizations experienced when candidly responding to the health care and medical research needs associated with infected gay men and intravenous drug users.[12] Within this analysis, the moralistic and homophobic stigmatization of nonreproductive sexual behaviors and intravenous drug use is a major but not the only contributor to the breakdown of organizational compassion and efficiency in the 1980s.

The preceding summary of some of the conspiracy theories circulating in the African American and gay communities indicates that in their status as subjugated knowledges, they offer standpoints on the politics of AIDS in the United States which are partially warranted by historical precedents that reveal extreme discriminatory practices toward gays and lesbians and people of color. Far from mere paranoid fantasies, these theories and legends will circulate as long as public policy discourses and the mainstream media continue to disclose the profound indifference to minority populations that has characterized such discourses in the recent past. I turn to one such disclosure of official indifference and perhaps intentional neglect, the effects of which activists in minority communities must continue to contend with.

PUBLIC POLICY RHETORIC

In February 1993, the National Research Council's Panel on Monitoring the AIDS Epidemic published its definitive report, *The Social Impact of AIDS in the United States*. Across the United States, local media coverage of the report cited these conclusions:

> If the current pattern of the epidemic holds, U.S. society at large will have been able to wait out the primary impact of the epidemic even though the crisis period will have stretched out over 15 years. HIV/AIDS will "disappear," not because, like smallpox, it has been elimi-

> nated, but because those who continue to be affected by it are socially invisible, beyond the sight and attention of the majority population. (Jonsen and Stryker 1993, 9)

Americans suddenly encountered a new metaphor, the "synergism of plagues," coined in an article (Wallace) that is cited in the report. This metaphor was embedded in a passage especially favored by the press:

> HIV is concentrating in pools of persons who are also caught in the "synergism of plagues": poverty, poor health and lack of health care, inadequate education, joblessness, hopelessness and social disintegration. (Jonsen and Stryker 1993, 7)

Thus in a series of news releases in February 1993, the national media refigured AIDS as a denaturalized yet unintentional catastrophe that selectively attacks certain urban populations, a synergistic plague which can be "waited out" by the unafflicted as it rages exclusively among the "socially invisible" of our society.

To the publicized dismay of the panel that authored the book, the media uprooted this metaphor from the report's discursive context. David Kirp argues in his substantive analysis of *The Social Impact* that the book is a "policy tale" whose grim conclusions are intended for the Clinton administration, delivered as a "wake-up call to a dozing nation" (Kirp 1993). In this respect, the book can be interpreted as intended to deflate the social effects of the epidemic logic which I mentioned earlier. In nearly every summary passage, the report reassures the general public, yet appeals to the president, the federal government, and the Centers for Disease Control to initiate vast reforms in the areas of preventive education, clinical trials and research, and diagnostic health care in urban and rural regions.

When comparing AIDS to other epidemics, the report acknowledges that the "changes in the collective mind of society might be the most profound of all impacts" wrought by AIDS, yet it concludes:

> Our report suggests that, in some respects, the AIDS epidemic may be more like the influenza of 1918 than the bubonic plague of 1348: many of its most striking features will be absorbed in the flow of American life. But, hidden beneath the surface, its worst effects will continue to devastate the lives and cultures of certain communities. (Jonsen and Stryker 1993, 5–6)

Despite this palliative language, the National Research Council's report does not simply advocate the status quo of administrative neglect toward socially marginalized groups. Full chapters are devoted to the battles fought by AIDS activists to reform the drug approval protocols of the FDA (Food and Drug Administration) and NIH (National Institutes of Health), and to the successes of the gay community in cultivating safer sex practices and a grassroots health care and research movement. The report indicts the failures of U.S. mainstream religions to respond compassionately to the epidemic and the failures by federally financed researchers and policymakers to "appreciate the interaction between social, economic, cultural conditions and the propagation of HIV/AIDS disease." These failures, the report remarks, have resulted in public misunderstanding and policy mistakes about the epidemic (Jonsen and Stryker 1993, 8). The report urges the extension of AIDS activists' efforts on behalf of those inner-city populations that are and will be ravaged by HIV and its synergism of plagues in the foreseeable future.

The panel's conclusions appeal to the prosaic imaginations of public health officials, who are urged to recommend that the war on AIDS be fought with an enlightened use of the manual weapons of condoms, clean needle campaigns, and safer-sex education programs tailored to the vernaculars of affected neighborhoods and age groups. In March 1993, *The New York Times* ran the headline "Experts Are Urging a Neighborhood-Based Attack on the Spread of AIDS"; the accompanying story included the demographic map of the concentration of HIV/AIDS in New York City, originally shown in the panel's report (Kolata 1993). According to the report, the only "disconcerting" social lack is what Dr. James Curran, the associate director for HIV/AIDS at the CDC, has termed the lack of "political will" to fund and implement targeted prevention programs (Kolata 1993, 16). Curran's plea for a new "political will" invites the resurgence of a coalitional politics and dovetails with feminist concerns about the impact of the epidemic on socioeconomically disadvantaged women, as well as with the organizing efforts of gay activists beset by the neoconservative "no special rights" initiatives sprouting in state legislative battles across the United States.

Ironically, at the same time that this document addresses a sort of depravity of political will exemplified by heterosexual white middle-class America and our public policy institutions toward the decimation of "others" by HIV infection, this report also blandly asserts that this indifference will have no lasting ill effects on the public institutions from which white middle-class heterosexual Americans benefit. The report asserts:

> The HIV/AIDS epidemic, although often compared to the Black Death, has not affected U.S. social institutions to any such extent. Although it had by the end of 1991 infected perhaps 1 million people, brought devastating sickness to 206,392, and death to 133,233, it had not significantly altered the structures or directions of the social institutions which we studied. . . . It is the panel's opinion that the limited responsiveness of institutions can in part be explained because the absolute numbers of the epidemic, relative to the U.S. population, are not overwhelming, and because U.S. social institutions are strong, complex, and resilient. (Jonsen and Stryker 1993, 7)

The report's language contradictorily implies that what is at stake is the resiliency of our social institutions rather than the depravity of political and moral will which manifested in the first wave of the epidemic and continues to manifest itself today.

CONSPIRACY OR LACK OF POLITICAL WILL?

The foregoing analysis discloses an institutional use of language which is perilously similar to the sort of self-deceptive locutions identified by Berel Lang to be characteristic of the genocidal uses of language by totalitarian regimes. Although I do not claim that U.S. public policy agendas or institutional processes are totalitarian, I find the institutional language exemplified by the National Research Council to approach, in Lang's words, a muteness "with respect to its own voice, detached from any sense of its own origins or purposes" (Lang 1991, 158). The report's understated contradictory ethical messages seem to exemplify language applied as "a political instrument which in its own structure would incorporate the features of moral violation that otherwise constitute [a] lie" (Lang 1991, 172).

Foucault's paradigm of genocide, the corporate and governmental disallowance of life by a society's specific regulatory mechanisms, is a more appropriate paradigm for understanding and countering our "undemocratic afflictions" than the totalitarian paradigm which Lang examines. Yet Lang's misgivings about the politicized, institutional uses of language that incorporate ethical self-deceptions and that broadcast ambiguous double-talk to policy-making agencies are compatible with and illuminate genealogical efforts to understand how genocidal regulatory mechanisms are participating in the degradation of the health status of women and minority communities. At stake is not only survival but also the qualitative enhancement of people's capacities to participate in democratic processes such as health care reform and the reform of local communities' socioeconomic status.

Feminist AIDS-related genealogical practitioners share with Evelynn Hammonds the sense that "I've been afraid to know more about this story." This is the opening phrase in her exploration of the details of nurse Eunice Rivers's complicity in the Tuskegee Syphilis Study. Conspiracy theories feature giant actors and small victims, some of whom are complicit with overriding agendas of annihilation or neglect. Hammonds calls for a more thorough contextualization of Rivers's participation in the Public Health Service's experiments in order to shed light on the ways that the African American community can invent self-determinative strategies of self-protection and self-care. Hammonds writes:

> If we do not speak out, then another generation will be perfectly justified in asking us, as we today ask those involved in the Tuskegee

Study, why blacks stood silent while our people die. (Hammonds 1994, 331)

The conspiratorial public masque of overweening perpetrators and passive victims must be contextualized by an analysis of the drama's actual power relations. Subjugated knowledges should become the stuff of contemporary legends that work to counter institutional betrayals, betrayals intertwined with women's and minority communities' limited access to health care.

NOTES

1. For useful discussions, see Watney (1989, 1993) and Crimp (1992, 1993).

2. For examples of alternative women's sex education videos that are tailored to the sexual vernaculars of minority communities, see the annotated bibliography in Saalfield (1990) and accounts by Juhasz (1992) and Mohammed (1992). For earlier AIDS activist media efforts, see Crimp (1987), Klusacek and Morrison (1992), and Miller (1992).

3. For examples of feminist assessments, see Treichler (1988), Patton (1990), Squire (1993), Watstein (1991), Bury et al. (1992), Huber and Schneider (1992), and Jewell (1993).

4. See Alonso and Koreck (1993), Hemphill (1991), and Doyle et al. (1994).

5. Queer theory and queer activism are umbrella terms for antiheterosexist theories and activisms that incorporate critiques of identity politics and critiques of essentialist views of sexuality and gender. At its best, queer theory and activism hold antiheterosexist positions which imply antiracist and antisexist assumptions as well. For examples, see Crimp (1993[B]), Warner (1993), Ringer (1994), Fuss (1991), and Gever et al. (1993).

6. For a description and defense of genealogical feminism's capacities to critique and oppose contemporary eugenics movements and neoconservative "family values" propaganda, see Quinby (1994, 31–51). For an incisive review of the Reagan-Bush Administration's assault on civil rights, see Eisenstein (1994).

7. For his elucidation of countermemory as the genealogical displacement of systems of subjugation, see Foucault (1977). For his view of subjugated knowledges, see Foucault (1980 [B]). For a thorough discussion of the relevance of Foucault's analysis of biopower for contemporary feminism, see McNay (1992).

8. See The ACT UP/NY Women and AIDS Book Group (1990, 139–55, 199–209). On the development of the punitive "fetal rights" juridical precedents in the 1980s, see Faludi (1991, 400–54). For a full account of the evolution of the Bedford Hills activist community, featuring the exemplary efforts of Katrina Haslip, see the interwoven narrative in Corea (1992). For the elucidation of the punitive aspects of "pediatric AIDS" toward HIV-positive women, see Corea (1992, 46–51).

9. See also Robinson (1960).

10. For a full account of this systematic exclusion of women, see Jonsen and Stryker (1993, 80–116) and Corea (1992).

11. See Lederer (1987–1988), Cantwell (1988, 1993), Chirimuuta and Chirimuuta (1989), and Farmer (1992).

12. See Guillén (1990, 11–44, 127–51), Lauritsen (1993), Nussbaum (1991), Brandt (1988).

REFERENCES

Abelove, Henry, Michele Aina Barale, and David Halperin, eds. 1993. *The lesbian and gay studies reader*. New York: Routledge.

ACT UP/NY Women and AIDS Book Group. 1990. *Women, AIDS and activism*. Boston: South End Press.

Almaguer, Tomas. 1993. Chicano men: A cartography of homosexual identity and behavior. In *The lesbian and gay studies reader*. See Abelove et al. 1993.

Alonso, Ana Maria, and Maria Teresa Koreck. 1993. Silences: "Hispanics," AIDS, and sexual practices. In *The lesbian and gay studies reader*. See Abelove et al. 1993.

Barak, Gregg, ed. 1989. *Crimes by the capitalist state: An introduction to state criminality*. Albany: State University of New York Press.

———. 1991. *Gimme shelter: A social history of homelessness in contemporary America*. New York: Praeger.

Barbee, Evelyn L., and Marilyn Little. 1993. Health, social class and African-American women. In *Theorizing Black Feminisms*. See James and Busia 1993.

Brandt, Allen. 1988. AIDS: From social history to social policy. In *AIDS: The burdens of history*. See Fee and Fox 1988.

Bury, Judy, Val Morrison, and Sheena McLachlan, eds. 1992. *Working with women and AIDS: Medical, social, and counseling issues*. New York: Routledge.

Butcher, Kate. 1994. Feminists, prostitutes and HIV. In *AIDS: Setting a feminist agenda*. See Doyle et al. 1994.

Cantwell, Alan. 1988. *AIDS and the doctors of death: An inquiry into the origin of the AIDS epidemic*. Los Angeles: Aries Rising Press.

———. 1993. *Queer blood: The secret AIDS genocide plot*. Los Angeles: Aries Rising Press.

Chirimuuta, Richard, and Rosalind Chirimuuta. 1989. *AIDS, Africa and Racism*. London: Free Association Books.

Collins, Patricia Hill. 1991. *Black feminist thought: Knowledge, consciousness, and the politics of empowerment*. New York: Routledge.

Corea, Gena. 1992. *The invisible epidemic: The story of women and AIDS*. New York: HarperCollins.

Crimp, Douglas, ed. 1987. *AIDS: Cultural analysis, cultural activism*. Cambridge: MIT Press.

———. Portraits of people with AIDS. In *Cultural Studies*. See Grossberg et al. 1992.

———. 1993(A). Right on, girlfriend! In *Fear of a Queer Planet*. See Warner 1993.

———. 1993(B). Mourning and militancy. In *Out there*. See Ferguson et al. 1993.

Crimp, Douglas, with Adam Rolston. 1990. *AIDS demographics*. Seattle: Bay Press.

Dalton, Haron L. 1990. AIDS in blackface. In *Living with AIDS*. See Graubard 1990.

Doyle, Lesley, Jennie Naidoo, and Tamsin Wilton, eds. 1994. *AIDS: Setting a feminist agenda*. Bristol: Taylor & Francis.

Duh, Samuel V. 1991. *Blacks and AIDS: Causes and origins*. Newbury Park: Sage.

Eisenstein, Zilla. 1994. *The color of gender: Reimaging democracy*. Berkeley: University of California Press.

Erni, John Nguyet. 1994. *Unstable frontiers: Technomedicine and the cultural politics of "curing" AIDS*. Minneapolis: University of Minnesota Press.
Faludi, Susan. 1991. *Backlash: The undeclared war against American women*. New York: Anchor.
Farmer, Paul. 1992. *AIDS and accusation: Haiti and the geography of blame*. Berkeley: University of California Press.
Fee, Elizabeth, and Daniel M. Fox, eds. 1988. *AIDS: The burden of history*. Berkeley: University of California Press.
Ferguson, Russell, Martha Gever, Trinh T. Minh-ha, and Cornel West, 1993. *Out there: Marginalization and contemporary cultures*. Cambridge: MIT Press.
Foucault, Michel. 1980[A]. *The history of sexuality, vol. 1*, trans. Robert Hurley. New York: Vintage.
———. 1980[B]. Two Lectures. In *Power/knowledge: Selected interviews and other writings 1972–1977*, ed. Colin Gordon, trans. Colin Gordon, Leo Marshall, John Mepham, and Kate Soper. New York: Pantheon.
———. 1977. Nietzsche, genealogy, history. In *Language, counter-memory, practice: Selected essays and interviews*, ed. Donald F. Bouchard, trans. Donald F. Bouchard and Sherry Simon. Ithaca: Cornell University Press.
Fraser, Nancy. 1989. *Unruly practices: Power, discourse and gender in contemporary social theory*. Cambridge: Polity Press.
Fuss, Diana, ed. 1991. *Inside/out: Lesbian theories, gay theories*. New York: Routledge.
Gever, Martha, John Greyson, and Pratibha Parmar, eds. 1993. *Queer looks: Perspectives on lesbian and gay film and video*. New York: Routledge.
Graubard, Stephen R., ed. 1990. *Living with AIDS*. Cambridge: MIT Press.
Grossberg, Lawrence, Cary Nelson, and Paula Treichler, eds. 1992. *Cultural studies*. New York: Routledge.
Hammonds, Evelyn M. 1994. Your silence will not protect you: Nurse Eunice Rivers and the Tuskegee Syphilis Study. In *The Black Women's Health Book*. See White 1994.
Hemphill, Essex, ed. 1991. *Brother to brother: New writings by black gay men*. Boston: Alyson.
Huber, Joan, and Beth E. Schneider, eds. 1992. *The social context of AIDS*. Newbury Park: Sage Publications.
James, Stanlie M., and Abena P. A. Busia. 1993. *Theorizing black feminisms: The visionary pragmatism of black women*. New York: Routledge.
Jewell, K. Sue, *From Mammy to Miss America and beyond: Cultural images and the shaping of U.S. social policy*. New York: Routledge, 1993.
Jones, James H. 1981. *Bad blood: The Tuskegee syphilis experiment*. New York: Free Press.
Jonsen, Albert R., and Jeff Stryker, eds. 1993. *The social impact of AIDS in the United States*. National Research Council Panel on Monitoring the Social Impact of the AIDS Epidemic. Washington, D.C.: National Academy Press.
Kirp, David. 1993. Killing the messenger. *The Nation*. March 15, 1993, 345–46.
Klusack, Allen, and Ken Morrison, eds. 1992. *A leap in the dark: AIDS, art and contemporary cultures*. Montreal: Vehicule Press.
Kolata, Gina. 1993. Targeting urged in attack on AIDS. *The New York Times*. March 7, 1993, 16.
Lang, Berel. 1990. *Act and idea in the nazi genocide*. Chicago: University of Chicago Press.
———. 1991. *Writing and the moral self*. New York: Routledge.

Lauritsen, John. 1993. *The AIDS war: Propaganda, profiteering and genocide from the medical-industrial complex*. New York: Asklepios Press.

Lederer, Robert. 1987–1988. Origin and spread of AIDS: Is the west responsible? *CovertAction* 28–29: 43–54, 52–65.

Lobbia, J.A. 1993. Anti-smear campaign. *The Village Voice*. July 20, 1993, 15.

MacKinnon, Catherine. 1993. Crimes of war, crimes of peace. In *On Human Rights*. See Shute and Hurley 1993.

McNay, Lois. 1992. *Foucault and feminism: Power, gender and the self*. Boston: Northeastern University Press.

Miller, James, ed. 1992. *Fluid exchanges: Artists and critics in the AIDS crisis*. Toronto: University of Toronto Press.

Mohammed, Juanita. 1992. WAVE in the media environment: Camcorder activism in AIDS education. *Camera Obscura* 28: 153–54.

Nussbaum, Bruce. 1991. *Good intentions: How big business and the media establishment are corrupting the fight against AIDS*. New York: Viking Press.

Patton, Cindy. 1990. *Inventing AIDS*. New York: Routledge.

———. 1994. *Last served? Gendering the HIV pandemic*. Bristol: Taylor & Francis.

Penley, Constance, and Andrew Ross, eds. 1991. *Technoculture*. Minneapolis: University of Minnesota Press.

Perrow, Charles, and Mauro F. Guillén. 1990. *The AIDS disaster: The failure of organizations in New York and the nation*. New Haven: Yale University Press.

Quinby, Lee. 1994. *Anti-apocalypse: Exercises in genealogical criticism*. Minneapolis: University of Minnesota Press.

Ringer, Jeffrey, ed. 1994. *Queer words, queer images: Communication and the construction of homosexuality*. New York: New York University Press.

Robinson, Nehemiah. 1960. *The genocide convention*. New York: Institute of Jewish Affairs.

Saalfield, Catherine. 1990. AIDS videos by, for, and about women. In *Women, AIDS and activism*. See ACT UP/NY Women and AIDS Book Group 1990.

Shilts, Randy. 1993. *Conduct unbecoming: Lesbians and gays in the U.S. military, Vietnam to the Persian Gulf*. New York: St. Martin's Press.

Shute, Stephen, and Susan Hurley, eds. 1993. *On human rights: The Oxford Amnesty Lectures 1993*. New York: Basic Books.

Singer, Linda. 1993. *Erotic welfare: Sexual theory and politics in the age of epidemic*, ed. Judith Butler and Maureen MacGrogan. New York: Routledge.

Solomon, Alisa. 1992. The politics of breast cancer. *Camera Obscura* 28: 157–77.

Squire, Corinne, ed. 1993. *Women and AIDS*. Newbury Park: Sage.

Stein, Zena, and Erica L. Gollub. 1993. Commentary: The new female condom—item one on a women's AIDS prevention agenda. *American Journal of Public Health* 83: 498–500.

Thomas, Ruth Morgan. 1993. HIV and the sex industry. In *Working with women and AIDS*. See Bury et al. 1993.

Treichler, Paula. 1988. AIDS, gender, and biomedical discourse: Current contests for meaning. In *AIDS: The burden of history*. See Fee and Fox 1988.

———. 1991. How to have theory in an epidemic: The evolution of AIDS treatment activism. In *Technoculture*. See Penley and Ross 1991.

Turner, Patricia. 1993. *I heard it through the grapevine: Rumor in African-American culture*. Berkeley: University of California Press.

Wallace, R. A synergism of plagues: "Planned shrinkage," contagious housing destruction and AIDS in the Bronx. *Environmental Research* 47: 1–33.

Warner, Michael, ed. 1993. *Fear of a queer planet: Queer politics and social theory*. Minneapolis: University of Minnesota Press.

Watney, Simon. 1989. *Policing desire: Pornography, AIDS and the media*. Minneapolis: University of Minnesota Press.

———. 1993. The spectacle of AIDS. In *The lesbian and gay studies reader*. See Abelove et al. 1993.

Watstein, Sarah Barbara, and Robert Anthony Laurich, eds. 1991. *AIDS and women: A sourcebook*. Phoenix: Oryx Press.

———. 1991. Prostitutes and AIDS. In *AIDS and women: A sourcebook*. See Watstein and Laurich 1991.

Wermuth, Laurie, Jennifer Ham, and Rebecca L. Robbins. 1992. Women don't wear condoms: AIDS risk among sexual partners of IV drug users. In *The social context of AIDS*. See Huber and Schneider 1992.

White, Evelyn C. 1994. *The black women's health book: Speaking for ourselves*. Seattle: Seal Press.

12

Pornography

An Uncivil Liberty?

ALISA L. CARSE

In recent years, a vocal movement has emerged within feminism advocating the legal regulation of pornography in the interest of the equality of women. More precisely, the aim is to draft antipornography laws classifying pornographic speech as a civil rights violation.[1] These laws would treat pornography as an exception to First Amendment protection, making the production, sale, display, and distribution of pornographic materials civilly actionable, and making it possible for people harmed by pornography to collect for damages through civil suits.[2]

The proposal to draft new legislation classifying pornography as a civil rights violation puts an interesting twist in the debate concerning pornography and the law. Traditionally, objections to pornography have been made on grounds of obscenity. It has been the defenders of pornography, not its critics, who have appealed to civil rights—in particular, to the constitutional right of pornographers to free speech. This recent feminist tactic shifts the focus away from the rights of pornographers and onto the rights of women. Pornography, it is claimed, is not only implicated in the physical and psychological abuse of women; it also fosters bigotry and contempt, contributing to the exclusion of women from full and equal participation in civic life.[3] Because of its sexual content, pornography is viewed as an especially powerful force in the creation and support of women's oppression.

My aim in this essay is to defend these new harm-based objections to por-

Hypatia vol. 10, no. 1 (Winter 1995) © by Alisa L. Carse

nography on moral grounds but at the same time to raise questions about the proposal to address pornography's harm by legal means.[4] I argue that though pornography's harm is sufficiently alarming to provide a principled basis for a prohibitive legal strategy, the nature of the harm pornography does and the mechanisms by which it does harm make it a poor candidate for legal correction. Moreover, the introduction of prohibitive legislation would risk legal safeguards crucial to the ability of feminists, among others, to speak out and, thus, to pursue social reform.

It does not follow from this, however, that we must tolerate pornography. I sketch strategies of intolerance that I believe would be both more promising and less dangerous to feminist ends than the legal strategy. I argue that the struggle against pornography cannot be effective unless it is joined by a struggle against other practices as well, including other forms of speech, that contribute in powerful ways to the denigration and subordination of women in our society.

POSITIONS IN THE CURRENT DEBATE

An observer of the current pornography debate may feel overwhelmed by the morass of arguments and counterarguments being exchanged. It is useful, therefore, to fix in broad terms the key points of opposition at the center of the debate. The opposing positions fall into two basic groups, which I will refer to as "protectionists" (those who advocate protecting pornography under the law) and "restrictionists" (those who advocate restricting pornography under the law).

Among protectionists, we can distinguish *absolute protectionists* (or, broadly, civil libertarians) and *qualified protectionists*. Some, but not all, who advocate "absolute protection" of pornographic speech are more global "First Amendment absolutists."[5] By "absolute protectionists," I mean in this context to refer to those who view any attempt on the part of the government to restrict or regulate pornography a threat to the commitment to free expression embodied in the First Amendment. Absolutists tend to give expressive freedom overriding value, rejecting as illegitimate the approaches that would balance alleged "harms" of speech against the liberty interests of speakers.[6] They also reject distinctions between "political" and "nonpolitical" speech, arguing that First Amendment protection extends equally to all speech, including pornography. Thus, restricting pornographic speech is, on this view, nothing short of moral tyranny.

Unlike absolute protectionists, qualified protectionists advance an interpretation of the First Amendment according to which restrictions on speech are appropriate when the speech is harmful, but only if the harm prevented through the restrictions is greater than the harm introduced by the restrictions.[7] Just how this assessment of harm is to be made differs on different views, but in general personal rights are to be balanced off against various individual and social goods in which the state is taken to have an interest, including the good of freedom itself. In the context of the current pornography debate, qualified protectionists tend to believe that, though many find pornography unpalatable, even debased, it is on balance a relatively harmless representation of sexual fantasy.[8] Some qualified protectionists go so far as to claim that pornography provides a healthy outlet or "safety valve," an opportunity for catharsis, to those who might otherwise be driven to act out harmful sexual fantasies, and thus that pornography can actually help minimize harmful sexual behavior.[9] In general, qualified protectionists see restrictions on pornography as "hurting" producers and users of pornography, by illegitimately curtailing their expressive freedom.

Among restrictionists, there are what I will refer to as *offense-based restrictionists* and *harm-based restrictionists*. In the context of the current debate, offense-based restrictionists standardly appeal to obscenity law as a ground for the legal restriction of pornography. Because they view pornography as an obscene form of speech (in fact, they *define* pornography by appeal to standards of obscenity), offense-based restrictionists hold that pornography is not protected by the First Amendment, and is thus justifiably subject to legal restriction. Offense-based restrictionism, supportive of antiobscenity statutes, grounds a powerful antipornography movement in the United States. It has included among its proponents such groups as the Moral Majority, the Christian Coalition, the National Federation for Decency, and the Eagle Forum—all groups that have had considerable political clout.

Harm-based restrictionists, in contrast to offense-based restrictionists, tend to reject obscenity law and offense-based objections to pornography. Like qualified protectionists, harm-based restrictionists hold that restrictions on speech are to be justified on grounds of harm. However, unlike qualified protectionists, they view the harm of pornography as, on balance, serious enough to justify its legal restriction. Harm-based restrictionists tend to be concerned both with harm done to women working in pornography[10] and with the broader social ramifications of pornographic speech itself. Here I concentrate on the latter issue. The restrictionists with whom I am principally concerned are those who argue that pornography is "harmful" in being sexually discriminatory, that it sexualizes violence and coercion, and in so doing fosters the degradation and subordination of women in our society.[11]

My discussion will center on points of opposition arising between absolute protectionism, qualified protectionism, and harm-based restrictionism. I will raise worries about each of these positions in turn. In the end, I argue for a version of qualified protectionism. Only *unlike* traditional protectionists, I argue not that those hurt would be purveyors and consumers of pornography but rather that they would be feminists and others trying to fight the understanding of sexuality and gender that pornography helps promote.

SHIFTING THE FOCUS FROM OFFENSE TO HARM

Let me begin by saying something about offense-based restrictionism to indicate why the argument developed here will not focus on this position. As mentioned, offense-based objections to pornography fall under obscenity law in the current legal context. The legal definition of "obscenity" was set out by the Supreme Court in 1973, in *Miller v. California*, 413 U.S. 15, 24. According to this definition, obscenity is "sexually explicit material" that "appeals to prurient interest" as measured by "an average person, applying community standards," that depicts or describes sexual conduct "in a patently offensive way," and that "taken as a whole, lacks serious literary, artistic, political, or scientific value." Thus, offensiveness is a *criterion* of obscenity.

Offense-based restrictions on sexually explicit speech, invoked through antiobscenity law, raise quandaries complex enough to merit their own discussion.[12] Because I want here to examine the feminist proposal to institute legal restrictions of pornography on grounds of self-protection and civil equality, I focus on the issue of harm and its ramifications for the legal regulation of pornography. It is important to note, however, that opposition to obscenity law, and more broadly to what I have called offense-based restrictionism, is registered within both restrictionist and protectionist camps by proponents of each of the other positions I have specified. For all the disagreement among these groups, there is agreement on one point: we may not legally restrict forms of sexual expression simply because we find them repugnant by our community's standards of sexual propriety. Feminist foes of pornography, in particular, argue that we must shift the emphasis of the pornography debate *away* from the issue of offense onto the issue of harm. As Susan Brownmiller writes:

> The feminist objection to pornography is not based on prurience . . . and we certainly believe that explicit sexual material has its place in literature, art, science and education. . . . No, the feminist objection to pornography is based on our belief that pornography represents the hatred of women, that pornography's intent is to humiliate, degrade and dehumanize the female body for the purpose of erotic stimulation and pleasure. (1980, 253–54)

In this context, the appeal in obscenity law to "contemporary community standards" *simpliciter* is unacceptable, not only because this marks an exceedingly vague standard but also because, in the struggle against pornography, some of our community standards themselves are in question. Moreover, offense-based restrictions are not directed to undercutting the sexual abuse and denigration of women, which should be our chief concern.

DEFINING "PORNOGRAPHY"

Central to the debate about the legal status of pornography is the definition of "pornography." If we are going to shift our focus away from offense and onto harm, we need a working definition of "pornography" which does not appeal to obscenity criteria. Thus, let me state how I construe pornography for the purposes of this discussion. My focus is on heterosexual material involving adults only, in which the sexualized object is female.[13] By "pornography," I mean the explicit representation of sexual behavior that has as a characteristic mark "the degrading and demeaning portrayal of the role and status of the human female."[14] By "degrading and demeaning portrayal," I mean, roughly, the portrayal of behavior that is intentionally injurious or hurtful, physically or psychologically coercive, or which disregards or denigrates the desires and experiences of the other, thereby treating the other as "a mere sexual object to be exploited and manipulated sexually" (Longino 1980, 42–43). Following the specifications of the Dworkin and MacKinnon ordinance, I include in the category of pornography representations of "women dehumanized as sexual objects, things, or commodities; enjoying pain or humiliation or rape; being tied up, cut up, mutilated, bruised, or physically hurt, in postures of sexual . . . servility . . . presented in scenarios of degradation, injury, torture; shown as filthy or inferior; bleeding, bruised, or hurt in a context that makes these conditions sexual" (MacKinnon 1987, 176).

I want to note that this definition does not extend to all sexually explicit material. We can contrast "pornography," understood in this way, with "erotica," taking "erotica" broadly to refer to forms of sexual depiction that, at a minimum, do not sexualize coercion, violence, or denigration.[15] Moreover, we can contrast it with educational materials, literature, position papers, or protest pamphlets, for example, all of which might contain sexually explicit representations, including portrayals of assault or degradation, without being "pornographic" in the stipulated sense. What is crucial to the designation of material as "pornographic" is that the abuse and degradation depicted is also, even if only implicitly, *endorsed* or *recommended*.[16] Determining how and when material recommends the abuse or degradation it depicts is a dicey matter, which contributes to worries I address later about seeking legal recourse against "pornography."

Clearly, this is not an uncontroversial definition of pornography, but I do not think we can formulate an uncontroversial definition. Let me, therefore, say a few things in defense of this definition in the context of our discussion. First, an etymological note: if we look to the origin of the word "pornography," we see the emphasis on the subordination of women to be on target. "Pornography" derives from the Greek roots *porne*, which means "sexual slave" or "harlot," and *graphos*, which means "description of." Thus, pornography means a description of sexual slavery or the purchase of sex from women, both of which involve an imbalance of power, paradigmatically between women and men. While the word "pornography" has a broader meaning than this in everyday usage, much pornography, even when it takes as principal sexual objects children, men, or animals, is modeled on a male-female, master-slave paradigm.[17] Second, this definition departs from obscenity criteria in focusing on standards of abuse and degradation rather than on prurience and offensiveness, thus emphasizing the inequality of the sexes and the subordination of women depicted and recommended by pornography. Finally, this definition leaves open the type of connection there exists, if any, between pornography and actual (as opposed to depicted) forms of harm.

PORNOGRAPHY, LIBERTY, AND THE FIRST AMENDMENT

If we are even to take seriously the question of harm in connection with the restriction of pornographic speech, we should first have something to say to the absolute protectionist. I want to claim that, at the very least, simple appeals to the First Amendment are not decisive in defending absolute protectionism, and moreover, there are good reasons for rejecting this position. As Cass Sunstein has recently written, the First Amendment should not be seen to function as "a talismanic or reflexive obstacle" to constraints on speech, particularly insofar as those constraints represent "strategies for achieving free speech goals" (1993, 81). The question, of course, is just what we take "free speech goals" to be. In addressing this question, I will note a number of things about how the First Amendment works and explore a broad vision of free speech goals that can provide a moral framework for recent feminist arguments appealing to the Constitution to justify restriction.

How exactly does the First Amendment protect freedom of speech? "Congress," it reads, "shall make no laws abridging the freedom of speech." What exactly this amounts to has been a matter of great controversy historically.[18] It is important to note that the First Amendment has in recent history been interpreted principally as a procedural safeguard against the *prior restraint* of speech by the government. As a safeguard against prior restraint, it prohibits the government from undertaking action to control or censor speech in advance.[19] Thus, the government cannot, for example, require licensing of written materials before their publication or by a court-ordered injunction prohibit a speaker from speaking. Action may be taken against speech, but only after the fact, and after it has been demonstrated to be an instance of an unprotected or relatively unprotected class of speech.[20]

The feminist proposal, then, is simply to add pornography to the list of unprotected classes of speech, which includes personal libel, "fighting words," slander, incitement to violence, perjury, bribery, criminal solicitation, false advertisement, obscenity, and shouting "fire" without cause in a crowded movie theater—all of which are, under current law, treated as exceptions to First Amendment protection on the grounds that they are harmful or that their exercise violates others' rights. If nothing else, these existing exceptions indicate that the interpretation of the First Amendment as a qualified rather than an absolute safeguard of free speech is the dominant interpretation.[21] Of course, absolute protectionists can reject this interpretation of the First Amendment as wrong.[22] The question is, What is at stake in doing so?

Let us suppose we do view freedom of speech as an absolute right. What would having such an "absolute right" involve? Among other things, it would involve being able to "say" what one wants, free from all legal restriction. Suppose, on the other hand, that we view freedom of speech not as an absolute right but as a qualified right, which may at times be restricted. Why should one opt for one view rather than the other? One thing at stake in these two views is our conception of liberty itself. Helen Longino argues that in construing freedom of speech as an absolute right, we imply that freedom of speech is a basic right, "part of what we mean by liberty," rather than a right derivative from a prior, more basic right to liberty. In supporting this claim, she invokes Ronald Dworkin's distinction between liberty construed as "license," that is, freedom "from . . . legal constraint to do what [one] might wish to do," and liberty construed as "independence," that is, "the status of a person as independent and equal rather than subservient."[23]

Now, I want to propose that this distinction corresponds in a suggestive way to one framed by Isaiah Berlin between what he calls "negative liberty," or freedom from the interference of others, and "positive liberty," or autonomy, the freedom "to be moved by conscious purposes which are one's own." Berlin gives eloquent expression to his notion of positive freedom:

> The 'positive' sense of the word 'liberty' derives from the wish on the part of the individual to be his own master . . . a subject, not an object . . . deciding, not being decided for, self-directed and not acted upon by external nature or by other men as if I were a thing, or an animal, or a slave incapable of playing a human role, that is, of conceiving goals and policies of my own and realizing them. (Berlin 1984, 23)

Now, if we understand liberty *negatively*, as *license*, we may well interpret the right to free speech as an absolute right, as the right to say what one wants to say, free from legal constraint.[24] If, however, we interpret liberty *positively*, as *independence* or self-mastery, freedom of speech ("negatively" understood as freedom from legal constraint to say what one wants to say) is not entailed by liberty; it is not a basic right, in Longino's sense. Rather, freedom of speech is at most one expression of our liberty and, as such, a right we have in virtue of a *more basic* right to liberty understood as independence or self-mastery. The First Amendment is, then, a safeguard of the more basic right to positive liberty, of which free speech is one expression. The right to free speech must then be protected by the First Amendment only insofar as doing so protects liberty, positively construed. On this view, it would follow that the right to free speech is a qualified right.[25]

In support of Longino, let me note that there is a strong precedent to be found in liberal history for the view that civil liberty is not to be understood as freedom from all constraint, to do as one pleases. If we look to liberal forebears such as Locke, Mill, or Tocqueville, we find an insistence that each person possesses negative liberty, some realm of personal freedom that may on no condition be violated. But we also find the acknowledgment that freedom so understood cannot be unlimited. We are not, for example, free to interfere boundlessly with the freedom of others. "The only freedom which deserves the name," Mill writes, "is that of pursuing our own good in our own way, so long as we do not attempt to deprive others of theirs, or impede their efforts to obtain it" ([1859] 1978, 12). Moreover, Mill argues not only that one cannot have liberty to interfere with the liberty of others but also that one cannot have liberty to give up one's liberty; one cannot, for example, freely sell oneself into slavery ([1859] 1978, 101). To claim this is to presuppose a positive conception of liberty, according to which to be free is to be the instrument of one's own, not another person's, will, to be master of oneself. In selling oneself into slavery, one forfeits one's liberty, positively understood.

I want to suggest, therefore, that it is consonant with both current law and significant strains of liberal history to reject absolute protectionism and to embrace a conception of the right to free speech as a right intended to secure not only (limited) negative liberty, to "say" what we please, but also positive liberty, thus protecting us as citizens against the unreasonable interference by the state in order that we might all be free, within bounds, to "be our own masters," to be respected as "independent and equal rather than subservient" to other people.

This interpretation of the First Amendment can provide a moral framework for much feminist restrictionism, because its implication for pornography is this: if we do interpret our right to free speech as subject to limitation on grounds of harm, and if we interpret this right as a guarantee of our status as "independent and equal rather than subservient," then if our status as independent and equal can be "harmed"—in this case by pornography—there are principled grounds for restricting pornographic speech in the name of the goals of the First Amendment itself.[26]

This is not to suggest that the debate among legal scholars is settled about how best to interpret the First Amendment and balance it off against other constitutional guarantees. Among harm-based restrictionists, there has been an emerging emphasis on the Fourteenth Amendment's equal protection clause. Rather than appealing to a view of First Amendment guarantees as protections of equality, some restrictionists pit the Fourteenth Amendment's equal protection clause against the First Amendment's protections of free expression, arguing that if the free speech of some injures the equal status of others (through degrading them, for example, or promoting violence against them or contempt for them), then the constitutional interest in equality trumps constitutional guarantees of expressive freedom, justifying curtailments on freedom of speech, particularly "low value" speech such as pornography.[27]

I do not want here to adjudicate between these several tactics. Whether one appeals to the First Amendment itself as a safeguard of independence and equality, or to the Fourteenth Amendment's equal protection clause, these positions are in accord, at the very least, in asserting that there are compelling *constitutional* grounds for affirming legal restrictions on pornography in the name of the civil equality of women.

PORNOGRAPHY'S HARM

Two questions now arise: (1) Is pornography harmful to women in a way that threatens our status as independent and equal? (2) Suppose pornography is harmful in this way, should our strategy against pornography be directed to its legal restriction? The first question concerns the justificatory basis of those versions of qualified protectionism that claim that pornography isn't harmful enough to merit restriction; the second concerns the wisdom of harm-based restrictionism. I consider each in turn.

First, a caveat. In reflecting on these questions, we need to keep firm a threefold distinction between (a) the harm done to women involved in the production of pornography (e.g., models and actresses); (b) harm that is *depicted* in pornographic material; and (c) harm that is done through the use of pornography or the widespread dissemination, display, and enjoyment of pornographic images of women. While crimes committed in pornographic production raise extremely difficult and important questions,[28] we are here concerned with the possible impact of pornographic materials and their use on attitudes and behavior in our society. And though pornography might be said to be *intrinsically* morally abhorrent in its portrayal of women in ways incompatible with their status and worth as persons, this is a judgment of its *content*. Historically, our courts have in most cases eschewed matters of content as alone providing a sufficient basis for the legal restriction of speech.[29] Let us, therefore, assume that, relevant to the legal restriction of pornography, the harm of pornography cannot consist only in the harmful behaviors pornography depicts and recommends. Rather, its depictions and recommendations of this harm must themselves be harmful.[30]

The view of pornographic speech that I dispute is the view I have attributed to qualified protectionists, namely, that though some people find pornography tasteless, even debased, it is, on balance, a relatively harmless representation of sexual fantasy, enjoyed by consenting adults.

A growing number of research studies have documented positive correlations between the exposure to violent pornographic images (e.g., of rape, bondage, molestation involving weapons, mutilation) and positive reactions to rape and other forms of sexual violence toward women. Studies suggest, for example, that exposure to violent pornography can significantly enhance arousal in response to the portrayal of rape, that exposure to films depicting sexual violence against women can act as a stimulus for aggressive acts against women, and that prolonged exposure to pornography (of a violent or nonviolent kind) leads to increased callousness toward victims of sexual violence, a greater likelihood of having rape-fantasies, and a greater likelihood of reporting that one would rape women or force women into unwanted sex acts.[31] These indications are not surprising. The practices of using pornography do, after all, provide powerful reinforcements of the behavior pornography depicts: male camaraderie, exciting music and visuals, and sexual arousal are often an integral part of its use. To deny any relation between pornography and attitudes, and attitudes and behavior, would be to deny standard conceptions of learning according to which repeated exposure to phenomena, especially when such exposure is made vivid and compelling as it is through sexual arousal, tends to lead to acceptance and habituation.[32]

Many who support the legal restriction of pornography see a strong connection between the pervasive violence on the part of men toward women and the unequal status of women in our society. They urge that we continue our research into this violence to determine more precisely how pornography contributes to it. There is faith that once the results are in, we will have a strong case against pornography. But critics question the legitimacy of extrapolating from laboratory findings about attitudes and sexual arousal patterns to "real-life" behaviors; they argue that we can at best hope to establish correlations, rather than causal connections, between pornography and violence;[33] and they question how successfully we can separate pornography's role as a cause of women's abuse in our society from the ways that exposure to pornography reinforces and exploits *existing* misogyny.[34]

It is my view that we should not ignore the connections between pornography and violence when they are demonstrated. At the same time, we must be aware of the inherent limitations of such research in revealing the nature and extent of pornography's harm. Even violent pornography must be distinguished from crimes of rape, incest, or battery themselves, which are direct and tangible acts against individuals.[35] The harmful effects of pornography are in the main not direct and individualized, but indirect, cumulative, and as such, inextricably bound up with other social practices and conditions figuring in the abuse and degradation of women.[36] Except in rare and extreme circumstances, the harm of pornography cannot be tested for in studies of the direct effects of pornography alone, let alone individual pieces of pornography.

I want to suggest, therefore, that consonant with the way we have defined pornography, we accept a broadened conception of harm, which includes but extends beyond direct physical injury and coercion to the contempt for and degradation of women collectively, as women. Let me explain what I mean. Pornography, as we have construed it for the purposes of this discussion, is material that portrays, among other things, behaviors that degrade and subordinate women in such a way as to endorse those behaviors, often through the highly charged context of sexual use. Our conception of harm can in this way involve an understanding of degradation which presupposes the positive notion of liberty. The conception of the person in terms of which the degradation (harm) of pornography can be cashed out is arguably precisely the conception the Constitution defends, namely, one that holds paramount the status of each person as independent and equal. The question then is this: Does pornography, in portraying and endorsing the degrading treatment of women, degrade women?

In her book *The Pornography of Representation*, Susanne Kappeler argues that there exists a shared understanding, a "pornographic" way of "seeing" women, which is the "root" of the problem:

> Man the action-subject is identical with man the viewing subject. . . . what men are doing in the world is continuing to . . . see women as objects of their pleasure. . . . The fundamental problem at the root of men's behavior in the world, including sexual assault, rape, wife battering, sexual harassment . . . treating them as objects for conquest and protection—the root problem behind the reality of men's relations with women, is the way men see women. (1986, 61)

Whether or not we agree with Kappeler that men's view of women is *the* "root" of the problem, if we understand pornography to embody and encourage a way of "seeing" women, then we must address the narrow literalism of our traditional conception of harm as consisting in direct and individualized physical injury or psychological assault. What is wrong with pornography is not solely a matter of its connection with direct and individualized forms of injury; it is also a matter of the view of women that pornography both reflects and fosters and that is enacted in pornographic practice. Regardless of the actual plots of pornographic books, films, or shows, or the representational content of pornographic images, the focal point and purpose of heterosexual pornographic practice is male sexual pleasure. Even when women's pleasure is of issue, it is found in the satisfaction of men's desires, in doing anything and everything that men want or order to be done (Kappeler 1986, 57). Women are objectified and subordinated in the attainment of men's ends. At the center of pornography is an eroticization of male dominance.

Consider the repeated images in pornography of the woman spread-eagled, stalked, bound, beaten, mutilated, gagged, or raped, and of the woman accepting such treatment, and (often) being sexually aroused by it.[37] Even in soft-core and less graphically violent pornography, the subordination of women to men is a unifying theme, expressed through women's sexual servitude, their roles as sexual toys and playthings of men, objects of access and use, whose purpose is to serve men sexually. As MacKinnon writes, in pornography,

> Subjection itself, with self-determination ecstatically relinquished, is the content of women's sexual desire and desirability. Women are there to be violated and possessed, men to violate and possess us. . . . On a simple descriptive level, the inequality of hierarchy, of which gender is the primary one, seems necessary for sexual arousal to work. . . . What pornography *does* goes beyond its content: it eroticizes hierarchy, it sexualizes inequality. (1987, 172)

> Because pornography is sexual it is not like the literature of other inequalities. It is a specific and compelling behavioral stimulus, a conditioner, and reinforcer. The way it works is unique: it makes orgasm a response to bigotry. It is a major way that the dominance and submission—a daily dynamic of social hierarchy, particularly of gender inequality—are enjoyed and practiced and reinforced and experienced. (1987, 200)

Even if individual women identify with the male pornographic view of women, it is a view that places the man's desires at the center and men in positions of dominance and power. Pornography standardly conveys the message that women are suitable subjects for sexual use, that women desire and enjoy being treated in an abusive way (and even when they don't that they are nonetheless "asking for it")—that they need and want to be forced to submit. We need not deny the claim that some women find "male" pornography arousing. Finding male pornography arousing is fully compatible with giving expression to one's sexual desires as a woman. But to the extent that we do, as women, find our desires represented by pornography, our desires may be incompatible not only with our own safety but also with a self-understanding as independent and equal.

We are now in a position to see the connection between pornography and the denial to women of equal civil status. Pornographic materials and the practices surrounding them are themselves an affront to the dignity of women, not least because women are viewed as objects, dehumanized and depersonalized instruments for the satisfaction of men's sexual desires and whims. Pornography may *reflect* the way we see ourselves as women and men, but it also *teaches* ways of seeing and ways of being; it shapes and fosters attitudes, expectations, patterns of desire, of sexual arousal and response, and other overt behaviors that can result in harm to women—not only physical violence and forcible sex but also disdainful and dismissive treatment, incompatible with our status as equals. To see pornography as mere fantasy is to overlook the powerful way pornography reinforces *and shapes* our understanding of gender differences and gender roles. It is not just in the pornographic context that women's equal status is undercut; pornography underwrites a more pervasive denigration of women, by helping to foster and reinforce expectations about women and men in domains that extend beyond the expressly pornographic or even sexual domains. The harm of pornography, broadly speaking, is "the harm of the civil inequality of the sexes *made invisible as harm* because it has become accepted as the sex difference" (MacKinnon 1987, 178; my emphasis; see also Longino 1980, 45–47).

Not only, then, has research revealed notable correlations between the use of pornography and attitudes and arousal patterns which may bolster coercive or violent sexual behavior, but there is arguably a more general connection between the pornographic understanding of women and the degradation of women collectively, as women—the denial to women of equal status as persons. An objection to pornography on grounds of its degradation of women, so construed, is a far cry from an objection on grounds of "prurience" and "patent offensiveness." The strength of this argument is that it extends the conception of harm to cover forms of degradation without advocating a narrow legal moralism: the conception of the good to which it appeals is arguably the very conception of equality that is to be protected by the Constitution.

LEGAL RESTRICTIONISM: PRACTICAL LIMITATIONS AND POLITICAL DANGERS

We see, then, that there is reason to reject not only absolute protectionism but also those versions of qualified protectionism holding pornography to be relatively harmless. The question now arises, What should we do about pornography once we recognize it to be harmful? Should we seek its legal restriction? Though there are, as I have argued, compelling grounds *in principle* for doing so, there is still the question whether legal restriction would be pragmatically wise. I argue that it would not be. First, legal restrictions can be expected to be largely ineffective against pornography and the pornographic view of women; second, legal restrictions would risk endangering, among other things, the struggle against pornography itself. Thus, the harm prevented through the introduction of restrictions will likely fail to outweigh the harm introduced by restrictions, with little promise of gain.

There are at least two significant ways the legal restriction of pornography can be expected to be ineffective. First, recall that the First Amendment is taken to prohibit the prior restraint of speech. Given this prohibition, general injunctions against pornography would be impermissible. Courts would not be permitted to restrain pornography prior to an independent judicial determination for each case of suspect speech that it is "pornographic," and hence harmful. Without general injunctions against pornography, we can expect that little could be done legally to disrupt the pornographic industry, and hence to protect us from its effects.[38]

Now, it might be responded that although we cannot, through legal restriction, hope to undercut the stability and profitability of the pornographic industry as a whole, we can still hope to do some good. The Dworkin-MacKinnon ordinance, for example, is intended to give individuals recourse through civil law to sue for the ban of specific kinds of sexually explicit materials and to collect damages from pornographers for the harm done by those materials. Under this ordinance, a civil injunction can stop future sale of a piece of material when it has been demonstrated to be harmful. The alleged benefit of this kind of ordinance would at least be this: it could secure reparations for particular victims of pornography and facilitate the general protection of people from particular pieces of pornography, even though it would not effect a general disruption of the industry. Moreover, the threat of civil liability could be expected, it is claimed, to serve as a powerful economic disincentive to those who traffic in pornography.[39]

In response, there is no doubt that the individualized approach, such as that developed by the Dworkin-MacKinnon ordinance and its offshoots, might in some cases succeed in securing damages to women or stopping future sales of pieces of pornography. Perhaps this would create a threat of civil liability great enough significantly to curtail the availability of pornography. But perhaps it would not: as long as there is a demand for pornography, it is just as reasonable to assume that legal regulation would instead run pornography underground, where it could become even more profitable than it is already.

This brings us to a still more serious problem. As suggested earlier, the harm of pornography is often not direct and individualized, but indirect and cumulative, due to the pervasive presence in our society of pornographic images, and to the widespread acceptability and enjoyment of these images. Though the inequality of women is surely reinforced by, and even crucially dependent on, debased cultural conceptions of women to which pornography vividly contributes, we must ask how much can be accomplished by taking legal action against isolated instances of pornography. This worry is reinforced by the extent to which a "pornographic" view of women—and a message of female inferiority—is expressed in forms of speech that are not themselves instances of pornography (e.g., advertisements, music videos, and women's romance novels), which glorify and eroticize female submission and male domination, but which would not be subject to antipornography laws.[40] We must remain sober about the extent to which reducing the (legal) availability of pieces of pornography, narrowly defined, can fundamentally alter the expectations and roles of women in our society or reduce the number of sex crimes committed against women.

It might be responded that though the legal restriction of pornography would alone be insufficient effectively to disrupt a huge and entrenched pornography industry, or to abolish the cultural representations and social conditions that help undermine women's equality, we might still advocate fighting for the legal restriction of pornography, if the fight were to be *accompanied by* educational efforts and reform programs aimed at changing deep-seated sexist attitudes and eliminating discriminatory social practices.

The question is, What price are we willing to pay for the legal opportunity to restrict pornography and collect for damages? If the benefits of introducing restrictions are likely to prove minimal, this is an important consideration, particularly if the costs of introducing restrictions are potentially high.

This brings us to the second set of worries, concerning the potential costs or *dangers* of supporting legislation against pornography. In assessing just what the price of legal restrictions might be, we need to consider the fact that the institution of legislative restrictions could present a positive risk to the feminist movement, and specifically, to the sorts of exploratory educational and reform programs that would be needed to transform attitudes and conditions subversive of women's equality.

What do I mean by this? Surely, one might object, restrictions against pornography need not threaten the struggle for women's equality generally, for very different grounds from those invoked in the case of pornography would be required to justify limitations on feminist political expression unrelated to sexuality (for example, appeals for comparable pay, for the just inclusion of women in medical research, and for quality, accessible day care). Thus, the objection would go, the legal control of pornography would not inevitably serve as a precedent for controlling political speech so long as distinctions between pornography and other sorts of speech are explicitly maintained and observed.

But one problem with this line of response is this: the struggle for women's equality is *not* narrowly political. It is a struggle, among other things, for sexual choice and freedom of expression. Such legal restrictions could strike at its very core. Once pornography is deemed unprotected by the First Amendment, what would prevent legislatures from restricting as "pornographic" lesbian erotica, sexually explicit literature, protest pamphlets or treatises, pamphlets on birth control, public messages about the use of condoms in helping to prevent AIDS, or texts such as *Our Bodies Ourselves*, or even MacKinnon's *Only Words*? (see English 1980, 20). What is to stop a judge from determining that any graphic or explicitly sexual material involving women, irrespective of its expressive content or the context of its use, is "pornographic," and hence an assault on women's dignity? Decisions about whether material degrades women are sufficiently controversial to raise genuine worries about how much faith feminist foes of pornography should place in government officials to make these decisions in a way sensitive to feminist ends.

In a society in which to be a woman is, among other things, to be an "object of sexual access" (Brownmiller 1980), subject regularly to uninvited sexual innuendo and insinuation, to sexualized intrusions (e.g., catcalls on the street, pinches and worse in school stairwells), and to the continual threat (and fear) of sexual violence, the avenues into self-possession and sexual reclamation may be various and unpredictable. As Robin West writes, invoking a quote from Ellen Bass, "Women's natural, playful, and affective eroticism . . . 'a basic and vital impulse—the desire to be seen, to be known, naked, in sexual sharing'" is "shattered" by "our pornographic, incestuous, sexually abusive culture" that "identifies sexuality with female degradation, helplessness, mutilation, and, in the extreme, with injury and death" (1989, 91). We need, in seeking to secure positive liberty, to respect the importance of sexual exploration and expression to self-possession and self-mastery. We must be on guard against seeking legislation that can be used to support a strenuous politics of silence and repression, thereby limiting not only pornography and other forms of harmful speech, but also free experimental discourse about sexuality, as well as expressive, playful, exploratory sexuality.[41]

These worries are not merely academic ones. The fate of the Minneapolis ordinance introduced by Dworkin and MacKinnon, which does not involve prior restraint, provides a poignant example of how antipornography legislation can end up hindering the very goals for which it is created. In bringing the power of the state against pornography, feminists helped foster a battle that sought to establish narrow norms of expressive correctness and that may, in the end, have posed more of a threat to feminist interests, including the struggle against pornography, than to pornography itself. When the Dworkin and MacKinnon bill, after being vetoed by the mayor in Minneapolis, moved to Indianapolis, no attempt was made to represent the ordinance as a "feminist bill." As a result, the bill was backed by forces hostile to feminism, the ERA, and lesbian and gay rights. This appropriation and perversion of the original spirit of the bill was not confined to Indianapolis. In Suffolk County, legislator D'Andre, in seeking to "restore ladies to what they used to be," introduced a version of the bill asserting that pornography causes "sodomy" and "destruction" of the traditional "family unit," along with crimes such as rape and incest "inimical to the public good" (quoted in Duggan et al. 1984, 42).[42] This ordinance is just one case,[43] but it highlights the importance, in embracing political strategies, of designing those strategies so as to avoid bolstering forces hostile to the very ends being sought.

Finally, once we introduce concerns about equality and, in particular, appeal to the broad-based harm that pornography does to the equal status of women in our society, it is hard, as I have already suggested, consistently to deny that forms of speech other than pornography pose similar, and perhaps even more pervasive, subtle, and insidious, threats. As Richard Posner writes, "Much of the production of the American film and theater industry, a fair amount of cable television, a huge number of videocassettes, some greeting cards, some advertising, and even an occasional opera would have to be removed from the market. . . . It would require . . . not a smattering of Indianapolis-style local ordinances, but a law enforcement effort on the scale of the Prohibition or the 'war on drugs,' and with the same dubious prospects of success. Would it be worth it?" (1993, 34).[44] Posner is, by my lights, understating the point: it would involve massive regulation of culture. We have reason to worry about undertaking a legal strategy against pornography on grounds which, if consistently applied, would open the floodgates to state control of speech.

If we abide by the justificatory condition that legal constraints on the freedom of speech are justified only if the institution of such constraints protects against harm that outweighs the harmfulness of the constraints themselves, then it is only on the condition that the introduction of legal constraints is not assessed as itself potentially more harmful to our objectives than is pornography that the introduction of such constraints is justified. There is good reason to believe this condition cannot be met. While qualified protectionism is wrong insofar as it takes pornography to be, on balance, relatively harmless, harm-based restrictionism is unwise in advocating the legal restriction of pornography, for it would risk putting in place measures that could be used to suppress not only pornography but many other forms of speech as well, including some important to the struggle against pornographic harm.[45]

STRATEGIES OF INTOLERANCE

If we reject harm-based restrictionism, what options do we have left? We must acknowledge the peculiar force and vivacity of pornographic speech, the power it has in virtue of its sexual content, to teach and habituate. As Diana E. H. Russell writes, "How can we stop rape and woman-battering by staffing rape crisis centers and refuges when there are thousands of movie houses, millions of publications, a multibillion dollar business that promote the idea that violence and rape of women is sexually exciting to men and that we like it, too?" (1980a, 303). We must pay attention to the messages pornography sends and the practices it engages all of us—men and women—in. The question remains, therefore, What should we do about pornography once we recognize it as a threat?

I think that the feminist struggle against pornography should be focused centrally on education, expressive exploration, and protest. What would this involve? First, it would involve pursuing aggressive consciousness-raising campaigns. We can develop powerful private strategies to discourage the view of women as victims and commodities on the part of friends, relatives, and neighbors who use pornography.[46] If we, as sisters, brothers, friends, mothers, aunts, lovers, wives, and fellow citizens speak up against pornography, our families, friends, and neighbors are going to notice. Undertaking an aggressive consciousness-raising campaign about pornography is prerequisite to creating the sort of social awareness necessary if the fight against pornography is to be properly maintained as a fight for women's equality.

Second, we can seek an empowering response to pornography through the creation of alternative erotica. The fight against pornography must, I think, be a movement to inspire the expressive and exploratory endeavors of women, to encourage women to engage with vitality and joy in sexual speech and experimentation of their own. Pornography helps undercut the equal status of women by depicting us over and over again in silenced roles, as the willing sexual handmaidens and play toys of men, thus leaving us invisible as persons in our own right. In educating ourselves and others about pornography, we come to have a say about it and thus to gain a voice; in expressing ourselves through erotica of our own making, we can begin to change the contours of sexual speech.

Of course, in fighting pornography, we are not only attempting to redefine sexual values and sexual tropes; we are also fighting a *powerful* economic force. This suggests that we must continue to develop aggressive strategies against pornographic industry and commerce,[47] organizing disruptive picket lines, writing and distributing pamphlets, and speaking out against pornographic films and media on the streets where they are shown as well as in public halls, on television, in newspapers, and in high schools, colleges, and universities. We may need to engage in collective civil disobedience to draw public attention to misogyny in the media. In these ways, we can make headway in stirring public consciousness, generating awareness, and provoking discussion. By drawing attention to misogyny in the media, we can give expression to the ways in which many women think and feel and thus help break the pattern of objectification pornography promotes. The process of change will undoubtedly continue to go slowly, for it will need to challenge the very heart of male dominance in our society, requiring fundamental transformation of the ways we understand and comport ourselves as women and men in relation to each other.

This last point highlights the importance of recognizing that, powerful as pornography is in virtue of its sexual content, we will have to do much more than fight pornography if the demand for and use of pornography is to abate and the violent abuse and denigration of women in our society is to end. The fight for women's liberty and equality must continue to be a fight for protection against sexual abuse and battery in the home and against harassment on the job; for safe neighborhoods and streets, for comparable pay and decent working conditions, for more active participation on the part of men in the nurturing and rearing of children, and much more—it must, in short, be a struggle to improve the material conditions of women's lives (see, e.g., Burstyn 1985). We must continue to organize against pornography, but we must not allow the battle to consume us or leave us blind to the constellation of factors that figure in the subordination and abuse of women in our society.

CONCLUSION

We have seen that simple appeals to the First Amendment will not justify the protection of pornography. In objecting to absolute protectionism, I invoked Helen Longino's proposal that the sort of liberty the Constitution is to protect is not license plain and simple, but political independence, "the status of all persons as independent and equal rather than subservient." As Longino suggests, once we understand liberty in this way, the "civil liberties" themselves can be understood as means to our realization of liberty. The implication for freedom of speech is this: if the exercise of freedom of speech in some way threatens our liberty, our status as independent and equal, then we have reason to restrict that exercise in the name of liberty itself. Against the background of this suggestion, I have interpreted recent feminist objections to pornography as extending our notion of harm to include not just physical and psychological injury but also threats to the independence and equality of women. I have tried to show that pornography harms in this way, as one of the forces that helps sustain the systematic domination of women by men in our society. Thus, I have argued against a version of qualified protectionism on grounds that I believe appeal to the very conception of civil equality that it is one object of the Constitution to protect.

However, at the same time that we recognize that there are moral grounds consistent with the Constitution for introducing legal restrictions of pornography, we must question whether the legal strategy is pragmatically optimal. The issue of restricting pornography raises the distinction between what we can and should affirm in principle, and what we ought actively to pursue in practice, given the facts of our social and political reality. Recent feminist arguments against pornography are on target in insisting that we cannot expect equality for women in a society that tolerates the pervasive portrayal of women as second-class citizens: pornography *is* an uncivil liberty. We should fight against pornography and against the violent abuse and denigration of women it fosters. But we should not, in doing so, overestimate the effectiveness of the law or underestimate its potential dangers.

One payoff of greater sensitivity to pornographic harm may be the heightened awareness of the extent to which the message of woman's inferiority floods prime-time television and mainstream media of all sorts. We need to be on the watch, not only for the explicitly sexual images, but all the images—in daytime soaps, situation comedies, lipstick billboards, car advertisements, and in the countless depictions of women as ditzes fixed on getting clothes clean and floors shiny—that convey the message that women are the contented servants of children and men. *Sexually explicit* images that demean women are, in some ways, uniquely threatening; as MacKinnon has put it, pornography "is a specific and compelling behavioral stimulus, a conditioner, a reinforcer . . . *pornography makes sexism sexy*" (MacKinnon 1987, 171; my emphasis). But pornography is just one form in which the blithe degradation of women is made invisible through our attachment to debased conceptions of gender and gender roles. We must continue to grow more alert to all the ways in which the second-class status of women is promoted and maintained in our society. In the words of Thomas Jefferson, "The price of liberty is eternal vigilance."

NOTES

I am indebted to Donald Ainslie, Kurt Baier, Bill Blattner, David Boonin-Vail, Alice Crary, Lauren Deichman, John Hasnas, Tamara Horowitz, Maggie Little, Terry Pinkard, Madison Powers, Geoff Sayre McCord, Ashby Sharpe, Nancy Sherman, Susan Stocker, Kathy Taylor, and Lynne Tirrell for generous and helpful comments and discussions.

1. This legal approach to pornography is forcefully defended by MacKinnon (1987) and (1993). See also A. Dworkin (1989) and Longino (1980).

2. The paradigm of such legislation is the Dworkin-MacKinnon ordinance, introduced in the Minneapolis City Council in 1983, versions of which were considered in half a dozen other cities. For discussion of this ordinance and the controversy surrounding it, see MacKinnon (1987) and Blakely (1985). In addition to the trafficking provision, the Dworkin-MacKinnon ordinance addresses coercion, force, and assault, both of women working in pornography and of women by consumers of pornography, making provisions, among other things, for monetary restitution to those harmed, and for the removal from public availability of those materials implicated in such harm. See Blakeley (1985). After the ordinance was signed and passed in Indianapolis, it was challenged by a coalition of publishers and distributors known as "The Media Coalition." The ordinance was found unconstitutional in two separate decisions. See *American Booksellers v. Hudnut*, 598 F. Supp. 1316 (S.D. Ind. 1984); *Hudnut v. American Booksellers*, 771 F 2d 323 (7th Cir. 1985).

3. See MacKinnon (1987, esp. 176–77).

4. My concern here will be with the proposal to designate pornographic speech an unprotected class of speech, rather than with regulations on the zoning, distribution, and display of pornographic materials.

5. I should note, however, that "First Amendment absolutism" may well be a mis-

nomer, for few if any have maintained that absolutely no restrictions on speech can be supported. Even self-declared "absolutists" tend, for example, to support restricting criminal solicitation or the publication of troop movements in wartime.

6. In the context of pornography, many absolutists maintain that though pornography may *depict* harms, it does not in virtue of that *do* harm. An editorial in *Playboy*, for example, argues in defense of pornography that "porn doesn't rape people, people rape people. Images are not acts. Punish the crime and the criminal, not the image" ("Politically Correct Sex" 1986). It should be noted here that it would not, of course, be the image that is "punished" under restrictive legislation, but the producer of that image, the pornographer. The pornographer, unlike the pornography image *is* an agent who has acted in producing the image, and who can in principle accept responsibility for harm resulting from that action. The pornographer also benefits from the sale of the pornography, so the question arises whether the pornographer benefits at an unacceptable cost to others.

7. The four positions I'm outlining cut across feminist lines. The Feminist Anti-Censorship Task Force (F.A.C.T.), for example, could be viewed as a qualified protectionist group. F.A.C.T. questions the causal connection between pornographic imagery and violent acts, and has argued, partly on this basis, against the restriction of pornography.

8. For example, a brief issued by F.A.C.T. states that "even pornography which is problematic for women can be experienced as affirming of women's desires and of women's equality"; "pornography can be a psychic assault . . . but for women as for men it can also be a source of erotic pleasure. . . . A woman who enjoys pornography . . . is in a sense a rebel, insisting on an aspect of her sexuality that has been defined as a male preserve" (A Brief *Amici Curiae* of Feminist Anti-Censorship Task Force et al. 30, *Hudnut v. American Booksellers*, 771 F.2d 323 (7th Cir. 1985), quoted in MacKinnon [1987, 236 n. 35]). F.A.C.T. is in effect claiming that, even if we grant that pornography itself "can be a psychic assault," the benefits of protecting it outweigh the benefits of restricting it, even for women.

9. This argument is used, for example, in *The Report of the Commission on Obscenity and Pornography* (1979) issued by the U.S. government.

10. See Lederer (1980), sect. 2, "Pornography: Who Is Hurt," for a collection of interviews and accounts by women who have worked as models in the pornographic industry.

11. There is an important dimension of the harm-based argument against pornography as it is articulated in the Dworkin-MacKinnon ordinance, which I do not examine here, i.e., the claim that "pornography *is* the graphic sexually explicit *subordination of women*" (my emphasis). For detailed attempts to examine and reconstruct this claim, see Vadas (1987) and Langton (1993). See Parent (1990) for a response to Vadas's paper.

12. See Sunstein (1993), A. Dworkin (1989), and Baier (1979).

13. A further discussion of the subject of pornography might pursue the extent to which the analysis offered here can apply to lesbian and gay pornography including lesbian and gay S/M and transsexual material.

14. This is a simplified version of a definition formulated by Longino (1980, 42), which is based on the definition formulated in the *Report of the Commission on Obscenity and Pornography* (1979, 239). I do not wish to suggest that I support the conclusions of the commission, which denies that pornography has an adverse effect on men's attitudes toward women. As should become clear, I reject this view.

15. Gloria Steinem suggests that we contrast "pornography" with "erotica," citing the Greek root of "erotica" in *eros*, meaning "sexual desire or passionate love, named for Eros, the son of Aphrodite." Eros, unlike pornography, she claims, "contains the idea of love" (1986, 250). Whether or not we want to build love into our notion of erotica, which seems on the face of it to capture far too narrow a conception, a distinction of this kind serves a useful purpose. If we take "erotica" to refer to forms of sexual depiction in which, in contrast to pornography, the features of coercion and violence are not present, then erotic materials would be those conveying *at least* respect (if not also trust, warmth, or tenderness), expressed through minimal regard each of the subjects is depicted as having for the desires, feelings, and experiences of the other(s), a recognition of the basic dignity and personhood of the other(s) (Longino 1980, 42). Respect, so understood, would at least preclude the treatment of women abusively, coercively, or as mere sexual slaves or toys of men. Much more would need to be said on this subject, however. Some believe that pornography depicts the woman's point of view, that is, that women want and need to be subordinated, used, forced, and made to submit. Others would argue that a principal danger of pornography is that it reinforces precisely this view of women's desires. Also, among advocates of S/M, some emphasize the enhanced trust and respect required by the "top" if appropriate limits are to be observed in enacting that role.

16. MacKinnon writes: "Pornography sexualizes rape, battery, sexual harassment, prostitution, and child sexual abuse; *it thereby celebrates, promotes, authorizes and legitimizes them*" (1987, 171; my emphasis). The importance to pornography of its recommendation (or "endorsement") of the behavior it depicts and the contextual mechanisms by which material conveys a recommendation or endorsement are developed and defended by Longino (1980, 43–4).

17. An important question is whether the sorts of pornographic depictions of women to which I here refer in the heterosexual context have the same significance in the lesbian context. My own view is that they do not, which is not to say that *some* of the concerns I raise here would not extend to the lesbian context.

18. See Sunstein (1993) for an excellent discussion of the historical vicissitudes in the interpretation and implementation of the First Amendment.

19. Here I follow Kaminer (1980) and Sunstein (1993) who offer clear treatments of this thorny matter.

20. Sunstein argues that one can see in court decisions a system of "free speech 'tiers'": certain forms of "high value" speech lie squarely inside the free speech "core" (e.g., political speech) and may be regulated only on "the strongest showing of harm"; other "low value" forms of speech lie at the "periphery" of constitutional protection (e.g., commercial advertisement) or outside constitutional protection altogether (e.g., obscenity, attempted bribes, criminal solicitation). The presumption that a regulation of speech is invalid becomes progressively weaker as one moves from core to periphery, from "high value" to "low value" speech (1993, 8–11). Sunstein claims that apart from occasional appeal to the contribution of a form of speech to democratic political ends, the court has offered no clear, consistent, principled basis for the categorization of some forms of speech as "top tier" (1993, 11).

21. Indeed, First Amendment absolutism has never been the law.

22. Many do. For a list of references on the interpretation of the First Amendment, see MacKinnon (1987, 262–63 n. 3; 275 n. 8; 183–84 nn. 52, 53).

23. See Longino (1980, 51–52) and R. Dworkin (1977, 262–63). Also see R. Dworkin (1993, esp. 41–42) for a discussion of what he calls the First Amendment's "egalitarian role," that of "protecting equality in the processes through which the moral as well as political environment is formed." It is notable that Dworkin here considers the view MacKinnon defends, namely, in his words, that "pornography works insidiously to damage the standing and power of women within the community," and hence injures their equality, but defends the pornographer's right to contribute "equally" to the "processes through which the moral as well as the political environment is formed" (1993, 42). When there is conflict, liberty rather than equality should, he claims, be privileged if we are to avoid "the despotism of thought-police" (1993, 41).

24. Though, as I hope will become clear, negative liberty does not entail unlimited license; thus, it does not follow from embracing a negative conception of liberty that one would hold that the right to free speech (as one protection of such liberty) is an absolute right.

25. For a discussion of various attempts to interpret the First Amendment as protecting autonomy, see Sunstein (1993, 137–44; and, for references, 274 n. 20 and 275 n. 24). One conception of autonomy, Sunstein writes, "is a form of self-mastery, through which people are permitted to be, roughly speaking, authors of the narratives of their own lives. This form of autonomy can be abridged not only by the obvious forms of government tyranny, but also by . . . conceptions of the good that are produced by social deprivation" (1993, 138).

26. For example, in MacKinnon's early work, she writes, "The assumptions the law of the First Amendment makes about adults—that adults are autonomous, self-defining, freely acting, equal individuals—are exactly those qualities that pornography systematically denies and undermines for women" (1987, 181). The Dworkin-MacKinnon antipornography ordinance, she claims, which "enunciates a . . . recognized governmental interest in sex equality," "aspires to guarantee women's rights *consistent with the First Amendment*" (1987, 177–78; see also 195). On this strain of MacKinnon's analysis, it is in effectively undermining women's expressive liberty, "positively" understood, that pornography renders women unequal: "Pornography . . . devastates women of credibility . . . we are stripped of authority and reduced and devalidated and silenced" (1987, 193). Sunstein argues for a similar view. The commitment to free expression embodied in the First Amendment is, he claims, "closely connected to the central constitutional goal of creating a deliberative democracy" (1993, 18). He thus focuses more narrowly on what he claims to be the role of the First Amendment in setting up the conditions for democratic self-government, which among other things presupposes "political equality." He argues that pornography subverts the equal status of women in causing violence against women, thus undermining the conditions for genuine democratic self-government (see Sunstein 1993, esp. 17–20, 23–29).

27. This second tactic is emphasized in MacKinnon (1993). MacKinnon claims that the free speech of pornographers protected by the First Amendment is "on a collision course" with the equality of women protected by the Fourteenth Amendment's equal protection clause (1993, 71), arguing that given the negligible value of pornographic speech, the state's interest in sex equality outweighs First Amendment safeguards of liberty in the case of pornography. Pornography is only one arena in which this claim is made; "hate speech" is another. See Delgado and Stefancic (1993), Matsuda et al. (1992), and Sunstein (1993).

28. Many women working as pornography models are young and in desperate financial circumstances; their work conditions are often terrible; they are frequently subject to coercion and abuse. Not only are they frightened to undertake the risk of further abuse and humiliation in initiating proceedings against their abusers, but they suffer credibility problems as well. See the U.S. Department of Justice, *Attorney General's Commission on Pornography: Final Report* (1986); Lederer (1980, esp. 55–115); and MacKinnon (1987, esp. 180–81). To the extent that the industry exploits models and that people working in the production of pornography are treated in ways that violate their rights to privacy or physical safety, the question arises whether others ought to have rights to that material or rights to make a profit from that material. These issues are addressed through the coercion, force, and assault provisions of the Dworkin-MacKinnon ordinance.

29. For the most part, anyway. There are exceptions, e.g., "obscene" speech.

30. MacKinnon argues that "pornography is more actlike than thoughtlike" (1987, 193); that pornography *itself* violates women.

31. Studies appeal principally to experimental evidence derived from testing peoples' responses (mostly their attitudinal, but in some cases, also behavioral, responses) to pornographic materials. They also appeal to statistical evidence, based in analyses comparing variations in crime statistics with variations in the availability of pornography, and anecdotal evidence found in reports of incidents in which a connection between pornography and criminal or coercive behavior has been claimed. See Donnerstein, Linz, and Penrod (1987), Donnerstein (1984), Donnerstein and Hallam (1978), Linz, Donnerstein, and Penrod (1987), Malamuth, Haber, and Feshback (1980), Malamuth and Donnerstein (1984), Mulvey and Haugaard (1986); and Zillmann and Bryant (1989). For additional references to research on the effects of pornography exposure, see MacKinnon (1987, 264–65 n. 9, 273 n. 59, 295 nn. 116, 132, 133) and Sunstein (1993, 280 n.8).

32. MacKinnon (1993) emphasizes the habituating effect of pornography, but she takes it to a behavioristic extreme I do not mean here to endorse. Attempting both to argue against pornography's expressive value as "speech" and to argue for the claim that it harms, she writes of pornography that "the way it works is not . . . through its ideas as such, at least not in the way thoughts and ideas are protected as speech. Its place in abuse requires understanding it more in active than in passive terms, as constructing and performative, rather than as merely referential or connotative. . . . The message of these materials . . . is addressed directly to the penis, delivered through an erection, and taken out on women in the real world" (1993, 21); "What was words and pictures becomes, through masturbation, sex itself" (1993, 24). Fundamental to MacKinnon's analysis is a view of pornography as alone having power, through use as a "masturbation tool," to habituate male sexual desire and arousal patterns in a way that subverts thought and is ineluctable. "Sooner or later," she writes, "in one way or another, the consumers want to live out the pornography further in three dimensions. Sooner or later, in one way or another, they do. *It makes them want to*. . . . Depending upon their chosen sphere of operation, they may use whatever power they have to keep the world a pornographic place so they can continue to get hard from everyday life" (1993, 19; my emphasis).

33. For a discussion of issues that arise in testing the social effects of pornography, see Bart and Jozsa (1980) and Mulvey and Haugaard (1986). See Schauer (1987) on the problem of causation and Sunstein (1993, esp. 218), for a general treatment of these issues.

34. See Parent (1990). Critics remark that those who would rely on causal arguments in objecting to pornography need to explain why violence against women is (allegedly) relatively rare in countries such as Sweden, the Netherlands, Denmark, and Japan, where pornography (including violent pornography) is widely available; whereas violence against women is relatively common in Ireland and South Africa, countries in which pornography is generally unavailable. See, for example, Feinberg (1986), Parent (1990), and Posner (1993). However, doubt has also been cast on the legitimacy of some of the statistical evidence educed in favor of this claim. See, for example, Court (1984, 150–69), Diamond (1980, esp. 199–200).

35. Here I follow Barry (1980, 307).

36. See Kaminer's argument that it is inappropriate to invoke the "clear and present danger standard" against pornography, which applies only to "tangible, immediate, and individualized danger" (1980, 245–46).

37. For example, in one content analysis of 428 "adult only" books, 20 percent of 4,588 portrayals of sexual encounter involved rape; 91 percent of the rapes were of females by males; 97 percent of these resulted in orgasm for the victims, and 75 percent of these were multiple orgasms. Detailed attention was given in these portrayals to the victim's terror, which was standardly portrayed as giving way through the rape to sexual arousal. Only 3 percent of the rapists faced negative repercussions for what they did, and many were rewarded with the "sexual devotion" of the victim (Smith [1976], cited in Bart and Jozsa [1980, 213–14] and Russell 1980b, 213–14]).

38. Kaminer argues along these lines (1980, 242–43).

39. Indeed, some have argued that the impact of such civil ordinances could be as severe in effect as criminal censorship laws, for they would permit court injunctions requiring the removal of materials that have been shown to be discriminatory, opening the door to "potentially endless legal harassment" of pornography producers and purveyors. See Duggan, Hunter, and Vance (1985, esp. 131), who argue against the Dworkin-MacKinnon ordinance and others like it on this ground. See also MacKinnon (1987).

40. As Skipper points out, "inequality can and has been romanticized, glorified, celebrated, patriotized, totemized, sacralized, proselytized, and aestheticized" (1993, 727). To the extent that women's internalization of the message of female inferiority is a piece of the problem, we might, he argues, worry even more about forms of speech, which, unlike pornography, are directed primarily to women.

41. A question that arises is whether we, as feminists, ought to affirm the eroticization of domination and subordination as a legitimate arena for exploration? Some feminists critical of the struggle for legal control of pornography argue that, as women, we must be left free to choose our sexual styles and modes, and even to enact or reenact subordinative sexual exchanges if that is what we desire to do. The fulfillment of forbidden desires, through the enactment of rape and bondage fantasies, it is argued, is not only for some an avenue into sexual arousal, especially charged in the light of patterns of inhibition and guilt, but also a way to take possession of one's own sexuality and to come to grips with one's sexual history, replete with its dark, abusive, or masochistic elements. Sexual experimentation and expression, when it involves playing subordinate roles on one's own initiative and using pornographic materials to this end, is one way to achieve self-possession and self-definition essential to self-owned sexuality and self-mastery. The question to be asked is whether such reenactments are exorcisms or rehearsals, occasions for further reinforcing troubling dispositions to engage in subordinative or self-effacing sexual encounters. I am grateful to Nancy Sherman for fascinating discussions about these issues.

42. See also Duggan, Hunter, and Vance (1985, 130–33) for a discussion of the history of the Dworkin-MacKinnon ordinance and the legislation it inspired.

43. It is also not the only example. For instance, the Canadian Supreme Court issued its decision in *Butler v. Her Majesty the Queen* (27 February 1992), defining "obscenity" by appeal to community standards of "harm," conceived to extend to degradation, influenced by and similar to those in the Dworkin-MacKinnon ordinance. The first arrest using the *Butler* decision was on April 30, 1992, of a manager of Glad Day Books, for selling a magazine called "Bad Attitude" produced by and for lesbians and containing depictions of bondage. On July 16, 1992, Judge Frank Hayes, of Ontario Court Regional Division, invoked *Butler* in reviewing gay magazines seized at the border, declaring anonymous homosexual encounters "harmful" to the community, and describing the sexual activity depicted in the magazines as "subhuman," and "degrading . . . without any human dimension" (*EXTRA* 23 December 1992). The censorship drama continues in Canada. Those keeping track of border seizures note that books from small presses and from certain earmarked companies—many of which are shipped to lesbian and gay bookstores—are "subject to higher levels of scrutiny and examination" (Lyall 1993). There is no question that Canadian policies grant less scope to expressive freedom than is currently granted in the United States. But the point is that the restrictive legal proposals we are considering here would move us in the direction of Canadian policy. See Rubin (1993, esp. 41–43) and *The San Francisco Chronicle*, Review (26 September 1993).

44. The recent appeal to the Fourteenth Amendment's equal protection clause on the part of feminist foes of pornography raises the question whether any form of speech—and not just sexualized speech—that helps create and maintain the second-class citizenship of any people or group, particularly those already disadvantaged, downtrodden, or oppressed in our society—is appropriately subject to state regulation.

45. Some would argue that these suggest at most that we must work harder to construct sufficiently narrow antipornography ordinances that could not be used to subvert the purposes for which they are designed. See, for example, Sunstein (1993, 225). Ultimately, this matter can only be settled empirically.

46. Russell (1980a, 305–6) argues along these lines. See also Kaminer (1980, 247).

47. Such as those that have been employed by Women Against Sexist Violence in Pornography and Media (in Pittsburgh), Women Against Pornography (in New York), Women Against Violence Against Women (in California), and others, which include forms of civil disobedience.

REFERENCES

The Attorney General's commission on pornography: Final report. 1986. United States Department of Justice.

Baier, Kurt. 1979. Response: The liberal approach to pornography. *University of Pittsburgh Law Review* 40(4): 619–25.

Barry, Kathleen. 1980. Beyond pornography: From defensive politics to creating a vision. In *Take back the night: Women on pornography*. See Lederer 1980.

Bart, Pauline B., and Margaret Jozsa. 1980. Dirty books, dirty films, and dirty data. In *Take back the night: Women on pornography*. See Lederer 1980.

Berlin, Isaiah. 1984. Two concepts of liberty. In *Liberalism and its critics*, ed. Michael Sandel. New York: New York University Press.

Black, Hugo. 1960. The bill of rights. *New York University Law Review* 35: 865ff.

Blakely, Mary Kay. 1985. Is one woman's sexuality another woman's pornography? Ms., April, 41–47, 120–22.

Brownmiller, Susan. 1980. Excerpt on pornography from *Against our will: Men, women and rape*. In *Take back the night: Women on pornography*. See Lederer 1980.

Burstyn, Varda, ed. 1985. *Women against censorship*. Vancouver: Douglas and McIntyre.

Court, John H. 1984. Sex and violence: A ripple effect. In *Pornography and sexual aggression*. See Malamuth and Donnerstein 1984.

Delgado, Richard, and Jean Stefancic. 1993. Overcoming legal barriers to regulating hate speech on campuses. *The Chronicle of Higher Education* 39(49): B1–B3.

Diamond, Irene. 1980. Pornography and repression: A reconsideration of 'who' and 'what.' In *Take back the night: Women on pornography*. See Lederer 1980.

Donnerstein, Edward. 1984. Pornography: Its effect on violence against women. In *Pornography and sexual aggression*. See Malamuth and Donnerstein.

Donnerstein, Edward, and John Hallam. 1978. Facilitating effects of erotica on aggression against women. *Journal of Personality and Social Psychology* 36(11): 1270–77.

Donnerstein, Edward, Daniel Linz, and Steven Penrod. 1987. *The question of pornography: Research findings and policy implications*. New York: Free Press.

Duggan, Lisa, Richard Goldstein, and Nat Hentoff. 1984. Forbidden fantasies. *The Village Voice*, 16 October, 1, 11–12, 14, 16–17, 22, 44.

Duggan, Lisa, Nan Hunter, and Carol S. Vance. 1985. False promises: Feminist antipornography legislation in the U.S. In *Women against censorship*. See Burstyn 1985.

Dworkin, Andrea. 1989. *Pornography: Men possessing women*. New York: Penguin, Plume.

Dworkin, Ronald. 1977. *Taking rights seriously*. Cambridge: Harvard University Press.

———. 1993. Women and pornography. *The New York Review of Books*, 21 October, 36–42.

Dyzenhaus, David. 1992. John Stuart Mill and the harm of pornography. *Ethics* 102(3): 534–51.

English, Deirdre. 1980. The politics of porn: Can feminists walk the line? *Mother Jones*, April, 20.

Feinberg, Joel. 1986. *Offense to others*. New York: Oxford University Press.

Griffin, Susan. 1980. Sadism and catharsis: The treatment is the disease. In *Take back the night: Women on pornography*. See Lederer 1980.

———. 1982. *Pornography and silence: Culture's revenge against nature*. New York: Harper and Row.

Kaminer, Wendy. 1980. Pornography and the First Amendment: Prior restraints and private action. In *Take back the night: Women on pornography*. See Lederer 1980.

Kappeler, Susanne. 1986. *The pornography of representation*. Minneapolis: University of Minnesota Press.

Langton, Rae. 1990. Whose right? Ronald Dworkin, women, and pornographers. *Philosophy and Public Affairs* 19(4): 311–59.

———. 1993. Speech acts and unspeakable acts. *Philosophy and Public Affairs* 22(4): 293–330.

Lederer, Laura, ed. 1980. *Take back the night: Women on pornography*. New York: William Morrow.

Linz, Daniel, Edward Donnerstein, and Steven Penrod. 1987. The findings and recommendations of the attorney general's commission on pornography: Do the psychological "facts" fit the political fury? *American Psychologist* (October): 946–53.

Longino, Helen. 1980. Pornography, oppression, and freedom: A closer look. In *Take back the night: Women on pornography*. See Lederer 1980.

Lovelace, Linda, and Michael McGrady. 1987. *Ordeal*. New York: Citadel Press.

Lyall, Sarah. 1993. Canada's morals police: Serious books at risk? *The New York Times*, 13 December.

MacKinnon, Catharine A. 1987. *Feminism unmodified: Discourses on life and law*. Cambridge: Harvard University Press.

———. 1993. *Only words*. Cambridge: Harvard University Press.

Malamuth, Neil and Edward Donnerstein, eds. 1984. *Pornography and sexual aggression*. Orlando: Academic Press.

Malamuth, Neil, Scott Haber, and Seymour Feshback. 1980. Testing hypotheses regarding rape: Exposure to sexual violence, sexual difference, and the 'normality' of rapists. *Journal of Research in Personality* 14: 121–37.

Matsuda, Mari J., Charles R. Lawrence III, Richard Delgado, and Kimberlè Williams Crenshaw. 1992. *Words that wound: Critical race theory, assaultive speech, and the First Amendment*. Boulder: Westview Press.

McCormack, Thelma. 1978. Machismo in media research: A critical review of research on violence and pornography. *Social Problems* 25(5): 544–52.

Mill, John Stuart. [1859] 1978. *On liberty*. Indianapolis: Hackett.

Mulvey, E. P., and J. L. Haugaard. 1986. *Report on the surgeon general's workshop on pornography and public health*. Washington: U.S. Department of Health and Human Services, Office of the Surgeon General.

Paglia, Camille. 1991. *Sexual personae: Art and decadence from Nefertiti to Emily Dickinson*. New York: Vintage.

Parent, W. A. 1990. A second look at pornography and the subordination of women. *The Journal of Philosophy* 37(4): 205–11.

Report of the Commission on Obscenity and Pornography. 1979. New York: Bantam.

Politically correct sex, an editorial. 1986. *Playboy*, October, 67–68, 85.

Posner, Richard. 1993. Obsession. *The New Republic*, 18 October, 21–32, 34–36.

Report of the Commission on Obscenity and Pornography. 1979. New York: Bantam.

Rubin, Gayle S. 1993. Thinking sex: Notes for a radical theory of the politics of sexuality. In *The Lesbian and Gay Studies Reader*, ed. Henry Abelov, Michele Aina Barale, and David Halperin. New York: Routledge.

Russell, Diana E. H. 1980a. Pornography and the women's liberation movement. In *Take back the night: Women on pornography*. See Lederer 1980.

———. 1980b. Pornography and violence: What does the new research say? In *Take back the night: Women on pornography*. See Lederer 1980.

Schauer, Frederick. 1987. Causation theory and the causes of sexual violence. *American Bar Foundation Research Journal* (4): 737–770.

Skipper, Robert. 1993. Mill and pornography. *Ethics* 103(4): 726–30.

Smith, Don. 1976. Sexual aggression in American pornography: the stereotype of rape. Paper presented at American Sociological Association. New York City.

Steinem, Gloria. 1986. *Outrageous acts and everyday rebellions*. New York: Signet.

Stoltenberg, John. 1990. *Refusing to be a man: Essays on sex and justice*. New York: Meridian.

Sunstein, Cass R. 1993. *Democracy and the problem of free speech.* New York: Free Press.
Vadas, Melinda. 1987. A first look at the pornography/civil rights ordinance: Could pornography be the subordination of women? *The Journal of Philosophy* 84(9): 487–511.
West, Robin. 1989. Feminism in the law: Theory, practice, and criticism. *University of Chicago Legal Forum*, 59–97.
Zillmann, Dolf and Jennings Bryant, eds. 1989. *Pornography: Research advances and policy considerations.* Hillsdale: Lawrence Erlbaum.

13

Beauty and Breast Implantation

How Candidate Selection Affects Autonomy and Informed Consent

LISA S. PARKER

Women's breasts and their decisions about them attract a great deal of attention in American culture and in the culture of American medicine. Breast cancer, for example, has become a highly politicized disease. Employed by politicians and researchers to redress inattention to women's health concerns and to reallocate federal research funds, breast cancer has galvanized groups of women into an effective lobby using political strategies of AIDS activism (Angell 1993; Gorman 1993; Laurence 1991; Marshall 1993). Moreover, prior to 1992 when the Food and Drug Administration (FDA) restricted access to silicone breast implants, women sought implantation at the rate of approximately 30,000 reconstructive mammaplasties and 120,000 augmentations annually, despite controversy about the safety, effectiveness, and propriety of breast implantation. In addition to constituting an obviously lucrative enterprise for aesthetic surgeons, breast surgery evokes strong sentiments among various parties. Feminists may view decisions to receive implants either as assertions of self-reliance and growing feminist consciousness (Davis 1991) or as extreme capitulations to prevailing cultural norms (Lorde 1980; Shapiro 1992). Some breast cancer patients view reconstruction as the final stage of their recovery (FDA 1992, 193), and FDA commissioner David Kessler termed it an integral part of breast cancer treatment (Kessler 1992). Both reconstruction and augmentation candidates frequently describe implantation as not only transforming their bodies

Hypatia vol. 10, no. 1 (Winter 1995) © by Lisa S. Parker

but also transforming their lives. Implantation alters their self-concept and their feelings of esteem, femininity, and confidence (Burk, Zelen, and Terino 1985; Davis 1991; Dull and West 1991; Ohlsén, Pontér, and Hambert 1979; Shipley, O'Donnell, and Bader 1977).

Women's access to breast implantation is constrained not only by their financial resources and the regulatory environment but also by two social practices within the clinical setting: candidate evaluation and informed consent. Before being permitted to transform their bodies, women seeking breast implantation must make their decision-making processes seem to conform to the normative requirements of these two practices. Moreover, critics of breast implantation have observed that women's decisions to seek implantation are themselves constrained by the cultural context of female beauty and by the social roles women occupy (Shapiro 1992; Young 1990), and some critics have concluded that, therefore, their decisions are importantly nonvoluntary or that they are not competent to make decisions to undergo breast implantation (Shapiro 1992).

In this essay I consider women's values and decisions concerning breast implantation, the cultural context within which their decisions are made, and the norms governing candidate evaluation and informed consent. First I outline some distinctive features of breast implantation and their influences on women's access to implantation and the process of informed consent. Next I examine whether the cultural context of female beauty influences surgeons' interpretation of data so that the information they disclose to candidates is such that women make substantially uninformed decisions about implantation. Further, I consider whether the cultural context of female beauty impugns women's ability to give informed consent either by rendering women incompetent to decide or rendering their decisions substantially nonvoluntary. Then I examine the norms informing candidate evaluation in the cultural context of female beauty. Finally, I consider the interplay between candidate evaluation and informed consent to determine whether these two practices place women in an untenable position where being deemed good candidates either undermines their ability to give informed consent or compromises their ability to act autonomously in a richer sense. This final inquiry is important because *even if* women can give valid informed consent to implantation, if the cultural norms governing candidate selection, the informed consent process, and breast implantation itself sufficiently undermine their abilities and opportunities to act autonomously, perhaps medicine's provision of breast implantation should be condemned.

INFORMED CONSENT, CULTURAL CONTEXT, AND DISTINCTIVE FEATURES OF IMPLANTATION

A focal point of the patients' rights movement of the 1970s, and now a cornerstone of medical ethics and law, the doctrine of informed consent evolved to protect patient welfare and preserve patients' rights of self-determination or of control over their bodies (Appelbaum, Lidz, and Meisel 1987; *Canterbury v. Spence*, 464 F.2d 772 [D.C. Cir. 1972]). Some commentators distinguish two senses of informed consent: it can be considered, first, as an autonomous authorization, an action, and, second, as a concept that may be analyzed in terms of the normative requirements governing it in particular policy or institutional contexts (e.g., hospitals or universities) (Faden and Beauchamp 1986). In general, this essay considers a sort of hybrid of the two senses. It treats informed consent as a social practice embedded in the social practices of other social institutions (including law, medicine, and particular health care institutions). It is, however, less concerned with informed consent as it is actually practiced (or even as it currently should be practiced according to prevailing norms); instead, it focuses on how informed consent might be practiced, were the desirability of promoting patients' abilities and opportunities for autonomous authorization taken seriously by those professionals and institutional structures participating in the informed consent process.[1]

As a social practice, informed consent may be analyzed in terms of five components: patient competence, disclosure of risks and benefits of a proposed intervention, understanding by the patient of these risks and benefits, voluntariness of patient decision making, and communication of that decision. The patient's competence to make the particular decision at hand serves as a prerequisite to the process of informed consent. In the informed consent process, a physician typically discloses the risks and benefits of various therapeutic options to the patient. The patient, understanding these options and appreciating their relative risks and benefits, weighs her options in the light of her own conception of the good or her stable set of values. She voluntarily makes and communicates her decision, her consent to or refusal of a particular therapeutic option, or her choice among several options.

Although informed consent to breast implantation generally follows this typical pattern, some features about breasts and breast implantation are distinctive (albeit generally not unique) and influence the process of informed consent, even though they do not alter its normative requirements, goals, or fundamental nature. First, breasts are rather distinctive body parts. Prior to any concern about breast disease or consideration of surgery, women and the society they inhabit typically have strong feelings about their breasts (see Young 1990). Breasts signal and signify the achievement of the biologically and socially constructed state of womanhood. They serve as symbols of women's stereotypical roles as mothers and as objects of sexual desire. Women experience their breasts, unlike most other body tissues, in a variety of ways. They observe their breasts' outward appearance, as well as the effects of others' observation of them. They experience their breasts both as connected to them physically (e.g., moving, swelling, providing erotic pleasure) and as connected to their identities, which are shaped by others' views, their own beliefs and values, and the constraints of a society that has strong and sometimes contradictory norms about female beauty and female breasts.

As a society we simultaneously believe, for example, that beauty is important and therefore should be sought and that beauty is a natural endowment and therefore should be effortless (Chapkis 1986). To be socially acceptable, women's care for their appearance must fall within narrow parameters. Too little care reflects low esteem; too much is either vain or pathological. Although female beauty is prized, women who seem too concerned with their appearance are viewed as selfish, immodest, or superficial. Women who seek beauty risk being simultaneously viewed as too aggressive and as asserting themselves over something trivial; they are both viewed as threatening barracudas and discounted as silly and inconsequential. Because men and women are led to believe that female beauty is a natural state, not an accomplishment, women who do not measure up to the supposedly natural norm are deemed inherently deficient, while those who expend energy and resources, or assume risks, to achieve the beautiful norm are deemed abnormal in virtue of both their efforts and the need for their efforts. We are, therefore, deeply ambivalent about whether a woman should seek beauty through breast augmentation. We suspect that her public body image should not matter so much, that her private body ideal is unrealistic, and that surgical relief of her beauty problems is too extreme a response.

In the light of their personal experiences of their breasts within this cultural context of female beauty, women are likely to have formed strong desires about their breasts' appearance by the time they seek breast implantation for either reconstruction or augmentation. Although some women deciding about reconstruction at the time of mastectomy (or following breast injury) face severe time constraints, implantation is generally not emergency surgery. Women are thus usually well-educated consumers with respect to breast implantation (Schain, Jacobs, and Wellisch 1984, 239). At least in contrast to those deciding about, for example, appendectomies or choosing between mastectomy or lumpectomy, women considering breast implantation know enough to want to consider the surgery (or, with augmentation, to seek it actively). They are, of course, likely to be better informed about the possible benefits of implantation than about its risks, not only because of the technical scientific nature of the risks but also because of the subjective nature of the primary benefits.

Indeed, a second distinctive feature of breast implantation surgery is the fact that its benefits are largely subjective and that the candidate is peculiarly authoritative about the nature and magnitude of the benefits that breast implantation may present to her. Without straying too far into discussion of the possibility of distinguishing between objective and subjective benefits, it may at least be claimed that in contrast to an emergency appendectomy, for example, breast implantation in most cases benefits a woman (or serves her interests) primarily if she thinks that it does.[2] Although the benefits of an emergency appendectomy might be determined with a fair degree of accuracy for most patients in most circumstances without knowing much about them, the benefits of breast implantation cannot be determined without knowing a great deal about the individual candidate, her circumstances, and her values. Her surgeon may inform her of the technical surgical possibilities and possible physical and likely emotional and psychological sequelae of the surgery, but the candidate herself will ultimately play a large causal role in achieving the desired affective responses to surgical outcomes. Thus preoperatively, she may be in a position, at least as good as anyone else's, to assess the likelihood of the desired results.

In the process of informed consent, the cumulative experience of the particular aesthetic surgeon consulted, as well as the cumulative experience of those practicing in the field as reported in the literature, is called upon to inform, assess, place in perspective, and even challenge the individual patient's own assessment of the anticipated benefits of her breast implantation. Nevertheless, she is not merely the final arbiter or weigher of the risks and benefits of the procedure; she and her personal experiences are also important sources of information about the nature and magnitude of the benefits (and perhaps some risks) of the surgery. Indeed, her values and desires serve to *constitute* the (possible) benefits of implantation *as benefits*.

The FDA's 1992 decision to grant different degrees of access to silicone breast implants to candidates for reconstruction and augmentation reflects, in part, a failure to recognize or to give sufficient weight to the subjective benefits of breast implantation for each purpose. Reconstruction may be viewed as the final step in a paradigmatic case of "make-you-good-as-new" acute care medicine. Unlike a reconstruction candidate's desire for implantation, an augmentation candidate's desire does not follow or "piggyback upon" the most socially and medically acceptable reason for seeking medical treatment—namely, to save her life.[3] Moreover, reconstruction seems much more *natural* than augmentation because it restores women to their previous natural (naturally more beautiful) breasted state; their previous state supplies the natural, biologically given, or objective norm at which surgery aims. In contrast, breast augmentation restores recipients to a social (and, in some cases, statistical) norm that is primarily aesthetic and is certainly not biologically defined in the case of the particular augmentation candidate. Reconstruction is, therefore, viewed as providing not only greater, but so-called objective benefits, while augmentation provides benefits of an inferior kind and therefore of a lesser magnitude—purely aesthetic, largely subjective benefits.[4]

A third distinctive feature of breast implantation concerns the scientific, legal, and public controversies surrounding the risks of implantation. Such controversies obviously affect the disclosure of risks during the informed consent process. Of course, controversy concerning the risks of a medical intervention is not unique to breast implantation; physicians have to disclose to patients (and research subjects) conflicting medical and scientific interpretations of data concerning other interventions. Nevertheless, it is unusual for such conflicting data to concern an intervention which has been available for thirty years and which approximately two million women have undergone; moreover, it is unusual for such conflicting data to inspire substantial and widespread fear among the public and to ground large settlements in lawsuits (Angell 1992, 1994; *Economist* 1992, 92–93; Feder 1994; Naik 1992; Ramsay 1994).

Although silicone implants, for example, have not been shown to present serious risks in relation to benefits, their safety and effectiveness has not been demonstrated according to the standards governing FDA approval of medical devices. Therefore, in 1992, in response to some consumer demands and in the light of evidence of misrepresentation of data by implant manufacturers, the FDA withdrew silicone breast implants from the open market and restricted access to them to women enrolled in clinical trials and registries (Galen 1992; Kessler 1992). Controversy persists, however, about the actual magnitude of risks of implantation.

In addition to the risks attending invasive surgery, there has been increased concern in recent years that "bleeding" of silicone gel from implants, either as a result of rupture or from the breakdown of the silicone cover, may be linked to increased incidence of cancer and connective-tissue and autoimmune diseases (Goldblum et al. 1992; Walsh et al. 1989; Weiss 1991). Other studies, however, have disputed the association of these implants with either cancer or connective-tissue disease in humans (Berkel, Birdsell, and Jenkins 1992; Deapen et al. 1986; Fisher and Brody 1992; Weisman et al. 1988). The frequency of rupture has also been disputed, with manufacturers reporting that it occurs in only 0.2–1.1 percent of asymptomatic women, while an FDA advisory panel suggested that 4 to 6 percent of devices may have ruptured (Kessler 1992; Skolnick 1992). Most recently, a study, published in June 1994 and described as providing the best data available thus far, found no association between breast implantation and connective-tissue and other diseases, such as cancers other than breast cancer (Gabriel et al. 1994; Angell 1994).

Fibrous capsular contracture is the most common complication of breast implantation, although the incidence of contracture has been variously reported as occurring in 10 to 70 percent of implant recipients (Rheinstein and Bagley 1992, 473; 50 percent in Burkhardt 1988a, 521). Accurate assessment of the data has been problematic for several reasons: measurement of contracture is difficult; no universal standard for measure has been accepted; incidence data collection has been incomplete; and no satisfactory animal model exists (Burkhardt 1988b, 72). Nevertheless, when the scar tissue that forms around the implant shrinks, compression, firmness, breast distortion, tenderness, and pain can result (Burkhardt 1988b, 72). In addition, severe contracture may distort the breast sufficiently to interfere with early diagnosis of breast cancer by mammography (Burkhardt 1988a, 521), and even without contracture, the presence of a breast implant may complicate early cancer detection by normal mammography, so that more sophisticated and expensive techniques or ultrasound may need to be substituted (Silverstein et al. 1988).

Finally, individual physicians' assessments of the conflicting data concerning the complications of breast implantation, and thus the risks they disclose to their patients during the informed consent process, are likely to be affected by the physicians' personal values. The effect of physicians' normative commitments on their interpretation of scientific data has been documented in other contexts. A study conducted in the late 1960s of physicians' interpretations of the scientific data concerning oral contraception, for example, revealed that those who viewed chemical contraception as immoral believed oral contraception to be much more unsafe and ineffective than those who viewed chemical contraception as moral (Veatch 1976). In a similar manner, how surgeons interpret the data reported about breast implantation is particularly likely to be influenced by their views concerning the lengths to which women may justifiably go to accomplish the goal of female beauty. In short, surgeons' views of and participation in the cultural construction of female beauty are likely to influence their interpretation, and subsequent disclosure during informed consent, of data concerning the risks of implantation.

Influenced by cultural norms that create and address women's desires to achieve a socially defined beauty norm, and faced with substantial controversy over data concerning breast implantation risks, a surgeon might tolerate a relatively high level of risk when interpreting breast implant data and might therefore consistently downplay the risks attending implantation when disclosing them during informed consent. Such a surgeon's risk-tolerant values, employed in interpreting data and disclosing risks, might poorly protect her patient's welfare and ability to make informed decisions. If this risk-tolerant response were uniform among aesthetic surgeons, in the light of cultural norms of beauty and conflicting data concerning implantation risks, women might generally be poorly protected. (Indeed, in the light of controversial interpretations of data and in response to concerns to protect women's welfare, in 1992 the FDA prescribed a standard "core disclosure" for individual surgeons to use in enrolling women in trials of silicone breast implants.) The concern raised here, however, is not merely a criticism of employing a professional or community standard of disclosure for informed consent; instead it highlights the implications for women's becoming informed about breast implantation risks if aesthetic surgeons were generally affected by cultural norms of beauty so as to truly believe that, in relation to the goals to be achieved, the risks of surgery were fairly minimal. The concern is not about a negligent or willful failure to disclose what patients would likely want to know; the worry is that surgeons' own roles within the culture of female beauty might lead them to adopt values that justify their toleration of higher levels of risk in their data interpretations, which upon critical reflection (or in the absence of cultural norms of beauty) they would not tolerate. (In addition, the integrity of the peer review process that governs the reporting of relevant data would be called into question if aesthetic surgeons, under the influence of cultural norms of beauty, were to adopt a uniform and uncritical or inappropriately biased stance toward research data.)[5]

WOMEN'S DECISIONS, CULTURAL CONTEXT, AND INFORMED CONSENT

It may be thought that the cultural context of beauty impugns women's informed consent to breast implantation by impugning their *competence* as decision makers or the *voluntariness* of their decisions. The present section explores these worries, but concludes that in spite of—perhaps even because of—the cultural constructions that influence women's decisions about breast implantation, it is generally correct not only to respect women's decisions to have their breasts reconstructed or augmented but also to respect those decisions as fulfilling the requirements of informed consent. As suggested in the previous section, however, there may be particular cases where because of the influence of cultural norms on surgeons' disclosures of the risks of breast implantation, women's opportunities to give their *informed* consent are indeed compromised. Moreover, the next section will critically examine the way that cultural norms of beauty influence surgeons' assessments of candidates for implantation surgery and thereby restrict women's *opportunities* to give informed consent to breast surgery, i.e., by deeming them inappropriate surgical candidates. Inadequate attention has been paid to the cultural influences on disclosure and understanding of information about breast implantation.[6] Commentators seem to assume that if women's decision making is seriously constrained by its cultural context, the cultural norms should be seen to operate directly on women's values and decision-making capacities, rather than operating indirectly by influencing physicians and others (in addition to candidates) who interpret and report data about implantation.[7] Cultural norms do indeed directly affect women's values and shape their decision making, but they do not thereby render women's informed consent invalid.

Several feminist commentators, however, clearly charge that the cultural context of female beauty undermines a woman's ability to give valid informed consent to breast implantation. Laura Shapiro, for example, states that "to 'choose' a procedure that may harden the breasts, . . . and introduce a range of serious health problems isn't a choice, it's a scripted response" (1992). Shapiro considers women who choose breast augmentation to be succumbing to society's dictates about what is beautiful. Iris Marion Young observes that it is "a phallocentric construction of breasts" that "privileges the look, their shape and size and normalcy" (1990, 201). Further, "phallocentric norms do not value a variety of breast forms, but rather elevate a standard; women are presented culturally with no choice but to regard our given breasts as inferior" (Young 1990, 202).[8] In a similar vein, Susan Bordo links norms governing beauty with practices of social control, including the practice of cosmetic surgery (Bordo 1989, 1990), and Wendy Chapkis highlights beauty's role in the oppression of women (Chapkis 1986). These feminist critiques of women's decisions to undergo breast implantation question the authenticity of their values, criticize the origin of their desires for implantation, and raise concerns about the ability of women, situated as they are in society and in the culture of beauty, to competently give consent that is voluntary or unconstrained.

A patient's competence is a prerequisite for her being able to give informed, voluntary consent. The type of competence generally demanded of patients in order for their decisions to be respected is related to the process of reasoning, not to the content of the decision reached; a competent decision is one that is the product of an appropriate reasoning process, not one that meets particular outcome-based criteria (e.g., being reasonable or being what the majority of decision makers would choose) (Buchanan and Brock 1989, 50–1). The capacities needed for a person competently to decide about health care are the capacities of *understanding* and *communication*, as well as those of *reasoning* and *deliberation*. In addition, a competent decision maker must have *a stable set of values or a conception of the good* in order to evaluate possible outcomes as benefits or harms and to assign relative weight to them (Buchanan and Broch 1989, 23–5). As Kathy Davis points out, feminist criticisms of women's decisions to undergo breast implantation typically fail to recognize that women must form their own conceptions of the good and make their choices within the prevailing cultural context (1991). Within the prevailing cultural context, physical appearance (beauty as well as deviation from norms of beauty) is not merely a difference worth noting but also a difference that is tied to social regard, self-esteem, love, power, employment, and security. Because, as Katha Pollitt notes, "self-esteem does not occur in a vacuum but in response to social pressures and rewards" (1992, 329), it is not only appropriate for women to take cultural values and social pressures and rewards into account if indeed those factors form a part of their own sets of values, it is indeed required by the norms governing competent decision making (Buchanan and Brock 1989, 25, 29–36; Davis 1991).

If women are to make decisions at all about whether to have breast implants, they should make their decisions on the basis of the risks and benefits of the procedure weighed in the light of what is important to them. For some women, small breasts, asymmetrical breasts, single-breastedness, averagebreastedness or even questions of their attractiveness are not of great importance. For others, these conditions may be of great importance because they are linked to their comfort, confidence, self-esteem, or perceived opportunities. For some, their unwillingness to perpetuate or to be influenced by prevailing norms of beauty will be crucial in their value systems. Whatever constitutes the set of values which are important to individual decision makers should be used by individual women in weighing their options about breast implantation.

Critics would respond that the cultural norms governing beauty are so pervasive and controlling that women's conceptions of the good which conform to them must be substantially inauthentic in virtue of how they are acquired and perpetuated. As George Sher points out, however, merely replacing women's socially conditioned values with spontaneously acquired preferences will not substantially increase their autonomy or control over their lives (1982, 47). What feminist critics must seek is a way to replace women's socially conditioned values with authentic values, values that they own in some relevant sense, values that are either the result of higher-order preferences or that survive critical self-interrogation. There is no guarantee, however, that women will not have higher-order preferences that lead them to prefer to conform to cultural norms, including norms of beauty (Sher 1982, 47).

Does a requirement of critical self-interrogation provide a criterion to distinguish women's authentic values? Sher, whose argument considers feminist criticisms of the content and genesis of the whole of "women's traditional preferences," concludes that this appeal to critical self-reflection cannot succeed. The argument for critical self-interrogation assumes that having traditional values precludes authentic autonomous decision making, which in turn is assumed to be marked by critical self-interrogation of the origin and content of one's preferences. If these assumptions are indeed correct, then critical reflection cannot provide the basis on which to choose between traditional (i.e., socially conditioned) and nontraditional preferences, because no women could engage in such critical self-interrogation while committed to traditional preferences. Because to engage in such critical self-interrogation is already to have chosen against adherence to traditional values, the justification for critical self-interrogation cannot reside in its making such choice possible. Therefore, its justification must instead lie in the belief that preferences resulting from critical self-interrogation are superior in some other dimension. The appeal to critical self-interrogation thus "tacitly prejudges the very question it seeks to answer" (Sher 1982, 48).

While such authenticity-guaranteeing wholesale critical self-interrogation may be impossible, critical interrogation of particular values and preferences—for example, those concerning beauty—may be possible. However, such a partial critical interrogation cannot be what feminist critics of women's breast implantation decisions have in mind, for it would be only a somewhat more deep interrogation of the values concerning beauty and consideration of the risks and benefits of implantation than is required by informed consent. As Kathy Davis suggests, women are not "cultural dopes"; in general, they are well aware of the cultural construction of their desires for breast implantation (1991, 30). If this degree of critical reflection were all that feminist critics required to deem women's decisions to undergo implantation authentic, then most women's choices would fulfill this criterion of authenticity, and there would be no question of women's competence to give informed consent to breast implantation. Although these critics are likely to remain unsatisfied, this partial critical self-interrogation is, as Sher's argument implies, all that is possible; there is no Archimedean point from which to examine the whole of their values or those concerning female beauty. Nevertheless, the desirability of a woman's critically reflecting on the content and genesis of her values as a means of ensuring her autonomous decision making suggests an important criticism of the candidate evaluation process, which is examined in the next section.

If the cultural context of beauty does not render women incompetent to give informed consent to breast implantation by rendering their conceptions of the good inauthentic, perhaps it places such substantial external pressures on them that their decisions are nonvoluntary. There are cases in which the external other who is influencing a woman's decision to have breast implantation can be easily identified: the lover who threatens to leave or the employer who threatens to fire a woman if she does not enlarge her breasts. Nevertheless, it is not clear that in these cases the woman's choice of implantation is rendered substantially nonvoluntary. If women who thought they might retain employment or achieve a secure relationship by enlarging their breasts were generally unsuccessful in doing so, this information might form one set of data from the cumulative experience of the surgical profession that could and should be disclosed to prospective patients. But even if this were true, the decision of whether to receive an implant in hopes of beating such odds should still remain that of the individual implant candidate. Although she may be wrong about her chances of finding a partner or even of increasing her self-esteem, she is in as good a position as anyone else to predict her chances and to weigh those chances in the light of her other options and her feelings of risk aversion or risk-taking.

In addition to external conditions that influence, but do not control, women's decisions, various "role constraints" may influence breast implant candidates' decision making (Faden and Beauchamp 1986, 368–72). Because roles assigned within particular social structures can constrain autonomous action, and because breast implant candidates occupy two such socially constructed roles—as patients and as women—it may be thought that role constraints impugn the voluntariness of their consent. Ruth Faden and Tom Beauchamp comment that because all actions are in some ways constrained by social experience, it is important to distinguish general circumstances of social and role constraint from those that occur in particular contexts, but that it is impossible to specify "threshold criteria that identify when the intentional features of role constraints function to push acts over the line of substantial noncontrol" (1986, 372). Nevertheless, in addition to identifying those roles and individuals occupying roles who are at high risk for experiencing substantial nonvoluntariness in their decision making because of role constraints and carefully analyzing their individual decisions, those concerned to promote patients' autonomous decision making should seek to ensure that medical practices do not replicate the role constraints or reinforce the passivity inherent in some roles. As the next section suggests, the practice of candidate evaluation for breast implantation unfortunately replicates the normative constraints of being a relatively passive patient and of being a woman in society.

The cultural norms governing conceptions of female beauty generally do not render women incompetent to decide to undergo breast implantation, nor do they usually render their decisions nonvoluntary. A woman's choice of implantation will, of course, help construct a culture in which women's (re)constructions of their bodies, at risk to their health, are acceptable responses to other cultural constructions. As unacceptable as the perpetuation of these cultural values may be, the alternative of not respecting women's choices to have breast implants as voluntary, competent decisions is even more unacceptable. As Faden and Beauchamp comment, "Perhaps the most important test of the adequacy of an analysis of autonomy is how well the analysis would function in the moral life, where it will inescapably be connected to the principle of *respect* for autonomy" (1986, 265). To refuse to accept women's consent to breast implant surgery as valid, one would have to either deny their agency or their competence as decision makers, or return to a model of medical paternalism deemed unacceptable during the past two decades.

CANDIDATE EVALUATION, INFORMED CONSENT, AND WOMEN'S OPPORTUNITIES FOR AUTONOMY

Obtaining informed consent for breast implantation occurs only in the later stages of the entire interactive process of preoperative consultation with an aesthetic surgeon, a process that involves discovering the candidate's expectations for and the anticipated subjective benefits of surgery. This process is often described in the aesthetic surgery literature as "assessing 'good candidates'" (Dull and West 1991, 60; Edgerton and Knorr 1971). Whereas the goals of informed consent are to protect the interests and promote the autonomy of the individual patient, the candidate assessment process has mixed, albeit not necessarily incompatible, goals. In addition to identifying candidates for whom the surgery is likely to afford the benefits sought, the surgeon seeks to ensure a track record of good surgical results and to avoid malpractice liability exposure.

Accounts of the candidate assessment process highlight both the largely subjective nature of the benefits of implantation and the influence of the cultural context of female beauty on medical practice. Candidate evaluation undercuts women's autonomous action with respect to their breast implantation decisions in several ways. First, it reinforces the passivity that (traditionally) accompanies their roles as women and as patients; candidate evaluation exacerbates the problems of role dependency. Second, through the candidate evaluation process, surgeons act as "gatekeepers" restricting access to implants and to the opportunity to give informed consent to surgery. Third, the candidate evaluation process may discourage some candidates from becoming as informed about their surgery as they would like to be. Finally, the process discourages women from engaging in a critical self-interrogation of the sources of their desires for implantation.

"Good" candidates display "'appropriate' levels of concern" about their appearance and realistic expectations about surgical results (Dull and West 1991, 60). They seek breast implantation "for themselves," to increase self-esteem or to improve self-image or confidence, not to attract others (Dull and West 1991, 61; Schain 1990). "The claim that there are 'appropriate' levels of concern for specific problems sustains the belief in objective, factual, transsituational grounds for aesthetic improvement—even as these are constructed from the particulars of the case at hand" (Dull and West 1991, 61). As one surgeon reports, "In cases where the patient's feature is physically unattractive in a manner about which there can be little disagreement, the request for surgery is usually granted—if the requested changes are surgically feasible, at a high level of confidence" (Edgerton and Knorr 1971, 555). In contrast, in dealing with patients whose deformity is both *congenital* (rather than acquired because of injury or disease) and *subjective*, the surgeon must

> fathom in each instance, as clearly as possible, exactly what this patient seeks and why he seeks it! Then he must make an educated guess as to whether or not he can surgically meet the demand. Often, when the subjective deformity is minimal the decision will involve difficult value judgments from the patient, surgeon, psychiatrist, and spouse. . . . Though these patients are difficult and the margins for surgical error are small, our experience . . . over the past 15 years have shown that many with definite neuroses (and occasionally, a psychotic patient) may receive substantial benefit from careful plastic surgery. (Edgerton and Knorr 1971, 552)

One motivation for this assessment process, then, is to place aesthetic surgery within the context of the traditional medical model whereby the tools of medicine are used to restore the patient to some statistical, discoverable, or given norm of health.

Where no such norm is "given," or when deviation from a statistical norm is not obvious, as when an average-busted woman seeks breast augmentation, surgeons (re)construct a norm by constructing a portrait of the good surgical candidate whose personality and behavior conforms to accepted norms of behavior for female patients and whose desired surgical outcome conforms to cultural norms of female beauty. The notion of the good aesthetic surgical candidate thus functions both descriptively and prescriptively. In the typical clinical context, as Faden and Beauchamp observe, "being a good patient may, in some cases, not be compatible with acting autonomously. By contrast, the 'bad-patient' role has often been described as a behavioral pattern in which the patient insists on exerting his or her autonomy. The bad-patient role is likened to a consumer-rights role, with the patient insisting on his or her right to criticize and to be informed" (1986, 371). In the context of *evaluating* the prospective patient, this disciplinary power of defining who constitutes a good patient is all the more constraining of the dependent patient's autonomous expression.

This discipline of breast augmentation candidates is especially striking. They must successfully walk the tightrope of the assessment process to get the opportunity to consent to surgery. They must be concerned, but only appropriately so; they may seek to be confident, but not directly seek outcomes that might come with increased confidence, like a mate or a job; and they must be strongly motivated, but neither externally pressured nor inappropriately internally motivated. As Kathy Davis writes: "The woman who wants to change her appearance by surgical means will find herself having to justify her decision with accounts of extreme suffering. However, even these will require some special handling if she is not to appear psychologically unstable or overly dependent on the approval of men" (1991, 24). Particularly disturbing is that augmentation candidates may be especially discouraged from asking questions about their surgeon's qualifications and patient satisfaction rate and from revealing their true expectations of surgical results for fear of appearing litigious or unrealistic. In this way, the candidate evaluation process itself may inhibit women's abilities to give informed consent, because it may prevent them from becoming informed. Moreover, to the extent that candidate evaluation places physicians in the gatekeeper role and creates an adversarial physician-patient relationship, the practice almost certainly erodes the basis for mutual trust.

Furthermore, a rejected augmentation candidate who is medically sophisticated and who has sufficient financial resources may learn from initial rejections how to "shop around" to find a surgeon willing to accept her as a candidate.[9] As a result, more sophisticated and better educated women, as well as those with greater financial resources, may gain access to breast implantation, while their less sophisticated, less educated, and poorer counterparts may not. To the extent that breast implantation is linked to economic opportunities and enhanced self-esteem, this inequitable access to implantation as a result of an institutionalized practice may exacerbate existing social inequalities.

Finally, out of pressure to conform to the norms of a good surgical candidate, women may be disinclined to question their motivations for seeking implantation, even in the light of new information about implantation's risks and benefits that they receive during the candidate evaluation and informed consent processes. To the extent that critical self-interrogation of their desires for implantation constitutes women's best means of ensuring some degree of authenticity in their decisions to undergo implantation, it is ethically problematic that the candidate evaluation process reinforces their roles as passive patients and as women within the culturally constructed contexts of beauty and of the general subordination of women. It is the practice of candidate evaluation, not the practice of breast implantation per se, that perpetuates cultural norms reinforcing the passivity or subordination of women.

CONCLUSION

From the perspective of respecting women as autonomous decision makers, it is candidate evaluation as it is often practiced, not breast implantation, that should be condemned. Candidate evaluation for breast implantation imposes norms on women which are directly contrary to those inherent in autonomous decision making and promoted by the informed consent process. Instead of condemning women for choosing to have breast implants or condemning breast implantation for perpetuating cultural norms of female beauty, commentators who are concerned about women's autonomy should encourage aesthetic surgeons to develop protocols for candidate evaluation that take seriously a candidate's values and reasons for seeking implantation, that interrogate her reasons *from a perspective informed by her own values*, and that encourage her to become informed about the risks of breast implantation. In this way, the norms informing candidate evaluation for breast implantation and those grounding the process of informed consent may be rendered consistent, and the process of candidate evaluation may be less likely to impugn a candidate's ability and opportunity to give an autonomous authorization to implantation.

NOTES

I thank Jennifer Bushee and Molly Sear for their research assistance. Earlier versions of this paper were presented at the Conference on Feminist Ethics and Social Policy, Pittsburgh, Pennsylvania, November 5–7, 1994; at Georgetown University, Washington, D.C., February 1, 1994; and at the Association for Practical and Professional Ethics annual meeting, Cleveland, Ohio, February 24–26, 1994. I thank members of those audiences for their comments.

1. Because the discussion is concerned with informed consent as a practice within

health care institutions, for example, much of the discussion of the normative requirement that an implant candidate understand the risks and benefits of implantation focuses on their disclosure. At the same time, however, because of the argument's commitment to promoting patients' autonomous authorizations, attention is also paid to the fact that women seeking breast augmentation are typically very well informed prior to approaching a surgeon. The candidate assessment process is criticized to the extent that it encourages women to act passively, to avoid asking questions, or to hide their prior understanding.

2. Some possible benefits of breast implantation may, however, be objective. Keeping or gaining employment, or earning more money, would be deemed objective benefits of breast implantation, especially augmentation.

3. Acute care and life-saving medicine are not the only sources of so-called objective medical benefits; they simply present the most stark examples of what are assumed to be objective benefits of medical intervention. There is wide agreement that life and life-saving are presumptive goods or benefits. Whether they are thereby *constituted* as good (and thus are properly called intersubjectively defined goods) or whether there is some (other) sense in which they are "objective" goods is not an issue that I wish to engage here. I am inclined toward the first view, and thus refer to "so-called objective benefits," but I realize that in order to criticize a policy for inappropriately employing this perceived distinction between objective and subjective benefits, it is necessary to refer to the perceived difference between the two.

4. That patients' personal values, beliefs, and circumstances constitute the benefits of medical interventions is, perhaps, most evident in cases of aesthetic surgery or other elective procedures undertaken in response to personal and cultural values (e.g., treatment with human growth hormone, prenatal testing, or carrier screening for genetic conditions), but nonelective, noncosmetic medical interventions have a larger component of subjective or value-dependent benefits than is often recognized. The magnitude of their subjective benefits (and harms) is, however, often obscured by the very presence of objective or intersubjective, widely recognized benefits, in much the same way that breast reconstruction's association with cancer treatment obscures the fact that such implantation is performed on a presumably healthy, cancer-free breast in response to a mastectomy patient's personal desires to avoid flat-chestedness or asymmetry. Obvious consensus concerning so-called objective benefits of a treatment not only obscures the subjective nature of the treatment's benefits; in current practice it also tends to make the process of informed consent less dialogical or interactive in these noncosmetic, nonelective medical contexts. Instead, the expert discloses *the* risks and benefits, i.e., the standard set of risks and benefits that a reasonable person in similar circumstances would want to know ("core disclosure" [Faden and Beauchamp 1986, 308]), and the patient communicates her decision.

5. I recognize that all data interpretation reflects some bias at least in the sense of reflecting theoretical and normative commitments; it is when these commitments are uncritical or self-serving that they may be particularly ethically, as well as scientifically, problematic (see, for example, Veatch 1994).

6. Young (1990) is a noteworthy exception in this regard; she raises concerns about the quality and culturally influenced sources of the *information* on which women base their implantation decisions.

7. Faden and Beauchamp (1986, 276) correctly note that patients may gain the understanding requisite for giving informed consent by means other than the disclosure

of therapeutic options, risks, and benefits during informed consent. However, because my general argument is concerned with informed consent as a socially embedded practice, I shall treat disclosure and understanding as intimately connected. Moreover, insofar as patients gain their understanding of at least the risks of surgery, and perhaps the benefits, from data interpreted and reported in the lay press and medical literature, their understanding of these risks is ultimately affected by the influence that cultural norms have on the interpretations of physicians, scientists, reporters, activists, and others.

8. Unlike Shapiro (writing with Springen and Gordon), however, Young does not judge women's decisions to augment their breasts to be nonvoluntary.

9. In this regard, of course, they are not unique. Rejected candidates for transsexual surgery, couples seeking fetal sex determination, or organ transplant candidates may, if sophisticated and wealthy, eventually learn how to behave in order to receive access to the medical resources they desire.

REFERENCES

Angell, Marcia. 1992. Breast implants: Protection or paternalism? *New England Journal of Medicine* 326(25): 1695–96.

———. 1993. Caring for women's health—What is the problem? *New England Journal of Medicine* 329(4): 271–72.

———. 1994. Do breast implants cause systemic disease? *New England Journal of Medicine* 330(24): 1748–49.

Appelbaum, Paul S., Charles W. Lidz, and Alan Meisel. 1987. *Informed consent: Legal theory and clinical practice*. Oxford: Oxford University Press.

Berkel, Hans, Dale C. Birdsell, and Heather Jenkins. 1992. Breast augmentation: A risk factor for breast cancer? *New England Journal of Medicine* 326(25): 1649–53.

Bordo, Susan. 1989. The body and the reproduction of femininity: A feminist appropriation of Foucault. In *Gender/body/knowledge*, ed. Alison Jaggar and Susan Bordo. New Brunswick, NJ: Rutgers University Press.

———. 1990. Reading the slender body. In *Body/politics*, ed. Mary Jacobus, Evelyn Fox Keller, and Sally Shuttleworth. New York: Routledge.

Buchanan, Allen E. and Dan W. Brock. 1989. *Deciding for others: The ethics of surrogate decision making*. Cambridge: Cambridge University Press.

Burk, Judith, Seymour L. Zelen, and Edward O. Terino. 1985. More than skin deep: A self-consistency approach to the psychology of cosmetic surgery. *Psychology of Cosmetic Surgery* 76(2): 270–77.

Burkhardt, Boyd R. 1988a. Capsular contracture: Hard breasts, soft data. *Clinics in Plastic Surgery* 15(4): 521–32.

———. 1988b. Breast implants: A brief history of their development, characteristics, and problems. In *Postmastectomy reconstruction*, ed. Thomas D. Gant and Luis O. Vasconez. Baltimore: Williams and Wilkins.

Chapkis, Wendy. 1986. *Beauty secrets*. Boston: South End Press.

Davis, Kathy. 1991. Remaking the she-devil: A critical look at feminist approaches to beauty. *Hypatia* 6(2): 21–35.

Deapen, Dennis M., Malcolm C. Pike, John T. Casagrade, and Garry S. Brody. 1986.

The relationship between breast cancer and augmentation mammaplasty: An epidemiologic study. *Plastic and Reconstructive Surgery* 77(3): 361–67.

Dull, Diana and Candace West. 1991. Accounting for cosmetic surgery: The accomplishment of gender. *Social Problems* 38(1): 54–70.

Economist. 1992. Implanting the seeds of doubt. 29 February, 92–93.

Edgerton, Milton T., Jr. and Norman J. Knorr. 1971. Motivational patterns of patients seeking cosmetic (esthetic) surgery. *Plastic and Reconstructive Surgery* 48(6): 551–57.

Faden, Ruth R. and Tom L. Beauchamp. 1986. *A history and theory of informed consent*. New York: Oxford University Press.

Feder, Barnaby J. 1994. Three awarded $27.9 million over breast implants. *New York Times*, 4 March.

Fisher, Jack C. and Garry S. Brody. 1992. Breast implants under siege: An historical commentary. *Journal of Long Term Effects of Medical Implants* 1(3): 243–53.

Food and Drug Administration (FDA). 1992. General and Plastic Surgery Devices Panel Meeting. 18–20 February. Bethesda, Maryland.

Gabriel, Sherine E., Michael O'Fallon, Leonard T. Kurland, Mary Beard, John E. Woods, and L. Joseph Melton, III. 1994. Risk of connective-tissue disease and other disorders after breast implantation. *New England Journal of Medicine* 330(24): 1697–702.

Galen, Michele. 1992. Debacle at Dow Corning: How bad will it get? *Business Week*, 2 March, 36–37.

Goldblum, Randall M., Ronald P. Pelley, Alice A. O'Donell, Debra Pyron, and John P. Heggers. 1992. Antibodies to silicone elastomers and reactions to ventriculoperitoneal shunts. *Lancet* 340: 510–13.

Gorman, Christine. 1993. Breast-cancer politics. *Time*, 1 November, 74.

Kessler, David A. 1992. The basis of the FDA's decision on breast implants. *New England Journal of Medicine* 326(25): 1713–15.

Laurence, Leslie. 1991. The breast cancer epidemic: Women aren't just scared, we're mad. *McCall's*, 1 November, 24–40.

Lorde, Audre. 1980. *The cancer journals*. Trumansburg, NY: Crossing Press.

Marshall, Eliot. 1993. The politics of breast cancer. *Science*, 5 April-28 June, 616–17.

Naik, Gautam. 1992. Woman receives $25 million judgment in Bristol-Myers breast implant suit. *Wall Street Journal*, 24 December.

Ohlsén, Lennart, Bengt Pontén, and Gunnar Hambert. 1979. Augmentation mammaplasty: A surgical and psychiatric evaluation of the results. *Annals of Plastic Surgery* 2(1): 42–50.

Pollitt, Katha. 1992. Implants: Truth and consequences. *Nation*, 16 March, 325–29.

Ramsay, Sarah. 1994. Breast implant settlement. *Lancet* 343: 1153.

Rheinstein, Peter H. and Grant P. Bagley. 1992. Update on breast implants. *American Family Physician* 45(2): 472–73.

Schain, Wendy S. 1990. Discussion of 'Reasons why mastectomy patients do not have breast reconstruction' by Neal Handel, Melvin J. Silverstein, Ellen Waisman, and James Waisman. *Plastic and Reconstructive Surgery* 86(6): 1123–25.

Schain, Wendy S., Ellen Jacobs, and David K. Wellisch. 1984. Psychosocial issues in breast reconstruction: Intrapsychic, interpersonal, and practical concerns. *Clinics in Plastic Surgery* 11(2): 237–51.

Shapiro, Laura. 1992. What is it with women and breasts? *Newsweek*, 20 January, 57.

Sher, George. 1982. Our preferences, ourselves. *Philosophy and Public Affairs* 12(1): 34–50.

Shipley, Robert H., John M. O'Donnell, and Karl F. Bader. 1977. Personality characteristics of women seeking breast augmentation. *Plastic and Reconstructive Surgery* 30(3): 369–76.

Silverstein, Melvin, Neal Handel, Parvis Gamagami, James R. Waisman, Eugene D. Gierson, Robert J. Rosser, Robert Steyskal, and William Colburn. 1988. Breast cancer in women after augmentation mammaplasty. *Archives of Surgery* 123(6): 681–85.

Skolnick, Andrew A. 1992. Ultrasound may help detect breast implant leaks. *Journal of the American Medical Association* 267(6): 786.

Veatch, Robert M. 1976. *Value-freedom in science and technology*. Missoula, MT: Scholars Press.

———. 1994. Incommensurability: Its implications for the patient/physician relation. *Journal of Medicine and Philosophy* 20(4).

Walsh, Frank W., David A. Solomon, Luis R. Espinoza, Glenn D. Adams, and Henry E. Whitelocke. 1989. Human adjuvant disease: A new cause of chylous effusions. *Archives of Internal Medicine* 149(5): 1194–96.

Weisman, Michael H., Thomas R. Veccione, Daniel Albert, Lawrence T. Moore, and Mary Rose Mueller. 1988. Connective tissue disease following breast augmentation: A preliminary test of the human adjuvant disease hypothesis. *Plastic and Reconstructive Surgery* 82(4): 626–30.

Weiss, Rick. 1991. Breast implant fears put focus on biomaterials. *Science*, 5 April-28 June, 1059–60.

Young, Iris Marion. 1990. Breasted experience. In *Throwing like a girl and other essays in feminist philosophy and social theory*. Bloomington: Indiana University Press.

14

Sex-Selective Abortion

A Relational Approach

GAIL WEISS

As new reproductive technologies are being discovered, refined, and implemented on a daily basis both in the United States and abroad, it is imperative that the new moral issues generated by them be discussed and addressed not just by the physicians and technicians implementing the procedures but also by the families making use of them and the communities that are affected by them. Sex-selective abortion (hereafter referred to as SSA) depends on the ability of a physician or technician to determine the sex of the fetus before birth, something that could not be done reliably before the advent of ultrasound and amniocentesis.[1] Given that SSA is made possible by these two procedures, the conflicts and contradictions that surround both the justifications for and the condemnations of SSA also "rebound" upon the use of ultrasound and amniocentesis as sex predictors. In this essay I will try to untangle what I take to be the most important and most confused aspects of the current debate regarding the morality of SSA through a critical discussion of Mary Anne Warren's argument in *Gendercide: The Implications of Sex Selection* (1985) for SSA as a moral right and through an application of Sarah Ruddick's cognitive-materialist account of "maternal thinking" (1980 [1983]). In accordance with Ruddick's emphasis on social acceptability as a crucial component of maternal thinking, I argue that SSA is never an individual decision but that it must be understood and evaluated through the family and community practices that make it appear to be a desirable (and, for many, the only viable) option. Through an examination of the complex manner in which SSA both reinforces and opposes the stated (and unstated) values of a given community, I conclude that SSA is a "moral mistake" for which individual blame cannot be assessed due to the fact that the decision to undergo the procedure is directly tied to community beliefs and practices that performatively construct differential values for males and females.[2]

SEX-SELECTIVE ABORTION: AN INTERNATIONAL PROBLEM

On July 21, 1993, this striking headline appeared on the front page of *The New York Times*: "Peasants of China Discover New Way to Weed Out Girls."[3] In the article that followed, the Chinese peasants interviewed stated that doctors would conduct ultrasounds on pregnant women in the community for a "bribe" roughly equivalent to thirty-five to fifty dollars in order to determine the sex of the fetus. "Then," one peasant announced, "if it's a girl, you get an abortion" (Kristof 1993, 1). The article's author, Nicholas Kristof, goes on to add: "In the China of the 1990s, the modern machine that is having the most far-reaching effect on society is probably not the personal computer, the fax or even the car. It is the ultrasound scanner" (Kristof 1993, 1).

Indeed, more and more ultrasound scanners are being made and distributed in China each year, and the increasingly skewed sex ratio in China (in 1992 it was 118.5 boys for every 100 girls—13 points higher than the international norm, which suggests that there are around 1.7 million girls unaccounted for in China per year) is directly tied to the growing availability of what in India is commonly referred to as the "sex test." In Bombay, clinics have proliferated in lower-income areas of the city offering "cut-rate prices" on amniocentesis. To aid in their advertising, the clinics exacerbate "the fear of dowry with such slogans as 'better 500 rupees now than 500,000 later'" (Bumiller 1990, 115). For those too poor to afford the "sex test" or for whom prenatal testing is unavailable, there is yet another alternative. Rajeshwari, a young mother who let her mother-in-law put her second daughter "to sleep" right after she was born, rationalized her family's decision to commit female infanticide in the following way: "Abortion is costly. And you have to rest at home. So instead of spending money and losing income, we prefer to deliver the child and kill it" (Bumiller 1990, 108).

What differentiates a sex-selective abortion[4] from an abortion undertaken for reasons that are independent of the sex of the fetus is that those who choose SSA would not be terminating the pregnancy if the fetus was not a member of the unwanted sex.[5] In India and China, countries where SSA is practiced quite widely, the majority of those who choose SSA indeed plan to have more children, but what they want are sons. Despite the very realistic possibility that new technologies will be developed in the coming years making it possible to *preselect* the sex of one's child, it is still unlikely that SSA will ever become as popular in the United States as it is in China and India. That will be due not to the lack of acceptance for such a procedure among health professionals, ethicists, and clergy but rather to the vast differences in the lives of females in the United States and in these other countries.

Although remnants of the dowry system can be seen in the United States in marriage traditions such as the bride's family paying all wedding expenses (which often amounts to thousands of dollars and which remains an expectation even if the groom's family has more money than the bride's), the stereotypical response of the groaning father pulling out his checkbook (dramatized by Steve Martin in the popular movie *Father of the Bride*) is still a far cry from the attitude of millions of Indian and Chinese families for whom a daughter is seen as "an investment with little return" (Bumiller 1990, 102). Warren argues that son preference is directly tied to the existence of a patriarchal society in which

> a daughter is usually only a temporary member of her family of origin, since she will leave it as soon as she is old enough to marry. Her children, like her labor, will belong to her husband's family, not that of her father or mother. Even if her husband is required to pay a bride-price to her parents, this is not usually enough to cover the cost of her upbringing. If, on the other hand, her parents are required to provide a dowry, the cost of raising daughters is apt to be perceived as far greater than any resulting benefits. (Warren 1985, 14)

China's strictly enforced quotas on the number of children a married couple may have and the extreme poverty of the majority of Indians make it even more apparent why SSA and female infanticide have become so prevalent in these countries. Indeed, there are an increasing number of villages in both India and China about whom the following claim, uttered by a Chinese peasant, can be made: "Last year we had only one girl born in the village—everybody else had boys" (Kristof 1993, 1). When these villagers are questioned about the possibility that their sons will not be able to find wives in twenty years' time, the villagers do not appear worried. Their immediate concern is to have sons who can help out in the fields, take care of them in their old age, and who will continue the family line. As Warren notes: "Wherever son-preference is especially pronounced, it is due in large part to powerful economic motivations. Even in societies which provide some social support for the aged, sons are often an important part of old-age security" (Warren 1985, 85).

Poverty and birth quotas are not the only motivating factors that lead to SSA and female infanticide. The social pressure to have sons rather than daughters and the associated prestige that comes from having sons also play a key role in most families' decisions to undergo SSA or to commit female infanticide, even when the birth of another daughter does not represent an economic hardship. In response to the growing use of the "sex test" (amniocentesis) in order to perform SSA on female fetuses, the state legislature of Maharashtra, India (which includes Bombay), passed a law in May 1988 banning the use of prenatal testing for purposes of sex determination. Many Bombay feminists, who had lobbied long and hard for such a law, were enthusiastic about its adoption but also had concerns about the serious difficulties associated with enforcing it.

The existence of this law in Maharashtra, India, which has nationally been regarded as a qualified success and a possible model for other state legislatures to adopt, raises some interesting policy questions that need to be addressed with regard to the use of SSA in the United States. Evans et al., in a 1991 article on SSA appearing in the American Journal of Obstetrics and Gynecology, claim that the United States needs to develop a coherent public policy that balances prohibitions against SSA and abortions performed for the use or sale of fetal tissue with protection of the "rights of parents (with the expert help of physicians) to make difficult choices in difficult situations" (Evans et al. 1991, 1099). Defining the difficulty of the choice and the difficulty of the situation is the crux of the problem, however, for both the choice and situation differ radically from one family to another and from one country to another.

THE CONFLICTS AND CONTRADICTIONS OF SSA

The most obvious challenge SSA represents for pro-choice feminists is the difficulty of reconciling a pro-choice position with moral objections one might have to SSA (especially since it has been used primarily on female fetuses), much less the advocacy of a law banning SSA. Warren claims that there is no way to resolve this tension satisfactorily, and this leads her to adopt what many may regard as a rather extreme position:

> If, as I have argued, early abortion raises no serious moral issues, then early sex-selective abortion is morally no more problematic than preconceptive sex selection. Furthermore, because even late-term fetuses are not yet persons, and because all persons have a basic moral right to "control their own bodies,"—i.e., to defend, and make decisions affecting, their own physical integrity—a woman has a moral right to choose even late abortion for any reason which she regards as sufficient. Thus, she has a moral right to use even late abortion as a means of sex selection. Of course, she also has the right not to. No one else has the moral right to coerce her in either direction. (Warren 1985, 104)

Throughout her book, Warren approaches the issue of SSA from within a traditional ethical framework that acknowledges two basic models for evaluating its acceptability: a utilitarian (consequentialist) paradigm and a Kantian (deontological) scheme. She moves rather quickly to the conclusion that deontological arguments against SSA are unsound, and, in a more systematic manner, she rather convincingly demonstrates that consequentialist arguments against SSA are not compelling either because, despite the predominance of son preference in almost every contemporary society, we are unable to be sure that the dire predictions individuals have made concerning widespread use of SSA primarily to guarantee the birth of sons rather than daughters will ever come to pass.

Although she does not find SSA morally objectionable during the first trimester of a pregnancy, Warren is against performing SSA on second and third trimester fetuses because she views them as sentient. And, she claims, "It requires a stronger reason than sex-preference to justify the killing of a sentient human being—even one which is not yet a person" (Warren 1985, 104). Warren's own position is fraught with tension, however, because it is difficult to reconcile her restriction on SSA in the second or third trimesters of a pregnancy with her previous claim that "a woman has a moral right to choose even late abortion for any reason which she regards as sufficient" (Warren 1985, 104). Warren tries to dissolve this tension by making a distinction between acting within one's rights and "doing the right or morally optimal thing." She implies that late SSA may be an instance of the former but not the latter; this distinction between having a right to choose and being right to choose requires more clarification, however, and the lack of such clarification further complicates, rather than resolves, the issue at hand.

Despite her moral objection to late SSA (she is opposed to legal prohibitions against late SSA), Warren states that we must not blame the women who opt for this procedure since

> very few women would submit to a late-term abortion for trivial reasons. However, in a highly patriarchal society, sex selection may *not* be a trivial reason for abortion. It may be an extremely compelling reason, from the viewpoint of the individuals who must make the decision. Under some circumstances, having a child of the "wrong" sex may be a misfortune of major proportions, and a female child, if born, may have little prospect of leading a decent life. In such circumstances, the blame must attach not to the individuals who opt for sex-selection abortion, but to the society which has created these circumstances. We should feel only compassion for women who find it necessary to accept such an extreme measure in order to prevent the birth of an unwanted daughter. (Warren 1985, 105)

According to Warren, it is patriarchal society and its oppressive institutions and practices which we must blame for the use of SSA to terminate female fetuses. Although this is a very appropriate target for blame, it is difficult on either a utilitarian or deontological model to know how to assess this blame, since both models rely heavily on the notion of an autonomous moral agent responsible for her or his choices. Warren herself appeals to the autonomy of the pregnant woman to justify the morality of early abortion in general and early SSA in particular. When it comes to assessing responsibility for SSA, however, a practice that she does regard as an "evil" (albeit a morally acceptable evil and often the lesser of two evils), she introduces contextual features of the situation that she views as largely responsible for the decision to undergo SSA in the first place.

The internal inconsistencies of Warren's own position as well as the more general conflicts that anyone discussing SSA from a pro-choice standpoint must grapple with make the prospect of developing a coherent position on SSA rather daunting. Nonetheless, there is a way of clarifying the central issues surrounding SSA and of coming to terms with them, but not from within the traditional ethical framework Warren uses. This is because the presupposition of an autonomous moral agent is precisely what must be challenged in evaluating the decision to perform SSA, since, as Warren herself realizes, this decision is never made independently of a given social reality, and, I argue, it is almost never made by the pregnant woman alone. In fact, many of the conflicts surrounding SSA stem from a failure to see the interdependent relationships that link the pregnant woman with her fetus, with the father of her child, with her other children, with her parents and (possible) parents-in-law, and which link all of these other individuals with one another. And the only viable way to understand the role these relationships play in SSA is to appeal to a standpoint that begins with these relationships rather than with isolated individuals. At the same time, it must be recognized that these relationships themselves take place within a larger social context that profoundly influences the values and priorities that emerge from these relationships.

"MATERNAL THINKING" AS A MODEL FOR UNDERSTANDING SSA

Given the centrality of familial relationships and the normative role played by community practices in the decision to undergo SSA, it is imperative that SSA itself be evaluated from an ethical position that *begins* with these relationships rather than viewing them as additional features of the situation that are considered on a post hoc basis in one's moral theorizing.[6] What unites the various moral theories that have been associated with an ethic of care is the primacy they give to familial and community relationships. One of the most successful models in doing justice to the role these relationships play in everyday moral decision making is Sara Ruddick's model of maternal thinking (see Ruddick 1980 [1983]). Not only is a model that centers on maternal thought extremely applicable to the issues surrounding SSA (since SSA marks the termination of a relationship between a fetus and its prospective mother), but an informed understanding of maternal thinking, as Ruddick has convincingly shown in her work on peace and nonviolence, can also serve as a guide to reconceptualizing much more than the relations between parents and children. In her discussion of maternal thinking, Ruddick acknowledges that some maternal interests are nonrelative in the sense that they must be minimally secured to ensure a young child's survival, but she also recognizes that there are a variety of culturally specific ways in which these interests are expressed and realized.

> Some features of the mothering experience are invariant and nearly unchangeable; others, though changeable, are nearly universal. It is therefore possible to identify interests that seem to govern maternal practice throughout the species. Yet it is impossible even to begin to specify these interests without importing features specific to the class, ethnic group, and particular sex-gender system in which the interests are realized. (Ruddick 1980 [1983], 214–15)

There are three primary interests Ruddick identifies as central to maternal practice and thought. Preservation, she claims, is the most primary and invariant, since it involves fulfilling a young child's basic needs to guarantee its continued survival.[7] Although a concern for the preservation of one's offspring remains an ongoing priority for whoever is raising the child, as an infant develops, maternal thought also expands to encompass "an interest in fostering the physical, emotional, and intellectual growth of [the] child." Moreover, Ruddick adds, "although rarely given primary credit, a mother typically holds herself, and is held by others, responsible for the *malfunction* of the growth process" (215). The third interest that plays an increasingly important role in maternal thought as the child becomes old enough to initiate and sustain interactions with individuals outside of her/his immediate family is social acceptability. With regard to acceptability, Ruddick maintains that the mother (who is usually but need not be female) "must shape natural growth in such a way that her child becomes the sort of adult that she can appreciate and others can accept" (215).

Ruddick believes that all three of these interests need to be realized, even though she acknowledges that they function in a more general fashion as ideals that guide maternal thought, leaving open a variety of strategies for putting them (and failing to put them) into practice. To say that these three interests guide maternal thinking is not to say that "all mothers are, as individuals, governed by these interests," since, as just one example, "severe poverty may make interested maternal practice and therefore maternal thinking nearly impossible" (216). What further complicates the process of simultaneously realizing all three of these interests is the fact that "interests in the preservation, growth, and acceptability of the child are frequently and unavoidably in conflict" (216).

Ruddick's observations that not all mothers seek to realize these three interests and that even if one does try to realize them, they often come into conflict with one another, are particularly salient for understanding the issues surrounding the practice of SSA. Extreme poverty is an especially apt example of why a mother may fail to pursue one or more of these interests, since it points up the fact that one can be *unable* to fulfill them rather than merely *unwilling* to do so (although, obviously, many mothers are unwilling to do so even when they have the requisite ability). Indeed, a major justification that is provided for the widespread practice of both SSA and female infanticide in India is the lack of economic resources that would allow the family in question to provide for not only this daughter in particular but the family as a whole. That is, the choice to undergo SSA or commit female infanticide is, for many poor Indian families, a choice to *pursue* the three interests Ruddick mentions in regard to the children already born into the family, accompanied by a conviction that one will be unable to pursue them for any of the children (old as well as new) if SSA or female infanticide does not take place.

A primary and unifying motive for poor, middle-, and upper-middle-class families to pursue SSA in countries such as India and China is to increase the family's acceptability in its community. Indeed, in U.S. journalist Elizabeth Bumiller's interviews with Indian families who had decided to proceed with SSA should the fetus turn out to be female, it became clear how powerful acceptability is as a maternal interest and how often it "wins out" when it comes into conflict with the other two interests, preservation and growth (Bumiller 1990, 101–124). Ruddick, in her work, not only refrains from directly suggesting which interest should prevail when conflicts arise but would, most likely, refuse to make such a suggestion insofar as each conflict is different and cannot be resolved in the abstract by claiming that one interest should always "trump" the others. However, given her claim that the interest in preservation is the most fundamental and the most invariant of the three, there is only so far it can be compromised if and when such a conflict should arise.

While Ruddick focuses her discussion of maternal interests on actual mothers (though the former need not be female or birth mothers, as she often notes), her theory seems to provide for its own extension to the relationship between fetuses and their prospective families. Indeed, although Warren and many others stress the moment of birth as especially significant, since this is when fetuses "become" (recognized as) persons, there is no reason why maternal *interests* should suddenly come into play at this moment. Indeed, interests in the fetus's preservation, growth, and eventual acceptability are often of paramount concern to many prospective parents. In SSA, the preservation of the fetus is actively chosen against by its prospective family. The interest in growth, as far as the fetus is concerned, suffers a similar fate. However, as we noted earlier, all three interests may indeed be realized for the family as a whole if SSA is chosen, because this decision, made by extremely poor families who cannot afford dowries but who feel compelled to provide them for their daughters, may indeed promote the preservation, growth, and acceptability of the existing family members and the family unit itself. Thus the conflict in maternal interests that Ruddick acknowledges to be both frequent and unavoidable can and often does become much more complicated when realizing these interests for one child (or fetus) may involve denying them for another child or the family as a whole.

Even if the family is agreed in its decision to pursue SSA or female infanticide, however, this is no *guarantee* that SSA or female infanticide will in fact secure the family's preservation, foster its growth, and enhance its social acceptability. Deciding to undergo SSA and actually having SSA performed are two entirely different things, and it is quite possible that what appeared to be a less problematic decision earlier on can become a source of serious regret for one or both parents, leading, in more serious cases, to divisiveness and disruption within the family.[8] On the other hand, the mother's consenting to terminate her pregnancy if the fetus turns out to be female, because she herself has suffered severe oppression for being female, may be a source of personal empowerment.[9]

Deniz Kandiyotti, in an article entitled "Bargaining with Patriarchy," coins the term "patriarchal bargain" to describe how women strategize when confronted with severe constraints within patriarchal societies (Kandiyotti 1988, 274–90). The classic form of patriarchal bargaining Kandiyotti describes involves a woman's acquiescing to inequalities within her marriage in order to maximize her security within the marriage, thereby leaving open the possibility of a future "payoff" for losses suffered now. Openly rebelling or refusing to put up with the inequity, on the other hand, may lead not only to the end of the marriage but also to loss of social status and severe economic privation, especially if the woman belongs to a society that will not provide her with employment as a single woman. Here, patriarchal bargaining may be her only viable option, and, as Kandiyotti, Judith Lorber, and others have shown, it can indeed be a source of empowerment for women, even though outside observers may view the woman as passively accepting an inequitable situation (see Lorber and Bandlamudi 1993). A woman may possibly go along with her family's decision to pursue SSA in order to win concessions that will improve and strengthen her own position within the family unit on a long-term basis as well as the socioeconomic status of the family within the community.

Ruddick's model for maternal thinking, although it acknowledges that one need not be female or a biological mother to be engaged in maternal practices, still is described in terms that suggest that there is one primary caregiver who both views herself and is viewed by society as largely responsible for fostering the preservation, growth, and acceptability of her child or children. Ruddick laments that more fathers do not engage in maternal thinking and that both the burdens and the pleasures of mothering tend to fall so heavily on the actual mother of the children; and yet, by discussing maternal thinking and practices almost exclusively in reference to individual mothers, Ruddick does not do justice to some of the thornier issues that arise when the mother is treated more as a servant whose actions are carefully controlled and supervised than as an independent decision maker.

In *Maternal Thinking: Toward a Politics of Peace*, Ruddick does, however, focus at some length on the experience of "maternal powerlessness," which stems in part from the realization that "as their children grow older, mothers can neither predict nor control the intellectual skills, moods, tastes, ambitions, friendships, sexuality, politics, or morality of their children" (Ruddick 1989, 34). She claims that a sense of maternal powerlessness is also attributable to "the fact and feeling of social impotence" that arises out of a mother's awareness of the power of economic and social policies directly to affect her and her children's lives without her input or control. Nonetheless, despite her acknowledgment of the potentially debilitating consequences that can result from a feeling of maternal powerlessness, Ruddick continues to speak of mothers as if they were autonomous moral agents, and, regarding the inevitable conflicts that occur when these mothers try to secure all three maternal interests simultaneously, she asserts that "although some mothers deny or are insensitive to the conflict, and others are clear about which interest should take precedence, mothers typically know that they cannot secure each interest, they know that goods conflict, and they know that unqualified success in realizing interests is an illusion" (Ruddick 1980 [1983], 216).

For those mothers whose own interests have no way of being expressed, much less realized, and who are expected to follow the orders of other family members even with regard to decisions about their own children, it is almost impossible to conceive of them as being unaware from early childhood that "unqualified success in realizing interests is an illusion." For such mothers, acquiescing to SSA may reflect both a lifelong conviction that these interests will never be successfully achieved for the as yet unborn child and an altruistic desire not to bring another female into a world that does not want her. Indirectly, SSA may also symbolize a rejection of the mother's own fate, when a more direct means of refusal is unavailable.[10]

According to Ruddick, realizing that conflict cannot be avoided in aiming to secure the simultaneous preservation, growth, and acceptability of one's child leads to a sense of humility, "a metaphysical attitude one takes toward a world beyond one's control." More specifically, "humility implies a profound sense of the limits of one's actions and of the unpredictability of the consequences of one's work" (Ruddick 1980 [1983], 217). Ruddick views humility as a positive virtue when it results in "clear-sighted cheerfulness" in the face of conflict, a cheerfulness that allows one to accept the conflict and helps one work through it rather than being paralyzed by it. She also acknowledges that the source of the conflict may include tension among competing expectations that one has for one's children, contextual features of the situation (e.g., accidents and natural disasters) that unexpectedly change the situation and its demands, or the unpredictability of the children themselves, who do not always respond the way one expects them to. As opposed to the response of "defensive denial," which refuses to accept the conflict as a normal aspect of everyday life, "cheerfulness is a matter-of-fact willingness to continue, to give birth and to accept having given birth, to welcome life despite its conditions" (Ruddick 1980 [1983], 218).

Although, as Ruddick describes it, a healthy sense of humility does indeed seem to be a positive experience that promotes flexibility in the face of the contingencies of life, too much humility may make both clear-sighted cheerfulness and defensive denial impossible. That is, while a sense of humility can serve as a bellwether that keeps one from being too hard on oneself when one fails to exhibit the composed qualities of the "perfect mother," humility as a predominant response to life (one that is inculcated from early childhood) may actually make one less flexible, to the extent that one becomes unable to see how conflicting maternal interests can ever be satisfactorily resolved. Indeed, this seems to be a central problem for many Indian mothers, who see SSA as the only viable resolution to the conflicts entailed by the birth of another daughter.

To perceive SSA as the only alternative to a life of misery, deprivation, and degradation for one's unborn child and one's family does not mean, however, that SSA is indeed the only alternative available. One of the strongest aspects of Ruddick's position lies in her realization that the three primary maternal interests—preservation, growth, and acceptability—are not on a par with one another. While there are certain basic needs that must be met to preserve the life of any child, and while the emotional, intellectual and physical growth of a child cannot occur without "attentive love and loving attention," the criterion of acceptability is the most variable from one culture to another, and adherence to a standard of acceptability varies greatly from one family to another.

Even within a given culture, what is deemed acceptable conduct for members of the community can change from one generation to the next. For instance, the institution of the dowry, once largely confined in India to upper-middle- and middle-class families, has now spread across castes and classes, creating a staggering burden for lower-income families and serving as a primary impetus for SSA. And although a society may change its standards within a relatively short period, this does not mean that members of that society feel free to act against those standards, especially when acceptance of the standards is seen as essential to one's self-respect as well as community respect for one's family.

Although the changing nature of what is deemed acceptable conduct for members of a community and the awareness that other communities do not share one's own social standards seems to make maternal interest in acceptability more flexible than the other two, a desire to have oneself and one's family regarded as full-fledged members of the community may not only override maternal interests in preservation and growth, but may even be viewed as the precondition for the pursuit of these latter interests. In the face of such a conviction, outsiders to that community who are opposed to the community's standards of acceptability are placed in a difficult dilemma. On the one hand, they may feel bound to state their opposition and may try to work with members of the community to change the standards they view as oppressive; on the other hand, it is important for them to acknowledge that, as outsiders, they are not in a position to come in and change the community's practices by force. To do so, as Hadjikhani (1993) notes, is to forget their own sense of humility and to be guilty of a "cultural imperialism" that almost inevitably leads to increased resistance on the part of members of the community to the proposed change.

CONCLUSION

Although Ruddick views preservation, growth, and social acceptability as three interdependent interests that must be harmoniously reconciled with one another, she does not view any one of them as encompassing the other two. To do so would be to ignore the different demands these interests make on one and on those with whom one stands in relation. Thus a strong implication of Ruddick's work is that the only way to relate authentically to others is to refuse to relativize either the relationships themselves or the competing interests that arise from them. Instead, adopting a relational framework means that one is committed to exploring all aspects of the situation which contribute to the very definition of the situation as such and to exploring how these various aspects of the situation affect and are affected by the individuals with whom one is relating.

It is the symbiotic relationship between family interests and community standards played out through a maternal interest in social acceptability that is largely responsible for presenting SSA as the only viable option to giving birth to a baby of an unwanted sex. Too uncritical an acceptance of the normative practices of one's community not only leads to a problematic conflation of community interests with family interests but can also prevent one from distinguishing significant areas of conflict between actual and perceived interests on both the family and community levels. And, as I have noted, too strong an emphasis on social acceptability as an overriding maternal interest can result in the exclusion of other maternal interests from consideration altogether.

With respect to SSA, the facts about the procedure itself (most notably, terminating a pregnancy because the fetus is of the undesired sex), the complex web of interests at stake in the decision, and the underlying community standards which help shape and define those interests together make it impossible to condone the procedure as the only viable alternative available to a family. And yet to refuse to condone SSA as an acceptable moral response to, for instance, the oppression of women in a highly patriarchal society does not mean that those who undergo (or perform) the procedure should be subject to punitive measures. For one, as Warren cogently argues, punishing these individuals will not address the roots of the problem, since these individuals find themselves within a social situation that presents SSA as a viable (and appealing) alternative, so it is the situation itself that needs to be directly addressed. Second, the only way to resolve the disparity between the perception that SSA is the only route to securing the family's interests and the fact that there are other ways of securing the family's interests besides resorting to SSA is to work with these families to explore the alternatives rather than punishing individuals for failing to see them.

Where Warren views SSA as a moral right that may not always be right, a position that presupposes an autonomous moral agent who is the bearer of this right and who may fail to act "rightly," I prefer to see SSA as a "moral mistake." Such a notion need not rely on the problematic rights language that creates difficulties for Warren, since her distinction between having rights and being right requires a thorough elaboration that never appears in her text.[11] Unlike an immoral act, a moral mistake involves a recognition that the wrong decision has been made but leaves open the possibility that the individuals who have made the decision did so in good faith. To call SSA a moral mistake is to acknowledge that the individuals who have decided to pursue SSA are not acting in a random or capricious manner (although some may indeed be doing so, and they are in a different category altogether) but are indeed making their decision in the light of moral considerations regarding how best to secure the material interests of their families. It is a mistake because the practice of SSA guarantees the very conflict between interests that it is presented as a solution to; it opposes the interests of the fetus to the interests of its future family based on a contingent fact about the fetus (its sex), and the elimination of the fetus altogether does not diminish but actually reinforces the social conditions that gave rise to the conflict in the first place. Thus SSA ends up working against not only the interests of the fetus but also the interests of the family and of the society as a whole.

This does not mean that SSA cannot be a source of empowerment for oppressed women or that it cannot, in the short term, save a family from a devastating economic burden. The point is rather that SSA can only secure some interests at the expense of others and that the prior conflicts that exist in the society which make SSA appear to be the only viable alternative to an impossible situation are not in any way resolved (but are actually exacerbated) by the procedure.

Viewing SSA as a moral mistake does not imply that no one is responsible for the mistake, but it also does not require that any one person shoulder the entire burden of the mistake. Ruddick offers us a compelling model for understanding how a family can believe that SSA is the only viable alternative—an alternative that seems to be in their immediate and even long-term interests—to the prospect of raising a child of the "wrong" sex. But to the extent that SSA pits not only the fetus's interests against the interests of the family but also the actual interests of the family against its perceived interests and the perceived interests of the society against the actual interests of the society as a whole, SSA cannot provide the resolution of the conflicts that it is responding to. It runs the risk of transforming the positive virtue of "clear-sighted cheerfulness" into a callous response to a procedure that issues in the death of the fetus, a death that is contingent on its sex alone, and it leaves no room for renegotiating either the fetus's interests, the family's interests, or the community's interests so as to harmoniously resolve the conflicts among them. Finally, it widens the gap between actual and perceived interests by misconstruing the latter for the former. In so doing, the procedure inevitably undermines its own goals, and this, more than anything else, will hopefully lead communities to take a more proactive role in altering their standards for social acceptability.

Restricting the practice of SSA will require a humble willingness on the part of international, national, and local communities to find new ways of altering the social acceptability of SSA in a nonpatronizing manner that continues to "maintain the caring relation" between the community as a whole and the individuals and families who are members of it. For, as Rosemarie Tong notes in the abstract to her short essay "Blessed Are the Peacemakers: Commentary on Making Peace in Gestational Conflicts," "an individual's ability to care is largely a function of whether her community cares for her. We must care for others to enable them to care for themselves and their loved ones—born or unborn" (Tong 1992, 329).

NOTES

The topic for this essay arose out of a proposal I coauthored with Professor Jacqueline Glover of the Department of Health Sciences at George Washington University for a November 1993 conference on Feminist Ethics and Social Policy at the University of Pittsburgh. The discussion in this essay was greatly influenced both by numerous conversations between myself and Jacqueline Glover and by the very stimulating conversations we had with students in our summer 1993 Feminist Ethics seminar.

1. Of course, there has always been a plethora of "tests" a woman could appeal to to verify the sex of her fetus which continue to circulate widely, the majority of which are

tied to bodily needs and dispositions, including what kind of foods the pregnant woman desires, whether the hair on her legs (if she shaves them) grows faster or slower during pregnancy, how she carries the baby (low or high, straight-ahead or off to the side), how much indigestion she experiences, and whether the baby moves more or less. In a recent visit to a maternity clothing store, I discovered a book displayed prominently by the cash register that offered a number of such tests that could be easily performed by the expectant mother. Almost every mother I have encountered, not surprisingly, has had the experience of being told (usually by a perfect stranger) that she will *definitely* be having a boy or girl, based upon some aspect of her appearance. Although sometimes the "predictions" are accurate (indeed, the odds are in favor of the prediction coming out right quite often), the fact that for one person a given symptom "means" a boy and for another it "means" a girl makes this form of diagnosis extremely unreliable. Nonetheless, many women not only enjoy hearing these "predictions" but are affected by them, becoming depressed or joyful upon hearing the pronouncement of the self-appointed authority. One friend of mine was told by her dentist that her gums indicated a girl, and the fact that this prediction was generated by a doctor seemed to make it much more compelling than one given by a nonmedical person. Given that she did have a female baby, it is impossible to say whether her dentist could indeed "read" the sex from her gums—did he just happen to guess right or did her body reveal the sex of the fetus through this rather indirect means? In any case, curiosity regarding the sex of the fetus has a long history, and the new reproductive technologies only allow for a greater degree of reliability in the prediction, since the predictions by folk practices have occurred for centuries and continue to occur within and across cultures in an unabated fashion.

2. While it is beyond the scope of this essay to discuss the various processes through which these differential values are enacted and codified, Judith Butler's "feminist genealogy," worked out in both *Gender Trouble* (1990) and *Bodies That Matter* (1993), shows how these constructed values pose as originary, inevitable, and therefore unalterable.

3. The headline alone compels attention. The equation of girls with weeds that need to be rooted out is clearly a rhetorical tactic on the part of the headline writer to dramatize the seriousness of the problem, but it also contributes, however unwittingly, to the dehumanization and consequent devaluation of all female human beings.

4. For the purposes of this essay, I restrict the term *sex-selective abortion* to those abortions performed purely because the family does not want a fetus of that particular sex, male or female. It does not include cases in which the fetus has a sex-linked disease; such cases also qualify as sex-selective abortions but the decision is motivated by the existence of the disease rather than the sex of the unborn child.

5. In this essay the term *family*, although usually employed in reference to a heterosexual, married couple, their children, and immediate relatives, is not restricted to this definition. Every individual, married or unmarried, young or old, homosexual or heterosexual, is a member of a family and to suggest, as I do in this essay, that SSA is a family decision does not mean that those who make the decision are members of a "traditional" nuclear family; nor does it presuppose that any two families are alike.

6. Often this gets done by taking familial and social pressures into account when ascertaining how much to blame the prospective mother for her decision, a move that Warren herself makes in *Gendercide*. Even though it is precisely these pressures that lead Warren to conclude that we ought not to blame these prospective mothers for undergoing SSA, my point is that these pressures are so strong that they make it impossible ever to view the prospective mother as an autonomous decision maker, a necessary presupposition of consequentialist and deontological theories.

7. There has been surprisingly little change over the centuries in either the need for preservation or the basic elements necessary to preserve a young human life; preservation does indeed seem to be one of the universals that "govern[s] maternal practice throughout the species" even though it has been pursued and presented in a variety of ways.

8. For example, given the high infant mortality rate in India and the close spacing between siblings, it is entirely possible that shortly after SSA is performed, a family may lose one or more of its existing children to a fatal disease and may wish that the terminated pregnancy had been continued.

9. I am indebted to Neda Hadjikhani for this point. In her unpublished paper on the practice of female circumcision in Africa, she notes that international efforts to halt this "initiation rite" have to date not been very successful. She attributes some of the resistance to eradication of the practice to the individual African women for whom female circumcision "may be the one act she authors and controls" (Hadjikhani 1993, 6).

10. If the mother views her daughter as a "mirror" through which her own life is revealed and validated, as some feminists have suggested—see Irigaray (1992), Kristeva (1989, 1987), and Chodorow (1974)—then choosing against a daughter is also a choice against being mirrored and perhaps invalidated by what is seen through the mirror. It is also a choice not to be a mirror for one's daughter through which she will learn the lessons of submission and disempowerment.

11. One could raise the question of whether or not individuals have a moral right to make moral mistakes, and thereby bring SSA back within the compass of moral rights language; however, I would argue that this approach sidesteps the concrete relationships and interests at stake in the decision to undergo SSA in favor of an abstract discussion of what it means to have a right to make the wrong decisions. On a more general level, this type of move represents an attempt to subsume a relational approach within a rights model, which cannot work except at the expense of the relationships that form the basis for the relational approach.

REFERENCES

Bumiller, Elisabeth. 1990. *May you be the mother of a hundred sons: A journey among the women of India.* New York: Fawcett Columbine.

Butler, Judith. 1993. *Bodies that matter: On the discursive limits of sex.* New York: Routledge.

———. 1990. *Gender trouble: Feminism and the subversion of identity.* New York: Routledge.

Chodorow, Nancy. 1974. Family structure and feminine personality. In *Woman, culture, and society,* ed. Michelle Zimbalist Rosaldo and Louise Lamphere. Stanford: Stanford University Press.

Evans, Mark, et al. 1991. Attitudes on the ethics of abortion, sex selection, and selective pregnancy termination among health care professionals, ethicists, and clergy likely to encounter such situations. *American Journal of Obstetrics and Gynecology* 164(4): 1092–99.

Hadjikhani, Neda. 1993. On humility: Engaging the moral agency of non-Western women. Unpublished paper.

Irigaray, Luce. 1992. *Elemental passions,* trans. Joanne Collie and Judith Still. New York: Routledge.

Kandiyotti, Deniz. 1988. Bargaining with patriarchy. *Gender and Society* 2(3): 274–290.

Kristeva, Julia. 1989. *Black sun: Depression and melancholia*, trans. Leon S. Roudiez. New York: Columbia University Press.

———. 1987. *Tales of love*, trans. Leon S. Roudiez. New York: Columbia University Press.

Kristof, Nicholas D. 1993. Peasants of China discover new way to weed out girls. *The New York Times*, July 21, 1.

Lorber, Judith, and Lakshmi Bandlamudi. 1993. The dynamics of marital bargaining in male infertility. *Gender and Society* 7(1): 32–49

Ruddick, Sara. 1989. *Maternal thinking: toward a politics of peace*. New York: Ballantine.

———. 1980 [1983]. Maternal thinking. In *Mothering: essays in feminist theory*, ed. Joyce Trebilcot. Baltimore: Rowman and Littlefield.

Tong, Rosemarie. 1992. Blessed are the peacemakers: Commentary on making peace in gestational conflicts. *Theoretical Medicine* 13: 329–35.

Warren, Mary Anne. 1985. *Gendercide: The implications of sex selection*. Totowa, N.J.: Rowman and Allanheld.

CONTRIBUTORS

Alisa L. Carse is Assistant Professor of Philosophy at Georgetown University. She teaches and writes in the areas of social and political philosophy, ethical theory, feminist theory, and moral psychology.

Judith Wagner DeCew is Associate Professor of Philosophy at Clark University. She is co-editor of *Theory and Practice*, and her articles have appeared in such journals as *Ethics*, *Law and Philosophy*, *Philosophical Studies*, and *Hypatia*.

Patrice DiQuinzio is Assistant Professor of Philosophy and Director of Women's Studies at Muhlenberg College. Her work on feminist theory and mothering has appeared in *Hypatia* and *Women and Politics*, and she is the author of the forthcoming book *The Impossibility of Motherhood*, a critical analysis of feminist accounts of motherhood.

Sharon E. Hartline is Assistant Professor of Philosophy in the Department of Philosophy and Religious Studies at Radford University.

Janet R. Jakobsen is Assistant Professor of Women's Studies and Religious Studies at the University of Arizona. She previously worked as a lobbyist and policy analyst in Washington, D.C. Her essays have appeared in *Journal of Feminist Studies in Religion* and *Journal of Religious Ethics*.

Eva Feder Kittay is Professor of Philosophy at the State University of New York, Stony Brook, and a dependency worker who relies on other dependency workers in order to write and teach. She is the author of *Metaphor: Its Cognitive Force and Linguistic Structure* and co-editor of *Frames Fields and Contrasts: New Essays on Lexical and Semantic Structure*. She is writing a book on dependency and equality entitled *Equality and the Inclusion of Women*.

Carolyn H. Magid is an Associate Professor of Philosophy at Bentley College. She owes her interest in comparable worth to her experience working with clerical workers in the early 1980s. Her current research explores justice issues in policy proposals about public education and welfare.

Kate Mehuron is Associate Professor of Philosophy and Women's Studies at Eastern Michigan University. She is co-editor of *Free Spirits: Feminist Philosophers on Culture* and author of numerous articles on feminist theory and HIV-related issues.

Uma Narayan is Assistant Professor in the Department of Philosophy at Vassar College. She has written articles on surrogacy, affirmative action, homelessness, colonialism, and punishment. She is co-editing, with Mary L. Shanley, a book on feminist political theory. She is also working on a book dealing with tensions between respect for women and respect for cultures.

Lisa S. Parker is Assistant Professor of Human Genetics and History and Philosophy of Science at the University of Pittsburgh. Her research focuses on informed consent in particular contexts, the ethics of genetic research and the provision of genetic services, and the cultural contexts of medicine and bioethics.

Selma Sevenhuijsen is Professor of Women's Studies and Social Sciences at the University of Utrecht. She is co-author of *Child Custody and the Politics of Gender* (with Carol Smart) and *Equality Politics and Gender* (with Elizabeth Meehan). Her current research is on feminist ethics and politics, especially the epistemological aspects of the ethic of care, and on moral discourses on gender and reproductive technology.

Mary L. (Molly) Shanley is Professor of Political Science on the Margaret Stiles Halleck Chair at Vassar College. She is the author of *Feminism, Marriage and the Law in Victorian England* and co-editor of *Feminist Interpretations of Political Theory*. She is working with Uma Narayan on a collection of essays reinterpreting central concepts in Western political theory.

Anita Silvers is Professor of Philosophy and Special Assistant for University Strategic Planning at San Francisco State University. She is the co-author of *Puzzles about Art* and has published a number of essays on the philosophy of art, moral philosophy, and public policy.

Gail Weiss is Assistant Professor of Philosophy at George Washington University. She is working on a book on the body image and is co-editing a book entitled *Perspectives on Embodiment*.

Iris Marion Young is Professor of Public and International Affairs at the University of Pittsburgh. She is the author of *Justice and the Politics of Difference* and *Throwing Like a Girl and Other Essays in Feminist Philosophy and Social Theory*. Her articles on justice, democracy, and women's issues have appeared in *Ethics*, *Signs*, *Social Theory and Practice*, and *Feminist Studies*.

Naomi Zack is Assistant Professor of Philosophy at the University of Albany, State University of New York. She is the author of *Race and Mixed Race* and *Bachelors of Science: Seventeenth Century Identity, Then and Now*. She is also the editor of *American Mixed Race: The Culture of Microdiversity* and is editing a collection of new theories of sex and race.

INDEX